HUMAN RESOURCE MANAGEMENT IN RECREATION, SPORT, AND LEISURE SERVICES

HUMAN RESOURCE MANAGEMENT IN RECREATION, SPORT, AND LEISURE SERVICES

BY

MARGARET ARNOLD, REGINA GLOVER,
AND CHERYL BEELER

VENTURE PUBLISHING, INC.

Library of Congress Catalogue Card Number: 2012934541
ISBN-10: 1-892132-97-4
ISBN-13: 978-1-892132-97-0

Dedication

To our students

TABLE OF CONTENTS

PREFACE

David Culkin and Sondra Kirsch wrote in the preface of their book, *Managing Human Resources in Recreation, Parks, and Leisure Services* (1986), "The problem is simple. Most park, recreation, and leisure services professionals require a considerable understanding of the principles and practices needed to manage full-time, part-time, and seasonal personnel and volunteers. Unfortunately, most professionals have not had sufficient training and development in this area." Here we are some 25 years later and we can make this same argument today.

Regina Glover, Cheryl Beeler, and I have taught many years in the area of recreation administration with particular emphasis on human resource management. We have often shared our frustration about searching for the perfect textbook. The three of us have been known to create reading packets for students that contained a collection of information from various textbooks, journals, agencies, and magazines. During a conversation at an NRPA conference, Regina and I both admitted to still using portions of the Culkin and Kirsch book despite the 1986 publication date. We agreed their book still had useful information and felt the topics, design, and layout of the book had not been obsolesced by its relative age. Furthermore, our students liked the practicality of it and found it easy to read and absorb. It was during that conversation at an NRPA conference that we committed to writing a book based largely on the previous work by David Culkin and Sondra Kirsch's *Managing Human Resources in Recreation, Parks, and Leisure Services*. We secured copyright permission from the authors, who graciously agreed to pass the torch along to us. Knowing the magnitude of this project we immediately asked Cheryl to be a co-author. We also invited Mary Tomaselli, an expert in employee and organizational development, to contribute a chapter on training and development.

Like Culkin and Kirsch, while writing the book we constantly asked the question, "What do our students, and ultimately our practitioners, need to know in order to manage their human resources effectively?" Hopefully, the result is a book that is substantive and practical but easy to understand and absorb. Obviously, we could not cover everything, but the student should certainly receive a solid foundation on which to build upon.

Margaret Arnold, Ph.D.

ACKNOWLEDGMENTS

The authors wish to acknowledge the efforts of several individuals who contributed to the development of this book. Without their support, insight, and professional competence, this textbook would not have been possible. Therefore, we must begin by thanking David Culkin and Sondra Kirch. If not for their book, *Managing Human Resources in Recreation, Parks, and Leisure Services*, the groundwork would not have been laid to develop this book. David and Sondra provided us with full copyright permission and encouraged us to continue where they left off. Thanks to their good work we feel as though this book had done them justice. We are thankful for all of your contributions—both past and present. In addition, we wish to thank Venture Publishing, Inc., under the leadership of Drs. Frank Guadagnolo and Geof Godbey, for their support and encouragement. Thank you to Dan Threet, Richard Yocum, and Kay Whiteside.

Margaret Arnold would like to thank those who were willing to share their time, expertise, and resources in order to make this book relevant and meaningful to students. A special thank you to Liz Vance, Deputy Director of the Ithaca Youth Bureau; Andrea Dutcher, Campus Recreation at Cornell University; the entire Office of Human Resources at Greek Peak Ski Resort; Lana Morse, Administrative Assistant for the Department of Recreation and Leisure Studies at Ithaca College; Laura Lefebvre and Julia Melrose, two precocious student workers; and Mary Tomaselli, Director of Employee and Organizational Development at Ithaca College, who contributed an outstanding chapter on training and development. And finally, a personal thank you to Peggy and David Williams who provided constant encouragement and support, and a peaceful venue for me to write.

Regina Glover wishes to thank the many practitioners who were willing to offer advice, answer questions, and share stories in the preparation of this text. A special thank you to Nancy Aldrich, Superintendent of Human Resources, Arlington Heights Park District; Kurt Carmen, Interim Director, Ohio State University Recreational Sports; Julie Stauthammer, Human Resource Manager, Big Brothers, Big Sisters of Eastern Missouri; and Randy Osborn, Director Carbondale Boys and Girls Club of Carbondale, Illinois. A thank you also to the Department of Health Education and Recreation at SIUC; to Linda Patrick, administrative clerk; and to three outstanding graduate assistants: Ksenia Novikova, Zakiya Newton, and Patrick Beezley.

Cheryl Beeler would like to extend a heartfelt thank you to "BB" for the generous support provided during the writing of this project. The encouraging words and willingness to listen to ideas, brainstorm examples, read sections of the chapters, and offer honest opinion are greatly appreciated. Two graduate assistants, Katie Cruikshank and Priscilla Alfaro, were instrumental in designing the graphics of the book. Appreciation is also extended to several professionals working in the recreation and parks field who were generous with their time in sharing their expertise, giving examples, and providing policy statements and formal documents. Sara Hensley, Director, City of Austin (TX) Parks and Recreation Department; Joan Byrne, Director, Largo (FL) Recreation, Parks, and Arts; Karen Paulus, Director, City of Tampa (FL) Parks and Recreation; Sarah Perkins, Superintendent, Broward County (FL) Parks and Recreation Department; and Phyllis Bush, Supervisor II, Tallahassee (FL) Parks and Recreation Department.

INTRODUCTION

Managers of recreation, sport, and leisure services perform a variety of activities. Perhaps the most essential of these activities is the management of human resources. Every person associated with an organization, directly or indirectly, is a resource. These people might be recreation directors, event planners, sport managers, park supervisors, therapeutic recreation specialists, or outdoor leaders. They might have full-time, part-time, seasonal, or voluntary status. It is a mistake to assume that these individuals will automatically fit together into a cohesive, coordinated team. Furthermore, it is an error to assume that people will automatically perform the appropriate tasks and perform those tasks in the most desirable manner. An effective team effort is essential to the operation of any organization, and it is the responsibility of the manager to make this happen.

Most professionals require considerable understanding of the principles and practices needed to manage full-time, part-time, and seasonal personnel and volunteers. Unfortunately, many professionals in our field have not had sufficient training and development in this area, which is known as human resource management (HRM). Although some organizations may have a full-time HRM specialist, the majority do not and therefore must rely on the recreation and sport manager to have the necessary knowledge, skills, and abilities.

Recently, a group of experienced recreation and sport managers were asked if they would hire a female to coach a soccer team knowing that she is pregnant. Half of the managers said they would not hire her because she would not be able to fulfill her coaching responsibilities, yet the other half indicated they had to hire her if she was the most qualified. Plus, they admitted to fearing a potential lawsuit. No one in the room knew for sure what the law states in this situation. Another example lends itself to college students. An increasing number of students are claiming that unlawful questions are being asked of them during internship and job interviews. That is, professionals in our field are asking non-job-related questions that are not only inappropriate but also *illegal* during the interview. Regardless of these anecdotal examples, the authors believe we need to better prepare our students, who are our future professionals, in managing human resources. Thus, *Human Resource Management in Recreation, Sport, and Leisure Services* is intended for students who are being exposed to human resource management for the first time. Topics covered in this book include the legal environment, supervision, planning and staffing, recruitment, selection, motivation, performance appraisals, compensation, grievances, ethics, and employee well-being. Throughout the chapters we attempt to provide basic information, principles, and case studies that have application to a wide variety of operations. Whatever recreation or sport organizations students choose to go into—private or public, for-profit or nonprofit—they should be able to relate to the material presented in this book.

It should be noted that we use the terms 'supervisor' and 'manager' interchangeably throughout the book. The term 'supervisor' is usually associated with the lowest level of management. In the early days of the Industrial Revolution, the supervisor's primary responsibility was to watch the workers carefully and make sure that they did their jobs. Today, most people working at the lowest level of management do not have their jobs defined so narrowly. For example, they may also be asked to make decisions in the areas of technology, finance, resource allocation, policy development, and public relations. Also, the need for understanding the management of human resources is not confined to the lowest level of management. Every manager, including the top manager, is responsible for the supervision of people lower in the organization. Every manager, from top manager to supervisor, needs to have a basic understanding of the principles of managing personnel. Therefore, we use the terms 'manager' and 'supervisor' interchangeably.

In summary, this textbook prepares students—whether they intend to work in commercial recreation, therapeutic recreation, outdoor recreation, governmental recreation, youth services, sports management, or event planning—with a solid foundation for human resource management. Theory and practice are combined to assist students in gaining a greater understanding of the many complexities they will encounter in the workplace.

Please contact Venture Publishing, Inc. (814) 234-4561 to obtain a CD of comprehensive instructors' materials.

1

LEGAL ENVIRONMENT: EQUAL EMPLOYMENT OPPORTUNITY

The legal complexities involved with managing human resources can seem daunting. The law changes daily, the law is vague, and sometimes the law is inconsistent. Regardless, laws, regulations, and court decisions dictate what a recreation and sport supervisor can and cannot do. In a spirited effort to correct some of the serious social problems in American society, a significant amount of our nation's legal activity has focused on employment practices. Although the laws that attempt to correct unfair employment practices have not always achieved their objectives, they are reflected in a significant part of recreation and sport organization's policies and procedures.

All of us, concerned about the people we work with as well as the people we serve, have both a moral and a legal obligation to carry out fair employment practices. To function otherwise places ourselves and our organizations outside the law and enhances the risk of facing investigation or litigation by some federal or state regulatory agency. In addition, unfair employment practices frequently foster resentment, anger, and frustration in our work force and do nothing to promote the worth and dignity of each individual human being. As a result, many recreation and sport organizations are committed to reducing and eliminating discriminatory practices by requiring multicultural and diversity training programs.

Unfortunately, it is very difficult to keep track of our legal obligations. Even the well-intended person may violate the law because he or she is unaware of exactly what the law requires. But, as we all know, ignorance of the law is no excuse. Hence, the purpose of this chapter is to provide the recreation and sport professional with a broad overview of the most important legal aspects of managing human resources.

If legal problems arise, most recreation and sport managers will have access to the expertise of lawyers and human resource management specialists. It is to our advantage, however, to prevent legal problems from arising in the first place, and we cannot expect lawyers and human resource (HR) specialists to constantly monitor our day-to-day activities. We need at least a basic knowledge of the legal aspects of managing personnel. An understanding of this chapter is a good starting point, but ultimately supervisors should (1) continue to read and keep current with changing laws, and (2) develop a good working relationship with their legal counsel and HR specialists in order to anticipate and eliminate potential problems.

INTRODUCTION TO THE CHAPTER

We opened this chapter by referring to laws, regulations, and court decisions. All three taken together make up the legal environment. Laws are usually written in broad terms, and an agency under the executive branch of government is assigned the task of writing the special regulations that put the new law into action. The agency assigned to this task is either a new agency created by the law or an already existing agency. Court decisions also come into play in that they assess the constitutionality of laws and interpret their meaning.

The reader will soon understand why this chapter is presented in the beginning of this book. On numerous occasions we will refer back to this chapter. Compliance with the law will frequently dictate what we do and how we do it in the area of human resource management.

UNDERSTANDING EQUAL EMPLOYMENT OPPORTUNITY (EEO)

Equal employment opportunity (EEO) refers to the responsibility of organizations and managers to keep the work environment free from discrimination. EEO is a broad concept holding that individuals should have equal treatment in all employment-related actions. Everyone has the right to obtain work, earn fair wages, and receive fair treatment in all areas on the basis of ability, work performance, and potential to learn on the job. One persistent stumbling block in accomplishing the objectives of EEO is the existence of prejudices. In order that the reader may better understand how prejudices can lead to employment discrimination and why the United States government has produced so much legislation pertaining to discrimination in the past, a brief discussion of the history of employment discrimination in the U.S. is presented.

U.S. History of Employment Discrimination

Following the Civil War, the Fourteenth Amendment to the Constitution was passed to guarantee everyone the right to equal protection of the law. Initially, however, this amendment was neither obeyed nor enforced. During the middle decades of the twentieth century, antidiscrimination orders were issued by Presidents Roosevelt, Truman, and Eisenhower, and 31 northern states passed antidiscrimination laws. On occasion, even the judicial branch of government addressed discrimination. In the 1940s, the Supreme Court banned several state laws that discriminated against minorities. Nevertheless, these legal actions did not curb the flow of pervasive discrimination in housing, education, recreation, and employment because government did not seek to enforce the laws.

Frequently, employment practices were discriminatory. Too often, recruitment for new employees was conducted primarily by word of mouth, or it was aimed at specific schools or newspapers that did not represent minorities. Although discrimination was not always the intent of these practices, the recruitment results eliminated most minorities from knowing about position openings.

If prospective minority applicants did learn about job vacancies, they were confronted with complicated application blanks which too often asked unfair questions, making the applicant appear inferior. For example, some application questions inquired about the heritage and education achievements of the parents. A question about the length of time at present residence inferred that something might be wrong with a person who had moved frequently. Those questions referring to home ownership focused on the poor economic status of many minority members. Similarly, questions concerning years of education and degrees earned were often intimidating to those having little education. Columns of questions concerning political memberships and drinking habits required the applicant to acknowledge personal lifestyles.

The criteria used to screen applicants were equally discriminatory. Unskilled jobs often required high school degrees, thus eliminating culturally and economically disadvantaged candidates. Tests were frequently used which might ask applicants to solve algebraic problems when only simple math would be required on the job. An applicant who could verbalize in English and follow spoken instructions might not be able to read or write English well enough to pass the test.

Traditionally, therefore, only the backbreaking, dirty jobs were available and sought by minorities and immigrants: jobs such as collecting trash, cleaning streets, working in blast furnaces, or cleaning homes. Educated minorities took jobs for which they were overqualified. Learning that certain organizations and certain jobs were closed to them, minorities confined job hunting to low-status occupations.

Similar standards existed for training and promotion practices. Many minorities and immigrants were excluded from apprenticeships in the building trades because those trades required a high degree and the passing of examinations. In the South, two seniority rosters were frequently kept: one for white employees and one for black employees. Blacks could not seek white positions and whites could not seek black positions. White jobs were better paid, however, and offered better working conditions (Strauss & Sayles, 1980).

Many African Americans and women, once they were hired, often faced dead-end jobs. Agencies and companies could show compliance to equal-employment-opportunity legislation by calling attention to their minority representatives in personnel departments or public relation offices. If women or African Americans were promoted to supervisory or management positions, complaints from subordinates, requests for transfers, or resignations frequently resulted.

It took the courageous actions of individual African American leaders and the civil rights movement to draw serious attention to the problems of discrimination in this country. As early as 1945, one young black Air Force officer challenged segregation regulations at Duke Field, Kentucky. Later he faced charges of mutiny when he and a fellow black officer tried to integrate the officer's club. The charges were eventually dropped, and Daniel (Chappie) James, Jr. went on to become the first African American four-star general in the history of this country. The late Thurgood Marshall, the attorney for young "Chappie," became the first African American Supreme Court justice, and William Coleman, the law student who assisted Marshall, became U.S. Secretary of Transportation in the Ford administration (Calvert, 1979). It was not until 1963, when hundreds of thousands of civil rights' supporters demonstrated in Washington, D.C., before a television audience of millions, that the federal government sought to right past wrongs. That was the turning point, particularly for African Americans. President Kennedy and then President Johnson pushed for civil rights legislation, and the Civil Rights Act was passed in July 1964.

Today, the legal spotlight continues to focus on women, and racial and ethnic minorities in its search for discrimination. But other minority groups have emerged in demanding attention and an end to bias in hiring and personnel practices. The **"protected class"** are individuals within a group who are identified for protection under equal-employment laws and regulations. These groups include individuals with disabilities, women, individuals 40 years of age and older, veterans, and in some states, marital status and sexual orientation. Despite legal action towards an end to prejudice and discrimination, race, sex, ethnicity, sexual orientation, age, and religion have had a history of inciting prejudicial behavior.

Prejudice and Discrimination Defined

The U.S. history of employment discrimination is riddled with prejudice and discriminatory acts of behavior. Therefore, it is paramount that we understand these two concepts before we introduce the Equal Employment Opportunity (EEO) laws and concepts.

Prejudice

According to Webster's dictionary (2012), prejudice is "preconceived judgment or opinion"; "an adverse opinion or leaning formed without just grounds or . . . sufficient knowledge"; and "an irrational attitude of hostility directed against an individual, a group, a race, or their supposed characteristics."

Prejudices do not necessarily lead to acts of discrimination. A recreation or sport manager who prejudges another person but allows that other person to move about and live as he or she wishes, is not discriminating. In our society, personal beliefs are highly valued, as long as those beliefs do not infringe on the rights of others. Consequently, *laws to change the acts of discrimination should not begin by trying to change personal beliefs.* It was evident from the discussion of past employment practices that prejudices were not legislated away because of constitutional amendment,

presidential orders, or state legislation. Only the acts of discrimination can be made illegal—specific acts toward specific protected-class members.

An awareness of one's prejudices sometimes prevents acts of discrimination. Putting oneself into the shoes of a minority person, even for a short while, can lead to better understanding of the frustrations and problems of minority-group members. The classic example is the role-shift study conducted by sociologist John Howard Griffin. Griffin darkened his skin in order to pass himself off as a southern African American man. He learned that constant rejection eventually leads to self-image and behavioral changes, and he eventually became fearful, clumsy, and self-rejecting in his role as a black man. In his book, *Black Like Me*, Griffin concluded that those characteristics which whites assign to blacks are not the result of differences in races, but rather the result of differences in environmental factors. Examples of prejudices are common in the field of sport and recreation; the owner of a professional sport team may have a bias against hiring a woman as the general manager; or the fitness club manager may have a bias against the qualified candidate who happens to use a wheelchair; or the staff member who refuses to work alongside an openly gay coworker.

Discrimination

Holding unreasonable, preconceived convictions and acting upon them when making employment decisions is the difference between the terms "prejudice" and "illegal discrimination." Simply put, illegal discrimination occurs when the supervisor or manager allow their personal prejudices to influence employment decisions.

The definition of discrimination has evolved over the years and has undergone three distinct changes worth mentioning:

1. The courts initially defined discrimination as "committing harmful acts against a person because the person belongs to a group that is disliked." The emphasis was on the word "because," which implied that the intent was to treat someone differently based on his or her group membership.

2. When it became difficult to prove that someone intended to harm another person, the courts defined discrimination as "unusual treatment" or treating persons differently because of their race, color,

gender, religion, or national origin (Jain & Sloane, 1981). The emphasis shifted from the "prejudicial intent to harm" to the actual treatment of employees. Different treatment was the commonly accepted definition, referred to as "disparate treatment." It was assumed that the inequalities would be eliminated by removing different treatment based on race, color, and sexual orientation of staff and supervisors. Thus the same standard of employment was applied to all applicants and all employees. But this definition led to unequal results. When equal standards, such as requiring a high school diploma, were applied to everyone, it resulted in unequal effects on certain minority groups.

3. The terms "disparate treatment" and "disparate impact" emerged to differentiate forms of discrimination. Disparate treatment (intentional discrimination) refers to treating protected-class members differently during the hiring process. For example, if a female applicant is asked certain questions that are not asked of male applicants, then disparate treatment may be occurring. The term "disparate impact" emerged from the famous Supreme Court case, *Griggs v. Duke Power Co.* (1971). Duke Power used what was believed to be a neutral, color-blind technique in determining promotions. Every applicant was treated the same, blacks and whites. Everyone had to pass two nationally recognized tests. A passing score was considered the national median score for high school graduates. This equal treatment, however, resulted in unequal impact on African Americans, who were less likely to have a high school education and consequently, less likely to pass the tests. The Duke Power Company had evidently interpreted the Civil Rights Act to mean that the use of any test from a reputable publisher of psychological tests was permitted by law.

What is Prejudice?

The word *prejudice* refers to prejudgment: making a decision before becoming aware of the relevant facts of a case or event.

What is Discrimination?

DISCRIMINATION: The process by which people are treated differently based solely on their differences. In terms of employment, it is illegal to discriminate against people on the bases of their race, color, religion, sex, national origin, and in some cases, sexual orientation.

••••

DISPARATE TREATMENT: Members of one group overly and intentionally treated differently than members of another group. If an African American employee leaves the recreation center early without permission four times and is discharged, but a white coworker leaves work the same number of times and is not fired, the result is disparate treatment for the African American.

••••

DISPARATE IMPACT: Indirect or unintentional adverse impact on members of one group who are deprived employment opportunities because of a particular rule or practice. Requiring a college degree in order to work as a park laborer may rule out a disproportionate number of people in a protected class.

Figure 1.1
Definitions of the Terms Prejudice and Discrimination

Disparate impact (unintentional discrimination) occurs when substantial underrepresentation of protected-class members results from employment decisions that work to their disadvantage. The Supreme Court addressed the definition of disparate impact when it interpreted Congress's intent to eliminate not only disparate treatment over discrimination, but also those practices that, while appearing to be equal, lead to unequal consequences for different groups. Although Duke's tests were not intended to discriminate, the Court ruled that the tests operated to exclude African Americans. Good intentions, therefore, are not sufficient reasons to excuse employers from violating the law. Congress was directing the law to the *consequences* of employment practices, as well as intent. Thus, disparate treatment and disparate impact are both illegal discriminatory practices (see Figure 1.1).

Introducing Equal Employment Opportunity (EEO) Laws and Concepts

The legal implications of Equal Employment Opportunity (EEO) laws have changed the role of supervisors and managers in recreation, park, and leisure organizations. Therefore it is useful to review those EEO laws, regulatory directives, and court decisions (Table 1.1) that attempted to rectify

Table 1.1
Major Equal Employment Opportunity Laws and Regulations

ACT	SUMMARY OF PURPOSE
Equal Pay Act (1963)	Requires equal pay for men and women performing similar work
Title VII, Civil Rights Act of 1964 (Amended in 1972)	Prohibits discrimination in employment on the basis of race, color, religion, sex, or national origin
Age Discrimination in Employment (1967) (Amended in 1978 and 1986)	Prohibits discrimination against persons who are over age 40 and restricts mandatory retirement requirements, except where age is a bona fide occupational qualification
Executive Orders 11246 (1965) and 11375 (1967)	Requires federal contractors and subcontractors to eliminate employment discrimination through affirmative action
Executive Order 11478 (1969)	Prohibits discrimination in the U.S. Postal Service and in various government agencies on the basis of race, color, religion, sex, national origin, handicap, or age
Vocational Rehabilitation Act (1973) (Amended in 1974)	Prohibits discrimination against persons with disabilities and requires affirmative action to provide employment opportunity for persons with disabilities
Americans with Disabilities Act (1990)	Requires employer accommodations for individuals with disabilities
Vietnam Era Veterans' Readjustment Assistance Act (1974)	Prohibits discrimination against veterans by federal contractors and the U.S. government and requires affirmative action
Pregnancy Discrimination Act (1978) with regard to benefits and leave policies	Requires that pregnancy be treated as any other medical condition
Immigration Reform and Control Act (1986) (Revised in 1990, 1996)	Establishes penalties for employers who knowingly hire illegal aliens and prohibits employment discrimination on the basis of national origin or citizenship
Older Workers Benefit Protection Act (1990)	Prohibits age discrimination in early retirement and other benefit plans
Civil Rights Act (1991)	Overturns many past Supreme Court decisions and changes damage claims provisions
Family and Medical Leave Act (1993)	Grants to qualified employees the right to unpaid leave for specific family or health-related reasons without fear of losing their jobs

past employment injustices. It is important to understand that EEO is a broad concept holding that all individuals should have equal treatment in all employment-related actions. Thus, recreation and sport supervisors and managers must be familiar with EEO laws and regulations and ensure that their practices are nondiscriminatory. It is equally important to understand that there are certain individuals who are covered under the equal-employment laws and are therefore protected from illegal discrimination. As previously mentioned, these individuals who fall within a group identified for protection are known as the protected class. Essentially, protected class members are certain individuals who are protected from employment discrimination by law. The federal law protects employees from discrimination or harassment based on sex, race, age (age 40 and over), disability, color, creed, national origin, or religion. Some states extend protected class to include marital status and sexual orientation. Every U.S. citizen is a member of some protected class and is entitled to the benefits of EEO law. However, the EEO laws were passed to correct a history of unfavorable treatment of women and minority group members.

Title VII, Civil Rights Act of 1964 as Amended by the EEO Act of 1972

The Civil Rights Act of 1964, especially Title VII, Sec. 703, provides the cornerstone for EEO employment. This law makes it unlawful for employers to hire, refuse to hire, discharge, or discriminate in employment practices against anyone because of race, color, religion, sex, or national origin. The law also prohibits employers from retaliating against the employee who files a charge of discrimination, participates in a discrimination investigation, or opposes an unlawful employment practice. In other words, acts of discrimination, whether deliberately planned or accidentally executed, are illegal.

What This Means for Recreation and Sport Supervisors

Title VII prohibits discrimination in various employment practices that include job recruitment, the job application process, the employee selection process, promotion, demoting, discharging, compensating, assigning work, scheduling time-off, providing job training and development opportunities,

A female maintenance worker with a high school diploma worked for a city park for seven years, receiving good performance evaluations. She was never offered an opportunity to attend training programs, nor was she ever notified about vacancies in better-paying positions. After witnessing the third promotion of male employees with less seniority and noting that their expenses had been paid to attend a maintenance workshop prior to each of their promotions, the female complained to her supervisor. The response was, "Aren't you happy in your present job? I didn't think you wanted extra training or a promotion."

Was the supervisor guilty of unfair equal employment opportunity practices under the law?

performance appraisals, and any other terms, conditions, and privileges of employment. Title VII covers most employers in the United States. If a recreation or sport organization meets any one of the following criteria, then it is subject to rules and regulations based upon this act:

- All private employers of 15 or more persons who are employed 20 or more weeks per year
- All educational institutions, public or private
- State and local governments
- Public and private employment agencies
- Labor unions with 15 or more members
- Joint labor/management committees for apprenticeships and training

Exemptions to Title VII

Title VII offers three exceptions in which preferential hiring is permitted. Court decisions have interpreted these exceptions very narrowly. If an employer can demonstrate that religion, sex, or national origin is necessary to do the job, the employer may "discriminate" on the basis of these three factors. A bona fide occupational qualification (BFOQ) is a legal exception to an otherwise discriminatory hiring practice that is reasonably necessary to the normal operation of a particular business. The BFOQ may be requested if the essence of the business operation would be undermined if the business eliminated its discriminatory policy. For example, recruiting female models for women's clothing line or hiring a male as the men's locker room attendant would be permitted. Race and color are not permissible exceptions in the law. It is important to note that *with a BFOQ the burden of proof always lies with the employer.* Figure 1.2 provides more details of BFOQs as they relate to race, religion, gender, and age.

Sexual Harassment Guidelines, Title VII

> *"Sabrina, I'll be happy to pay for your conference registration fee and give you administrative leave to go, if you want to share my room for the five days while we are in San Antonio." Sabrina filed a complaint against her boss, Tom.*
>   *Will anyone take her complaint seriously?*

This supervisor is demonstrating an overt act of sexual harassment. He is requesting implied sexual favors as a prerequisite condition to granting approval and financial support for professional development opportunities. Sexual harassment is a form of discrimination in violation of Title VII of the Civil Rights Act of 1964. Guidelines issued later in 1980 by the Equal Employment Opportunity Commission (which is discussed later in this chapter) place the responsibility on the employing agency, as well as the supervisor, to provide a work environment free from unwelcome sexual advances. Furthermore, several Supreme Court cases have illustrated that sexual harassment is intolerable and is considered a form of sexual discrimination and victims or survivors are entitled to legal assistance. Therefore, Sabrina has a valid complaint against both her boss and the organization for which she works. Figure 1.3 (see p. 8) identifies other examples of where sexual harassment may occur.

As previously mentioned, Title VII covers all employers who hire 15 or more employees who work 20 or more weeks per year at the federal, state, and local levels of government, as well as public and private educational institutions. According to the Equal Employment Opportunity Commission (EEOC), the group that interprets and enforces the sexual harassment guidelines, the definition of sexual harassment is:

> *Unwelcome sexual advances, requests for sexual favors, and other verbal or physical conduct of a sexual nature constitute sexual harassment when this conduct explicitly or implicitly affects an individual's employment, unreasonably interferes with an individual's work performance, or creates an intimidating, hostile, or offensive work environment.*

RACE: The law specifically states that it is unlawful to discriminate on the basis of religion, gender, or national origin, except where any of these factors is "a bona fide occupational qualification reasonably necessary to the normal operation of that particular business or enterprise." Race can never be a bona fide occupational qualification.

••••

RELIGION: Religion could be considered a bona fide occupational qualification when membership in a certain religion is reasonably necessary to the performance of a job. For example, a religious sport camp might be allowed to insist on hiring staff of the particular religion represented by the camp. But the organization who sponsors the summer camp could not refuse to hire a maintenance worker because of his or her religion, as it would not be "reasonably necessary" to the operation of the business.

••••

GENDER: The gender as a bona fide occupational qualification causes more difficulty than any of the other provisions of this section of the law. Various state laws limiting the jobs women are allowed to do and regulating their wages and hours are now largely invalidated because they were based, in large part, on the traditional separation of "man's work and woman's work." On several occasions, the Equal Employment Opportunity Commission has said it will take a very narrow view of this exemption.

••••

AGE: The Age Discrimination in Employment Act (ADEA) prohibits employers from discriminating against workers who are 40 years of age or older. The purpose of the Act is to promote the employment of older workers based on their ability rather than their age, to prohibit arbitrary age discrimination in employment, and to help employers and workers find ways of resolving problems arising from the impact of age on employment.

Figure 1.2
BFOQs as They Relate to Race, Religion, Gender, and Age

Prevention is the best tool to eliminate sexual harassment in the workplace. Recreation and sport managers should clearly communicate to employees that sexual harassment will not be tolerated. The message of zero tolerance may occur by providing sexual harassment training, by establishing an effective complaint or grievance process, and by taking immediate and appropriate action when an employee complains. It is important to note that it is unlawful to retaliate against an individual for filing a discrimination charge, testifying, or participating in any way in an investigation, proceeding, or litigation under Title VII.

Equal Employment Opportunity Commission (EEOC)

To administer and enforce the Civil Rights Act of 1964, Title VII, an independent federal organization was created, the Equal Employment Opportunity Commission. The United States Equal Employment Opportunity Commission (EEOC) is a federal agency charged with ending employment discrimination.

1. The sexual harasser may be male or female. The victim does not have to be of the opposite sex.

2. The harasser can be the victim's supervisor, a supervisor in another area, a coworker, or a non-employee.

3. The victim does not have to be the person harassed but could be anyone affected by the offensive conduct.

4. The harasser's conduct must be unwelcome.

5. Some examples of specific sexual behaviors that have been found in violation of sexual harassment in recreation and sport organizations include:

   • Sending sexually explicit, offensive e-mails to coworkers

   • Unnecessary and unwanted patting or pinching of an employee

   • Making sexual requests for favors

   • Sharing sex-related stories or jokes that are unwanted and offensive

   • Making unwanted remarks about clothing, body, or sexual activities

Figure 1.3
Circumstances of Sexual Harassment

The EEOC investigates discrimination complaints based on an individual's race, color, national origin, religion, sex, age, disability and also investigates allegations of retaliation (e.g., demotion, termination, discipline, harassment) for reporting a discriminatory practice.

Originally, EEOC only investigated complaints of alleged discrimination and, through conciliation, persuasion, and negotiation, tried to resolve charges. When these methods failed, EEOC lacked authority to take cases to court. This lack of authority was the major weakness of the 1964 Civil Rights Act. Employers often ignored the Civil Rights Act and EEOC, hoping that wronged individuals would not have the knowledge or financial resources to pursue their complaints through litigation. The Equal Employment Opportunity Act of 1972 addressed these weaknesses and extended the authority of the EEOC, enabling it to take organizations directly to federal district courts.

According to the EEOC's website (http://www.eeoc.gov), the Charge Processing Procedures are summarized:

The employer is notified that the charge has been filed. From this point there are a number of ways a charge may be handled:

• A charge may be assigned for priority investigation if the initial facts appear to support a violation of law. When the evidence is less strong, the charge may be assigned for follow-up investigation to determine whether it is likely that a violation has occurred.

• EEOC can seek to settle a charge at any stage of the investigation if the charging party and the employer express an interest in doing so. If settlement efforts are not successful, the investigation continues.

• In investigating a charge, EEOC may make written requests for information, interview people, review documents, and, as needed, visit the facility where the alleged discrimination occurred. When the investigation is complete, EEOC will discuss the evidence with the charging party or employer, as appropriate.

• The charge may be selected for EEOC's mediation program if both the charging party and the employer express an interest in this option. Mediation is offered as an alternative to a lengthy investigation. Participation in the mediation program is confidential, voluntary, and requires consent from both charging party and employer. If mediation is unsuccessful, the charge is returned for investigation.

• A charge may be dismissed at any point if, in the agency's best judgment, further investigation will not establish a violation of the law. A charge may be dismissed at the time it is filed, if an initial in-depth interview does not produce evidence to support the claim. When a charge is dismissed, a notice is issued in accordance with the law which gives the charging party 90 days in which to file a lawsuit on his or her own behalf.

How Does EEOC Resolve Discrimination Charges?

• If the evidence obtained in an investigation does not establish that discrimination occurred, this will be explained to the charging party. A required notice is then issued, closing the case and giving the charging party 90 days in which to file a lawsuit on his or her own behalf.

- If the evidence establishes that discrimination has occurred, the employer and the charging party will be informed of this in a letter of determination that explains the finding. EEOC will then attempt conciliation with the employer to develop a remedy for the discrimination.

- If the case is successfully conciliated, or if a case has earlier been successfully mediated or settled, neither EEOC nor the charging party may go to court unless the conciliation, mediation, or settlement agreement is not honored.

- If EEOC is unable to successfully conciliate the case, the agency will decide whether to bring suit in federal court. If EEOC decides not to sue, it will issue a notice closing the case and giving the charging party 90 days in which to file a lawsuit on his or her own behalf.

What Remedies Are Available When Discrimination Is Found?

The "relief" or remedies available for employment discrimination, whether caused by intentional acts or by practices that have a discriminatory effect, may include:

- back pay,
- hiring,
- promotion,
- reinstatement,
- front pay,
- reasonable accommodation, or
- other actions that will make an individual "whole" (in the condition s/he would have been but for the discrimination).

Remedies also may include payment of:

- attorneys' fees,
- expert witness fees, and
- court costs.

(Taken directly from EEOC website on January 13, 2012)

Civil Rights Act of 1991

The Civil Rights Act of 1991, like the Civil Rights Act of 1964, states that employers are required to show they use job-related employment practices. The act clarifies that the individual who is bringing the discrimination charges must identify the intentional hiring practice or workplace discrimination and must show only that protected-class status played some factor.

Two provisions of the Civil Rights Act of 1991 are worth noting here—*compensation/punitive damages and jury trials*, and *race norming*. The first provision clarifies that protected-class members who feel they have been discriminated against are allowed to have a jury trial and to sue for punitive damages if they can prove intentional hiring and workplace discrimination. Compensatory damages usually include payments for emotional pain, mental anguish, loss of enjoyment of life, or inconvenience. Nongovernmental entities, if found guilty, may be required to pay "punitive" damages if deemed by the court. All attorney fees and court costs are paid by the organization if found in violation of the law. The second important provision prohibits discriminatory use of employment tests and test scores. Race norming is the practice of giving every applicant for employment the same skills test, but then grading the test differently depending on the applicant's race or gender. This provision addresses the concern of using different passing or cutoff scores for protected-class members than those individuals who are not considered to be in protected classes.

The Glass Ceiling Commission also evolved from the Civil Rights Act of 1991. For years, women's groups have claimed that discriminatory practices have prevented women and other protected-class members from advancing to upper-level management positions in recreation and sport organizations. The "glass ceiling" is a term used to describe the invisible barrier that impedes women and minorities from career advancement. The Glass Ceiling Commission is comprised of a 21-member body and was appointed by President Bush and Congressional leaders. Its mandate was to identify the glass ceiling barriers that have blocked the advancement of minorities and women, as well as the successful practices and policies that have led to the advancement of minority men and all women. It is important to note that the commission examines opportunities for women and minorities, and it also addresses the preparation they receive to be qualified for upper-level management.

Many recreation and sport organizations are committed to breaking the "glass ceiling" since many

1. Establishing formal mentoring programs for women and racial/ethnic individuals.

2. Allow for job-sharing, job-rotation, and flex-time schedules to help balance the work/family responsibilities.

3. Provide job and career rotation opportunities within the organization.

4. Increase visibility of women and minorities on boards and membership affiliations.

5. Develop clear retention programs for protected-class members and hold supervisors accountable for implementing and achieving the intended goals of the program.

Figure 1.4
Innovative Programs to Eliminate the Glass Ceiling Barrier

of these agencies continue to be severely underrepresented with regard to women and minorities in the highest management positions. Some innovative programs attempting to shatter the glass ceiling are found in Figure 1.4.

Equal Pay Act of 1963

A female sport director was promoted to facilities manager after the male manager resigned. The three-step increase in salary was not made at the time of her promotion, although the duties and responsibilities remained the same for the facilities manager position. When she sought to correct this oversight, she was told, "We have decided to reclassify this position down three steps from what it had been previously. Consequently, you are not entitled to any salary increase."

Did this action violate EEO laws?

The sport facility that acted to pay the female three steps less in salary than the former male manager was in conflict with the Equal Pay Act. The female held the same position and performed the same responsibilities as her predecessor; therefore, she was entitled to the same salary.

The Equal Pay Act of 1963 and the Equal Opportunity Acts of 1972 and 1977 were all amendments to the Fair Labor Standards Act of 1938. To avoid confusion over the different titles of the same law, we will refer to the law as the Equal Pay Act.

This act provides even broader coverage than the Civil Rights Act of 1964. It covers all state and local governments and public agencies, schools, hospitals, and businesses with sales in excess of $362,500. *Under the Equal Pay Act, all employers are required to pay equal wages to men and women performing similar work.* The work does not have to be identical to be considered similar work. The law defines similar work as: Equal work on jobs, the performance of which requires equal skill, effort, and responsibility, and which are performed under similar working conditions, except where such payment is made pursuant to (i) a seniority system; (ii) a merit system; (iii) a system which measures earnings by quantity or quality of production.

The issue is not always one of exact duties in exactly the same environment, but whether or not any differences in duties are significant enough to warrant different wages. Should a male community center director be paid more than a female community center director because his center has 5,000 more square feet, offers different facilities, and requires an extra person to assist in operating the center? Probably not, because all major job functions, levels of responsibility, and required education and experience remain the same for both centers. However, an employee could pay a female sport director more in San Francisco than a male working in the same position in Portland, Maine, even if the jobs were the same, because of the cost-of-living difference.

Exceptions to the Equal Pay Act

The Equal Pay Act permits employers to pay differential wages when wages are based on established seniority or merit systems. If a male sport director had been a director several years longer than the female sport director, the agency can pay him a high salary, as a result of legitimate longevity pay increases. Similarly, if two sport directors were hired at the same time, but the male employee performed in an outstanding manner the first year while the female employee only performed her duties satisfactorily, the agency with an established merit system could reward the male employee with a greater salary increase.

Another important aspect of the Equal Pay Act relates to differential pay according to the risk of bodily harm on the job. Some organizations provide greater remuneration to the employee facing possible danger. This may or may not be considered legal. For example, one agency requires park rangers to assign camp sites, collect fees, patrol park areas, present interpretive programs, and perform related duties. Male rangers in that agency are more frequently scheduled to patrol isolated park sites late at night, and occasionally encounter disorderly park patrons breaking park regulations. Although both male and female rangers are charged to patrol park areas, the likelihood of the male ranger finding himself in a potentially confrontational situation late at night is greater. The courts generally have been unsympathetic to situations such as the one just cited, where male employees have been paid higher wages than females based on the possibility that the males are exposing themselves to greater danger. A number of court cases have resulted in back-pay awards to women who were targets of unequal pay discrimination. A listing of factors that permit pay distinctions are found below:

Equal Pay Act permits pay distinction based upon

- Unequal responsibility
- Differences due to seniority
- Dissimilar work conditions
- Differences resulting from merit pay systems
- Differences based on production

In January 2009, President Barack Obama signed a gender pay equity law referred to as the Lilly Ledbetter Fair Pay Act that makes it easier for workers to sue organizations for pay discrimination. The bill amends the Civil Rights Act of 1964 stating that the 180-day statute of limitations for filing an equal-pay lawsuit regarding pay discrimination resets with each new discriminatory paycheck.

The reason for the Equal Pay Act is because of the continuing disparity between the earnings of men and women. According to Dolliver (2004), in 2003 the median weekly earnings for female workers were 80% of their male counterparts, which is up from 65% in 1979. Other more recent studies show that when differences between work experience, education, and length of employment of men and women are analyzed, female workers earn approximately 90% of what comparable male workers earn.

Age Discrimination in Employment Act of 1967, as Amended in 1978 and 1986

> *"Shane, don't be angry about not being considered for the golf superintendent's job. Carl is fifteen years younger than you and has more energy. Besides, a guy at age 56 doesn't need all that added stress and responsibility."*
>
> *How does this statement violate the law?*

The Age Discrimination in Employment Act of 1967 (ADEA) originally prohibited job discrimination against workers between the ages of 40 and 65. The 1978 amendment provided protection for workers between the ages of 40–70, and the 1986 amendment prohibits job discrimination against workers who are 40 years of age or older. The ADEA applies to employers with 20 or more employees for 20 or more weeks per year, unions with 25 or more members, and federal, state, and local governments. The EEOC is the investigating and enforcement agency for this act, and not surprisingly age discrimination is the leading category of discrimination files charged. Over 16,000 claims have been filed costing organizations more than $75 million. It is unlawful to retaliate against an individual for opposing employment practices that discriminate based on age or for filing an age discrimination charge, testifying, or participating in any way in an investigation, proceeding, or litigation under the ADEA.

The Age Discrimination in Employment Act protection applies to both employees and job applicants. Under the ADEA, it is unlawful to discriminate against a person because of his or her age with respect to any term, condition, or privilege of employment, including hiring, firing, promotion, layoff, compensation, benefits, job assignments, and training. Questions asked about an applicant's age or birth should be avoided unless there is concern for child labor laws. For example, an applicant applying for a camp counselor position may be asked "Are you under the age of 18?"

Presidential Executive Orders 11141, 11246, 11375, and 11478

Presidential executive orders (PEO) are directives issued by U.S. presidents that have the force of law, even though Congress did not enact them. Some of these orders pertain to EEO and federal contracts with private organizations. Local and state governments who receive federal monies are also covered.

In 1941, President Franklin D. Roosevelt was the first president to try to prohibit employment discrimination nationally. Through executive order, he created a Fair Employment Practices Committee which investigated complaints of discrimination in defense industries that held federal contracts. The committee settled thousands of cases by conciliation, but it lacked the authority to enforce the executive order. Those presidents who followed Roosevelt established similar committees, but it was not until President Kennedy took office that an investigating committee was given the authority to cancel government contracts or to penalize contractors who chose to continue to discriminate in employment practices (Beach, 1980).

Presidential executive orders prohibit discrimination in employment by agencies with federal contracts or subcontracts valued at $10,500. These employers are not allowed to discriminate based on age (PEO 11141), race, color, religion, or national origin (PEO 11246), sex (PEO 11375), or political affiliation, marital status, or disability (PEO 11478). In addition, PEOs also require all employers whose government contracts exceed $10,500 to implement affirmative action plans.

It is important to note that PEOs apply to state and local governments with 15 or more fulltime employees. Recreation and sport agencies receiving federal monies from any federal agency are responsible for those private contractors who contract for facility development, operations, maintenance, or programming. If a private contractor discriminates in any employment practice and a violation is reported, the recreation and sport agency could be investigated, become involved in a formal hearing or lawsuit, and possibly lose federal financial support.

Affirmative Action: Presidential Executive Order 11246, as Amended by Executive Order 11375

As we have now learned, the Presidential Executive Order 11246 was established to provide equal opportunity in federal employment for all qualified individuals regardless of race, color, religion (formerly referred to as creed), or national origin. A major revision to PEO 11246 requires employers to abide by this non-discriminatory policy should they received federal financial assistance (e.g., loans, grants, contracts). *Affirmative Action*, which was stipulated by PEO 11246, provides organizations with an opportunity to remedy past discrimination by taking

positive steps to ensure that an applicant or an existing employee receives fair treatment with regard to race, creed, color, or national origin. According to Mathis and Jackson (2008), "Through affirmative action employers are urged to hire groups of people based on their race, age, gender, or national origin to make up for historical discrimination" (p. 147). This includes such areas as recruitment and selection, training and development, and promotion. To not abide by the affirmative action policy could mean severe penalties. If, for example, a federal contractor is found in violation of affirmative action, the contract can be terminated or suspended. In addition, it is highly probable that the contractor maybe found ineligible to receive future government contracts.

> The cruel disease of discrimination knows no sectional or state boundaries. The continuing attack on this problem must be equally broad. It must be both private and public—it must be conducted at national, state, and local levels—and it must include both legislative and executive action.
>
> *John F. Kennedy*
> *February 28, 1963*

Affirmative Action Landmarks

The need for affirmative action is a subject for debate throughout the United States. Proponents of affirmative action claim it helps to overcome past injustices while opponents of affirmative action believe it penalizes certain individuals such as white males. Some recreation and sport organizations have instituted affirmative action voluntarily, while others are simply required to do so. Nevertheless, by the late 1970s, flaws in the policy began to show up amid its good intentions. Reverse discrimination became an issue, epitomized by the famous *Bakke v. Regents of the University of California (1978)*. Allan Bakke, a white male, had been rejected two years in a row by a medical school that had accepted less qualified minority applicants—the school had a separate admissions policy for minorities and reserved 16 out of 100 places for minority students. The Supreme Court outlawed inflexible quota systems in affirmative action programs, which in this case had unfairly discriminated against a white applicant. But a later landmark ruling on affirmative action involved the *University of Michigan*. In short, two cases were tried in federal courts in 2000 and 2001—one involving the undergraduate program *(Gratz v. Bollinger)* and the other its law school *(Grutter v. Bollinger)*. The Supreme Court (5-4) upheld the University of Michigan Law School's policy, ruling that race can be one of many factors considered by colleges when selecting their students. The Supreme Court, however, ruled (6-3) that the more formulaic approach of the University of Michigan's undergraduate admissions program, which uses a point system that rated students and awarded additional points to minorities, had to be modified. In these two cases, the Supreme Court ruled that although affirmative action was no longer justified as a way of redressing past oppression and injustice, it promoted a compelling state interest in diversity at all levels of society. As Sandra Day O'Connor wrote for the majority, "In order to cultivate a set of leaders with legitimacy in the eyes of the citizenry, it is necessary that the path to leadership be visibly open to talented and qualified individuals of every race and ethnicity."

Affirmative Action Compliance

Affirmative action plans (AAP) are required by government contractors to ensure that protected-class members are represented in their organization. An affirmative action plan is a formal report that organizations submit to enforcement agencies. Usually contractors with at least 50 employees and $50,000 in government contracts annually must supply these plans to appropriate agencies. It is important to note that some recreation and sport organizations voluntarily have AAPs, but employers who have government contractors must have such a plan. AAPs are discussed in more detail later in this book.

The Debate Rages on About Affirmative Action

Affirmative action is an opportunity for recreation and sport organizations to help remedy past discrimination. The debate continues to rage on as supporters of affirmative action argue that without it, women, minorities, and members of other protected groups will continue to be discriminated against. Opponents of affirmative action argue that preferential treatment or selection for protected-class members over other individuals who are equally qualified is unfair.

Research shows the majority of Americans feel that affirmative action has been good for minorities and is still necessary to achieve diversity at work. Regardless of whether or not one supports or opposes affirmative action programs, it is clear that affirmative action is a controversial subject that will likely be debated for years to come.

Vocational Rehabilitation Act of 1973 (as Amended by the Rehabilitation Act of 1974) and the Americans with Disabilities Act (ADA) of 1990

> *A young college graduate with a degree in outdoor adventure leadership with a certification in wilderness first responder (WFR) applied for a seasonal position as a back-country ranger. The response to his inquiry about why he was not considered for the position was, "You are a diabetic and we can't take a chance that you might endanger yourself or others out in the 'brush' if you should require medical care."*
>
> *Was the agency justified, legally, in offering this reason for not hiring the applicant?*

In the case of the diabetic applicant who was not considered for the position of back-country ranger, the agency could be courting a lawsuit for discrimination. The agency had the right to ask the applicant if he had any medical conditions that might impair his ability to perform his duties, but not until after the agency had decided that the applicant did or did not meet all the necessary requirements for the position. If the applicant was not considered for the position solely because of his diabetic condition, he could claim discrimination because he was not able to demonstrate that a diabetic in the "brush" is not a medical risk, nor that it requires reasonable accommodation on the part of the agency.

For individuals with disabilities, the Vocational Rehabilitation Act of 1973 (amended by the Rehabilitation Act of 1974) and the Americans with Disabilities Act (ADA) of 1990, is their counterpart of Title VII in prohibiting employment discrimination. Too often recreation and sport managers incorrectly overlook qualified individuals who happen to have disabilities. This occurs due to the lack of knowledge most managers have regarding specific disabilities. In an attempt to protect persons with physical and mental disabilities against employment discrimination, the Vocational Rehabilitation Act (VRA) legislation passed to covered federal agencies and government contractors.

- Section 503, as amended in 1974, required employers with contracts or subcontracts over $2,500 to include affirmative action clauses in the contracts. If the contract was $50,000 or more and the employer had at least 50 people on the payroll, the employer had to submit an affirmative action plan for hiring the person with a disability.

Although the rehabilitation legislation passed during this time is considered by many to be the civil rights law for persons with disabilities, the laws often were limited in scope in that they only applied to organizations receiving federal financial assistance.

The Americans with Disabilities Act (ADA) passed by Congress in 1990 sought to broaden coverage and expanded employment regulations to further protect people with varying degrees of disabilities. Title I of the Americans with Disabilities Act of 1990 prohibits private employers, state and local governments, employment agencies and labor unions from discriminating against qualified individuals with disabilities in job application procedures, hiring, firing, advancement, compensation, job training, and other terms, conditions, and privileges of employment. The ADA affects employers with 15 or more employees working 200 or more weeks during the calendar year including part-time employees. The act applies to private employers, employment agencies, and labor unions. The ADA's nondiscrimination standards also apply to federal sector employees under section 501 of the Rehabilitation Act, as amended, and its implementing rules.

The basic provision of the ADA prohibits organizations from discriminating against qualified person with disabilities who can perform the essential functions of a job. Therefore, it is essential that recreation and sport managers clearly identify the "essential" job functions of each position and identify other functions that are nonessential as "desirable."

According to the U.S. Equal Employment Opportunity Commission, an individual with a disability is a person who:

- Has a physical or mental impairment that substantially limits one or more major life activities;
- Has a record of such an impairment; or
- Is regarded as having such an impairment.

A qualified employee or applicant with a disability is an individual who, with or without reasonable accommodation, can perform the essential functions of the job in question. Reasonable accommodation may include, but is not limited to:

- Making existing facilities used by employees readily accessible to and usable by persons with disabilities.
- Job restructuring, modifying work schedules, reassignment to a vacant position;
- Acquiring or modifying equipment or devices, adjusting or modifying examinations, training materials, or policies, and providing qualified readers or interpreters.

An employer is required to make a reasonable accommodation to the known disability of a qualified applicant or employee if it would not impose an undue hardship on the operation of the employer's business. "Undue hardship" is defined as an action requiring significant difficulty or expense when considered in light of factors such as an employer's size, financial resources, and the nature and structure of its operation.

An employer is not required to lower quality or production standards to make an accommodation; nor is an employer obligated to provide personal use items such as glasses or hearing aids.

Title I of the ADA also covers:

- *Medical Examinations and Inquiries.* Employers may not ask job applicants about the existence, nature, or severity of a disability. Applicants may be asked about their ability to perform specific job functions. A job offer may be conditioned on the results of a medical examination, but only if the examination is required for all entering employees in similar jobs. Medical examinations of employees must be job related and consistent with the employer's business needs.

- *Drug and Alcohol Abuse.* Employees and applicants currently engaging in the illegal use of drugs are not covered by the ADA when an employer acts on the basis of such use. Tests for illegal drugs are not subject to the ADA's restrictions on medical examinations. Employers may hold illegal drug users and alcoholics to the same performance standards as other employees.

It is also unlawful to retaliate against an individual for opposing employment practices that discriminate based on disability or for filing a discrimination charge, testifying, or participating in any way in an investigation, proceeding, or litigation under the ADA.

Veterans' Employee Rights: Vietnam Era Veterans' Readjustment Assistance Act of 1974 and the Uniformed Services Employment and Reemployment Rights Act of 1994

> *A female applied for a position at a coastal state park and was told she was one of five top candidates and would be called soon for an interview. When she was never notified, she contacted the park superintendent and learned that two veterans had "bumped" her from the interview list.*
>
> *Did the state park system violate federal law?*

The Vietnam Era Veterans' Readjustment Assistance Act (VEVRAA) of 1974 parallels the Vocational Rehabilitation Act. According to the U.S. Department of Labor, the VEVRAA prohibits employment discrimination and requires federal contractors to take affirmative action to hire and promote Vietnam-era veterans. More specifically, the Vietnam Era Veterans' Readjustment Assistance Act of 1974, as amended, states that contractors and subcontractors with a federal contract or subcontract in the amount of $100,000 or more, entered into on or after December 1, 2003, for the purchase, sale, or use of personal property or non-personal services (including construction), take affirmative action to employ and advance in employment qualified covered veterans. In addition, VEVRAA requires contractors and subcontractors to list their employment openings and requires affirmative action protocol.

The employment rights of military veterans and reservists are also included in the Uniformed Services Employment and Reemployment Rights Act (USERRA) of 1994. This act states that employees must notify their employer of military service obligations. Employees serving in the military must be provided leaves of absences and have reemployment rights for up to five years. However, this does not mean that an employer is required to compensate the employee while he or she is on active military leave. Most often the employee is reinstated in the same job position that he or she had prior to leaving for military serve obligations.

The state park system, therefore, did not violate federal legislation when it followed its state veterans' preference law and placed two qualified veterans on the list ahead of the female. Whenever veteran applicants meet minimum job qualifications, they may be given a point advantage, even if such practice appears to discriminate against women and those male non-veterans who may have been disqualified from military service because of some disability. The example given did violate good recruiting and selection personnel practices. An applicant should not be kept anticipating a promised call for a job interview. She should have been notified when her position changed on the list of applicants.

Pregnancy Discrimination Act of 1978

> *A female sports information director for a private agency took all her vacation and sick leave to have her second child. Because the agency's insurance policy did not include pregnancy disability benefits, which would have paid her a percentage of her salary while she was out having the child, she planned to return to work immediately after childbirth. However, medical complications ensued, and when she finally planned to return to work two months later, she learned the sport agency had hired someone else in her position.*
>
> *Was this action fair? Was it legal?*

Legislation passed in 1978 amends Title VII of the Civil Rights Act of 1964 and attempts to eliminate employment discrimination against employees who are pregnant. The Pregnancy Discrimination Act (PDA) requires that employers treat maternity leave the same as other personal or medical leaves. Thus, the recreation or sport manager may not engage in discriminatory employment practices against an employee who is affected by pregnancy, childbirth, or any related medical condition (including abortion and adoption). The PDA relates a great deal to employee benefit plans and requires that women who are affected by pregnancy, childbirth, or any subsequently related medical conditions will receive the same benefits as any other disability in the fringe benefit program of the employer. Although pregnant women are not disabled because they are pregnant, there is a period of disability associated with every childbirth. Medical insurance must now cover pregnancy as fully as it covers other medical disability conditions. In summary, the Pregnancy Discrimination Act states that women who are affected by pregnancy, childbirth, or abortion must be treated the same as all other employees (or applicants) on the basis of their ability or inability to work. This law protects all females, single and married.

In the case of the female sports information director, the agency *prior to PDA* would have been within their legal rights not to provide pregnancy disability benefits in their insurance coverage. The Supreme Court in *General Electric v. Gilbert* (1976) struck down an EEOC guideline, Sex Discrimination—Part 1604. This guideline stated that pregnancies were temporary disabilities and should be covered under any health plan. The Court ruled that such guidelines were in conflict with interpretations of the Equal Pay Act, and that difference in benefit plans between men and women were legal. However, with the passage of PDA two years later in 1978, Congress mandated that pregnancy be treated like any other disability in health insurance plans.

Therefore, if the sport agency provided 60 percent salary benefits for 60 days for any disability, the female sports information director would be entitled to those same benefits during the two months she experienced medical complications following childbirth. Furthermore, the agency could not discharge her from her position during that time period, even if she had used all sick and vacation leave. Explanations of the guidelines can become complex and will not be explained in detail here. Each case should be considered independently with EEOC prior to any discharge decision, to avoid future complaint or lawsuit.

Immigration Reform and Control Act of 1986, as revised in 1990 and 1996

The Immigration Reform and Control Act (IRCA) prohibits employers from hiring individuals who are not legally authorized to work in the United States and requires employers to verify the eligibility of all new employees. That is, any new employee must provide documentation to prove they are eligible to work in the U.S. by completing and signing an I-9 form to certify their eligibility. One intention of IRCA is to prevent discrimination when hiring and discharging individuals based upon their national origin and citizen status. Further, IRCA prevents discrimination against foreign-looking or foreign-sounding job applicants.

Family and Medical Leave Act of 1993

The Family and Medical Leave Act (FMLA) applies to all government employees regardless of their number and to private employers with 50 or more employees who live within 75 miles of the workplace. The FMLA enables qualified employees to take up to 12 weeks a year of unpaid leave during a 12-month period for family and health reasons.

The law is intended to help employees balance work demands without hindering their ability to attend to personal and family needs. Employees may be full-time, part-time, or those already on leave. Only employees who have worked at least 12 months and 1,250 hours in the previous year are eligible for leave under the FMLA. An employee's health insurance coverage is maintained during the leave and the employee has the right to return to the same or an equivalent position after the leave. It is important to understand that both male and female employees are eligible for unpaid leave for:

- for the birth and care of the newborn child of the employee;
- for placement with the employee of a son or daughter for adoption or foster care;
- to care for an immediate family member (spouse, child, or parent) with a serious health condition; or
- to take medical leave when the employee is unable to work because of a serious health condition.

Note: In January 2008 the President made an amendment to permit a spouse, son, daughter, parent, or next of kin to take up to 26 workweeks of leave to care for a member of the Armed Forces, including a member of the National Guard or Reserves, who is undergoing medical treatment, recuperation, or therapy, is otherwise in outpatient status, or is otherwise on the temporary disability retired list, for a serious injury or illness.

Serious Health Condition

The FMLA protects employees who need to care for themselves or a family member due to a serious health condition. Recreation and sport organizations have the right to require employees to provide medical certification or verification should they choose to request a leave under FMLA. In this context, "serious health condition" means an illness, injury, impairment, or physical or mental condition that involves the following:

- any period of incapacity or treatment connected with inpatient care (i.e., an overnight stay) in a hospital, hospice, or residential medical care facility; or

- a period of incapacity requiring absence of more than three calendar days from work, school, or other regular daily activities that also involves continuing treatment by (or under the supervision of) a healthcare provider; or

- any period of incapacity due to pregnancy, or for prenatal care; or

- any period of incapacity (or treatment therefore) due to a chronic serious health condition (e.g., asthma, diabetes, epilepsy, etc.); or

- a period of incapacity that is permanent or long-term due to a condition for which treatment may not be effective (e.g., Alzheimer's, stroke, terminal diseases, etc.); or,

- any absences to receive multiple treatments by, or on referral by, a healthcare provider for a condition that likely would result in incapacity of more than three consecutive days if left untreated (e.g., chemotherapy, physical therapy, dialysis, etc.).

Summary

1. The primary purpose of EEO legislation is to ensure that every person has the right to fair treatment as a job seeker and as an employee.

2. Employment practices shall be based on a person's ability, work performance, and potential to learn the job rather than on his or her age, sex, race, religion, color, national origin, or disability.

3. An employment practice is discriminatory if it (a) treats people differently, or (b) leads to unequal consequences for different groups.

4. The Civil Rights Act of 1964 outlawed discriminatory acts regardless of whether they are deliberately planned or accidentally executed.

5. Protected class refers to individuals within a group who are identified for protection under equal employment laws and regulations. These groups include individual with disabilities, women, individuals 40 years of age and older, veterans, and in some states, marital status, and sexual orientation.

6. The EEOC, established by the 1964 Civil Rights Act, has responsibility for (a) issuing the regulations that ensure compliance with the Act, and (b) processing complaints of discrimination.

7. Under the Equal Pay Act, employers are required to pay equal wages to men and women performing similar work requiring similar skill, effort, and responsibility. The Lilly Ledbetter Fair Pay Act (2009) makes it easier for workers to sue organizations for pay discrimination.

8. Employers may pay differential wages when those wages are based on an established seniority or merit system.

9. Whereas both the Civil Rights Act and the Age Discrimination Act provide for exemptions from the law or "bona fide occupational qualifications" (BFOQs), employers and supervisors should exercise caution in taking advantage of these permissible exceptions. Remember, race and color are not permissible BFOQs.

10. Affirmative Action urges employers to hire groups of people based on their race, age, gender, or national origin to make up for historical discrimination.

11. Recreation and sport organizations should not award contracts to contractors who cannot provide evidence of obeying presidential executive orders which serve to eliminate employment discrimination. Ignorance of discriminatory practices is not excusable under the law. Affirmative Action Plans should be used.

12. According to the Americans with Disabilities Act (ADA), employers are expected to make reasonable accommodations for people with disabilities, unless an undue financial hardship would be imposed on the hiring organization. The laws do not expect the employers to jeopardize the safety or health of employees

and the public in order to hire a person with a disabling condition.

13. State and federal veterans' preference laws were passed to compensate those who spent time in active military service. These laws have been upheld as legal by the Supreme Court and the Civil Rights Act.

14. Organizations that provide employee disability health insurance benefits must provide the same benefits for pregnant employees who may be absent from work due to pregnancy- or child-related medical problems.

15. Employers should develop written policies and grievances and disciplinary procedures concerning sexual harassment. These must be communicated to all employees. Knowledge of sexual harassment without taking measures to eradicate it places the employer in violation of the law.

16. The Family and Medical Leave Act enables qualified employees to take up to 12 weeks a year of unpaid leave during a 12 month period for family and health reasons.

Discussion Topics

1. Why should recreation and sport organizations comply with EEO laws and regulations?

2. What is the difference between disparate treatment and disparate impact?

3. What is meant by "job relatedness" and "business necessity"? How might these concepts apply to organizations? What impact does ADA have on these issues?

4. Under what conditions would "good-natured fun" constitute sexual harassment?

5. Under what conditions can an employer be held responsible for sexual harassment of its employees?

6. Where do you stand on the debate of affirmative action?

7. When could employees make a case for reverse discrimination?

8. Should government impose a mandatory retirement age? Provide an argument against such an act.

9. What is the difference between prejudice and discrimination?

10. Assume that you are the manager of a county athletic program. You are responsible for hiring, training, supervising, and evaluating a staff of full-time and part-time personnel. List a number of discriminatory practices that you should avoid.

References

Beach, D. (1980). *Personnel: The management of people at work*. (4th ed.). New York, NY: Macmillan Publishing Co.

Calvert, R. (1979). *Affirmative action: A comprehensive recruitment manual*. Garrett Park, MD: Garrett Park Press.

Dolliver, M. (2004, November 8). And women used to be such a good bargain! *Adweek, 45*, 34.

Jain, H. & Sloane, P. (1981). The structure of labor markets, minority workers and E.E.O. legislation. *International Journal of Social Economics, 3*.

Mathis, R. & Jackson, J. (2008). *Human resource management* (12th ed.). Thomson South-Western.

Strauss, G. and Sayles, L. (1980) *Personnel: The human problems of management* (4th ed.). Englewood Cliffs, NJ: Prentice-Hall, Inc.

Train Managers and Executives to Avoid Legal Danger Zones. (2006, August). *HR Focus, 83*, 4–7.

U.S. Department of Equal Employment Opportunity Commission. Retrieved from http://www.eeoc.gov

Webster's New Collegiate Dictionary. (2012). Springfield, MA: G&C Merriam Co.

LEGAL ENVIRONMENT: EMPLOYEE CONCERNS

While EEO legislation has received the most attention in recent decades, federal laws and regulations have influenced human resource management since the 1920s, when the federal government and court actions attempted to intervene in the disputes between organized labor and employees. Just as Chapter 1 focused on EEO legislation, this chapter attempts to give the reader an overview of the magnitude of governmental legislation that also influences the supervision and management in recreation and sport organizations. An awareness of these laws may be all that is required of supervisors. However, as a supervisor accepts greater responsibility within the organization, moving up into middle- and top-management, the need to interact with attorneys, personnel, and labor relations specialists is magnified and additional information and training should be sought. At all levels, supervisors should understand the significance that these laws play in maintaining a work environment which will maximize employee motivation and concern for health and safety, compensation, and civil liberties. Many of these laws are revisited in Chapter 9 as a way to reinforce the importance of understanding the legal environment. First, let us begin with an introduction to labor relations.

LABOR RELATIONS

The following discussion provides a brief description of the most important labor laws. The recreation and sport supervisor should be aware that employees have the right to freely organize and bargain collectively even though the federal government has taken action to both help and hinder unions. Simply stated, *a union is a formal association of workers that promotes the interests of its members through collective action.*

National Labor Relations Act of 1935 (Wagner Act)

The primary purpose of this law was to give employees more bargaining power. Known as the Wagner Act, it has served as the basic federal statement of policy towards labor-management relations. To administer the Wagner Act, the National Labor Relations Board (NLRB) was established. The NLRB is an independent federal agency created by Congress in 1935 to administer the National Labor Relations Act (NLRA), the primary law governing relations between unions and employers in the private sector. The statute guarantees the right of employees to organize and to bargain collectively with their employers, and to engage in other protected concerted activity with or without a union, or to refrain from all such activity.

Labor-Management Relations Act of 1947 and 1974 (Taft-Hartley Act)

Congress passed this law after employers complained that the Wagner Act not only favored unions too much, but failed to address unfair union practices. Thus the Taft-Hartley Act, as it is frequently called, attempted to establish a balance of power between the labor union and the employer. One of its most notable provisions recognized the right of employees not to join unions. It also prohibits strikes during national emergencies.

Labor-Management Reporting and Disclosure Act of 1959 (Landrum-Griffin Act)

In an effort to prevent improper union practices and the abuse of power by some union officials, the Landrum-Griffin Act was passed to protect employees and regulate the internal affairs of unions. It included provisions that controlled union elections, membership dues, and member conduct.

Federal Employees and Labor Relations

Although employees in the private sector have been governed by federal legislation for many years, federal government employees were excluded from those labor relations laws discussed previously in this section. Now federal employees are protected under executive orders and covered by congressional law.

President Kennedy in 1962 established the first labor relations regulations for federal employees. Executive Order (EO) 10988 recognized employees' right to organize and collectively bargain, although employees were forbidden to strike. Agency heads had the final authority over all grievances. Orders 11491, 11616, and 11838 amended EO 10988, clarified collective bargaining regulations, and created a Labor Relations Council to hear appeals and discuss personnel practices and working conditions. Federal employees still did not have the same rights as those of workers in the private sector, however, because they could not bargain for salaries or benefits, and their respective agency heads still made the final decisions on all matters.

The Civil Service Reform Act, passed by Congress in 1978, superseded previous executive orders and became the basic law governing labor relations for federal employees. The act created the Federal Labor Relations Authority (FLRA). This federal agency was created by Title VII of the Civil Service Reform Act of 1978. The statute allows certain non-postal federal employees to organize, bargain collectively, and to participate through labor organizations of their choice in decisions affecting their working lives.

State and Local Government Employees

Most states have passed laws pertaining to the collective bargaining rights of state and local public employees, although the coverage and permissiveness varies from state to state. While some state laws protect all public employees, others only specify and cover certain groups, while exempting other groups. The rights of public-sector employees, as those rights relate to collective bargaining, have not been as extensive as those in the private sector, but the greatest growth in unionization in recent years has been public-sector labor organizations. It is important to keep in mind that legislation varies widely from state to state. Therefore, a recreation and sport supervisor who works for a state or local agency would be well advised to ascertain and understand the laws specific to their situation.

Health and Safety

It is important for the reader to understand that supervisors must accept responsibility for maintaining a healthy and safe work environment for employees. In this section we address two key health-related areas for legislation: workers' compensation (WC) and workplace safety, which was the target of the Occupational Safety and Health Act (OSHA). In addition, we introduce health and safety concerns as they relate to child labor laws. Many youth are employed within recreation and sport organizations, and the supervisor must be aware of the legal ramifications of using child labor in the workplace.

Workers' Compensation Laws

Until 1970 and the passage of the Occupational Safety and Health Act (OSHA), health and safety on the job had been governed by individual state laws, although some effort had been made by the federal government to control safety conditions in certain industries. Workers' compensation (WC) laws vary considerably from state to state, but certain provisions are similar in all states. These laws are designed to compensate employees for job-related illnesses or injuries, whether temporary or permanent; to provide rehabilitation services to reclaim the injured workers' capabilities; and to award death benefits to survivors. In addition, workers' compensation coverage has been expanded in many states to include the emotional well-being of employees who suffer psychological loss due to job-related injury, stress, pressure, and anxiety.

Not all states make employer participation compulsory. In some cases, employers are self-insured. Where the employer does provide coverage for employees, the employer pays all the costs through insurance premiums based in part on a rate set according to the organization's past safety and health record. The employer, through each supervisor, must maintain a safe work site in order to reduce accidents and thereby reduce workers' compensation costs. Fewer accidents mean a healthier workforce and a financial saving for the employer.

Since every state has a different WC law, the two questions for the recreation and sport supervisor to ask are: "In my state, who is covered?" and "What are work-related injuries?" Workers' compensation problems most often stem from vague or confusing language in the laws themselves. The standard verbiage "arising out of and in the course of employment" leaves open the question: "What are work-related injuries?"

Injuries that take place during employer-sponsored recreation programs are covered. The courts have upheld these decisions based on the premise that company-sponsored recreation promotes morale, loyalty, and better productivity, conditions that are of value to the employer.

There are several other interesting points for recreation and sport employers and managers to remember about workers' compensation. Injuries incurred while driving to different work sites or while living on the recreation site (e.g., a park ranger's cabin) are also covered. If a sports manager stops to check in on the outdoor basketball league while driving home from work, any injuries sustained during that trip should be compensated. River guides, camp managers, or therapeutic recreation specialists who must reside at the work site or live at an institution (e.g., group home) are also covered by WC, especially if their services may be called upon at any time.

Generally, part-time recreation, park, and sport employees, however short their period of work, are covered by workers' compensation if the employer is contributing financially to a program. Volunteers would not usually be covered unless (1) the insurance company agrees and/or extra premiums were paid, or (2) the volunteer receives some form of recompense, such as a free lunch, free use of facilities, or a stipend. Court cases have supported the contention that when the work is performed within the course of business hours and represents an integral part of the recreation or sport operation, the person should be covered, like any other wage-earning employee. And finally, although not widely known, employees who work at home are typically covered under workers' compensation, providing the employee is injured while doing employer-related work.

Occupational Safety and Health Act of 1970

It was not until the 1960s that the federal government seriously concerned itself with safety in the private sector. Prior to the passage of the Occupational Safety and Health Act (OSHA) of 1970, employee safety was regulated by state workers' compensation laws; laws often obsolete and lacking in enforcement. As a result of a coal mine explosion in 1968 and a significant increase in injuries on the job during the previous decade, unions became active in lobbying for job-safety legislation. Congressional lawmakers were convinced that work environments were unsafe after bearing considerable evidence on black lung disease, work accidents, and job-related mortality rates.

According to the Occupational Safety and Health Administration (U.S. Department of Labor, 2012) the purpose of OSHA is to preserve resources

by ensuring, as far as possible, safe and healthy working conditions for all workers (see Figure 2.1, p. 22). The act consists of three main stipulations that employers must address:

1. Establish a safe work environment that is free from known hazards and harms to employees.
2. Obey all OSHA standards and regulations.
3. Maintain safety records or injuries and illnesses on the job.

State workers' compensation laws are designed to assist the worker after an accident, but OSHA regulations are designed to reduce the risk of accidents in the first place. This means that each non-government recreation employer must furnish his or her staff with a place of employment free from recognized hazards that are likely to cause physical harm or death. Each employee must abide by the prescribed standards or face prescribed disciplinary action specifically permitted in OSHA regulations. The federal government regulates the employer, but the employer, through supervision, must ensure that employees are in compliance with the OSHA standards. Employees of federal, state, and local government are excluded in this law. Although the state and local governments are exempt, state governments are required to set up their own OSHA plan and have it approved by the federal government. These various state OSHAs must be at least as effective as the federal OSHA legislation and must cover all workers, including public employees in that state. Many states have their own OSHA plan which covers both private and public sector employees.

The administration and enforcement of this act is vested in the Occupational Safety and Health Administration within the Department of Labor. This agency establishes the standards, conducts on-site inspections, and issues citations for OSHA violations. An independent review commission functions like a court to hear appeals, and a national institute conducts safety standards research and trains inspectors.

The act itself is very brief, but the technical and complex regulations and standards number in the thousands and fill volumes. It would be impossible to provide the reader with all the basic provisions in the regulations and standards as they pertain to parks, recreation, sports, and leisure services. However, some examples of OSHA regulations that are written

Employers have certain responsibilities under the Occupational Safety and Health Act of 1970. The following list is a summary of the most important ones:

Provide a workplace free from serious recognized hazards and comply with standards, rules, and regulations issued under the OSHA Act.

Examine workplace conditions to make sure they conform to applicable OSHA standards.

Make sure employees have and use safe tools and equipment and properly maintain this equipment.

Use color codes, posters, labels, or signs to warn employees of potential hazards.

Establish or update operating procedures and communicate them so that employees follow safety and health requirements.

Provide medical examinations and training when required by OSHA standards.

Post, at a prominent location within the workplace, the OSHA poster (or the state-plan equivalent) informing employees of their rights and responsibilities.

Report to the nearest OSHA office within 8 hours any fatal accident or one that results in the hospitalization of three or more employees.

Keep records of work-related injuries and illnesses. (Note: Employers with 10 or fewer employees and employers in certain low-hazard industries are exempt from this requirement.)

Provide employees, former employees, and their representatives access to the Log of Work-Related Injuries and Illnesses (OSHA Form 300).

For 2002 only, post a copy of the totals from the last page of the OSHA 200 Log during the entire month of February 2002.

Provide access to employee medical records and exposure records to employees or their authorized representatives.

Provide to the OSHA compliance officer the names of authorized employee representatives who may be asked to accompany the compliance officer during an inspection.

Do not discriminate against employees who exercise their rights under the Act.

Post OSHA citations at or near the work area involved. Each citation must remain posted until the violation has been corrected, or for three working days, whichever is longer. Post abatement-verification documents or tags.

Correct cited violations by the deadline set in the OSHA citation and submit required abatement-verification documentation.

Figure 2.1
Summary of Important Employer Responsibilities of OSHA

for recreation-related activities include firework displays, swimming pools and spas, all-terrain vehicles, and playgrounds. For example, OSHA regulations address ways to keep lifeguards safe on-the-job and protect them from hazards and include safety issues such as testing the chlorine levels and pH balance of water in a swimming pool, spa, or hot tub; and wearing sunscreen, uniforms, and hats to protect against sun exposure.

OSHA standards also apply to construction activities and address topics such as fall protection, working on or around stairs and ladders, scaffolding, electrical, trenching and excavation, and motor vehicle safety on the worksite.

Child Labor

Just as OSHA has certain regulations that address ways to keep lifeguards safe on the job and protect them

from hazards, the Fair Labor Standards Act (FLSA), which is discussed in a later chapter, has child-labor provisions that directly affect employing full-time and part-time youth in recreation and sport organizations. Safety concerns are addressed in the child labor provisions, especially those under the age of 18.

The age of a youth worker determines which child-labor standards apply to the work week. For example, at the age of 18 or older, youth workers may perform any job for unlimited hours. Youth workers who are 16 or 17 years old may also work unlimited hours; however, these jobs must be non-hazardous. Examples of hazardous work may include storing explosives such as fireworks and dangerous chemicals, and using power-driven bakery machines and meat slicers.

At the age of 14 or 15, youth workers are limited during the school year to a total of 18 hours per week (3 hours per day on school days) and must be scheduled for work between the hours of 7 am and 7 pm. During the summer when they are not attending school, 14- and 15-year-olds may work 40 hours per week (8 hours per day) between the hours of 7 am and 9 pm. It is important for the recreation and sport supervisor to keep accurate records of the number of hours worked by youth workers. Supervisors should carefully schedule hours that will not place a youth worker in violation of exceeding the maximum number of hours worked per week. For example, it is irresponsible of a supervisor to schedule a youth worker to referee a basketball game when the youth is approaching 39 hours of work prior to the game. What happens if the game goes into overtime and pushes the number of hours worked by the youth over the maximum 40 hours? This situation could result in enforcement actions and a fine for violating the FLSA.

Benefits and Unemployment Compensation

Benefits other than wages did not exist at the turn of the century. Now they can consume as much as 30% or more of the employer's payroll (Bureau of Labor Statistics, 2011). Because they are so widely accepted as part of the cost of hiring employees, the term "fringe benefits" is no longer appropriate. No one would argue that benefits vary from employer to employer, some being more generous than others.

Recreation and sport supervisors can easily feel overwhelmed by the many federal and state laws, rules and regulations, and court decisions that surround benefits and compensation practices. Although Chapter 9 is devoted fully to the topic of compensation, here we begin by introducing the Social Security Act of 1935 followed by four key pieces of federal legislation related to health care. We conclude with an introduction to unemployment insurance. Again, it is easy to feel overwhelmed by the many laws that we are governed by, but a basic awareness of these regulations is critical for the recreation and sport supervisor.

Social Security Act of 1935

The Social Security Act of 1935 was passed near the end of the Great Depression, following public concern over economic security. The purpose of the act was to provide financial benefits to all workers in the United States. Today, most workers in the U.S. receive Social Security benefits once they retire and then collect a Social Security check once a month.

Initially, the plan was designed to force workers, through payroll deductions matched by the employer, to save for old age. At age 65 the worker could retire and receive a modest pension to supplement his or her own savings. Today, the plan not only covers retired workers, but it provides benefits to survivors of deceased workers, pays disability benefits, and covers payments for medical and hospital care for those 65 of age or older. The employers' contribution to the pension is the part that is considered a benefit.

Medicare is a federal health insurance program that covers most people 65 years of age or older, or those under the age of 65 with certain disabilities. Although Medicare covers most medical expenses such as doctor's visits, hospital stays, and drug and medical treatment costs, it does not cover most medical care given at home, in nursing homes, or in assisted-living facilities.

Employee Retirement Income Security Act of 1974

The Employment Retirement Income Security Act (ERISA) attempts to regulate the internal management of private pension plans in order to protect employees who have contributed to the plans. Not every employer is required to have a plan, but those who offer their employees this benefit are regulated by the federal government under this law. The basic provisions of ERISA require private employers to provide employees with a description of the pension plan written in specific, clear terms. ERISA also provides the detailed fiduciary responsibilities of those controlling and administering the assets of the pension plan. The ERISA applies to most private-sector employers providing employee health benefit plans.

Like OSHA, this law is very lengthy, complex, and highly technical. Some employers claim that pension plans are more expensive now because the law demands so much. This may be true, but most workers can now retire without fear that their pension program will not be able to pay out benefits when they most need the money.

Consolidated Omnibus Budget Reconciliation Act (COBRA) of 1985

COBRA is a federal law passed by Congress in 1985. It contains a provision allowing employees and their families who had been covered by their employer's healthcare plan to maintain coverage if a "qualifying event" occurs that makes them ineligible for coverage. Divorce, resignation, layoff, discharge, medical leave, death of the covered employee, or a dependent child reaching the age at which he or she is no longer covered are examples of qualifying events. When a qualifying event occurs and an employee no longer qualifies for the employer's healthcare plan, the employer is required to give qualified beneficiaries a period of time to decide whether to elect COBRA coverage. COBRA is discussed in fuller detail in Chapter 9.

Health Insurance Portability and Accountability Act (HIPAA) of 1996

The Health Insurance Portability and Accountability Act (HIPAA) of 1996 amended the Employee Retirement Income Security Act (ERISA) to provide rights and protections for employees and their families in group health plans. For example, HIPAA includes protection for employees who change jobs and need to continue healthcare insurance coverage due to pre-existing conditions. By law, employers are prohibited from excluding employees with pre-existing conditions for 12 months. If employees fail to enroll in a company-sponsored healthcare insurance program as soon as they are eligible, employers may impose exclusions for pre-existing conditions. HIPPA applies to most private-sector employers providing health benefit plans.

Pension Protection Act (PPA) of 2006

According to the Internal Revenue Service (IRS), the Pension Protection Act (PPA) of 2006 is the most sweeping pension legislation in over 30 years and includes a number of tax incentives to enhance and protect retirement savings for millions of Americans. Simply stated, *a pension is a sum of money paid regularly by an employer to an employee who has retired and is eligible to receive the retirement benefit*. Employers are not required to offer a pension plan and roughly half of all privately employed workers in the United States have no employer-provided retirement plan. The PPA contains provisions that deliberately strengthen the funding rules for defined benefit pension plans.

Unemployment Compensation

The seasonal nature of recreation and sport in both the private and public sectors places an economic strain on the underemployed worker who can find work only during specific months of the year. It can also place a burden on the employer, who must pay higher unemployment taxes. For these reasons, the reader should know how some management decisions make an impact on unemployment compensation rates: decisions such as whether to hire seasonal staff rather than full-time workers, and whether to hire or retain an employee.

Title VII of the Social Security Act of 1935 forced the states into enacting unemployment compensation laws. The federal government imposed a federal payroll tax on every employer, but permitted the employer to pay the tax into a state plan instead of paying the tax to the federal government. To keep the tax money in the state, each state established its own unemployment compensation plan by 1937.

Not only do the tax rates differ from state to state, but the tax rate for each employer also varies, based on the employer's own record of unemployment payments to discharged employees. This is referred to as an *experiencing rating system*. By terminating fewer employees, the employer pays taxes based on a lower rate.

The federal government sets minimum standards for both the dollar amount of weekly payments and for the length of time that payments should be made to each unemployed person. The U.S. Department of Labor (Bureau of Labor Statistics, 2012) also requires states to establish a state employment service and to develop a plan to train and find jobs for workers who happen to have disabilities.

To receive payments, a worker must:

1. Have worked a specified period of time for the employer.

2. Have been terminated through no fault of his or her own and not for on-the-job misconduct, or because the worker chose to leave without a good reason.

3. Have filed for benefits.

4. Be available and able to work should the state employment service locate another job.

5. Be making reasonable effort to find employment in the same or similar line of work.

Thus, if a sport director, terminated from a local recreation agency, met all these conditions, the employment service would expect her to be seeking work at prisons, private clubs, or youth-serving agencies. But if a seasonal interpreter for the National Park Service met all of the first four conditions, he would probably find it difficult to find similar work in an isolated area near the National Park that had formerly hired him.

Although we have placed an emphasis on seasonal employment as an example, it is important for the recreation and sport supervisor to understand that unemployment compensation provides temporary income payments to eligible employees who lose their jobs through no fault of their own, and are able and available to do work. Unemployment checks are typically collected when employees lose their jobs as a result of a company's decision to restructure and downsize, merge with another company, or sell the business. Unemployment payments are intended to serve as temporary income to allow an unemployed worker sufficient time to find a new job without major financial distress.

CIVIL LIBERTIES

A number of state and federal laws protect individual privacy and the right of individuals to freedom of speech. The balance between freedom of speech, employee privacy, and employer security has become very controversial in the work environment. In this section we address freedom of expression, privacy rights and employee records, workplace monitoring (such as tracking Internet use, using surveillance, and monitoring e-mail and voice mail), lie detector tests, and identity theft.

Freedom of Speech

The First Amendment guarantees freedom of speech for every citizen. However, that freedom is not necessarily an unrestricted one in the workplace. For example, blogs and wikis, whistle blowers, and employees with controversial views may be the exception. Using disparaging or threatening words on a blog about one's supervisor may be cause for disciplinary action. Whistle blowers, individuals who report real or perceived wrongs committed by their employers, may also find themselves facing disciplinary action. The same holds true for employees who advocate controversial viewpoints at work.

Conflicting court decisions have clouded freedom of speech in the workplace. Government employees, such as recreation professionals, may choose to publicly criticize their supervisors or elected officials and this can become controversial.

A so-called *balancing test* is usually applied in court cases on this issue. The balancing test examines the rights of employees as citizens to comment on public matters against any evidence that an official is unable to continue to provide services to the public. If a public official is unable to serve the public satisfactorily as a result of an employee's unfavorable remarks, the courts are not sympathetic to the employee's claim that "freedom of speech" was violated. Where employee statements do not affect their own performance, disrupt the harmony of the workplace, violate employer confidentiality, or damage the reputation of the agency, the courts have generally supported the employee's right to make public statements about the activities of the employer.

Privacy Rights and Employee Records

The Privacy Act of 1974 was passed to protect individual privacy rights. Although this law applies only to federal agencies, similar state laws have also been passed. In most states, the private sector (such as aquatic centers, ski resorts, spas) is less entitled to access personnel records than the public-sector organizations.

Employers are often required to acquire and retain sensitive, personal information about their employees. This information may include drug test reports, medical reports, information about disabilities for the American with Disabilities Act (ADA) purposes, workers' compensation records, and tax and financial information. With regard to the record keeping for medical reports, ADA has a provision that states:

> Information from all medical examinations and inquiries must be kept apart from general personnel files as a separate confidential medical record available only under limited conditions specified in the ADA.

Typically, personnel files and records should be maintained for about three years; however, it would behoove the recreation and sport supervisor to understand the specific requirements for specific records within the file. The legal and regulatory standards change for different types of records.

Workplace Monitoring

Workplace monitoring is on the rise, as issues of security and trust between the employer and employee become more convoluted, especially with the advancement of technology (Hymowitz, 2005). The increasing usage of cameras, computers, and tele-communication systems in the workplace is causing great concern as it relates to employee privacy rights. Monitoring the use of e-mail and voice-mail in the workplace is not uncommon by both private-sector and government employers. These supervisors have a right to monitor, search, and observe employees without a search warrant if they believe work rules have been violated.

The Internet has become widely used in the workplace and many employers have developed policies and procedures to ensure it is used appropriately. It is estimated that three out of four companies monitor their employees' use of the Internet, and nine out of ten employees admit to visiting non-work websites during work hours (Breeden, 2005).

Video surveillance systems are installed in workplaces areas such as parks, lobby areas of recreation departments, and dimly lit areas. Employer rights and employee privacy collide when the use of video surveillance is used in changing areas, restrooms, and other private areas. It is critical for employers to develop policies and procedures for the use of such video surveillance. Employees should understand the intent and purpose of this type of monitoring, when it occurs, and who is authorized to view the surveillance when necessary.

Monitoring e-mail and voice mail in the workplace is allowed by employers. Voice mail, e-mail, and computer files are provided by the employer and should be used for business purposes only. Court cases will continue to surface over e-mails that contain sexist, racist, and defamatory language. The use of any type of media for personal use should be prohibited in the workplace and employers have the right to monitor this media without notice.

Lie Detectors

The Employee Polygraph Protection Act (EPPA) prohibits the use of lie detectors in most employment situations. The lie detector includes polygraph equipment which can measure pulse, respiration, and perspiration. Other devices may analyze voice stress. The EPPA states that an employer may not request or suggest that an employee participate in a lie detector test. An employer who terminates or demotes an employee for refusing to take a lie detector test may open their agency to civil damages. Exceptions to the EPPA may take place only when employees of government con-

tractors have access to security, counterintelligence, and law enforcement functions.

Identity Theft

Identify theft is a serious and growing national problem. We have all heard stories whereby someone wrongfully obtained and used another person's personal data in a way that involved fraud or deception for economic gain. The United States Department of Justice (2010) states the following:

> In one notorious case of identity theft, the criminal, a convicted felon, not only incurred more than $100,000 of credit card debt, obtained a federal home loan, and bought homes, motorcycles, and handguns in the victim's name, but called his victim to taunt him -- saying that he could continue to pose as the victim for as long as he wanted because identity theft was not a federal crime at that time -- before filing for bankruptcy, also in the victim's name. While the victim and his wife spent more than four years and more than $15,000 of their own money to restore their credit and reputation, the criminal served a brief sentence for making a false statement to procure a firearm, but made no restitution to his victim for any of the harm he had caused. This case, and others like it, prompted Congress in 1998 to create a new federal offense of identity theft.

Unfortunately, most fraud is caused by theft of records from employers that house employee personal data. This information may include name, birth date, address, and Social Security number. Therefore, it is paramount that employers safeguard this personal information in order to protect employees from being victims of identity theft. Failure to protect employees could result in legal liability. Figure 2.2 identifies steps that can be taken by the recreation and sport supervisor in an effort to protect employee personal data.

The United States Department of Justice (2010) recommends the following suggestions to help individuals minimize the risk of becoming a victim of identity theft or fraud: Think "SCAM":

S   Be *stingy* about giving out your personal information to others unless you have a reason to trust them, regardless of where you are.

C *Check* your financial information regularly, and look for what should be there and what shouldn't.

A *Ask* periodically for a copy of your credit report. Your credit report should list all bank and financial accounts under your name, and will provide other indications of whether someone has wrongfully opened or used any accounts in your name.

M *Maintain* careful records of your banking and financial accounts. Even though financial institutions are required to maintain copies of your checks, debit transactions, and similar transactions for five years, you should retain your monthly statements and checks for at least one year, if not more.

Summary

1. Employees have the legal right to organize for their mutual benefit, but they may not be forced to join unions.

2. The Civil Service Reform Act of 1978 governs labor relations for federal employees. These employees are not permitted to arbitrate for salary, benefits, examinations, or appointments.

3. State laws covering public employees vary considerably in their permissiveness to bargain and strike.

---

1. Keep personnel records in a secure room. If employee information is maintained electronically, make sure the files are protected by a password. Medical records should be secured in a separate secured area from personnel records.

2. Conduct background checks on employees who have access to employee personal data.

3. Avoid allowing part-time, seasonal, volunteer, and temporary workers access to personnel records.

4. Do not use Social Security numbers for identification purposes (e.g., badges) or on employee paychecks. When necessary, only refer to the last four digits.

5. Allow employees to exclude personal information in your organization's directory or website.

6. Always shred obsolete records rather than merely discarding them into the trash.

Figure 2.2
Protecting Your Employees from Identity Theft

---

4. Workers' compensation laws are designed to compensate employees for job-related illnesses or injuries, whether temporary or permanent; to provide rehabilitation services to reclaim the injured workers' capabilities; and to award death benefits to survivors.

5. Employees' health and safety are protected by state workers' compensation laws and the Occupational Safety and Health Act (OSHA) of 1970. OSHA serves to prevent accidents and state laws provide compensation after an accident.

6. The purpose of the Social Security Act is to provide income for retired workers and their survivors, to pay disability benefits, and to cover medical expenditures. The Social Security Act also forces every state to establish a statewide unemployment compensation program.

7. Recreation and sport supervisors should be familiar with child labor laws and understand the number of hours certain youth are eligible to work depending on their age.

8. The Employee Retirement Income Security Act of 1974 (ERISA) attempts to regulate the management of thousands of private pension plans so that workers can retire and be guaranteed the benefits they invested in pension plans during their working years.

9. Recreation and sport supervisors should become familiar with state laws pertaining to employee civil liberties. Personnel departments and legal advisors are in the best position to provide employers with this information, as well as relevant interpretation of these laws.

Discussion Topics

1. Should federal employees have the right to bargain for salaries and benefits?

2. What is occupational health and safety? Provide several examples. Who is covered under OSHA?

3. How might an agency's unemployment compensation program be affected if it

chooses to reduce its number of full-time employees and hire more seasonals?

4. Who should be responsible for the cost of employee benefits: employees, employers, state government, or the federal government?

5. Is the Social Security system meeting its original intent? Explain.

6. Why was the Employee Retirement Income Security Act of 1974 (ERISA) a significant piece of legislation?

7. What are three key issues that the recreation and sport supervisors know about child labor laws?

8. List four important contemporary issues in the area of employee rights which have some relationship to recreation and sport organizations.

REFERENCES

Breeden, R. (2005, May 10). Small talk/internet time. *The Wall Street Journal*, B4.

Employer Costs for Employee Compensation. (2011). *U.S. Bureau of Labor Statistics*. Retrieved from http://www.bls.gov/news.release/ecec.nr0.htm

Employer Responsibilities. (2010). *U.S. Department of Labor*. Retrieved from http://www.osha.gov/as/opa/worker/employer-responsibility.html

Hymowitz, C. (2005, August 16). Balancing security and trust. *The Wall Street Journal*, B1.

Identity Theft and Identity Fraud. (2010). *U.S. Department of Justice*. Retrieved from http://www.justice.gov/criminal/fraud/websites/idtheft.html

Overview of BLS Statistics on Unemployment. (2010). *U.S. Bureau of Labor Statistics*. Retrieved from http://www.bls.gov/bls/unemployment.htm

Questions and Answers About the Association Provision of the Americans with Disabilities Act. (2010). *The U.S. Equal Employment Opportunity Commission*. Retrieved from http://www.eeoc.gov/facts/association_ada.html

U.S. Department of Labor. (2012). Retrieved from http://www.osha.gov

3

EMPLOYEE SUPERVISION

Ask anyone who has worked in a paid position—whether full-time, part-time, permanent or temporary—in the management ranks or at the entry level and most will say a good supervisor makes a huge difference in their attitude toward work and the way they perform their assigned job duties. Individuals who have had an opportunity to work for a great boss and describe him or her as someone who was competent, honest, had integrity, was fair, and cared about them as people are frequently the same ones who say they enjoy going to work, work hard while they are there, and are willing to do "extra" work if asked by the boss. On the flip side, those who have had a lousy relationship with their boss and describe him or her as someone who "doesn't know what he is doing, "says one thing and does another," "plays favorites," "meddles in my work," and "doesn't know or care if I'm at work" are most likely to be the ones who are looking for another job, frequently absent from work, often arriving late to work, and are doing only what is necessary to get by and no more.

Good supervisors, who have the ability to bring out the best in others and encourage their employees to achieve the goals of the organization, are of paramount importance to recreation, parks, and leisure services organizations. Because employees are the most valuable asset of human services organizations, it is important to treat them well and keep them highly motivated so they can deliver quality programs and services. Without competent supervisors, organizations find themselves with a host of headaches including low morale, high turnover, and a general lack of overall productivity.

Although good supervision is critical to an organization, all too often individuals with little or no proven supervisory experience or training are promoted to supervisory positions, and therefore they perform marginally. This chapter is designed to introduce supervision concepts, principles, and basic supervisory practices to enhance an understanding

of what it takes to become a good supervisor. The major sections in the chapter include: 1) understanding the unique role of supervision; 2) developing and improving supervisory relationships; and, 3) developing and improving personal skills to improve supervisory performance.

UNDERSTANDING THE UNIQUE ROLE OF SUPERVISION

Supervisors play a unique role in recreation, park, and leisure service organizations, and the skills required of individuals with supervisory responsibility are very different from those required of non-supervisory personnel. In this section we will cover the function of supervisors in the management of organizations, the major areas of responsibility and primary duties of supervisors, the qualifications required of supervisory positions, and the selection process that is used to employ supervisors.

Definition of Supervision and Function of Supervisors

"Supervision" is defined as *achieving desired results through the work of others*. A supervisory relationship typically occurs when an individual has been employed to oversee and supervise one or more employees within a specific unit (aquatics, youth sports, gymnastics) or division of an organization (athletics, recreation, parks). The essential function of a supervisor (supervisor of youth sports, supervisor of aquatics) is to work effectively with those in an assigned group to accomplish the goals and objectives of a specific unit or division. Supervisory positions can exist at every level of management—lower, middle, and upper—and the job duties and responsibilities among these different levels can vary extensively. It is difficult to know for sure whether an employee is a supervisor merely by knowing his or her official job title. Recreation, park, and leisure services organizations have a variety of positions and position titles (i.e., manager, coordinator, event specialist, crew leader, superintendent) and some, but not all, carry supervisory responsibility. The best way to determine if an employee has actually been assigned supervisory responsibility is to review the position description or examine the chain-of-command on an organizational chart.

Figure 3.1 is an organizational chart of a large recreation and park agency with three major divisions (Parks, Recreation, and Athletics) and four management levels. Supervisory positions exist in all three divisions and at all four management levels. For example, in the Athletics Division, there are three major units (Adult and Youth Sports, Gymnastics, and Aquatics) and supervisory positions are located in all management Levels 1 through 4. In the Aquatics unit at management Level 4, there are 3 Aquatics Center Managers with supervisory responsibility. Each manager is responsible for planning and organizing programs and services at an aquatics center, and has a supervisory responsibility to hire, train, and oversee personnel including lifeguards, swimming instructors, and pool attendants.

All three of the Aquatics Managers in Level 4 report to and are supervised by the Aquatics Supervisor at management Level 3. Notice that the Aquatics Supervisor has the highest-ranking position in the Aquatics unit and as such, has broader job duties and responsibilities than the individual aquatics managers at Level 4. The Aquatics Supervisor has a community-wide focus for aquatic programming and is expected to accomplish the goals and objectives of the entire aquatics unit. This person's supervisory responsibility includes not only recruiting, hiring, and overseeing the work of the three Aquatics Managers, but, ultimately, this person oversees and is held accountable for the actions, behaviors, and performance of all employees in the aquatics unit.

The Aquatics Supervisor, as well as the Gymnastics and Adult and Youth Sports Supervisors, reports directly to the Athletics Superintendent, a Level 2 manager. The job duties and responsibilities of supervisors in Levels 1 and 2 of management are much more complex and varied than at Levels 3 and 4. The Athletics Superintendent must have the skills to supervise division managers in three distinct units: Adult and Youth Sports, Gymnastics, and Aquatics. Ultimately, the superintendent will be held accountable for the performance of all employees in

the Athletics division whether or not they report directly to her. Rarely do supervisors at the higher management levels have the expertise or experience in all the areas they supervise. However, they typically prove themselves to be good managers with the supervisory skills required to motivate, coordinate and work with people to accomplish goals. It is this special talent that most likely enabled them to move to a Level 2 supervisory position, and it is this same talent that will be critical in obtaining promotion to Level 1 management.

In large organizations with several layers of management, top-level management is usually comprised of the highest-ranking person, such as the Director, and may also include one or more top-level assistant managers who report directly to that individual. As shown by Figure 3.1, the Director and Assistant Director occupy supervisory positions in management Level 1.

The supervisory focus of the Director's position is to provide effective leadership and direction to all divisions and units in the overall organization. The Director is expected to achieve the desired results of the organization by primarily working with and through the Assistant Director and the Level 2 Superintendents. However, ultimately it is the Director who is responsible for all personnel in all divisions. Individuals promoted to the Director's position are considered the "supervisor of all supervisors." Directors not only set the example for all supervisory personnel, but they also serve as role models for all others in the organization who aspire to a management position. To achieve the desired outcomes of an organization, the ultimate supervisor must have the ability to inspire, motivate, and lead all individuals, regardless of rank or position.

Supervisory Duties and Responsibilities

The specific duties and responsibilities of supervisors may vary depending on the level of the position on the organization's hierarchy (entry-level management, middle management, or upper-level management) and the particular assigned unit or division (athletics, aquatics, camps). Job responsibility is a term that refers to a person's main job or the areas of accountability. In general, the major responsibility of a supervisory position in the field of recreation, parks, and leisure services is to plan, organize, and provide supervision and oversight for an assigned area such as recreation activities, programs, services, facilities, and/or special events. Job duties are the tasks that a person does on a

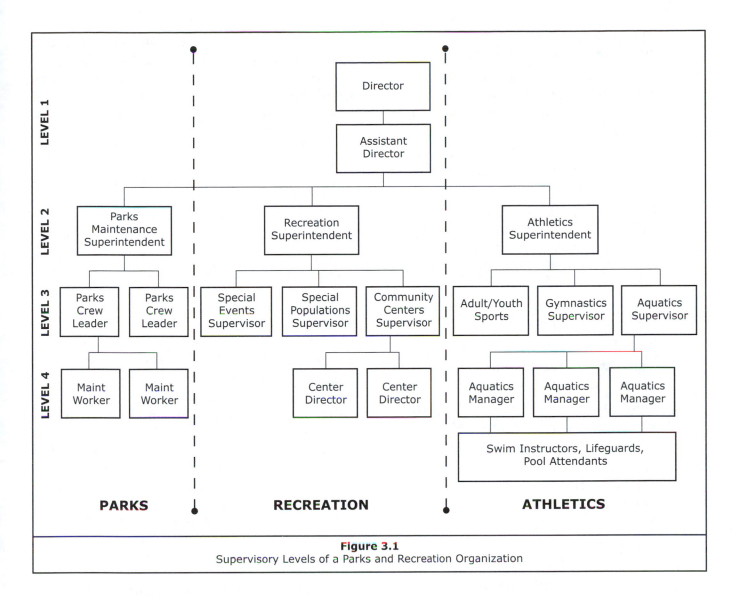

Figure 3.1
Supervisory Levels of a Parks and Recreation Organization

job. The key duties that are typically associated with supervisory position are to:

1. Plan and organize work

2. Set direction, provide leadership, and make decisions that are aligned with the mission of the organization

3. Recruit, interview, train, supervise, evaluate, and discipline employees

4. Provide ongoing supervision including building collaborative relationships, coaching, mentoring, motivation, and leading others.

To successfully perform the responsibilities required of supervisory positions, individuals must have the knowledge, skills and abilities to work effectively with those they directly supervise, as well as with others with whom they work closely, such as their boss, other upper-level managers, coworkers, and the organization's customers.

Qualifications of Supervisory Positions

Organizations expect individuals performing supervisory duties to have competencies that enable them to communicate effectively and work well with people. This expectation holds true of supervisory positions at every management level from entry-level managers at Level 4 to the top-level director in Level 1. Qualifications specifically established for supervisory positions are typically written in broad, general terms, and placed in the section of a job description reserved for special knowledge, skills, and abilities. Listed below are qualifications that are commonly found for supervisory positions in the field of recreation, parks, and leisure services:

1. Align talent of employees based on an organization's mission and goals

2. Inspire and foster team commitment, spirit, pride, and trust; facilitate cooperation and motivate team members to accomplish group goals

3. Develop networks and build strategic relationships across boundaries to achieve desired results

4. Develop the ability of others to perform and contribute to the organization by providing ongoing feedback and opportunities to learn through formal and informal methods

5. Identify and analyze problems, generate and evaluate alternative solutions, and make recommendations

6. Anticipate and take steps to manage and resolve conflicts and disagreements

7. Treat others with courtesy and respect, value diversity and leverage individual differences to achieve desired results

8. Have the ability to express oneself orally, clearly, concisely and in a convincing manner

9. Write in a clear, concise, organized and convincing manner

10. Behave in an honest, fair, and ethical manner; show consistency in words and action; remain optimistic and persistent, even under adversity

Employers often write job qualifications for supervisory positions in such a way as to leave open for interpretation whether they will hire only job candidates with "proven" ability or whether they will consider for selection someone with "potential" but unproven ability. In this way, organizations have much more flexibility during the selection process.

Selecting Supervisors

When selecting job candidates for positions that carry supervisory responsibility, organizations often give preference to those individuals who have a proven track record of effective supervision. Generally, successful past performance as a supervisor is the best indicator of future supervisory success. To determine the extent of successful supervisory performance, organizations establish procedures for checking references and

require a thorough investigation of the job candidate's competencies for supervisory work. Merely listing the number of years of supervisory experience or the number of employees directly supervised is not sufficient in determining whether an individual has been effective in a supervisory position.

Although organizations prefer to hire experienced supervisors, they often expand the pool of qualified candidates for various reasons to include individuals who lack direct supervisory experience, but who nonetheless are strong performers and show *promise* for future supervisory job success. Organizations that use this method of selecting supervisors accept other qualifications of the candidates, such as strong communication skills, a proven ability to *work cooperatively with others,* and a commitment to excellence to compensate for the lack of "proven" supervisory ability. Organizations must be very careful in making the false assumption that excellent performance in a non-supervisory position guarantees success as a supervisor. Excellent performers may be very capable of managing their own time and directing their own behavior but, to become successful supervisors, they also must be capable of motivating others to become as disciplined in their own work. Becoming a good supervisor requires competencies beyond those of being an outstanding individual performer. Additionally, not all people have the desire or discipline to develop and practice the skills required for effective supervision.

DEVELOPING AND IMPROVING SUPERVISORY RELATIONSHIPS

It is one thing to understand the unique role of supervisors, but it is quite another to successfully make the transition from a non-supervisory position to a supervisory one. To develop and to continually improve supervisory relationships with employees, it is imperative that supervisors 1) make an effective transition to the supervisor's position and 2) establish trust with employees.

Transitioning to a Supervisory Position

Making a successful transition to a supervisory position is not easy, especially for first-time supervisors. Most individuals see a promotion to supervisory management as a natural progression toward successively higher levels of status and pay, and they do not fully comprehend the complex nature of a supervisory job. Most enter the position without an adequate understanding or appreciation of the immediate challenges they will face in the transition or the additional "people" skills they will need to develop to become successful. Experienced supervisors, too, face challenges in making the transition to a new supervisory position, although the supervisory skills they have developed in prior positions should help lessen the adjustment period.

Recreation, park, and leisure service organizations must be mindful that new supervisors need training, support, and encouragement to perform successfully in a new supervisory role, especially those who are transitioning from a non-supervisory position. Most individuals will face some, if not all, of these common challenges in moving up to a supervisory position.

1. *Aligning with management.* Once a promotion to a supervisory position becomes effective, a new supervisor is instantly expected to align with management and leave behind the days as an individual performer. Behavior that may have been acceptable among coworkers—gossiping about supervisors, complaining about organizational policies, procedures, and rules, and disputing management decisions—is no longer appropriate for a supervisor and that behavior will need to change. New supervisors are immediately expected to switch their loyalty to management and to represent management's viewpoints to their employees, whether they agree with the opinions of management or not. Because new supervisors were most likely superstars in their former non-supervisory position, management expects these individuals to magically know what to do and how to do it, regardless of the lack of supervisory experience or training they have had. As new supervisors, individuals must adopt a proper attitude toward management and learn as much as possible about a management perspective to gain the confidence of their boss, the boss's boss and those in the higher ranking supervisory positions.

2. *Supervising friends.* Most newly appointed supervisors, especially those promoted to their first supervisory position, face difficulty transitioning to the new role and accepting and managing the transformation that inevitably takes place within interpersonal relationships. People who are promoted to a supervisory position from *within an organization* face the immediate challenge of dealing with friends who used to be their peers. Once a person accepts a supervisory position, the balance of power shifts and the social dynamic may need to change (Nefer, 2008). Social behavior that is common among coworkers—going to lunch, meeting for happy hour, playing together on the company softball team—may need to be re-evaluated in light of the new supervisory role. It is very difficult for even the best supervisors to remain impartial when assigning work and evaluating the performance of employees who are also close friends.

3. *Gaining acceptance and cooperation from employees.* Striking the balance between being a "boss" and being a "buddy" is also required of new supervisors working with people whom they do not know or do not know well. To make an impact and immediately achieve results for the organization, new supervisors need immediate acceptance and cooperation from those they supervise. Employees have needs too, and will want a new boss to like them and value their contributions. The challenge for new supervisors is developing professional relationships with individuals in their unit, while at the same time limiting social behavior with employees that may eventually compromise and impair their objectivity.

4. *Dealing with the resentful employees.* Another transition challenge that new supervisors confront is dealing with resentful employees within the organization. Individuals who applied, but were not selected for the job, may take exception to the new boss especially if they think they were well-qualified and should have been chosen. New supervisors who assume responsibility for a large division within an organization and who have little or no knowledge or experience

in one or more of the units may also expect to deal with discontented staff. If an aquatics supervisor, for example, is promoted to a superintendent of a division that includes aquatics, gymnastics, and youth and adult sports, it is likely that employees responsible for the adult softball league will have doubts about whether the person has adequate knowledge and skills in the areas other than aquatics to function effectively. They may also think the new superintendent will likely show favoritism toward employees in the aquatics unit. Jealousy, backstabbing, and insubordination are common challenges that new supervisors will face when dealing with the same people who used to be their buddies (Evans, 2003).

5. *Avoiding the temptation of doing work for others.* New supervisors must resist the temptation of doing work that should clearly be delegated to others. Individuals who have excelled in a non-supervisory position may find it very tempting as a supervisor to take on difficult work that others are supposed to do because they have done it before, it is easy, and they can get the work done quickly. However, an essential function of supervisors is to develop the ability of others to contribute to the organization by coaching, providing feedback, and providing opportunities for learning. New supervisors must meet the challenge of achieving desired results *through* others, not by performing the work themselves.

6. *Giving credit, rather than taking credit.* In a new supervisory role, individuals must make the transition from being in the limelight, receiving praise, and taking personal credit for accomplishments, to crediting successes to the new team and individual team members (Lisoski, 2006). The focus for new supervisors is inspiring team commitment, spirit, and pride, and placing the team on center stage for accolades. At the same time, the supervisor must take responsibility and accept the blame for blunders or inadvertent mistakes the team makes. Giving credit to the team for things that go well

and taking the heat for failures are difficult but important lessons to be learned by new supervisors.

Being a new manager and trying to get something accomplished in the first couple of months by working with people who are dissatisfied or just plain uneasy about their new boss can be very frustrating. New supervisors must be patient, show sensitivity to the attitudes, feelings, and circumstances of others, and look for ways to gain staff support. One lesson individuals will learn early in the transition period is that earning trust and establishing credibility are key to supervisory success.

Establishing Trust with Employees

Trust between supervisors and employees is essential for sustaining performance and effectiveness. When supervisors believe their employees can be trusted, they have more flexibility in the way they make everyday employment decisions such as assigning work, giving instructions, guiding the work, providing feedback, and evaluating performance. Similarly, when employees believe their supervisors can be trusted, they may be willing to take on additional responsibilities that benefit the unit, the division, and the entire organization. In this section, the reader will learn about trust, including what it is, why it is important, and what supervisors must do to earn the trust of their employees.

Concept Definition and Theoretical Framework

Researchers studying trust as a concept have defined the term in many different ways and have offered different explanations about how trust develops and how trust affects work relationships (Dirks & Ferrin, 2002). Generally, *trust* means that employees rely on the intentions of their supervisor to meet positive expectations. For example, employees who trust their supervisor have confidence that he or she will act in a fair, ethical, and predictable manner. Likewise, supervisors who trust their employees expect them to exhibit behaviors that are beneficial to the organization.

There are two primary perspectives that are used as a framework to understand trust between a supervisor and employee (Dirks & Ferrin, 2002). The first perspective is that trust operates according to a *social exchange* process. According to this theory, employees and supervisors enter into a social exchange relationship (Blau, 1964) because they perceive each other has something of value to contribute. In high-quality trusting relationships, the exchange between supervisors and employees is based on care, consideration, and the perception of mutual obligations. Researchers have used this social-exchange perspective in describing how the trust between a supervisor and employee affects both the attitudes and the work performance that benefit an organization. A second perspective of trust is the *character-based perspective.* Using this as a framework, researchers have focused on the perception of a leader's character and how it influences a follower's sense of vulnerability in an organization (Mayer, Davis, & Schoorman, 1995). This perspective implies that employees develop opinions about leadership characteristics (such as integrity, dependability, fairness, and ability) and these opinions impact their attitudes toward work and their actual work performance. Both perspectives are important and can be used as a framework for explaining why trust is essential to a relationship between a supervisor and employee and describing the components that comprise a trusting relationship.

Outcomes of a Trusting Relationship

Trust between a supervisor and employee has a significant impact on a variety of outcomes important to an organization. When employees believe their boss can be trusted, organizations benefit in four major ways.

1. *Increased organizational citizenship behaviors.* Organizational citizenship behaviors are a special type of work behavior that refers to the actions that employees take that are beneficial to the organization and are discretionary, or not directly or explicitly recognized by the organization's reward system (Organ, 1988). When employees trust their supervisor, they are willing to increase organizational citizenship behaviors; that is, they are more highly committed to their assigned tasks and they are willing to take on additional responsibilities (Chiaburu & Kim, 2008; Konovsky & Pugh, 1994). Employees who trust their supervisor tend to work hard, are conscientious, and "go the extra mile" on assignments. When asked by their supervisor to do things that are not within their scope of assigned duties (such as attending an important meeting, or helping a coworker who has a heavy work load), a trusting employee accepts without hesitation. Employees who trust their supervisor tend also to be the ones who do not spend a lot of time complaining about trivial matters.

2. *Higher-level job satisfaction.* Supervisors have a major impact on a person's job satisfaction, especially as it pertains to giving guidance and assistance with job responsibilities, training, giving informal feedback, and conducting performance evaluations. When employees have a supportive relationship with their immediate supervisor, they experience higher levels of job satisfaction than those who do not (Ting, 1997). They are also likely to feel more positive about the employment decisions the boss makes and are more willing to believe that the information is accurate. The extent to which an employee believes information from a performance appraisal is accurate hinges on the level of trust that has been established with his or her supervisor. Without credibility, supervisors are at a distinct disadvantage in communicating with employees and motivating them to work hard and produce high-quality work.

3. *Higher-level work performance.* Having a trusting relationship motivates employees to perform at a higher level. When employees believe their boss has integrity and is caring, they will be more comfortable engaging in behaviors that put them at risk (Mayer, Davis, & Schoorman, 1995). Taking initiatives on developing new programs or services or sharing a personal weakness with a supervisor during a performance evaluation are examples of risk-taking behavior that can have a positive impact on job outcomes.

4. *Decreased antisocial behavior.* When a trusting relationship is established, employees are also more likely to refrain from antisocial work behaviors (such as coming to work late, padding expense reports, stealing office supplies) and more likely to administer sanctions against someone who does (Thau, Crossley, Bennett, & Sczesny, 2007).

From an employee's perspective, trusting relationships with supervisors also bring them benefits. Supervisors take bigger risks with employees they trust more (Schoorman, Mayer, & Davis,1996). Supervisors are much more likely to assign "choice" assignments that give employees an opportunity to gain valuable exposure and work experiences at a higher level when trust levels are high. Trusted employees are typically the ones given more autonomy and resources to work on a wide range of initiatives.

Organizations, supervisors, and employees benefit from forming and sustaining trusting relationships, yet many supervisors do not have an understanding of the components of trust and the skills necessary for building trust with their employees.

Components of Developing Trust

For trust to exist, supervisors and employees must be confident that the other is competent, caring, and will act in a fair and ethical manner. Trustworthiness also assumes that supervisors will show support of employees and not take advantage of them by withholding or manipulating information. Supervisors cannot demand trust from their employees; they must earn it. Although it would be much easier and more productive for individuals if trust and respect were automatically granted to them when they accepted a supervisory position, the truth is, that trust-based relationships are much more complicated. To develop and sustain a trusting relationship, both supervisors and employees must understand the principles of trust and engage in practices that lead to increased trust. The principles of a trusting relationship are built on the elements of competency, honesty, integrity, fairness, and benevolence.

1. *Honesty.* Honesty in a supervisory relationship means that employees perceive their supervisors to be truthful in their principles, actions, and intentions. Because trust involves beliefs about honesty and the extent to which a supervisor might take advantage of an employee, it is likely to affect the extent to which employees are willing to believe the accuracy of information they receive from a supervisor (Dirks & Ferrin, 2002). Supervisors interact with their employees on a daily basis, delegating work, giving information, offering advice, and providing performance feedback. If honesty is not the cornerstone of a supervisory relationship, supervisors may soon discover that employees are not willing to perform delegated tasks to the best of their ability, ignore suggestions for improving their work performance, and question the rationale for every directive. For trusting relationships to develop and to be sustained over time, employees must perceive their supervisor as someone who is upright, fair, and consistently provides accurate and timely information.

2. *Integrity.* Integrity refers to a person who behaves in ways consistent with his or her values and beliefs. Individuals with integrity are consistent in word and deed and do what they say they are going to do. Kouzes and Posner (2008) tell us that integrity is essential to a trusting relationship between supervisors and employees. Supervisors often make promises to employees through the things they say— improvements they say they will make, tasks they will complete, and opportunities they will provide. However, too often supervisors break promises and do not follow through with their plans. To develop and sustain trust with employees, supervisors must do what they say they are going to do and ensure there is no difference in what they promise and what they produce.

3. *Competence.* Competence is defined as having requisite or adequate ability to fulfill the responsibilities of a position. If employees believe their supervisor is competent and has the skills and abilities to perform his or her job, an employee is more likely to develop trust. When a trusting relationship exists, employees have confidence in their supervisor's competence and are more willing to be influenced by their manager and commit to assignments that are delegated. (Bass, 1990). Employees perceive competent supervisors as those who have a track record of performing their job well, doing things in a capable manner, and performing tasks with skill (Sherwood & DePaolo, 2005). Supervisors who are not perceived as competent may find themselves with the challenges of working with employees who are reluctant to accept information, performance feedback, delegated tasks, or new assignments

4. *Fairness.* From an employee's perspective, fairness exists when supervisors are capable of making impartial decisions without showing favoritism or prejudice. Perry and Mankin (2007) determined that where trust between employees and supervisors was high, employees emphasized fairness, ability, and an employee orientation as features of a fair supervisor. To earn and sustain trust of their employees, supervisors must consistently apply "fairness" in the ways they distribute rewards, adopt new procedures, and give feedback to employees in a timely manner (Forret & Love, 2008).

5. *Benevolence.* The term benevolence describes someone who desires to help others. Supervisors convey benevolence to their employees at work by doing such things as standing in support of their decisions, demonstrating genuine interest in their career interests, and remaining a confidant if they disclose personal information about their work performance. A trusting relationship exists when employees believe their supervisor is genuinely interested in them and motivated to seek mutually beneficial gains (Cunningham & MacGregor, 2000, Mayer, Davis & Schoorman,1995). To sustain a trusting relationship over time, supervisors must show support of employees and sustain an attitude of kindness and friendliness.

DEVELOPING AND IMPROVING PERSONAL SKILLS TO IMPROVE SUPERVISORY PERFORMANCE

Another important aspect of becoming a supervisor is developing and refining personal skills that help improve effectiveness. Although there are many skills that will be beneficial, the three that will be discussed in this section are effective delegation, time management, and managing meetings.

Effective Delegation

Delegation is a powerful tool that can be used to develop and motivate both employees and supervisors. The aim of this section is to provide information on delegation by addressing the following topics: definition of delegation, importance of effective delegation, reasons why supervisors often fail to learn or use delegation, steps involved in effectively delegating, and reasons why supervisors should not delegate.

Definition of Delegation

Simply defined, "delegation" takes place when a supervisor *assigns work to employees and holds them accountable for the results.* Although much of the work performed by employees is stated in general terms in their formal job description, there are many other tasks, committee work, and projects that are important to the organization but do not clearly fall within any one person's scope of job responsibility. Supervisors must realize they are responsible for prioritizing and delegating unassigned work, and for following through to make sure their employees achieve the desired results.

Importance of Effective Delegation

Many supervisors do not fully appreciate the importance of delegating work to others. Effective delegation brings benefits to both supervisors and employees. From the perspective of supervisors, the greatest advantage for delegating work is to free up time to invest in work activities that bring the most value to the organization (Yukl & Fu, 1999). If supervisors are bogged down in time-consuming activities that should be performed at a lower level, they may not have time to fully commit to "leading" the work group by performing important functions such as coaching, giving one-on-one feedback to employees, teambuilding, and problem-solving. The leadership component of supervisory positions is critical, and through effective delegation, supervisors have the opportunity to add more value to their organizations.

Effective delegation also brings many benefits to employees. Work delegated from a supervisor can serve as a motivator, especially if the work is challenging and offers employees an opportunity to gain knowledge and experience that makes them more marketable for a higher-level position (Yukl & Fu, 1999). An individual occupying a non-supervisory position who aspires to become a first-level supervisor would greatly benefit from delegated responsibilities that typically are performed in management. For example, chairing a committee that involves employees at different ranks and from different units of the organization can provide a person an excellent opportunity for developing interpersonal and oral communication skills, and learning techniques to motivate a team to accomplish a particular goal. Delegated work also may be welcomed by employees looking for work that is different from what they do on a routine basis and that allows them to use their own special talent to produce an end product such as a new event, program, or service. Supervisors may often take advantage of delegated work as a way of giving lower-level employees a different perspective of the organization from a higher level of management.

Supervisors must avoid falling into the trap of feeling like every time they have a job that needs to be delegated it will be perceived by employees as a burden. To the contrary, delegated work has the potential to be very effective in "broadening" employee perspectives and developing a more effective work group.

Reasons Why Supervisors Often Fail to Learn or Use Delegation

Although delegation is very valuable to supervisors and employees, many supervisors do not delegate as much work as they should. Below are five primary reasons supervisors fail to delegate:

1. Supervisors may lack an understanding of delegation as an essential component of supervisory work. All too often supervisors, especially those who are inexperienced, fail to recognize the value of developing effective delegation skills. Most individuals are promoted to their first supervisory position because of the excellence they achieved in performing non-supervisory job duties and responsibilities. They became very skilled in planning and organizing their own work and performing at a very high level. However, in a supervisory position, individuals are responsible for achieving desired results by working through others. To be effective, they must be motivated to delegate and capable of delegating work to others. This is especially challenging for inexperienced supervisors when many of the tasks, assignments, and projects that they could and should delegate are exactly the ones they enjoy, can do well, and can accomplish quickly. If supervisors choose to perform most of the unassigned work, they often fail to develop effective delegation skills and do not delegate enough (Urbaniak, 2005). The challenge

for supervisors is to gain an appreciation of delegation as an essential component of their supervisory jobs and develop effective skills that allow them to realize the full benefits that come from it.

2. Supervisors may lack confidence in employees' skills. In some cases, supervisors may not believe their employees have enough knowledge and skill to delegate work to them. Supervisors have a valid point in refusing to delegate important work if they have employees who are recently hired, learning new duties and responsibilities, or not comfortable with accepting additional tasks. Also, in the event that supervisors have employees who are unmotivated and have a track record of doing below average work, they often will not take the risk of assigning these individuals work that is important to the organization. However, if supervisors have competent and motivated employees but resist delegating work because they do not feel these individuals will measure up to their expectations, they must acknowledge this as a personal weakness and find a way to overcome it. It is not fair to deny employees opportunities for growth and development through delegated work because of a supervisor's own insecurities.

3. Supervisors believe delegation takes too much time. Delegating work requires supervisors to think through each step of the delegation process and make decisions about what tasks should be delegated, who should be assigned the work, what deadline should be set, and what criteria will be used to determine success. Communicating expectations, monitoring progress, and providing ongoing feedback are also time-consuming activities. Many supervisors decide not to invest the time required to delegate a responsibility even though in the end it would free up time for them to do other work. Choosing not to delegate because it takes too much time is a poor decision. Good supervisors see the long-term value of delegating work even if, in the short-term, it seems to take a lot of time.

4. Supervisors fear disappointing their boss and their employees. Supervisors often fail to delegate important tasks because they fear they will disappoint their boss, their employees, or both. Delegating work requires supervisors to let go of control and give it to someone else. If for some reason the delegated work does not get done, then the assigning supervisor's reputation could be discredited. Many supervisors, especially the inexperienced, would much rather perform the work themselves than run the risk of disappointing their boss. Also, most supervisors have had their share of bad experiences of delegating work that was not well-defined and probably should not have been delegated and then dealing with the aftermath of frustrated and perhaps jaded employees. Again, many supervisors would rather accomplish the work themselves rather than delegate an assignment and risk resentment from their employees.

5. Supervisors fear competition. Supervisors also resist delegation because of a fear of competition from talented employees. Supervisors, especially those who are inexperienced or are insecure in their positions, often refuse to delegate assignments particularly if they think one of their employees will perform well, attract attention from a higher-level boss, and perhaps eventually compete for the supervisor's own job.

Rather than finding reasons for not wanting to delegate, supervisors should invest time and learn the techniques for delegating effectively.

Steps Involved in Effectively Delegating

Effective delegation requires supervisors to take their time and carefully think through all aspects of the assignments they entrust to their employees. There are five steps involved in successfully delegating responsibilities.

1. *Consider, in detail, the work to be delegated.* The first step in effective delegation is for supervisors to analyze the work they intend to delegate. For inexperienced supervisors, it is important to choose tasks that are clearly defined with specific standards and an explicit deadline date. It is also helpful to choose tasks that do not require too much of the supervisor's time for follow-up. As individuals gain supervisory experience, they may gain more confidence to delegate work that is not well-defined and where measures of success are not readily available.

   Before work is delegated, supervisors must determine the kind and extent of authority that will be delegated to an employee doing the assigned work. "Authority" is the right and power to make decisions, seek input and give instructions to others regardless of their rank or position. For delegation to succeed, employees must know the authority they have in carrying out the assigned responsibility. During the planning stage, it is important for supervisors to specify the results they desire and think about the criteria they will use to determine how well the work has been done. Typically, supervisors assess the degree of error and misjudgment they can tolerate before assigning work. If the assigned work is expected to last several weeks or months, most supervisors establish benchmarks along the way and have an idea about what success looks like at each critical phase.

2. *Select the employee.* As supervisors analyze the work they will delegate, they also must carefully consider the person who will perform the delegated work. Research shows that delegation is more likely to occur when supervisors perceive employees as competent in undertaking the task demands and the associated risk (Schriesheim, Neider, & Scandura, 1998). For inexperienced supervisors, it is best to choose an employee who has a track record of being productive, cooperative, and responsive to accepting challenges. Supervisors should know the competency and motivation of each of their employees so that the delegated assignments fit the needs and talents of each one.

3. *Communicate the assignment.* Supervisors must be careful in the way they turn over assignments to individual employees. The goal is to clearly communicate, in detail,

the assignment and to achieve a common understanding of the desired results. For important assignments, supervisors should provide the details of an assignment in writing including specific items that need to be accomplished and the expected dates for completion. In this way, employees and the supervisor have a written record of the assignment and the supervisor's expectations. Also, for those important assignments, supervisors typically meet with employees in private and allow sufficient, uninterrupted time to review the details. Supervisors should consider the meeting a dialogue with an employee rather than a one-way exchange of information. Employees should participate in the discussion, provide input, and ask questions. In this step it is critical that the supervisor and employee have the same understanding of the assignment and the desired results.

4. *Hold employee accountable.* It is the supervisor's responsibility to monitor the progress that is being made by an employee on the assigned work and hold him or her accountable. Delegating work without some type of systematic monitoring often results in disappointed supervisors and dissatisfied employees. To establish accountability, supervisors must formalize a system for tracking progress as well as for giving and receiving feedback. Good supervisors set checkpoints to formally sit down with an individual and discuss an assignment, the progress that is being made, and any issues or concerns that might have a negative impact on the task. It is also important for supervisors to receive ongoing updates through formal and informal meetings during the duration of the assignment.

Establishing the level of accountability for delegated assignments is not always easily determined and supervisors must be perceptive to strike a delicate balance between taking too much control and not taking enough. Employees resent supervisors who want to "micro-manage" and be involved at every decision point. On the other hand, employees take offense at supervisors who turn over an assignment,

especially one that is communicated as "vital" to the agency, and then appear to be uninterested and unavailable for consultation. To be effective, supervisors must begin the delegation process with a formal accountability system and then be flexible enough to adapt the system to the situation as well as to meet the needs of their employees.

5. *Support employees.* For delegation to be successful, supervisors must maintain open lines of communication and provide adequate support to employees performing assigned work. Effective supervisors demonstrate their openness and support in a variety of ways. They make it a point to tell employees, through words and actions, that they are available to discuss problems that could arise. They back up an employee when others in the organization challenge his or her "authority." Good supervisors show support by giving employees a fair chance to prove their performance without meddling in their affairs. Further, they provide encouragement and give credit to those who do well. Another excellent way of demonstrating support is to look for ways to appropriately recognize and reward accomplishments made by individuals or groups involved in successful assignments.

Reasons Why Supervisors Should Not Delegate

There are some responsibilities that are suitable for delegation and others that absolutely should not be delegated. Supervisors must make good decisions about the type of work they pass along to their employees. Supervisors should not delegate tasks that involve sensitive personnel issues, such as resolving conflict between employees, disciplining an employee, or conducting employee performance reviews (Yukl & Fu, 1999). It is also not appropriate for supervisors to delegate duties that are associated with recognizing and praising employees. Employees would be outraged if a supervisor asked a lower-level employee to serve as a substitute at an employee awards ceremony to hand out service pins to those who had 5 years, 10 years, or 25 years of service.

Tasks that are sensitive and for which the supervisor cannot provide all the information or confer the appropriate level of authority should not be delegated. If the task requires the use of confidential information that the employee is not privileged to access, then it is an inappropriate assignment. Finally, it goes without saying, that a supervisor's personal chores should not be delegated. An employee should not be assigned the responsibility of managing the supervisor's personal rental property or making arrangements for the supervisor to have his or her house painted.

Learning to delegate effectively is not easy and many of the experiences bring mistakes, frustration, and disappointment. However, supervisors who are willing to put forth the effort, learn from their mistakes, and become successful delegators, are more productive and valuable not only to the organization, but also to themselves and the employees they supervise.

Effective Time Management

Time is a precious resource of supervisors and although all supervisors have the same amount of work time available to them (8 hours/day, 40 hours/week, 2,080 hours/year), some manage time better than others. *Time management* is defined as the act of planning and organizing work to improve efficiency and effectiveness. In supervisory work, there are many competing demands and it is important for supervisors to understand what they do at work that wastes time and prevents them from investing in the work that is most valuable to the organization. Also, supervisors must be constantly looking for ways to improve time management and adopt techniques that help better utilize their time to become more productive. In this section we will address the common things that we do at work that waste time and then present techniques and suggestions for resolving time management challenges.

Time Wasters at Work

Time is a valued resource and unless supervisors acknowledge the things they do (or do not do) that fritter away their time, they most likely are not working as productively as they could. The following is a list of activities that are considered "time wasters."

1. Unorganized computer files and e-mail. Chances are that if supervisors have not adopted a system for organizing their computer and clearing out old files and e-mails, they spend a lot of wasted time scouring the hard drive for particular documents they created several days or weeks ago.

2. Untidy and disorganized workplace. Many supervisors lose valuable time during the day searching for important documents that were misfiled or misplaced in a cluttered office. Some people are not well-organized and do not have a filing system to help them work swiftly and efficiently with important documents. Some supervisors are messy and spend wasted time rummaging through their desks looking for important documents. This type of work environment often creates an unfavorable impression especially, if supervisors constantly ask employees to resubmit their assignments.

3. Unwillingness (or inability) to prioritize work, establish a work plan, and stick to it. There are many supervisors who are unable or unwilling to plan and organize their work for the day. Rather than prioritizing their workload, they tend to respond to the "hot" topic of the day and leave important business unfinished. Some supervisors also have difficulty in establishing realistic time frames for completing their work. They tend to underestimate the time needed to complete assignments and, as a result, postpone deadline dates and important decisions. The time wasted by these supervisors often negatively affects their employees who are frequently forced to stop progress on their assignments until decisions are made by the boss.

4. Spending too much time on less important assignments and procrastinating the work that brings value to the agency. Most people at work, including supervisors, typically take on and complete work they enjoy doing first, and needlessly procrastinate on assignments they dislike or find difficult. This type of supervisory behavior is unproductive for the agency, especially if the work that is delayed is important and adds value to the agency. Some supervisors boast that they often procrastinate because they do their best work and produce the most when they are under pressure to meet a deadline. This, too, is unacceptable for supervisors because much of what they do, and most decisions they make, impact the work of their employees and others in the organization.

5. Spending too much time on the telephone or mobile phone. Most employees, including supervisors, bring mobile phones to work and leave them activated to respond to calls throughout the day. Spending an unreasonable amount of time on unimportant mobile phone conversations robs the employee and organization of productivity.

6. Spending too much time sending and receiving electronic mail. Some supervisors spend an excessive amount of time on electronic mail, constantly checking for messages and instantly responding. Also, with very good intentions, many supervisors add their names to electronic mailing lists sponsored by professional groups and then spend an inordinate amount of time reading and responding to messages that may only be remotely related to the "valued" business of the organization.

7. Spending too much time online. Most employees spend a few minutes each day shopping, checking current news, sports, stock prices, and other online "favorites" during the day, but it is not appropriate to waste hours of company time on personal business especially when other important work of the organization is being overlooked.

8. Unwillingness (or inability) to say "no" to requests to take on more "busy" work. Some supervisors are overly ambitious and have difficulty in saying "no" when asked to take on additional work that may not bring value to the organization. These requests may come from employees within an organization, coworkers, or from leaders in state and national professional groups. The inability to say "no" or negotiate a lesser assignment impacts the productivity of supervisors, especially when they attempt to do too much, become overwhelmed with the volume of work, and subsequently are unable to give any one assignment their best effort. This lack of discipline becomes a serious problem when the work most valuable to the organization is not receiving the supervisor's best effort. This time waster also impacts supervisory relationships in that supervisors who are overloaded do not have adequate time to mentor, coach, and motivate their employees.

9. Unwillingness (or inability) to delegate effectively. Supervisors who have not developed effective skills for delegating work often take on responsibilities and perform duties that could and should be delegated to their employees. As a result, these supervisors may not have the time to address the matters that would bring the most value to the agency.

10. Spending too much time in ineffective meetings. Many supervisors squander their time and the time of their employees when they fail to effectively plan and conduct staff meetings. (See the next section on effective meeting management).

11. Spending too much time talking with drop-in visitors. Supervisors can waste a great deal of time talking with people (employees, coworkers, customers, or vendors) who drop by for casual conversation. Unless supervisors have the tact and diplomacy to control uninvited interruptions and manage visitors who stay too long, they will lose valuable time during the day that could be used for higher priority work.

To overcome these and other time wasters, supervisors must treat "time" as a precious resource. They must be constantly aware of how they use their time and continually look for ways to use their time more efficiently and effectively. Effective supervisors use the following techniques and suggestions to help use their time more efficiently and effectively.

Techniques and Suggestions for Resolving Time Management Problems

There are many books, articles, and online information about time management with helpful suggestions and techniques for getting control of time at work. Effective supervisors constantly explore and experiment with time management techniques that best fit their personal style. Four such techniques and suggestions that supervisors use to resolve time-management problems are provided below.

1. Establish a plan of work. Effective supervisors establish a plan of work, set priorities, and establish a timeframe for managing work each day. By doing so, they are less

likely to procrastinate, and they may actually have a rationale for saying "no" to a person's requests to take on more work. Complex projects that require an extended period of time should be broken down into small, identifiable tasks. It is easier for supervisors to accomplish several work tasks within a shorter time frame, than it is to face an entire project that demands a large time commitment. Many supervisors establish priorities for their work by labeling tasks that are of the greatest value to the agency as priority "A," those tasks that are in the second tier of importance as priority "B," and those of least value, label "C." After establishing a system of priorities supervisors should use the plan as a *guide*, not a mandate, for performing work. Work with priority "A" should come first, and when "A" tasks are complete, the supervisor should shift attention to "B" tasks. This process of establishing a plan of work is most effective when supervisors establish a daily work plan that is based on a weekly work plan, which in turn is based on a monthly work plan, and so on. Most supervisors use more than one planning calendar and may actually color code the entries to help them stay focused on their priorities.

Another planning technique that is helpful to supervisors, if they have control over scheduling of their work, is to plan "A" tasks during their prime time. "Prime time" is that part of a person's day when he or she is most productive, thinks the clearest, and accomplishes the most work. For example, some supervisors prefer early morning hours and will come to work an hour early and use that quiet time to tackle "A" tasks. Other supervisors are more productive at mid-morning or late afternoon and schedule the highest priority work for that period of time.

One caution in establishing a plan of work is to recognize that rarely will everything go according to the way it was planned. Supervisors should expect to handle important interruptions and unexpected problems that disrupt the "flow" of work during the day. Supervisors must remain diligent, but at the same time stay flexible as they implement their plan of work.

2. Avoid unnecessary time on electronic mail and use software to manage the inbox. Today, supervisors are deluged with electronic mail not only from individuals working for the organization, but also from external contacts including professional colleagues, family, and friends. To gain control over incoming e-mails and daily priorities, effective supervisors learn methods of task and e-mail management through commercial software programs. These products have enhancements that help users manage an unruly inbox, prioritize daily tasks, schedule meetings, and make appointments. Effective supervisors take responsibility for reading tutorials, attending workshops, and learning the best practices to help them realize all of the benefits that an integrated information and e-mail system can provide.

To control the time spent on electronic mail, supervisors must be self-disciplined and handle e-mail correspondence only a couple of times a day, preferably at midday and later in the afternoon. To avoid constant interruptions, many supervisors turn off the audible alert and visual notification of incoming e-mails. They also prioritize incoming mail and make an immediate decision on how to handle non-business related messages. Some supervisors make an intentional choice not to immediately respond to some messages. Many times problems are resolved in a couple of days without the supervisor's input. Effective supervisors may also make a conscious decision never to respond to some of the messages they receive. In fact, many effective supervisors use filters and delete messages before they appear in the inbox. If supervisors give it serious thought, there are usually several messages they receive each day that will have little consequence if they choose not to read or respond to them. Effective supervisors also unsubscribe from electronic listservs that may generate interesting messages but that are not pertinent to the supervisor's essential job functions.

3. Limit use of the Internet to important job-related activities. Self-discipline is the answer to those supervisors who tend to spend too much online time for personal business. Effective supervisors limit personal use of the Internet and stay focused on the important work of the organization. Also, if they do take a few minutes out of their day to use the Internet for personal business, they make certain that any of the sites they access would not embarrass them or put themselves in a compromising position. Many organizations use tracking software to enforce company policies on Internet use and detect irregular and illegal activity. Supervisors should surf wisely and encourage their employees to do the same.

4. Control unwanted phone interruptions. To overcome the problem of unwanted telephone or mobile phone interruptions, supervisors first must determine who is calling and why. One technique that is commonly used by supervisors to complete this first step is to conduct a phone audit. As calls are received throughout the day, the supervisor maintains a log of the persons calling, the reasons for the call, and the amount of time spent on each call. The supervisor can then review the list and identify the type of calls that are unnecessary, unwanted, or unnecessarily lengthy. At that point, supervisors can develop a strategy for each type of problem. If employees are calling unnecessarily, the supervisor may want to delegate more authority or more clearly explain the authority that has been granted. If supervisors are receiving unwanted calls from people outside the agency (e.g., friends, vendors) and screening calls by a receptionist is not possible, a supervisor may want to develop a list of reasons to justify the need for concluding a conversation. Attending a meeting, keeping a previous appointment, or completing a report for upper management are examples of reasons that can be used to end unwanted conversations. Another effective technique for bringing closure to unwanted calls is for supervisors to point out the caller's busy schedule. This method transfers the burden of responsibility for the call from the supervisor to the caller.

The phone audit may also reveal that a supervisor's outgoing calls are too lengthy and time-consuming. To make the best use of time on the phone, supervisors should consider jotting down key words or phrases that trigger major points for discussion. This technique helps keep the conversation focused and reduces rambling. Still yet another technique to handle outgoing calls more efficiently is to establish morning and afternoon time blocks. During these blocks, supervisors can place all outgoing calls and respond to voice mail messages left earlier in the day.

Supervisors who are good time managers have several useful techniques for handling disruptive mobile phone calls. First, supervisors need to set boundaries and have a serious conversation with their family members and friends about calling during the work day for casual conversation. Using a mobile phone for personal calls during a lunch break is an effective way of preserving valuable work time. Many supervisors set their mobile phones to vibrate during the work day to prevent different ring tones from annoying others in the office. When in doubt about whether a call is important, let voice-mail pick up calls. Supervisors waste less time checking voice-mail than they do responding to every call they receive. Listening to other people's private mobile phone calls at work is annoying for most workers and for that reason many supervisors find somewhere else to talk other than at their desk when responding to personal calls. This technique is also a good reminder about the amount of time that is spent on personal calls.

5. Control the problem of too much "socializing." Most effective supervisors are committed to an "open door" policy and are accessible to their employees who want to "drop in" and discuss work-related issues. Also, to demonstrate interest and concern, many supervisors make it a point to visit and talk with employees at their various work locations. However, often the supervisor's accessibility can be a primary

cause of unwanted interruptions and long-winded conversations. This is a very delicate situation and supervisors must be very careful to use tact and diplomacy to achieve their business objectives while at the same time demonstrating support for their employees. One of the best ways to reduce the frequency and length of socializing conversations is for supervisors to approach their work in a professional, businesslike manner and give others the impression that work is important and their time is valuable. Successful supervisors are approachable, accessible, and make time to meet with their employees and yet at the same time, they model behavior that communicates that work is serious, they are serious about it, and unimportant conversations are undesirable.

Another technique that is helpful to minimize unwanted interruptions is to arrange the furniture in such a way as to take away direct eye contact from a passerby. Desks can be arranged to face a wall, not an open door. Since visitors usually prefer to sit while chatting, it is a good idea for a supervisor to intercept unwanted "socializers" before they enter the office door and then remain standing until the conversation can be ended. Supervisors may also control the length of a visit by ambling toward a water fountain, copy machine, or toward the visitor's own office.

Time is a valuable resource for supervisors. In a position where there is "too much to do" and "too little time to do it," supervisors must be persistent in understanding how they use their time. They must be vigilant, they must look for time-saving techniques, and they must use the company time efficiently and effectively.

Conducting Effective Staff Meetings

Most employees grimace and groan whenever they receive word of another meeting to attend. Employees already attend regularly scheduled meetings such as weekly staff meetings, in-service training meetings, project meetings, and special task force meetings, so to add another meeting to the work schedule is discouraging. The bad reputation that meetings earn is,

for the most part, well deserved. Most people dislike meetings because they feel like they are wasting time. Employees complain that meetings lack substantive agenda items, too much time is spent rehashing agenda items that have previously been discussed, discussions go off on tangents and decisions are never made, and people who have accepted assignments during a meeting never follow through with their commitments. Employees also grumble that meetings never start or end on time, the person leading the meeting is disorganized and a poor facilitator, and almost always there is someone in attendance who behaves inappropriately and is disruptive to others. Not only are meetings disliked, the waste associated with them is staggering. The organization not only loses productivity during the meeting (each person's hourly pay rate times the number of hours the meeting lasts), but also forfeits any benefits that could have been realized from good ideas conceived, but never actually implemented.

In the face of all these problems, meetings are still a fundamental way of conducting the business of an organization. Supervisors conduct meetings for many important reasons. First, a meeting is an efficient way of communicating information to a group when supervisors need face-to-face interaction. It is much easier for supervisors to convince, influence and persuade others when they can read nonverbal cues and gauge reactions directly. Second, the collective talent of individuals sitting in a meeting can be advantageous in generating ideas, resolving problems, and influencing others to accept a new idea. For supervisors, it is much more efficient to have the brainpower all in one room at one time rather than working one-on-one with individuals.

Planning and conducting meetings are essential skills for supervisors to develop. In this section, the focus is on conducting effective staff meetings. Basic principles and practices are covered in planning and conducting staff meetings, and completing the follow-up activities after the meetings. In Chapter 13, we will address two other important aspects of running meetings, including preparing for a formal presentation and introducing *Robert's Rules of Order*, a recognized guide for running meetings effectively and fairly.

Planning for a Staff Meeting

From the casual perspective of someone attending a staff meeting, it seems like they should be easy to arrange and conduct, but effective supervisors understand that successful meetings may only happen after careful planning. During the planning stage, supervisors should perform the following four tasks:

1. Establish clear objectives and outcomes. An important component of effective staff meetings is to have clearly stated objectives. Objectives are distinct from agenda items and are typically stated in terms of what needs to be accomplished. Objectives that are common for staff meetings are to: 1) communicate important policies, procedures, rules, or decisions; 2) train employees; 3) obtain employee feedback and hear expert opinion; 4) resolve a problem; 5) broaden awareness of employees; and 6) gain acceptance for a new idea, program, policy, procedure, or rule.

   To plan the objectives of a meeting, supervisors must first envision specific outcomes. For staff meetings, outcomes usually come in the form of a decision, a recommendation, a resolution, a new policy, a list of options, or a list of new ideas. For example, supervisors may want their employees to make a final decision on agenda items such as the date, time, and location of an event, or review the current fees and charges and recommend changes for the next fiscal year, or evaluate a recent program or event.

   Not all outcomes of a staff meeting must be specific and measurable, although most employees will judge the success or failure of a meeting based on their perception of whether something concrete was accomplished. It is common for supervisors to state objectives for a staff meeting that may not be easily perceived by those attending. For example, supervisors may have an objective to broaden employees' perspective of not only what goes on with other employees in the work group, but also the initiatives in other divisions of the organization. During the staff meeting the supervisor may ask each employee to give an update about what is happening in his or her job. The supervisor may also share information about activities in other divisions of the agency. This exchange of information may be perceived by employees as "not accomplishing much," but it does satisfy an important objective.

   During the planning phase, the bottom line for supervisors is knowing precisely the purpose and desired outcome of each agenda item. Pre-planning for staff meetings is not a one-time event or an activity that is done by the supervisor on an occasional basis. To earn the respect and trust of employees, supervisors must consistently demonstrate, week after week, that they plan, prepare, and care about what happens in staff meetings.

2. Prepare and distribute a written and prioritized agenda. The next step in the planning process is to prepare a written agenda that is based on the pre-established objectives for the meeting and to circulate it in advance. Items on the agenda should appear in priority order, starting with the most important first. Supervisors should also estimate the amount of time that is needed to accomplish each agenda item so that adequate time is allowed and discussions are not rushed. Supervisors typically send meeting agendas via an e-mail attachment in advance of the meeting, along with any supplemental documents that employees are expected to review prior to the meeting time. Any instructions that help employees to prepare for a staff meeting (items they should bring, ideas to consider) are also distributed with the agenda.

   It is very important that staff members have input into the topics addressed in staff meetings. Effective supervisors invite employees to review the agenda and contribute additional items by a deadline that is established prior to the meeting. This technique helps supervisors gauge the length of the meeting and eliminates the opportunity for "surprise" items from group members during the meeting.

3. Anticipate and prepare for inappropriate behavior that may interfere with the meeting. Prior to a staff meeting, it is important for supervisors to anticipate inappropriate behavior that might occur in reaction to an agenda item and to give thought to strategies that can help

to quickly resolve an issue, should it arise. In the workplace, it is considered rude and inappropriate to use mobile phones, Blackberries, and MP3 players during meetings (Agnew & Hill, 2009). Managers may need to discuss with staff the proper use of electronic devices and meeting etiquette. The idea that it is effective multitasking to sit in meetings and answer e-mails, text, or better yet, get up and walk out to take a mobile call, ignores the idea of working together or being part of a team. Other common behavior problems that meeting leaders should anticipate include employees who are aggressive and dominate discussion by sharing an opinion on every agenda item, as well as those who have good ideas and yet sit quietly, rarely engaging in discussion. There may be characters in the group who can be described as the "self-appointed expert," the "pessimist," or the "condescending critic." Supervisors may need to deal occasionally with an employee who brings a "hidden agenda," one that is contrary to the objectives of the meeting. Each of these individuals brings a different dynamic to the staff meeting, and it is the skilled supervisor who knows each employee and finds a way to capitalize on an employee's strengths, while not allowing the inappropriate behavior to interfere with the meeting's objectives and outcomes. A technique that many supervisors use to address inappropriate and disruptive meeting behavior is to work with the group to create a standard of conduct for meetings. Many organizations post a standard of conduct and meeting rules in each conference room to serve as a constant reminder.

4. Arrange the meeting room. It is the supervisor's responsibility to make certain that the meeting room is prepared prior to the meeting time. The supervisor should check the furnishings (tables, chairs) and make sure they are adequate and in an appropriate configuration. Any equipment or supplies needed for the meeting (computer, projection system, telephone for conference call, flip chart, marking and dry-erase pens) should be available and in good working order. The thermostat should be set in advance so the room is comfortable for the number of people expected at the meeting.

Pre-planning is essential to effective meetings, and without this effort on an ongoing basis, meetings lose their effectiveness and supervisors find it difficult to obtain their objectives. Employees want and deserve a supervisor who is well organized and who conducts efficient and effective meetings.

Conducting a Staff Meeting

Just as it is important to pre-plan for a meeting, it is equally important to perform well as a leader during the meeting. Successful meeting leaders use these principles and techniques for conducting meetings:

1. Start and end the meeting on time. Meetings should begin and end on time. Supervisors who choose to delay the start of a meeting communicate a message to those who are punctual that "time" is not a valued resource. And if meetings consistently start late, employees who do value their time may begin to intentionally wait a few minutes before coming to a meeting so they can continue to work at their office and not waste time sitting in a meeting room waiting on others to arrive. To deal with the problem of late arrivals, many supervisors will make a public statement reminding all in attendance that meetings start and end on time, and all employees are expected to be punctual. Supervisors should set in advance an ending time for staff meetings and then abide by the schedule. By ending meetings on time, supervisors are obligated to conduct business during a meeting efficiently.

2. Review the agenda and desired outcomes. At the start of the staff meeting, meeting leaders should review the purpose of the meeting and identify the desired outcomes. They may also review the time allocations anticipated for each of the agenda items and respond to general questions about the items. The technique of reviewing the agenda sets the tone for the meeting and gives employees the perception that the supervisor is organized and results are expected.

3. Appoint a person to take minutes. It is imperative to have notes of the meeting and typically the supervisor is responsible for arranging a note taker. If a staff person is unavailable for taking notes, the supervisor may establish a rotation system and have the schedule listed as part of the agenda. The note taker should keep a record of the outcomes of the meeting including the results of any decisions, assignments, or commitments that are made. Many supervisors also ask that a note taker keep a running record of discussion points and ideas that are brought up during the meeting. Once the meeting is adjourned, the published notes serve as a reminder of what needs to be accomplished before the next meeting. They also document the meeting for those unable to attend, including higher-level administrators.

4. Use humor and encourage fun. Meetings do not have to be dull and boring to be effective. To the contrary, much serious business can take place in a meeting where the leader encourages fun and uses humor as a way of communicating important messages. Some supervisors bring "brain teasers" or word puzzles, for example, when they are looking for employees to think creatively. Short video clips from a comedy or action film are often used to prompt employees to think in a different way. Providing healthy snacks for the meeting is another way that supervisors can facilitate a more relaxed and fun meeting setting. To break the monotonous routine, some supervisors move the location of regularly scheduled meetings to give employees a different perspective. In an effort to create a fun meeting environment, supervisors must make certain that anything that is said or done is appropriate and in good taste and achieves the desired result.

5. Maintain the focus of the meeting. During the meeting, supervisors are responsible for following the agenda and achieving the meeting objectives. In meeting discussions, it is common for group members to stray from a topic and go off on a tangent. Most of the time digressions are unintentional, although there are times when employees lose focus and are unable to make progress because the topic is too difficult. Unfocused conversations may be interesting to the group members, but when they drag on, they can be counterproductive in accomplishing a meeting objective. When discussions get off track, it is important for the meeting leader to recognize that it is happening and refocus the group discussion in a tactful way. Also, when good ideas emerge during a rambling discussion, they should not be lost. Many effective supervisors use a technique called a "parking lot." Rather than divert attention away from the agenda, they suggest to employees that good ideas be parked until adequate time is available to fully discuss them at a later meeting.

6. Recognize and end disruptive behavior. When inappropriate behavior disrupts a meeting, it is the responsibility of the supervisor to take immediate and appropriate action. If one or two people are dominating the discussion, the supervisor may remind the group that everyone's input is needed and solicit participation from those who are sitting quietly. When dealing with a pessimist who has nothing good to say, a supervisor might remind the entire group that positive energy and good thoughts are most conducive for accomplishing meeting objectives. If disruptive behavior repeatedly occurs, the supervisor should meet privately with the individuals after the meeting and deal with the problem as a discipline issue.

7. Be a good facilitator. As the facilitator of a meeting, supervisors must be careful not to dominate the meeting. The real purpose of the facilitator is to stimulate participation by all group members. Supervisors should not feel like they need to be on center stage and share an opinion on every agenda item. Most of the time, it is more productive for the group if the supervisor remains neutral and refrains from giving an opinion. Facilitators should encourage employees

to voice their suggestions and concerns during a meeting. They also should invite differing opinions and show support for individuals who express a minority view or cast a vote that goes against the majority. Rather than becoming absorbed in the discussions of each agenda item, good facilitators look for ways to stimulate group discussion by asking good questions. They also make certain that all sides of an issue are brought to light before final decisions are made.

8. Summarize action that was taken and decisions that were made. At the end of a discussion on a particular agenda item, meeting leaders should briefly review what was accomplished. They also summarize the commitments that were made, by whom, and when.

Following Up After a Staff Meeting

After a staff meeting adjourns, effective supervisors immediately begin follow-up activities such as the ones listed below.

1. Promptly distribute the minutes. The supervisor is responsible for promptly distributing the minutes of the meeting. Typically, the person recording the minutes provides a draft document and distributes it to everyone via an e-mail attachment. Once corrections are made, the supervisor circulates the final draft. As mentioned above, the minutes serve as a reminder to individuals as to what they have promised to do and by when.

2. Check on individual progress and keep everyone updated. When employees volunteer to accept assignments in a meeting, they should carry through with their commitments. However, it is common for employees to be very busy and actually forget what they said they were going to do in a meeting. It is the supervisor's responsibility to follow up on the actions of all those who made commitments and make sure the work is completed by the agreed deadline. Also, supervisors make it a point to keep the entire group posted on the progress on assigned tasks by sending periodic updates.

3. Provide individual feedback to employees. Supervisors should take the time to give feedback to individual employees following a staff meeting. The supervisor's intent is to recognize and praise the type of behavior that is desired in a staff meeting, and to try to correct behavior that is inappropriate and interferes with the group process before the next scheduled staff meeting. To those individuals in the meeting who helped lead the group discussion toward reaching an objective, the supervisor should recognize and give positive feedback. Most supervisors send a simple thank-you via e-mail, or drop by the person's office and say thank you in person. To the individuals who disrupted the meeting or showed inappropriate behavior, the supervisor should make the effort to meet with each one individually and give constructive feedback. Through this type of personal coaching, supervisors communicate to employees that the behavior is inappropriate, unacceptable, and needs to change. Typically, this type of informal counseling session is sufficient to deal with the problem and further disciplinary action is not required.

4. Evaluate the meeting. Supervisors should take time to evaluate meetings in terms of their effectiveness. The purpose of this exercise is to use the input as a way of improving future meetings. Supervisors should think about the meeting objectives and whether the intended outcomes were achieved. They should also focus on the interaction among employees and determine what could be done to improve team dynamics. It is also a good idea for supervisors to assess their own performance as a meeting leader. They should evaluate their ability to keep the meeting focused, control inappropriate behavior, and stimulate critical thinking. Good supervisors also solicit feedback from employees to help improve meeting effectiveness.

Follow-up activities are essential to effective meeting management. When supervisors pay attention to the details, they have a better chance of using the meeting to accomplish the important business of the agency. If follow-up steps are ignored, supervisors will, over time, face the challenge of trying to achieve desired objectives with employees who have a negative attitude and who resent attending meetings when little is accomplished.

As mentioned earlier, meetings are a fundamental way of conducting the business of the organization. The time spent in staff meetings can be perceived by employees as extremely valuable or as a major waste of time, depending on the meeting management skills of a supervisor. Supervisors must learn to make meetings work for them, not against them. They wisely must make use of meeting time by planning ahead, developing objectives, staying focused, using good facilitation techniques, managing inappropriate behavior, and following through on assignments. In short, they use meetings effectively as a way of producing results for the agency.

SUMMARY

1. Supervisors are responsible for working effectively with individuals assigned to them for the purpose of achieving the goals and objectives of their unit, department, or division.

2. Supervisory positions exist at all levels of management (lower, middle and upper).

3. The key duties of a supervisor are to: plan and organize work; provide the type of leadership for the unit that is aligned with the mission of the organization; and recruit, hire, motivate and retain talented individuals.

4. Qualifications for supervisory positions are typically written in broad, general terms which then allows for the possibility of hiring job candidates that may have the potential to become a good supervisor but have not yet proven themselves in a supervisory position.

5. Employees who have an excellent performance record in a non-supervisory position do not necessarily have the competencies or motivation to become successful supervisors.

6. Aligning oneself with management view points, supervising friends, striking the balance between being a "boss" or "buddy" with employees, and dealing with resentful employees are common challenges that first-time supervisors will have in transitioning to their new position.

7. Establishing a trusting relationship with employees is essential to successful supervision. When a trusting relationship exists, employees perform at a higher level, are more highly committed to their assigned duties, and more willing to take on additional responsibilities that benefit the unit. Supervisors who trust their employees have more flexibility in the way they delegate work and are more likely to assign "choice" assignments that allow employees to gain valuable work experience and exposure.

8. Honesty, integrity, competence, fairness, and benevolence are the primary components of developing a trusting relationship between supervisors and their employees.

9. Employees benefit from meaningful work that is delegated by their supervisors in that they have an opportunity to gain more knowledge, experience, and a different perspective that make them more marketable for a higher level position. Supervisors who are effective in delegating have more time to invest in work activities that bring the most value to the organization.

10. Supervisors often fail to develop effective delegation skills because they enjoy doing the tasks that they should be delegating. They may also resist delegating work because they fear disappointing their boss or are concerned about competing against other talented employees.

11. The key steps supervisors take in effectively delegating are to define the work that will be delegated, carefully select the person who will perform the work, clearly communicate the assignment and desired results, monitor the employee's progress and provide feedback, and provide support to the employee performing the assigned work.

12. Supervisors should avoid delegating work that involves sensitive personnel issues.

13. Time management requires supervisors to plan and organize their work in a way that improves efficiency and effectiveness.

Techniques for resolving time management problems include establishing a plan of work and setting priorities, developing a strategy or using software to efficiently manage electronic mail and documents, reducing or eliminating unnecessary socializing and procrastination, limiting the use of Internet searches to work activities that add value to the organization, and minimizing unwanted interruptions.

14. Supervisors are responsible for planning and conducting effective staff meetings. Establishing clear meeting objectives and meeting outcomes, preparing and distributing a prioritized meeting agenda, anticipating and preparing for inappropriate staff member behavior, and arranging for adequate meeting space and equipment are essential components in effective meeting management.

15. In conducting successful meetings, supervisors make a special effort to start (and end) a meeting on time, review the agenda prior to the start of the meeting, arrange for someone to take meeting notes, maintain the focus of the meeting, recognize and manage disruptive behaviors, facilitate the meeting effectively so that all group members have an opportunity to participate, and summarize major decisions and commitments that were made at the close of the meeting.

16. After a staff meeting adjourns, supervisors are responsible for making sure that meeting minutes are promptly distributed, following up on the actions of all those who made commitments, providing individual feedback to staff members who positively (or negatively) impacted the meeting, and evaluate the outcomes of the meeting against the meeting's goals and objectives.

DISCUSSION TOPICS

1. The qualifications of most supervisory jobs require job candidates to have 1–5 years of proven supervisory experience. What suggestions can you offer to individuals who aspire to supervisory positions and yet have limited or no experience in supervising full-time employees?

2. If you were the hiring authority for a recreation supervisor position, would you prefer to hire job candidate A who has adequate job experience in the area of responsibility (aquatics, camps, athletics) and shows clear evidence of successful supervisory experience, or job candidate B who shows extensive job experience in the area of responsibility but has no experience in supervising full-time employees? Justify your response and explain the level of support needed for either candidate who is selected for the job.

3. If you are promoted to a supervisory position which requires you to supervise peers from your previous job, what challenges will you face in supervising those individuals whom you consider to be good friends? Explain if, and how, your relationship with them will change.

4. Assume you have been promoted to a supervisory job that is considered a part of the management team. If you disagree with management's decisions and find it difficult to represent management's views, explain how will you deal with employees reporting directly to you? Explain how will you deal with your boss, your boss's boss, and other top-level managers?

5. How do supervisors develop and sustain trust with their employees? With their immediate boss? With their peers?

6. Is it possible for supervisors who have lost the trust of their employees to regain it? Explain.

7. Assume you have hired an individual for a supervisory position and he or she met only the bare minimum experience requirement of supervising full-time employees. What are the reasons why this individual might have difficulty in delegating work to the full-time employees working for him or her? What type of management support is needed for inexperienced supervisors to overcome their reluctance to delegate?

8. What are the top time-wasters of supervisors at work? What are the workplace time-wasters of employees? What strategies or techniques are recommended for addressing each of the time-wasters?

9. What are the reasons why meetings are ineffective? What strategies or techniques are recommended for making meetings successful?

10. What strategies or techniques are recommended for dealing with employees who behave in ways that are unproductive (dominating, condescending, pessimistic) during meetings?

References

Agnew, D., & Hill, K. (2009). E-mail etiquette recommendation for today's business student. *Proceedings of the Academy of Organizational Culture, Communications and Conflict, 14*(2), 1–38.

Bass, B. M. (1990). *Bass and Stogdill's handbook of leadership: Theory, research & applications.* New York, NY: Free Press.

Blau, P. (1964). *Exchange and power in social life.* New York, NY: Wiley.

Chiaburu, D. S., & Lim, A. S. (2008). Manager trustworthiness or interactional justice? Predicting organizational citizenship behaviors. *Journal of Business Ethics, 83*(3), 453.

Cunningham, J. B., & MacGregor, J. (2000). Trust and the design of work: Complementary constructs in satisfaction and performance. *Human Relations, 53*(12), 1575–1591.

Dirks, K. T., & Ferrin, D. L. (2002). Trust in leadership: Meta-analytic findings and implications for research and practice. *Journal of Applied Psychology, 87*(4), 611–628.

Evans, T. J. (2003). Transitioning from superstar to supervisor. *Supervision, 64*(9), 12–13.

Konovsky, M., & Pugh, D. (1994). Citizenship behavior and social exchange. *Academy of Management Journal, 37*, 656–669.

Kouzes, J. M., & Pozner, B. Z. (2008). *The leadership challenge.* San Francisco, CA: Jossey Bass.

Lisoski, E. (2006). Rising from the ranks to management: How to thrive versus survive. *Supervision, 67*(7), 20–22.

Mayer, R. C., Davis, J. H., & Schoorman, F. D. (1995). An integrative model of organizational trust. *Academy of Management Review, 20*, 709–734.

Nefer, B. (2008). Supervising friends. *SuperVision, 69*(10), 12.

Organ, D. W. (1988). *Organizational citizenship behavior: The good soldier syndrome.* Lexington, MA: Lexington Books.

Perry, R. W., & Mankin, L. D. (2007). Organizational trust, trust in the chief executive, and work satisfaction. *Public Personnel Management, 36*(2), 165.

Schoorman, F. D., Mayer, R. C., & Davis, J. H. (1996). Organizational trust: Philosophical perspectives and conceptual definitions. *Academy of Management Review, 21*, 337–340.

Schriesheim, C. A., Neider, L. L., & Scandura, T. A. (1998). Delegation and leader-member exchange: Main effects, moderators, and measurement issues. *Academy of Management Journal, 41*(3), 298–319.

Sherwood, A. L., & DePaolo, C. (2005). Task and relationship-oriented trust in leaders. *Journal of Leadership and Organizational Studies, 12*(2), 65–82.

Thau, S., Crossley, C., Bennett, R. J., & Sczesny, S. (2007). The relationship between trust, attachment, and antisocial work behaviors. *Human Relations, 60*(8), 1155–1180.

Ting, Y. (1997). Determinants of job satisfaction of federal government employees. *Public Personnel Management, 26*(3), 313–334.

Urbaniak, A. J. (2005). Giving others authority. *SuperVision, 66*(4), 3.

Yukl, G., & Fu, P. P. (1999). Determinants of delegation and consultation by managers. *Journal of Organizational Behavior, 20*(2), 219–232.

4

PLANNING AND ORGANIZING FOR HUMAN RESOURCES

Effective staffing decisions begin with a methodical approach to human resource planning (Anderson, 2004). *Human resource planning* is the process of analyzing and identifying the need for availability of human resources so that the organization can meet its goals and objectives (Mathis & Jackson, 2008). In an effort to assist the reader with understanding this process, we begin with a case study that will be used throughout the chapter in order to convey a practical application to the human resource planning process. After the steps involved in planning for human resources are covered, we discuss how the organization's overall workload is broken down into specific activities and then reassembled into a functional organizational structure.

Before we begin discussing the importance of goals as they relate to human resource planning and organizing, we must first address the importance of the vision and mission of the organization. Once an organization can define their preferred future (vision) and their purpose (mission), they are in a position to set goals for planning and organizing for human resources.

VISION STATEMENT

A vision statement projects the organization's preferred future. Vision statements answer the questions, where do we want to be, and what do we want to look like if we can achieve our true potential? Examples of vision statements include the following:

Texas State University Campus Recreation
During the next decade, Texas State Campus Recreation will continue to be recognized as a leader in recreational and leisure services on campus and in the state. We will develop a comprehensive program that supports student learning and lifelong participation and wellness. We value student development, collaboration, and professionalism.

American Therapeutic Recreation Association (ATRA)
The vision of the American Therapeutic Recreation Association is to be the premier professional membership association representing recreational therapists, consumers, and stakeholders.

MISSION STATEMENT

A mission statement describes the intended purpose of the organization. The statement is more detailed than the vision statement and it focuses supervisors, managers, and other employees in a single direction. Especially in times of unpredictable and fast change, employees should reflect upon the organization's mission statement for clarity and stability. Examples of mission statements include the following:

Monterey Recreation and Parks Department
The Monterey Recreation and Parks Department enriches lives and fosters harmony within the community through citywide programs. We believe quality of life is improved through healthy lifestyles, educational and recreational opportunities, public participation, respect, compassion, and enhancement of our urban forest. We accomplish this through community outreach, quality programming, activities and events, safe and well-maintained parks and facilities, and an aesthetically pleasing environment that is provided by professional and caring employees, contractors, and volunteers.

Utah State University Outdoor Recreation Center
To enable USU community members to experience the physical and mental benefits of safe, fun outdoor recreation by providing them with excellent equipment, instruction, and resources.

Goals

Once the vision and mission statements have been established, we can now move toward planning and organizing for human resources. Human resource planning and organizing must be directed toward some purpose. That purpose, the starting point for our discussion and the guiding force that gives human resource planning and organizing its direction, is the achievement of goals. *A goal is a statement of a desired future an organization wishes to achieve based upon the vision and mission statements.* It describes in specific terms what the organization is trying accomplish. Goals may be strategic (making broad statements of where the organization wishes to be at some future point) or tactical (defining specific short-term results for units within the organization). Defining organizational goals helps to conceptualize and articulate the future direction of the organization, thus allowing those responsible for setting that direction to develop a common understanding of where the organization is heading. Goals provide a way of assuring that an organization will get where it wants to go (McClelland & Burnham, 2003).

Having clearly defined goals is absolutely essential—not only for recreation and sport managers, but for almost anything we do in life. In any given work situation, we might have organizational goals, departmental goals, program goals, individual work goals, and individual career goals. In our case study below, Chief Valez has been presented with a new organizational goal: attract more out-of-state tourists. This goal provides Valez with a certain amount of direction, but he is still a long way from having sufficient information to be able to plan and organize his staff. The next step is to establish organizational *objectives* for each organizational goal. Objectives are specific targets that focus on the achievement of goals. For example, Chief Valez might work with his staff to establish a set of objectives for his new goal of attracting more out-of-state tourists. These objectives might include the following:

- To provide sixty lodge units in Fernie Park by January 1, 2015.

- To increase camp sites in Yoko Park by 50% by August 1, next year.

- To provide a ski slope and support services at Cranbrook Park within six years.

STATE PARKS NEED A PLAN

The division of state parks in a western mountain state currently operates 27 different parks, historic sites, reserves, and wildlife areas. The division was created fifty years ago and is managed by a contingent of professionals, mostly men.

An informal arrangement within state government allowed the division to function independent of the state's personnel department. For many years the division's chief took care of the little personnel work that was necessary. If site managers had a personnel problem, it was usually resolved with one telephone conversation with the chief. However, times have now changed.

A year ago the governor appointed a task force to review the operation and management of its natural resource areas. The task force's report recommended that the state should take steps to attract more out-of-state tourists.

Stacy Valez, the division's chief for the last six years, quickly realized that the current staff would be unable to meet these new challenges without considerable adjustment. After a great deal of soul searching, he identified some of the problem areas as follows:

- We are shorthanded in a number of staff positions, especially in the planning and programming sections.
- We lack expertise in certain critical areas. No one, for example, has a background or experience in marketing or research.
- The average age of our professional staff is 55. We need more young college graduates and a management training program.
- Our affirmative action record has been terrible: only one minority and two women professionals are currently on staff.

Although more definitive than goals, objectives still do not tell us exactly what employees will do. Therefore, each objective needs to be broken down into a number of activities. For the objective "to provide sixty lodge units in Fernie Park by January 1, 2015," Valez might delineate the following activities to be done:

- Perform feasibility study.
- Prepare master site plan.
- Develop construction specifications.
- Develop publicity material.
- Provide food service operation.
- Provide housecleaning services.

Activities are the units of work that must be accomplished in order to achieve an objective.

PLANNING AND ORGANIZING FOR HUMAN RESOURCES

Once Valez and his staff have clearly stated their objectives and compiled a complete list of all the activities to be accomplished, they are in a position to begin planning and organizing for staff. This arrangement is depicted in Table 4.1 (see p. 56).

Human Resource Planning (Steps 1-4)

As stated earlier, planning and organizing for human resources are two closely related procedures that usually happen simultaneously, but we will discuss planning first. Human resource planning is the process of anticipating human resource needs and establishing a sound procedure for filling those needs. Four steps are involved in this process (see Figure 4.1).

STEP 1: *Determine Human Resource Needs*

The first step is to forecast the number and type of employees needed by the organization. Several factors might influence the number of employees that will be needed. For example, if new facilities are acquired or constructed, programs are expanded, or the level of service is increased, it is likely that more employees will be needed. As Chief Valez and his staff look over the long list of activities that will need to be accomplished to attract more out-of-state tourists, they will most likely decide to request funding for new positions. Therefore, it is critical that Chief Valez scan the external environment. *Environmental scanning* is the process of studying the environment to determine external opportunities

and threats to the state parks. Valez must consider economic conditions, competition issues, government influences, and workforce composition, while he scans the environment.

Once an environment scan is conducted, Chief Valez must determine the *type* of staff that is needed within the state parks. The term "type of staff" refers to the knowledge, skills, and abilities of the work group. It might be that some important tasks are not now being performed because the organization's work group lacks the necessary knowledge. For example, an agency may not be administering construction contracts effectively because no one is knowledgeable about contract administration. Perhaps some changes in technology have occurred, but the organization is unable to utilize the new machinery because employees are unskilled in its use. A good example would be failure to use computers for such tasks as data analysis, GPS systems, financial analyses, and reservation software programs. In order for Chief Valez to determine the type of staff needed within the state parks, he must next assess the internal workforce within the state parks.

STEP 2: *Assess Internal Workforce*

The second step in the human resource planning process is to inventory and evaluate the current internal workforce. Up to this point, Chief Valez has scanned the external environment to help him determine what is

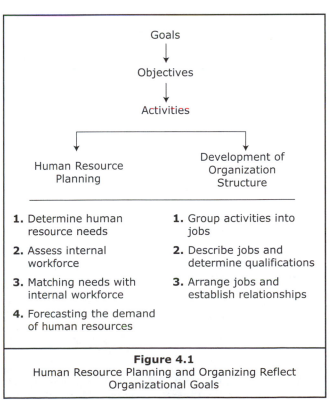

Figure 4.1
Human Resource Planning and Organizing Reflect Organizational Goals

needed as well as the human resources that are currently available within his division. *Human capital* is the collective value of the capabilities, knowledge, and skills of workers (Sullivan & Stevens, 2003). In order to analyze the human capital within the parks division, Chief Valez starts by conducting an evaluation of the internal strengths and weaknesses of the jobs that currently exist and he addresses the following questions:

- What jobs currently exist within the state parks under the chief's jurisdiction?

- How many employees perform each job?

- Who reports to whom?

- How essential is each job that exists?

- What jobs will be needed and what are the characteristics of these anticipated jobs?

It may also be fruitful if Chief Valez could refer to the park system's internal recordkeeping that provides information on each employee. Information on employees should include:

- Individual demographics

- Career progression, certifications

- Knowledge, skills, and abilities

- Training, education, and continuing education units

- Career goals

- Promotability

Most of the information can be gathered through the annual or semiannual performance appraisals and personnel files. A chart such as the one shown in Table 4.1 can be plotted to show the employee situation for an entire department.

Chief Valez has now allowed for a systematic scan of all the forces affecting the planning of human resources. This process refers to a SWOT analysis.

S = strengths inside the organization
W = weaknesses inside the organization
O = opportunities outside the organization
T = threats outside the organization

Examples of Chief Valez's SWOT analysis might reveal the following:

Strengths inside his organization may include seasoned and experience personnel. A weakness inside the organization may include that the average age of his workers is 55 and that they are predominately male. An opportunity outside the organization may include the state support to expand programs and services in order to attract out-of-state tourists. A threat outside his organization might be a rumored ski resort expansion by a neighboring state.

STEP 3: Matching Needs with Internal Workforce

The third step is to determine the extent to which the existing staff can fulfill the organization's needs. In other words, how well does the current staff match with current and future organizational needs of the state parks? One of the state parks found that its

Table 4.1
Assessing Promotion Potential for Management Personnel

Position	Current Occupant	Age	Promotability*	Current Personnel Capable of Filling Position
Level One				
Executive Director	D. Hooper	60	—	C. Korte, J. Riddle
Level Two				
Superintendent of Parks	C. Korte	57	A	
Superintendent of Recreation	J. Bonham	27	B	M. Patroni
Superintendent of Special Facilities	S. Stalnaker	61	C	L. Watts, M. Patroni
Support Services Manager	J. Riddle	51	A	L. Shenk, L. Watts, M. Patroni
Level Three				
Supervisor—North	N. Faessler	60	C	
Supervisor—South	C. Carlos	46	B	
Supervisor—Centers	D. Huisingh	30	C	
Supervisor—Programs	A. Barefoot	31	B	
Supervisor—Sports	L. Watts	47	A	
Supervisor—Culture	M. Patroni	29	A	
Business Manager	M. Johnson	50	C	
Planning Director	L. Shenk	45	A	

* A = ready for promotion; B = currently lacks training and experience for promotion; C = questionable promotability

maintenance staff had slowly shifted from multipurpose generalists to highly focused specialists. Because these specialists were only able to perform a narrow scope of work activities such as carpentry, landscaping, and painting, it greatly restricted management's capacity to obtain from its full-time employees a full day of work throughout most of the year. In this case, the staff's knowledge, skills, and abilities did not match well with organizational needs.

STEP 4: Forecasting the Demand for Human Resources

It is inevitable that an existing staff will never match perfectly with the human resource needs of the organization. Thus, the fourth step is to develop a plan to make changes in the work force. Forecasting usually takes into consideration when staff members leave positions because of promotions, transfers, turnovers, or terminations. Once Chief Valez and his staff have gone through the first three steps in the process, they are now in a position to develop a plan for forecasting human resources. This might include:

- Expand the position of park superintendents to include responsibility for publicity.
- Establish a training program for park superintendents on publicity and advertising methods.
- Establish a new position: Marketing Analyst.
- Retrain the office staff to perform database management using new computer software programs.

Depending on the size of the operation and its level of management sophistication, various organizations handle human resource planning in different ways. In larger operations especially, the maintenance of data on individual employees and the overall work group (Step 2) is done by the Office of Human Resources (HR). Primary responsibility for the other three steps usually rests with managers, although HR may provide managers and supervisors with assistance as needed. In small operations or departments within large operations, all the human resource planning steps may be the responsibility of the manager or owner. Regardless of the particular situation, any manager with supervisory responsibilities should be familiar with the four steps: determine human resource needs, assess internal workforce, match needs with internal workforce, and forecast the demand for human resources.

Development of Organizational Structure (Steps 1–3)

In addition to planning for human resources, managers need to develop the type of structure that will keep employees working together as a coordinated team, directed toward the achievement of organizational goals. An organization structure is the result of organizing. It is the final product we hope to achieve. To develop organization structure, we first break down goals into objectives and objectives into activities, and then follow these steps (see Figure 4.1, p. 55):

1. Group activities into jobs.
2. Describe the jobs and the qualifications needed by the people who are to perform them.
3. Assign jobs to organizational units or areas and establish the necessary relationships among jobs and units.

STEP 1: Grouping Activities into Jobs

Before we can understand how to group activities into jobs, it is important that the term 'job' be defined. According to Monday (2008), "a *job* is a group of tasks that must be performed for an organization to achieve its goals" (p. 91). A job in a recreation and sport organization may require the service of one person, such as an executive director, or the service of 25, such as youth coaches. A *position* "is the collection of tasks and responsibilities performed by one person; there is a position for every individual in an organization" (p. 91). Thus, in a work group consisting of an executive director, a sports programmer, and three soccer coaches, there are three jobs and five positions.

Recall that Chief Valez developed a list of activities for the objective "to provide sixty lodge units in Fernie Park by January 1, 2015." Some of the activities listed were:

- Perform feasibility study.
- Prepare master site plan.
- Develop construction specifications.
- Develop publicity material.
- Provide food service operation.
- Provide housecleaning services.

In reality, this list would be much longer. If you were in Mr. Valez's position, how would you go about grouping the activities into specific jobs and positions?

Your job would be much easier if you addressed the following:

- Which activities go together?
- Which ones use the same resources or space?
- Which ones closely depend on others?
- At what level in the organization should the activity be placed?
- What activities need supervision, and who should provide it?
- Who most needs to talk to and work with whom?
- What knowledge, skills, and abilities are needed to accomplish each activity?

Valez will probably give considerable time and thought to this matter, but eventually it will be possible to convert all of this information into real jobs and positions. The state's office of human resources will have trained personnel who are experts at developing and defining jobs. But since most of these jobs will be either managerial or professional, the final decision about them will still have to be made by Valez and his staff in the division. We cannot and should not expect HR specialists to know a great deal about activities involved in the provision of lodging services in a state park.

When jobs exist over a period of time, the next step is to conduct a *job analysis*. Since Valez is only at the starting point of determining the activities that will eventually arrange into jobs and then positions, we will defer our discussion of job analysis until later in this chapter.

STEP 2: Describing Jobs and Determining Qualifications

Once the activities have been grouped into jobs, it is common practice to prepare a job description. This description is a broad, general, and written statement of a specific job, based on the findings of a job analysis. It generally includes:

- job identification
- summary of duties and responsibilities
- essential functions performed
- job specifications
- working conditions
- relationships and key contacts
- qualifications (education and experience)

It is important to keep in mind that the content of job descriptions may vary depending on the purpose for which it will be used. Regardless, it is critical that job descriptions are always both relevant and current. Let us examine more closely these components.

Job Identification
The first part of a job description identifies the title of the job, the department or unit within the organization, location, the reporting relationship, and where appropriate, a job number or code. Additional items that often are found in this section include pay grade and the exempt or non-exempt status under the Fair Labor Standards Act (FLSA) and the EEOC.

Summary of Duties and Responsibilities
This section of the job description provides an overview of what the job entails. This concise paragraph identifies the content in general terms.

Essential Functions
This section of the job description is perhaps the most time-consuming. It identifies clear and accurate statements relating to the major tasks, duties, and responsibilities needed to perform the job. Essential functions directly relate to complying with the Americans with Disabilities Act (ADA).

Job Specifications
This component provides a description of the minimum acceptable qualifications of knowledge, skills, and abilities (KSAs) a person needs for the job. *Knowledge* is the acquired information background that a person must have to perform the job's duties and responsibilities. *Skills* refer to the capacity to use computers, machines, and equipment, such as a pool filter system or ball field equipment. *Abilities* are the capacity to perform based on natural talent or acquired proficiencies. The ability to react quickly and calmly under emergency conditions is an example of an ability that is typically required of an outdoor adventure leadership guide.

Working Conditions
This component is typically a concise statement that addresses any unusual working conditions or hazards.

Relationships and Key Contacts
This component addresses a concise statement of what position(s) the employee supervises and by whom the employee is supervised.

Qualifications

This component usually states the minimum qualifications needed for the particular job. For example, it may include a specific educational level (e.g., four year or master's degree) and/or the number of years of experience (e.g., two years minimum in supervisory position).

Importance of Job Descriptions

First, clear and accurate job descriptions are vital because they serve as a concise delineation of each position in the organization. In addition, job descriptions are essential for the following:

- Position classification and compensation
- Recruiting, testing, screening, and selecting employees
- Orientation
- Training and development
- Performance appraisal
- Compliance with legislation (such as ADA, FLSA)

Preparing Job Descriptions

When writing the duties and responsibilities, it is important to use precise action verbs. Words such as "initiates," "submits," "assists," and "attends" give a clear picture of what is expected. Words such as "does" and "handles" do not. Well-written duty statements contain action words which accurately describe what is being done.

Examples of duty and responsibilities statements are:

- *Compiles* reports on an annual basis
- *Adjusts* pool chemicals to ensure
- *Drives* park vehicles
- *Listens* to customer at counter

The degree of detail that should be included in a job description is a matter for constant debate. If it is very specific, a job description is helpful for certain things, such as orienting a new employee. The new person will be able to understand exactly what is expected of him or her. This is especially valuable for a young or inexperienced employee, who might need considerable direction. But if the job description is very specific, it leaves very little room for flexibility or creativity. Also, as an organization's goals and plans change, a very specific job description will quickly become out of date. Most recreation and sport organizations have chosen to develop job descriptions that are only moderately specific. On those occasions when more specificity is needed, detailed information can either be incorporated into a supplemental job description or included in the unit's operating manual—the document that explains day-to-day operating procedures. Please refer to Figure 4.2 (p. 60) and Figure 4.3 (p. 61) as examples of job descriptions.

Job Analysis

Before we go further, an important matter needs to be clarified. Previously, we stated that job descriptions are prepared after the activities to be accomplished have been arranged into jobs. This is true. But after jobs exist for a time, it is imperative that they be analyzed periodically to determine their accuracy and relevance. This is called a *job analysis*—a systematic way of gathering and analyzing information about the job as it relates to (1) content (2) context, and (3) the human requirements. The outcome of a job analysis usually entails a certain amount of adjustment in what a job holder is to do and the description of that job. To summarize, *new job descriptions are the product of jobs being formed, while revised job descriptions are the result of job analysis.* The relationship among job formulation, job analysis, job descriptions, and other management activities is depicted in Figure 4.4 (p. 62).

The purpose of job analysis is to address five important questions:

- What is the current content of this job; that is, what work is done and how is it being done?
- What physical and mental tasks does the worker accomplish?
- When and where is the job to be accomplished?
- Is the content of this job, including the qualifications, within the intended context?
- If current content is inappropriate or outdated, how should this job be redesigned?

To illustrate how these questions might be addressed, recall the case study on state parks. Chief Valez has been doing some serious thinking about his organization's new mandate. It would be nice to use

CORNELL UNIVERSITY
STAFF JOB DESCRIPTION

The university job title classification will be determined in accordance with the **Position Classification Process**. *Please refer to the* **Guidelines for Preparing the Staff Position Description** *prior to completing this document.*

Current Incumbent, if any: _____   Position #: _____

University Job Title: Wellness Program Coordinator   Pay Band: _____

Working Title (if different): Director of Cornell Fitness Center, Associate   Exempt: ❏   Nonexempt: ❏
Director of Recreational Services

Department Name: Athletics & Physical Education   Dept Code: _____

Immediate Supervisor's Name and University Job Title: Mgr. PE II – Dir. Helen Newman Hall

---

POSITION SUMMARY and **PREFERRED QUALIFICATIONS** are combined for any associated posting.

POSITION SUMMARY: Explain the purpose for the position and summarize the responsibilities.

The Cornell Fitness Centers (CFC) oversees all fitness sites (@12,000sf) and group exercise programs available to Cornell's staff and students on Cornell's main Ithaca campus. The CFC employs 225+ students to monitor the five fitness sites. CFC employees 6 full-time and 3 part-time benefits eligible staff as well as several part-time instructors and seasonal employees. The director is responsible for the organization, administration and supervision of all aspects of CFC including supervising all full-time staff (6), managing the annual ($1.3M) budget, managing the long-term equipment reserve fund, developing and adjusting policies and procedures, marketing and promotions, conducting special events, collaborating with other departments across campus for programming, and ensuring that all CFC programs adhere to the risk management plan.

As Associate Director of Recreational Services, the CFC Director assists when needed with the daily operations of Recreational Services and serves as the lead professional in the Director's absence.

REQUIRED QUALIFICATIONS: Specify required *minimum* equivalency for education, experience, skills, information systems knowledge, etc.

- Master's Degree in Exercise Physiology, Health, or Fitness with 2-4 years of professional supervisory experience or a Bachelor's degree with 5-7 years of experience.
- CPR, First Aid, AED Instructor certification. (Must be obtained within first year of employment.)
- Experience in facility management and fitness equipment purchase.
- Strong leadership and supervisory skills. Experience in long-term, strategic planning.
- Ability to mentor and coach a high-performing, very diverse professional and student staff.
- Excellent organizational and analytical skills. Facility with standard desktop applications.

PREFERRED QUALIFICATIONS: Specify preferred specialized education, field and/or certifications.

- Experience providing outstanding customer service and programming in a diverse and multi-cultural environment.
- Strong background in IT and web site management.
- Experience in being on the management team of a new recreation center or fitness facilities.
- Experience working at an institution of similar size with comparable professional and student staff.

Figure 4.2
First of a 4-page Wellness Program Coordinator Job Description

FUN CITY PARK DISTRICT
JOB DESCRIPTION

Position Title: Recreation Supervisor
Organizational Unit: Recreation Division
Code Number: G-8999

General Summary: Responsible for the planning, organizing, and supervising in the following areas:
                       Trips and tours, special events, adult leisure education program, and children and youth
                       programming.

Essential Job Functions:
    Directs a wide variety of activities for his or her assigned units of responsibility.
    Recruits, selects, directs, and evaluates recreation leaders and volunteers as needed.
    Conducts programs within adopted budget guidelines.
    Makes recommendations for Fun City recreation program and assists in the study of community wants and interests.
    Submits program reports, evaluations, inventories, and proposals to the superintendent of recreation.
    Establishes and maintains cooperative planning and work relationships with public and private nonprofit agencies
        serving Fun City, such as the YWCA, the school district, and the Chamber of Commerce.
    Provides all appropriate program publicity.
    Assists in the preparation of the budget and supporting material.
    Conducts workshops and in-service training programs as needed.
    Evaluates program areas using appropriate procedures.
    Reviews performance of leaders and volunteers and provides feedback as needed.
    Maintains current and accurate records of assigned program units.
    Performs other duties assigned by the superintendent of recreation.

Job Specifications:
    Ability to be flexible in all aspects of job responsibility.
    Ability to communicate effectively (oral and written).
    Skill in the operation of electronic technology including computers, registration software, GPS.
    Knowledge of basic management functions.
    Ability to set goals and objectives.
    Knowledge of the community's socioeconomic structure.

Supervision:
    Reports to the superintendent of recreation.
    Directly supervises part-time and seasonal leaders and volunteers.

Relationships and Key Contacts:
    Has frequent contact with the superintendent of recreation regarding goals and objectives, policy questions, and the
        coordination of program activities.
    Has frequent to moderate contact with the general public regarding program offerings.
    Has frequent contact with the other recreation supervisors regarding the coordination of program planning,
        scheduling, implementation, and evaluation.
    Has moderate contact with the news media and the general public regarding publicity and public relations.
    Has occasional to moderate contact with other groups serving the public regarding the provision of services.

Qualifications:
    Bachelor's degree in recreation, sport, or closely related field with two years of entry-level experience.

Review and Approval:

Approved by _____ Date _____

Approved by _____ Date _____

Figure 4.3
Job Description for a Recreation Supervisor

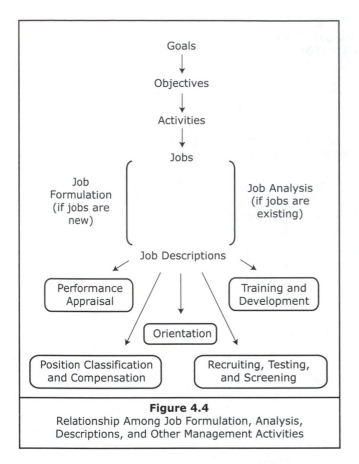

Figure 4.4
Relationship Among Job Formulation, Analysis,
Descriptions, and Other Management Activities

the state parks as a vehicle to attract more out-of-state tourists, but on the other hand, increased use of the parks might have a negative environmental impact.

Although the division does have an environmental-assessment analyst position, that person has been spending most of her time working on projects dealing with the acquisition of land for preservation purposes. Valez claims, "It's been a long time since we did a job analysis of the environmental-assessment analyst position. I think we need to do one." When conducting this job analysis, each of the questions we listed previously will need to be addressed. Perhaps this analysis will result in a change in the job and job description of the environmental assessment analyst to include certain new duties related to assessing the potential impact of increased park usage.

Responsibility for Job Analysis

Some recreation and sport managers, because they have access to an office of human resources (HR), allow job analysis to be performed by HR specialists. Other managers do not have access to human resource specialists but fail to perform job analyses either because they lack the ability or fail to understand its importance.

Managers should be involved in job analysis whether they oversee the entire process themselves

or assist and advise HR. In fact, one of the most significant benefits of job analysis is that it serves as an opportunity for managers and supervisors to discuss and debate the five questions mentioned previously. All recreation and sport managers should at least have a fundamental knowledge of how to perform a job analysis.

Performing Job Analysis

The employees whose jobs are to be analyzed and their immediate supervisors work together as a group to develop a preliminary statement for the essential functions of the job. For example, in the state park systems, Mr. Valez might ask his head of environmental interpretation and all the current environmental interpreters to work together in an effort to conduct a job analysis for the environmental assessment analyst position. *It is important to note that the job is being analyzed and not the person who occupies the position.* Considerable information will be needed to perform a comprehensive job analysis for the environmental-assessment analyst position.

Choosing a Job Analysis Method

In order to obtain the necessary information for a job analysis for the environmental-assessment analyst position, we must first understand the approaches used to collect such valuable information. Selecting a method should be directly related to how the information will be used (performance appraisal, pay increase, training, etc.). There are several commonly used methods of job analysis such as the interview, observation, questionnaires, computerized systems, and combination of methods (Brannick and Levine, 2004). Each of these methods will be discussed.

Interview

An understanding of the environmental-assessment analyst position could be gained by interviewing the person who holds the position by the head of environmental interpretation (her supervisor). A standardized interview form is used to record information accurately. If an HR specialist is available within the organization, it is highly suggested that this specialist interview the head of environmental interpretation to cross-check the accuracy of the information obtained from the employee and to clarify certain points. A standardized interview form is strongly recommended for this method.

Observation

When using the observation method, the head of environmental interpretation will watch the environmental-assessment analyst perform her tasks and record the observations. *Work sampling* allows the supervisor to randomly select times for observation. Another type of observation method might include the use of employee diaries or logs. This method of observation would require the environmental-assessment analyst to record her own performances. The use of this method is somewhat limited and is usually restricted to jobs that emphasize manual skills. For example, observing a budget manager would reveal very little about the requirements of the job, whereas observing the ball-field maintenance worker would reveal a great deal about the requirements of the job.

Questionnaires

The questionnaire method is widely used and economically attractive to organizations. In this instance, the environmental interpreters as well as the environmental-assessment analyst may be given a questionnaire to identify tasks performed by the position being analyzed. Typical areas covered in a job-analysis questionnaire might include: duties and percentage of time spent on certain functions, supervision (given to others and received), contact with other people (internal and external contacts), physical demands and working conditions, and the knowledge, skills, and abilities used on the job.

Computerized Systems

Computerized job-analysis systems are being used more frequently particularly in large organizations. Data is collected over a period of time and into a job-analysis system that helps to reduce the time it takes to write a job description. As the computerized systems become more commonly used, the more likely we will see this method implemented within recreation and sport organizations. Interestingly, a recent study found little variation between the information gleaned from the paper questionnaires and from computerized methods (Mackiney et al., 2003).

Combination of Methods

In the example of the state parks, the head of environmental interpretation may choose to use a variety of the methods previously mentioned. A combination of methods is often more appropriate and will aid the supervisor in receiving accurate descriptions and specifications of the job. It is important to note that each of the methods has strengths and weaknesses, and a combination of methods may be more advantageous than merely using a single method.

Behavioral and Legal Aspects of Job Analysis

Regardless of the job-analysis method selected by the recreation and sport supervisor or manager, it is critical that the analyst (the one conducting the job analysis) learn as much as possible about the job before the analysis takes place. This can be done by reviewing organizational charts and talking with individuals who are familiar with the job that is to be analyzed. It is very important that the analyst explain the purpose and process to the employee so that he or she will have a solid understanding of what is about to take place.

The goal of the job analysis is to get to the "core" of the job and to determine the essential job functions. Unfortunately, conducting a job analysis often instills fear among employees; they fear the results may lead to a job downgrade or possible elimination. As a result, anxiety may occur and there may be a tendency to inflate the importance and significance of the job. There is also a legal aspect that is connected to job analysis. Not only are the essential job functions a component to a job description, but the ADA requires that organizations identify these functions. Job analysis data are needed to defend decisions involving a variety of functions such as employee termination, promotion, transfers, and demotions.

To reiterate, the employees whose jobs are to be analyzed and their immediate supervisors should work together as a group to develop a preliminary statement for each of the key elements of the job. For example, Chief Valez might ask his head of environment interpretation and all the current environmental interpreters to work together. The key elements of a job analysis and an example of what the interpreters might generate for each of these elements is presented:

1. **Overall responsibility**
   Example:
   Organizes, guides, and instructs groups in nature study and wildlife education.

2. **Domain (a major area of job duties)**
   Examples:
   Program planning
   Scheduling
   Evaluation

3. **Duties**

Note: Each duty should begin with an action verb (e.g., prepare, consult, collect). Duties should reflec what needs to be done to best meet organizational goals.

Examples:
Domain: Program planning
Duty: Assesses the environmental features of the area
Domain: Scheduling
Duty: Conducts tours at those times that best explain the phenomena of nature
Domain: Evaluation
Duty: Maintains attendance records

4. **Supervision**
Examples:
Reports to the head of environmental interpretation
Responsible for volunteer leaders

5. **Relationships and key contacts**
Example:
Has occasional to moderate contact with park personnel to advise on matters of plant and animal life conservation

6. **Knowledge, skills, and abilities**
Example:
Knowledge of botany and zoology

7. **Desired education and experience**
Example:
Graduation from an accredited four-year college or university with a major in environmental studies, outdoor education, botany, or zoology

8. **Special requirement**
Example:
Cardiopulmonary resuscitation certification and First Aid

Hopefully, the reader has noticed that the key elements of a job analysis are also commonly used headings for job descriptions. (Domains may or may not be included in job descriptions.) This further illustrates the close relationship between job analyses and job descriptions.

Once the job elements are developed, a preliminary job description can be prepared by the office of human resources or a small group of managers. This preliminary description should reflect the standardized language used in each job description within the organization. The final version of a job description is usually subject to approval by upper-level management, policy makers, or the office of human resources.

STEP 3: *Arrange Jobs and Establish Relationships*

Now that we have assembled the jobs (Step 1) and accurately described them (Step 2), our third and final task is to assign jobs to organizational units and establish the necessary relationships among jobs and units to the overall organization.

Organizational structure depicts how job tasks are formally divided, grouped, and coordinated within an organization. In order to do this, we will now focus our attention on a variety of elements to consider when creating organizational structure. These five elements include span of control, unity of command, chain of command, departmentalization, and line and staff functions. In addition, organization charts can be an effective tool for understanding organizational structure. Therefore, organization charts will be discussed first because this tool will also be used to help explain the five elements.

Organization Chart

An organization chart is a graphic illustration of an organization's formal or informal structure. Charts serve as tools to indicate department names, identify the position that heads each department, and clarify how positions and departments are linked together (Burke & Bittel, 1981). No one correct or best way to draw an organization chart exists. Since the purpose of a chart is to depict an organization's structure accurately, it should be drawn in whatever form or style best achieves that purpose. Some charts are circular, some horizontal (from left to right), and some are pyramidal. The most common arrangement among recreation and sport organizations is vertical (from top to bottom). Positions and departments are indicated by rectangles. Lines, indicating the formal flow of decision-making authority, connect these rectangles into a network. Generally, vertical charts are drawn so that positions with greatest authority are shown at the top and those with less authority are shown at the bottom. Suggestions for the preparation of the traditional vertical organization chart are presented in Figure 4.5.

1. Identify the chart fully, showing the name of the organization, name of person responsible for preparation, name of person or group that granted authorization, and date of authorization.

2. Use rectangular boxes to show either an organizational unit or position.

3. For line units, vertical placements of rectangles show relative position in the organization hierarchy. No such pattern exists for staff or units that may be incorporated into the organization in various locations.

4. Any given horizontal row of boxes should be of the same size and should include only those positions having the same organizational rank. This rule is frequently violated due to space limitations.

5. Vertical and horizontal solid lines are used to show the flow of line authority.

6. Some organization charts may use dashed or broken lines to show technical relationships or critical advisory channels (see Figure 4.7).

7. Lines of authority enter at the top center of a box and leave at the bottom center; they do not run through the box. Exception: The line of authority to a staff position may enter the side of the box (see Figure 4.6).

8. The title of each position should be placed in the box. The title should be descriptive and show function. For example, "supervisor" is not sufficient as it does not show function. The functional area (e.g., sport) should be included even though it is not a part of the official title. Titles should be consistent; if necessary, revise titles so that they are both consistent and descriptive.

9. Include the name of the person currently holding the position (optional).

10. Keep the chart as simple as possible; include a legend if necessary to explain any special notations.

Figure 4.5
Suggestions for Preparing an Organization Chart

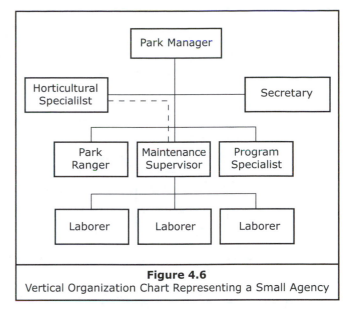

Figure 4.6
Vertical Organization Chart Representing a Small Agency

can be seen. Organization charts provide a summarized overview of the entire picture.

Another benefit is that it forces the people who are preparing the charts to think about how the organization can be most effectively structured. In fact, the analysis and discussion that goes into the preparation of the chart may be more valuable than the chart itself. Finally, charts seem to be most beneficial for people in the middle of the organization because relationships at this level seem to be the most complex.

Problems with Charts
It should be kept in mind that the organization chart represents only the officially sanctioned organization structure. Communications and even decision making sometimes take place outside normal channels. When this occurs, the principle of *chain of command* is violated. This principle will be defined and discussed in a later section.

Because some problems exist with charts, some managers are reluctant to use them. For one thing, if charts are simple, they are easy to use but provide little information. If they provide a lot of information, they are more informative but more difficult to use. Also, charts are difficult to keep up to date, and an out-of-date chart only explains "what was." Another criticism is that it makes some people feel superior and others inferior.

Circle Charts
The circle approach can be extremely effective in many types of operations. Picture a local recreation department such as the one in Figure 4.9 (p. 68). The recreation supervisor is in charge of a major special event: an ice cream social for the entire community to

The need for an organization chart varies considerably according to the size of the organization. The small park operation depicted in Figure 4.6 may have little need for a chart. A middle-sized organization, such as the recreation department shown in Figure 4.7 (p. 66), has a greater need for a chart. Figure 4.8 (p. 67) indicates a horizontally drawn chart for a resort operation. The need for this chart is obvious.

Benefits of Organization Charts
The primary benefit of organization charts is that they inform people of the network of relationships that exist throughout the organization. Each person can see how his or her position fits into the entire structure. Recall that job descriptions specify key relationships for each position. But as each person studies his or her own job description, only a small part of the picture

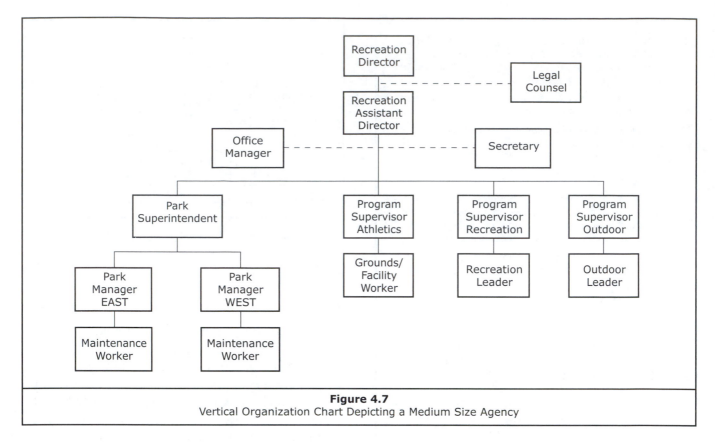

Figure 4.7
Vertical Organization Chart Depicting a Medium Size Agency

recognize a local Olympian. Usually, this means that most of the planning, organizing, and implementing is the responsibility of the recreation supervisor and all work is carried out at a lower level in the organization with recreation leaders and volunteers.

If the circle approach were used, the entire staff, including the executive director, would participate and assume a share of the work. Decision-making authority for that particular event would rest with the recreation supervisor. Individuals would be "assigned" to tasks based on their capabilities and expertise. For example, the museum supervisor, who has many contacts in the business community, might be in charge of finding a place to store a large amount of ice, and the executive director, who can be very persuasive, might be in charge of getting volunteers. The athletic supervisor may coordinate with the local high school athletic department to co-organize photo opportunities with the Olympian. Although the executive director always retains ultimate decision-making authority, he or she does not exercise that authority unless necessary or appropriate.

This type of organization structure (1) uses an inclusive and collaborative approach and thereby makes everyone on the staff feel he or she has an important role to play in the organization, (2) allows maximum utilization of individual capabilities and expertise, and (3) keeps jobs dynamic and challenging. The major prerequisite to a successful circle structure is that "upper-level" personnel must be willing to allow "lower-level" staff to share power, albeit for short periods of time. This structure is highly inclusive and collaborative with shared power and authority.

Span of Control

How many staff members should report directly to each supervisor or manager? In the organization chart presented at the top of Figure 4.10 (p. 69), 11 people report to the director of intramurals. Is this too many, too few, or just the right number? *The number of employees that a manager can supervise effectively is called span of control.* The 12 positions in the top portion of Figure 4.10 are all arranged on two levels and because of the way it looks, it is referred to as a "flat" structure. The same 12 positions could be arranged into a "tall" organization (as depicted in the bottom of Figure 4.10) by narrowing the span of control and adding a middle-management level.

For decades, management theorists tried to determine the optimal span of control. Many writers on organization believe there are a maximum number of employees a chief executive officer (CEO) can normally supervise effectively. Hendricks (2001) claims the number of employees that an executive can directly supervise is three to six people. For first-line

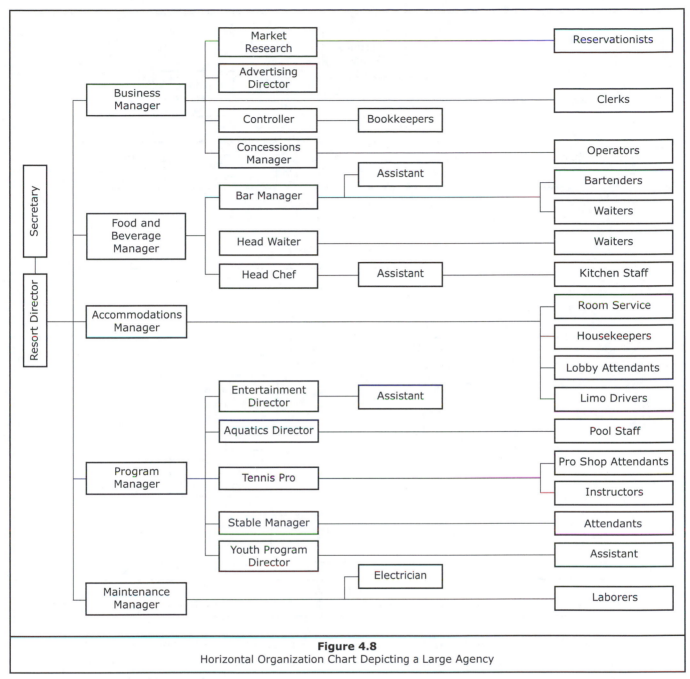

Figure 4.8
Horizontal Organization Chart Depicting a Large Agency

supervisors of routine operations, the maximum limit may be anywhere from 15 to 20. These numbers have little relevance, however, unless certain factors are taken into consideration for each situation. These factors are:

- Amount of time that a manager must spend on activities other than supervision

- Training and experience of the supervisor as well as the people being supervised

- Extent to which clear policies and plans exist to guide the people being supervised

- Complexity and importance of the activities being performed

- Amount of support staff assistance provided to both the supervisor and the staff

- Geographic distance between the manager and his or her staff

Another way to look at span of control is to consider the effects created by tall and flat organization structures. Flat organizations, caused by wide spans of control, have the advantage of rapid information flow. Since only a few people are involved, messages can move quickly up and down through the network. In addition, decision making tends to be closer to the

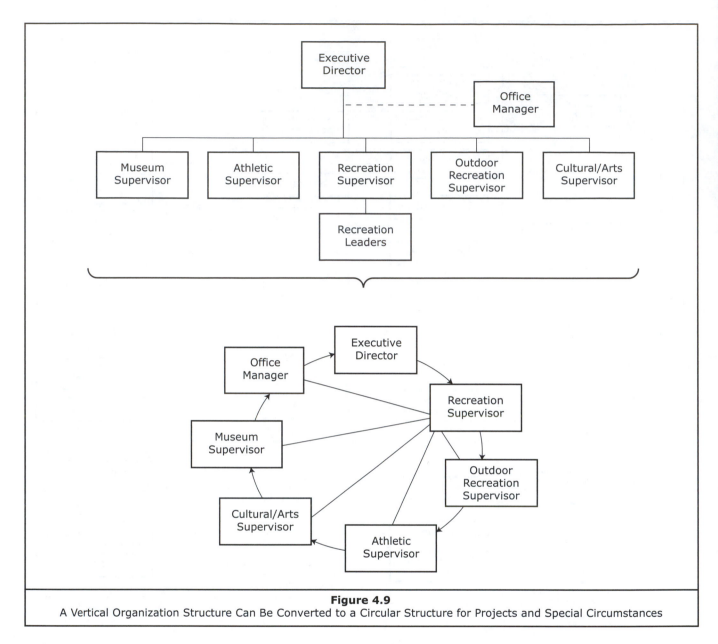

Figure 4.9
A Vertical Organization Structure Can Be Converted to a Circular Structure for Projects and Special Circumstances

clientele—the people being served. Flat organizations also have fewer managers, which may mean less office space, fewer support staff, fewer salaries, and greater savings to the agency.

Flat organizations also have some disadvantages. Because a large number of subordinates report to one person, subordinates may have difficulty gaining access to their supervisor. Also, during a busy season or in a crisis situation, a considerable strain may be put on the normal decision-making process. In some cases, decisions may get delayed, and in other cases, weak decisions might be made because of inadequate time for analysis and discussion.

Tall organization structures, caused by narrow spans of control, usually result in faster, more efficient problem resolution (Koontz, O'Donnell, & Weihrich, 1980). Also, decisions are made at higher

levels by generally more experienced managers. Since they have fewer people to supervise, managers have the time to become closely involved in their areas of responsibility and give very close supervision. But this can also be a serious disadvantage. In fact, this situation, usually referred to as *micromanagement*, is a serious problem in some recreation and sport organizations. When supervisors become too involved in specific day-to-day operations, it can stifle those employees who desire a more challenging and flexible role. In addition, when managers spend too much time on lower-level matters, upper-level matters such as policy development, goal setting, and organization planning can be badly neglected.

In summary, no easy answer exists for the question of how many employees should report to one supervisor. We understand there is a limit to the number of

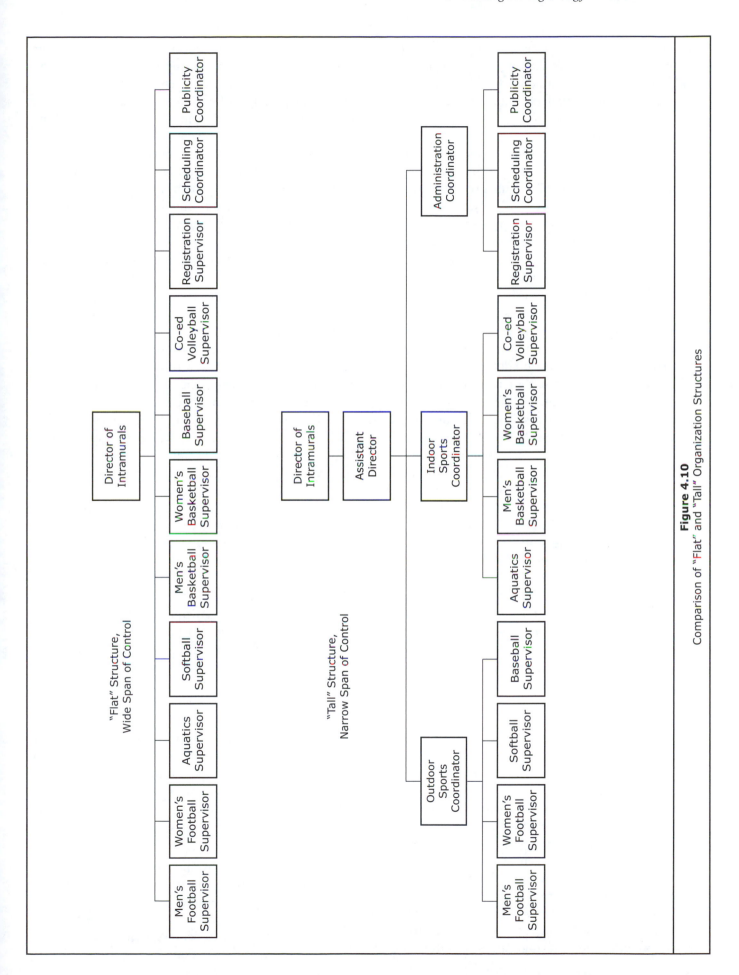

Figure 4.10

Comparison of "Flat" and "Tall" Organization Structures

persons an individual can effectively manage, but the exact number in each case will vary in accordance with the effect of underlying variables and their impact on the time requiremets of effective managing.

Unity of Command

Luther Gulick was a pioneer in management theory. In 1937 he wrote, "from the earliest times it has been recognized that nothing but confusion arises under multiple command" (1978, p. 57). By this he meant that each employee should have only one supervisor. Whenever an employee is required to take orders from more than one person, a real possibility exists that the orders will occasionally conflict. Therefore, the unity of command contends that each employee should be able to identify one supervisor to whom they are accountable.

Consider the following illustration that actually occurred in a campus recreation department. The outdoor recreation equipment center houses tents, skis, snow shoes, sleeping bags, etc. for college students to rent for weekend getaways. The office manager is a student intern who reports to two supervisors—the assistant director of campus recreation and the part-time manager of the outdoor center. The student intern was instructed by the outdoor-center manager to clean all equipment the weekend before spring break. At the same time, the assistant director of campus recreation instructed the student intern to organize the equipment for his employee weekend retreat. The student intern is reporting to two supervisors, and was given two different directives, and thus the communication becomes complicated. If the principle of unity of command had been observed, the student intern would report to either the manager of the outdoor center or the assistant director of campus recreation, but not to both.

Chain of Command

In an earlier section we pointed out that the lines of an organization chart indicate the formal flow of decision-making authority from the top to the bottom of an organization. One of these lines, going from the chief executive to the lowest level of personnel, is commonly referred to as a chain of command. We also stated that although organization charts represent the officially sanctioned arrangement, decision making sometimes takes place outside the chain of command.

We have used Figure 4.7 (p. 66) to illustrate. The *Outdoor Program Supervisor* frequently has lunch with one of the *Park Managers* and often they discuss current projects and exchange ideas. Recently they have been discussing projects they plan to implement and—further—for which they have sought funding from various community agencies. These activities violate the principle of chain of command, which says communications and decision making should follow the lines of authority specified by the organization chart. In other words, supervisors have the right to direct the activities of the employees immediately below them in their chain of command. In this situation, the Outdoor Program Supervisor should first communicate with the Assistant Recreation Director.

Depending on the desires of top management, the principle of chain of command is rigidly followed in some organizations while in others it is almost completely ignored. Persons new to an organization would be wise to find out early how closely the principle of chain of command is followed. Nowadays in the typical recreation and sport operations, people are encouraged to collaborate with other staff outside the chain of command when the need exists, while keeping direct supervisors informed.

The chain of command principle generally makes good sense and should not be needlessly violated. Sometimes employees attempt to jump over their immediate supervisor because they disagree with the directives they have been given by that person. This can be very risky. The supervisor may have very good reasons for his or her decisions and is not always in a position to explain those reasons fully to the persons whom they supervise.

Departmentalization

When developing organization structure, consideration should be given to how similar jobs are arranged into work units. This process is referred to as departmentalization. The work units might be called "divisions," "bureaus," "departments," "branches," or "units." For example, in a large recreation and sport operation, the largest work units might be referred to as "divisions," the subunits within the division might be called "departments," and the sub-subunits within departments might be called "units."

Different patterns can be used for grouping jobs. Four are most relevant to recreation and sport organizations:

1. *Organizing by primary purpose.* Work units are built around the major components of an organization's mission, be it parks, sports, or therapeutic recreation. Each unit would contain all the necessary elements to achieve that particular portion of the mission.

2. *Organizing by process.* Units are arranged according to specialized skills, such as programming, financing, marketing, and counseling.

3. *Organizing according to territory.* Units are organized by geographic location, such as the sections of a linear parkway, the quadrants of a city, or the branch locations of a rehabilitation center.

4. *Organizing by clientele to be served.* Working units reflect groups of people, such as children and youth, adults, senior adults, or males and females.

Different patterns can be used at different levels of an organization. Figure 4.11 shows an organization arranged using all four patterns

As you read through the description of the four patterns you may have perceived a certain amount of ambiguity. This is the major criticism of using these patterns to form departments. Is maintenance a primary purpose or a process? Is a program for children with developmental disabilities a primary purpose? Sometimes activities are hard to fit into neat categories; nevertheless, these four patterns do provide a basis for arranging activities into units for more effective handling.

Line and Staff

Another type of organization pattern deals with the concept of line and staff. Line personnel are all the people from the top to the bottom of the organization who are directly responsible for accomplishing the organization's mission. Their focus is inside and outside of the organization toward the clientele being served. Support staff are employees who assist the line staff to work more effectively to reach the mission of the organization. Their services are rendered within the organization, not outside it. Looking at Figure 4.7, the organization chart distinguishes the difference between line and staff with dashed lines verse solid lines. Dashed lines represent staff personnel (Office Manager, Secretary, and Legal Counsel) whereas all other positions are line personnel. Most modern administrators feel there is no need to make a big distinction between line and staff. It would be easy to argue that all personnel are important for the achievement of an organization's mission regardless of whether they run a program directly or assist indirectly by signing up participants or distributing towels. The important thing is not whether they fall into neat categories labeled "line" and "staff," but whether they fully understand their role in the organization and their work relationship with other people. Specifically, the work relationship should be clear concerning:

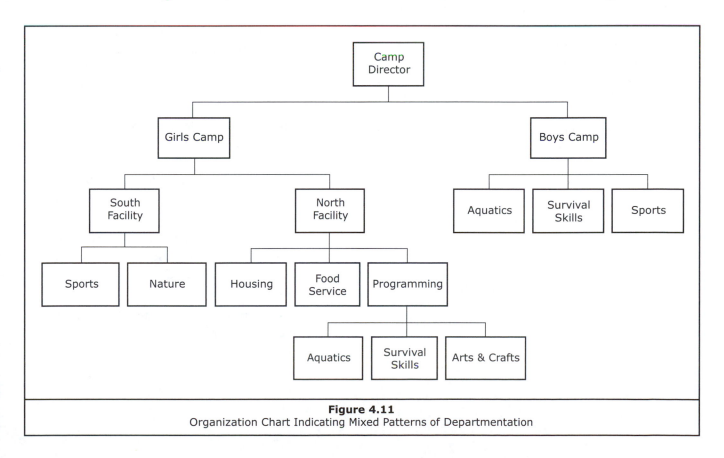

Figure 4.11
Organization Chart Indicating Mixed Patterns of Departmentation

- Who is consulted
- Who decides
- Who acts
- Who is informed of the results
- Who reports

Looking at Figure 4.8 (p. 67), the organization chart of a resort, it would be difficult to distinguish line and staff. But this distinction may not even be relevant if each person knows who is responsible for what and the degree of this responsibility. Organizations that emphasize effective communications, clearly defined objectives, cooperation, and mutual support will seldom have to debate questions of who is considered to be line and who is considered to be staff.

Summary of Organizational Structure

Organizational structure can be thought of as the fabric that keeps an organization coordinated and directed toward the achievement of organizational goals. In this chapter we have described the steps for human resource planning and the steps associated with the development of organization structure. But no magic formula exists for designing an organization and no one best structure exists. Each operation must be shaped to fit its unique circumstances.

In some cases, organizations are highly structured and people within that organization are not allowed to shape the organization but asked only to "fit in" to what exists. In other cases, recreation and sport supervisors will be required to play a key role in organizing whether it is an entire organization or only a small unit within an organization. Regardless, it is critical to understand the importance and complexities that go into planning for human resources and the development of organization structure.

Summary

1. Human resource plans and organization structures are based on and shaped by the organization's vision, mission, goals, and objectives.

2. The purpose of human resource planning is to anticipate personnel needs and develop a plan for meeting those needs.

3. Recreation and sport managers a) forecast human resource needs by scanning the environment and using the SWOT analysis, (b) determine if current personnel match current needs within the organization, and (c) make plans to correct problem areas.

4. Organizational structure is the fabric that keeps an organization coordinated and directed toward the achievement of organizational goals.

5. The basic procedures and concepts of organizing can be applied to small organizations and units within organizations as well as large operations.

6. Organizing is the process of breaking down broad goals into specific activities, arranging those activities into jobs, and then assembling those jobs into an organizational structure.

7. A job is a group of tasks that must be performed for an organization to achieve its goals, where as a position is the collection of tasks and responsibilities performed by one person.

8. A job description includes many components such as job identification, summary of duties and responsibilities, essential job functions, job specifications, working conditions, relationships and key contacts, and qualifications to perform the job.

9. Job analyses are done periodically to ascertain if jobs, as they are currently being done, are consistent with the goals of the organization. Several methods may be used to achieve these analyses and legal ramifications are included.

10. The primary benefit of organization charts is that they inform people of the network of relationships that exist throughout the organization.

11. Each employee should usually have only one supervisor.

12. The principle of chain of command should not be violated in matters of decision making without very good reason.

13. Departmentalization helps to organize similar jobs into work units. Different patterns can be used for grouping jobs.

14. It is not important that each job be labeled "line" or "staff," but it is important that employees understand their role in the organization and their work relationship with other people.

DISCUSSION TOPICS

1. Develop a hypothetical vision and mission statement, one goal, and three objectives for a sport and recreation organization of your choosing.

2. What role should a recreation and sport manager play in planning and organizing for human resources?

3. Discuss the process of environmental scanning and SWOT analyses in relation to planning for human resources.

4. What is the purpose of organizational structure?

5. Which of the following activities are most closely linked together and could conceivably be assigned to specific jobs? Explain your rationale for the linkages.

    (a) Prepare master site plan.
    (b) Develop construction specifications.
    (c) Develop publicity material.
    (d) Provide food service operation.
    (e) Provide housecleaning services.

6. What are the usual components of a job description? What is the difference between job specifications and job qualifications?

7. What is the link between job analysis and legal considerations?

8. If you were director of intramurals, which of the two organizational structures presented in Figure 4.10 would you wish to have? Which structure do you feel would make the most efficient use of limited financial resources? Why?

9. What factors can influence the span of control that a manager can effectively handle? Develop an example that will explain each factor.

10. Give several examples of the types of decisions and kinds of circumstances that may warrant (a) going outside the chain of command or (b) jumping over an immediate supervisor.

11. What is your ideal job after graduation? Pretend your supervisor will conduct a job analysis of that position. What methods should your supervisor use for these analyses?

12. Does the recreation and sport manager who is responsible for a small operation and a small staff (five to seven people) have to be as concerned about organization structure as does the chief executive officer of large operation?

REFERENCES

American Therapeutic Recreation Association (ATRA) vision statement. Retrieved from http://www.atra-online.com

Anderson, M. (2004, Winter). The metrics of workforce planning, *Public Personnel Management, 33,* 363–378.

Brannick, M. and Levine, E. (2002). *Job analysis: Methods, research, and application for human resource management in the new millennium.* Thousand Oaks, CA: Sage Publishing.

Burke, R., & Bittel, L. (1981). *Introduction to management practice.* New York, NY: McGraw-Hill Book Co.

Gulick, L. (1978). Notes on the theory of organization. In J. M. Shafritz & P. H. Whitbeck (Eds.), *Classics of organization theory*, p. 57. Oak Park, IL: Moore Publishing Co.

Hendricks, M. (2001, January). Span of control. *Entrepreneur.*

Koontz, H., O'Donnell, C., & Weihrich, H. (1980). *Management* (7th ed.). New York, NY: McGraw-Hill.

Mackiney, J. D. et al. (2003). Examining the measurement equivalence of paper and computerized job analysis scales. Paper presented at Society for Industrial and Organizational Psychology.

Mathis, R. & Jackson, J. (2008). *Human resource management*, 12th ed. Thomson South-Western.

McClelland, D. & Burnham, D. (2003). Power is a great motivator. *Harvard Business Review, 81*, (1), 117–126. Boston, MA: Harvard Business School Publishing Corporation.

Mondy, R. W. (2008). *Human resource management* (10th ed.). Upper Saddle River, NJ: Pearson Prentice Hall.

Monterey Recreation and Parks Department mission statement. Retrieved from http://www.ci.monterey-park.ca.us

Sullivan, A. & Sheffrin, S. (2003). Economics: Principles in action. Upper Saddle River, NJ: Pearson Prentice Hall.

Texas State University Campus Recreation vision statement. Retrieved from http://www.campus-recreation.txstate.edu/about/mission.html

Utah State University Outdoor Recreation Center mission statement. Retrieved from http://www.usu.edu/orc/mission

5

RECRUITMENT

A good staff is perhaps the single most important asset any organization can have. In leisure service settings the vast majority of staff comes into contact with customers either as service providers or facility managers. Your employees are a key element in the "experience" of the patron. Because of this, recruiting and selecting quality staff is a critical responsibility. The purpose of this chapter is to help recreation and sport managers (1) better understand recruitment, (2) comply with legal mandates, (3) differentiate between recruitment methods, (4) be able to prepare job announcements, and (5) work effectively with the personnel specialist in the Human Resource Department.

WHAT IS RECRUITMENT?

Recruitment is the process of finding qualified applicants and encouraging them to apply. Selection, the final stage of hiring, is choosing whom to employ out of the applicant pool and is the subject of the next chapter. Some people think recruitment is fairly easy, but it is not. Recruitment is a type of employment decision and an agency must be sure to follow appropriate legal guidelines. It is only with a well-planned recruitment program that an agency can be sure of having a strong applicant pool. The stronger the applicant pool, the better the chances of hiring the right person for the position. Effective recruitment minimizes agency turnover and saves the agency dollars. The agency's mission, personnel policies, and size of budget will all influence how recruitment is done. Gold's Gym, a well-known franchise operation, can approach and handle recruitment much differently than an independently owned fitness facility.

Recruitment is on ongoing process in many organizations. This is especially true in leisure service agencies, where positions are part-time and seasonal. Residential camps, ski resorts, national parks, campus recreation centers, and outdoor water parks are all examples of agencies with large seasonal staffing patterns. A great deal of staff time can be spent on recruitment.

Recruitment involves analyzing the open job, identifying job requirements, preparing job announcements, selecting recruitment methods, monitoring applications, and establishing a final applicant pool. In large agencies, Human Resource (HR) Department staff can assist the recreation and sport manager with some of these duties. However, it is the immediate supervisor of the open position who will most likely be the individual responsible for hiring and the one most familiar with the job, its requirements, and appropriate applicant markets.

LEGAL ENVIRONMENT

It is important to remember that several pieces of legislation presented in Chapter 1 impact employee recruitment and retention. The laws were passed in an effort to reduce discrimination in the workplace and promote equal employment opportunity (EEO). The most well-known piece of legislation is Title VII of the Civil Rights Act of 1964, which prohibits discrimination based on race, color, sex, religion, or national origin. The year prior, 1963, the Equal Pay Act was passed, requiring starting salaries, annual increases, and promotion adjustments to be equal for men and women who perform "substantially the same work." The Age Discrimination Act of 1967 originally prohibited discrimination in employment and advancement for those between 40 and 60 years of age. Now, age discrimination is prohibited regardless of age unless it is a bona fide occupational qualification. Individuals with disabilities are protected against discrimination in the workplace by both Sec. 501 of the Rehabilitation Act of 1973 and the American with Disabilities Act of 1990 (Noe, Hollenbeck, Gerhart & Wright, 2007).

Another key piece of federal legislation which impacts the recruitment and selection of personnel is the Pregnancy Discrimination Act of 1978. This law requires employers to view pregnancy, childbirth, and related conditions as "temporary disabilities." In other words, employers may not base personnel decisions on such conditions. The 1994 Uniformed Services Employment and Re-employment Rights Act requires employers to reemploy individuals who leave for military duty for up to 5 years. Upon their return from active duty, they are entitled to the job they would have held if they had not had required military service. They are to have the same seniority status and pay. Employees are subject to time limits in notifying employers of their wish to return to work. Veterans who are disabled in service have up to two years to recover and employers are required to make "reasonable accommodations" (Noe, Hollenbeck, Gerhart & Wright, 2007).

In addition to federal laws, you will need to be cognizant of relevant state and local laws which relate to employment. Though the federal government does not presently protect sexual orientation in the workplace, several state and local communities do so. Almost half of the states (21) and the District of Columbia prohibit discrimination in employment based on sexual orientation.

AFFIRMATIVE ACTION

There is a difference between the terms "EEO" (Equal Employment Opportunity) and "affirmative action." Simply, EEO means you cannot discriminate based on a protected factor, such as race, gender, or religion. Affirmative action, on the other hand, refers to proactive steps taken to achieve and maintain a diverse workforce. Following the passage of the 1964 Civil Rights Act, Presidential Executive Order #11246 was issued to aid in smoother implementation of the law. There were four key elements to the Order.

1. The Order established the federal Equal Employment Opportunity Commission (EEOC) to oversee discrimination claims.

2. The Order required the federal government, federal contractors, and subcontractors to take "affirmative action" in the hiring of employees.

3. The Order stipulated the development of affirmative action plans. Initially, plans were to identify under-represented groups, outline steps for increased recruitment, and set measurable hiring goals or quotas to move toward a more balanced and representative workforce.

4. The Office of Federal Contract Compliance Programs (OFCCP) was charged with overseeing affirmative action compliance.

The original intention of the Executive Order was to pave the way for those who had been discriminated against in the past to have the same opportunity for employment, advancement, and salary increases. Today, affirmative action plans may also be required of employers, both public and private, as the result of court judgments in discrimination cases.

Affirmative action is a complex issue. It was not long after Executive Order #11246 that cries of "preferential treatment" and "reverse discrimination" were heard and led to a landmark case being heard by the Supreme Court in 1978. In the case (Regents of the University of California vs. Bakke) a white male medical student failed to receive admission to the university medical school two years in a row, though less qualified minority students were accepted. Minority applicants were evaluated under a separate admissions policy and 16 of 100 slots were earmarked for minorities. The Court ruling banned the use of inflexible quota systems in the case.

Since then, many additional cases concerning affirmative action have come before the Supreme Court. The difficulty of fairly interpreting and implementing affirmative action is clear. For example, since the Bakke case, the issue of numerical quota has returned. In one case (*Fullilove v. Klutznick*), the Court ruled that "modest quotas" were constitutional and in another (*U.S. v. State of Alabama*), the Court ordered the implementation of quotas if "overt and defiant racism has been demonstrated." In 2003, the Court further dealt with the issue of preferential treatment. The University of Michigan's affirmative action policies in admission were questioned in two cases. In *Gratz v. Bollinger*, the court ruled that the university could no longer continue automatically awarding points for being part of an under-represented group on undergraduate applications. However, in the second case, *Grutter v. Bollinger*, the court ruled that the University of Michigan's Law School may continue to consider race in review of applications because the Law School's admission process included intensive "individual assessment" of the application (Riccucci, 2007).

While Americans say they support the elimination of discrimination, there seems to be a decline in support of *government-imposed* affirmative action. In

1996, California restricted the use of affirmative action by the state and local governments. Since then, Texas, Washington, and Florida have passed similar laws (Hirsch, 2009). However, though not required to do so, many public, private, and nonprofit employers have chosen to implement some type of affirmative action program (see Figure 5.1).

If you are employed by an agency with an affirmative action plan, you may be asked to follow specific procedures in the recruitment and selection of staff. Even if there is no affirmative action program in place, you as a manager still want to strive to maintain a workforce with diverse talents, skills, backgrounds, abilities, and interests. A diverse workforce can help with new markets, recruitment, and employee morale. Your staff should be at least as diverse as your clientele.

How Vacancies Occur

Within any agency, there are several ways vacancies can occur. An employee may be promoted or transferred to a new position, leaving the present position vacant. "Promotion" refers to a hierarchical move within the agency and "transfer" refers to a lateral move. Or, an employee may leave a position to accept employment

---

The YMCA is firmly convinced that people of color, minority groups, women, persons with disabilities, and other protected groups under municipal, state and federal law must be brought more fully into the mainstream of American social and economic life.

We are committed to a policy of taking all reasonable steps to steadily increase team member representation throughout our workforce from these groups. Our commitment is not based on obligation, but rather a conviction that affirmative action is the right thing to do.

Our affirmative action program is designed to ensure that:
- Recruiting, hiring and training for all job classifications are done without regard to race, color, creed, religion, national origin, sex, marital status, sexual orientation, status with regard to public assistance, membership or activity in a local human rights commission, disability, age or other legally protected status.
- Employment decisions further the principle of Equal Employment Opportunity.
- Promotion decisions further the principle of Equal Employment Opportunity and that non-discriminatory criteria for promotions are used.
- All Human Resource policies and procedures governing compensation, benefits, transfers, training and recreation programs are administered without regard to race, creed, color, religion, national origin, sex, sexual orientation, marital status, age, disability or other legally protected status.

Retrieved from: https://www.ymcatwincities.org/careers/diversity_and_inclusion/#AffirmativeAction

Figure 5.1
Twin Cities YMCA Affirmative Action Statement

---

elsewhere. The dismissal of an employee also results in a vacant position (Pynes, 2009). On a positive note, the expansion of a program, or the addition of a new facility, may create openings within the agency. In many leisure service agencies, there are annual vacancies due to the seasonal nature of the work (park laborers, lifeguards, sports officials, etc.).

What should you do when vacancies occur? First, a thorough review of the job description should be made to see if the position should remain as is, if it should be redesigned, or if it should be eliminated. Agencies and services change over time, and so will staffing needs. As customer demands change or new competitors appear, it is not uncommon for agencies to restructure their workforce. For example, over time there may be a decreased need for teen programs and increased need for fundraising within an agency. Rather than fill the Teen Programmer position when it becomes vacant, the agency decides to put the dollars towards a new position, that of Fundraising Coordinator.

Alternatives to Recruitment

Although the purpose of this chapter is to discuss recruitment, it should be kept in mind that not all employment needs have to be met by promoting current employees or hiring new ones. Recruitment and selection costs are high. In one study, the average cost of replacing an employee was found to be $17,000 and for employees earning over $60,000, the average cost rose to $38,000 (Bobinski, 2006). Depending on the level of the position, recruitment expenditures can include advertising, staff time, background check fees, travel expenses, employment agency fees, and/or relocation expenses.

To avoid these expenses, recreation and sport agencies have sought alternatives to the traditional pattern of full-time, permanent personnel. Some organizations have chosen to pay their existing employees overtime to meet peak seasonal work requirements. The danger in prolonged use of overtime is that employees will become fatigued and experience less energy and enthusiasm. Obviously, these can have an adverse impact on the quality of work performance and on the relationships with fellow workers and the public. The employee working overtime for a long period of time is often the last person to recognize the signs of fatigue, personality change, and decline in work effort.

Contracting out entire services or particular job functions is another alternative that is often used in the recreation field. Between 1978 and 2000, local government recreation agencies alone contracted out 94,000 full- and part-time positions (Crompton & Kaczynnki, 2003). It may be cost-effective because recruitment and selection expenses are eliminated and because the agency does not have to pay for full-time employee fringe benefits, which represent an additional expense. This practice, however, does have pitfalls. The agency loses direct control over the employees hired by the third party, the contracting group. Even more critical is the possibility of gradual erosion of agency image and effectiveness if the contractor is not effective.

A third staffing alternative is the use of temporary employees who may be found using one of the over 45,000 temporary help agencies in the United States. Temporary employees may not feel the same loyalty to your agency as do full-time employees, and they may not understand the goals of a park, recreation, or leisure organization. In spite of these minor disadvantages, temporary help is sometimes a good alternative to full-time employment. As workloads fluctuate, or as full-time employees take family medical leave, disability, jury-duty, or extended vacation leave, temporary specialists can keep the operation going until business returns to normal. The most common uses of temporary help in leisure service agencies are clerical and information technology individuals. Over 12.5 million workers were placed by temporary help agencies in 2005 (Bureau of Labor Statistics, 2009).

Hiring from Within

Organizations usually have certain choices concerning how to fill new or vacant positions. Collective-bargaining agreements may dictate that the agency recruit from within before recruiting from outside the agency. However, many organizations will always attempt to recruit from within their current pool of full-time, part-time, and seasonal employees even if not required to do so by a labor contract. There are other agencies that will always open their positions to individuals outside their agency. Each approach has certain advantages and limitations.

Advantages of Hiring from Within

Five major reasons exist for a policy of hiring from within the organization.

1. Strong performers can be rewarded for their efforts by being promoted. Employees will feel they can develop and advance without needing to leave the agency.

2. An organization knows the strengths and weaknesses of its own employees. It is easier to evaluate knowledge, skills, abilities, and work behavior of current employees from personnel records and supervisors than those candidates interviewing from outside the organization. Working with known information reduces the risk of making a poor selection decision.

3. The period of time needed for both recruitment and orientation are reduced when internal hiring occurs. The posting of jobs, the scheduling of interviews, and evaluation of internal candidates takes much less time than with external candidates. Once a hire has been made, the orientation can be tailored to address only job specific items and not include agency characteristics, lines of communication, and overall operating procedures, all of which are a must for an external hire.

4. In addition to time, dollars are saved with internal recruitment. It costs almost nothing to recruit internally. In most cases, all that is needed is staff time to post the opening. Dollars are also saved with reduced time spent in orientation.

5. For some agencies, internal hires allow for continued stability and connections with the community. Many nonprofit organizations value the continuity that internal hires provide with funding agencies.

Limitations to Hiring from Within

There are three inherent problems or limitations in *always* following a policy of filling vacancies from within the organization.

1. Depending on the hiring history of the agency, internal hiring may limit the ability of the organization to develop a diverse workforce. The limited diversity could be in terms of under-represented groups based on race, gender, or age. Or, it may be diversity in attitude and behavior. If an agency limits itself to only

internal hires, the opportunity to bring in fresh, new ideas exists only with entry-level positions.

2. Internal hiring limits the pool or number of candidates. Thus, the agency has to support a strong training and development program to be able to have employees capable of moving into new and often specialized positions. For example, many leisure service agencies found they could not fill new positions for IT specialists from in-house staff. Training and development programs are costly and many small agencies feel they cannot allocate major dollars to a highly developed training program. The other challenge for small agencies is that even if dollars exist, the number of employees who are able to be trained and promoted is small.

3. Even with a diverse workforce, it may be time to change the internal culture. A new voice from outside the agency can more easily bring about change. As subordinates move up in the organization, they bring to the new job the same thinking and practices under which they previously worked.

In light of the previous discussion, it would appear that the best policy for most agencies would be a flexible one in which the organization fills most positions from within, when qualified employees are available, but goes outside when appropriate talent is not available inside the organization. When filling upper-level positions, many agencies prefer to go outside to tap new ideas and bring fresh perspectives to the organization. If hiring from within, it is important that a climate of acceptance exists for lateral and upward moves. Employees should not feel ostracized by former coworkers if they leave for a new position or department within the agency.

E-Recruitment

E-recruitment is the term for using Web-based tools in the recruitment process. The process may be as simple as posting the job online. Or, it may be more complex, such as asking the applicant to apply online, submit references online, and complete online testing. The federal government, all 50 states, and most of the nation's large cities and counties maintain recruitment websites (Kim & O'Connor, 2009).

The federal government started USAJobs.com in 1996 in an attempt to better promote position vacancies. Between 1996 and 2002 the website was limited to just posting the vacancies nationwide. But, beginning in 2003, individuals became able to complete online applications and preliminary testing for federal positions. At the local level, a 2001 study found that 79% of city managers (cities over 50,000) prefer receiving applications on the web (Llorens and Kellough, 2007).

Benefits to E-Recruitment

Why the strong support for e-recruitment? First, the Web can greatly reduce hiring time. Once the decision has been made to announce a vacancy, it can be posted immediately rather than be delayed by the print schedule of a newspaper or journal. Online applications remove the time needed for postal delivery. Online testing eliminates the need for testing dates, times, and locations.

E-recruitment also reduces many of the traditional costs. The reduced costs include staff time, postage, telephone, supplies, advertising, and storage. The more extensive the use of web-based technologies in the recruitment process, the greater the savings.

Another advantage to e-recruitment is the ease in expanding the recruitment market. One way the market can be expanded is geographically, from local to regional to national. This becomes increasingly important as the skills and experience required becomes more specialized. The director of event planning for a major professional sporting team demands a different skill set and level of expertise than a director of programming for a Boys and Girls Club. Maybe more important than geography is the ability to more easily extend recruitment to underrepresented groups.

With e-recruitment, agencies have an opportunity to promote their image. Recruitment websites can provide the applicant with a wealth of information. Space is not an issue. The employment page of the National Outdoor Leadership Schools (NOLS) greets prospective applicants with a video entitled "Why we Work at NOLS." The page also provides a description of internships, in-town jobs, how to become an outdoor leader, and the NOLS jobs network. Or, if an agency uses an online job board such as the one provided by the Illinois Park and Recreation

Association, the agency can provide a direct link to their own home page. The amount of information an agency can provide about itself to an applicant far exceeds that possible with a print ad.

The ease for applicants is another plus for e-recruitment. Even if the only element of e-recruitment used is the online posting of positions, the applicant has the ability to more easily find the vacancy with the use of search engines and can search for jobs 24/7. If the recruitment process includes an online application, there is no need for the candidate to call or visit the agency to obtain an application form. Often, applicants need complete only one application form, even if they wish to be considered for multiple positions with an agency. With online applications, applicants are also able to easily update information as it changes. Applicant tracking systems can be designed to notify applicants quickly of receipt of materials, any missing items, and the scores of online test(s). Satisfaction studies of online recruitment with applicants produced high results with special emphasis given to the "notification" element of the process (Bingham, Ilg & Davidson, 2002).

Online application software also benefits the employer. To begin, a basic template for an application form can be adopted by the agency. It is then quite easy to tailor the template to individual positions. The basic template would include the information needed from all applicants such as name, contact information, education, experience, and references. The form for the position of a Recreation Therapist might add the question "Are you a certified therapeutic recreation specialist?" Or an application for summer day camp staff might include, "Are you at least 18 years of age?" Applicants who respond negatively to questions about required criteria are notified by the program that they are not eligible for the position. An online application program allows the agency to easily sort application in folders by position, staff member responsible for hiring that position, or by any other criteria selected. Staff are more easily able to contact applicants with e-mails and letters from the database of applicants. Applicant tracking is much easier with an automated system. Possible applicant tracking systems are People-Trak, NeoGov, Applitrack, or Staffing Soft (Aldrich, 2008).

Concerns with E-Recruitment

Just as there are benefits to e-recruitment, there are also concerns. E-recruitment more often than not increases the number of applications submitted. On the one hand, it is usually a good thing to have a large pool of applicants, but sometimes the increased number contains too many weak candidates. For example, online posting of a position with an application process of only submitting a cover letter and résumé could result in staff spending too much time discarding unqualified candidates. The same could hold true if a generic application form is used and no step exists within the program to delete by required qualifications.

E-recruitment is seen by some as unfair and a possible danger to Equal Opportunity Employment. Households with minorities, persons with disabilities, and low annual income are reported to show a difference in Internet access. Even if employment kiosks and Internet access are made available for applicants, online applications should not necessarily be used for all jobs. If computer use is not a regular part of the job or the education level required is minimal, why require applicants to be able to apply online? In recreation and sport settings, there are many seasonal, part-time, and low-level positions for which only having online applications might be discriminatory (Kim & O'Connor, 2009).

Any time online technology is used, privacy issues and data security are concerns. It is true that with paper-copy applications, staff had access to personal information. With online applications, however, the data is more vulnerable if proper precautions have not been taken in the design of the online application system.

Within the agency, the staff might hinder the use of e-recruitment. The lack of knowledge and understanding by present staff about e-recruitment might limit their willingness to use it. Or, staff might be excited and eager to move to e-recruitment but fail to gain administrative commitment. In the initial move to take e-recruitment beyond just the posting of vacancies, a great deal of staff time will need to be spent investigating and selecting software programs.

If application and pre-screening testing are done online, questions might be raised about the information entered. How, for example, do you know the test was completed by the applicant seeking the job? It is important in any application process to have a method by which you verify the information submitted. Reference and past employer checks often serve this purpose. For tests, a secondary, on-site test may be used to verify candidates' abilities. A second test is usually only done with the applicants who have made it through an initial screening.

The final concern with e-recruitment is the ever-famous "technical difficulties." With the use of technology in the recruitment process, there is no way to completely avoid the issue of technical problems. However, they can be minimized by assigning competent staff the responsibility for e-recruitment, investing in quality equipment and programs, and by planning ahead for technical difficulties.

INTERNAL RECRUITMENT PROCEDURES

If the decision is made to hire internally, one of two methods is used. One involves the circulating of job announcements throughout the agency. This is known as "job posting." Employees are invited to apply. If current employees are interested in a particular opening, they may inform the immediate supervisor of the vacant position or the Human Resource (HR) Department. Employees should also be encouraged to notify their present supervisor of their interest in a new position. Failure to do so may lead to some friction between the employee and the supervisor or between the two supervisors.

In large agencies, the HR department can serve as a clearinghouse to screen all applicants. HR can protect the confidentiality of applicants until it can be decided whether they are qualified enough to be actual candidates for the job. HR also screens out those who are not qualified, to prevent an excessive number of applicants from taking the time of the supervisor of the position opening. The principal value of this method of circulating job announcements throughout the agency is that it gives every employee a fair chance to obtain a better job. It also helps reduce employee selection based on special deals or favoritism.

The second method used to identify potential candidates from within the organization involves a careful review of agency personnel records and performance-appraisal forms and is called "managed movement" (Klaff, 2004). In this method, both management and HR work closely together to decide who might be eligible. The employees in question may not even know they are under consideration. This method avoids the sensitivities between supervisors and employees previously mentioned but runs the risk of overlooking potentially qualified employees.

Since all agencies are under the constraints of EEO legislation, and should want to give every employee a chance to advance, both methods (posting and managed-movement review) should be used. To do otherwise places the sport, recreation, or leisure services agency in a position where employees, unions, or interested parties could file a discrimination suit with EEOC because a protected minority-group member was denied equal opportunity to prove himself or herself capable of advancement.

THE EXTERNAL SEARCH FOR EMPLOYEES

In external recruitment, the Internet is now the primary recruiting method. A 2008 study by the Institute of Management and Administration found 87% of the companies surveyed recruited via the company website and 82% used Internet job sites. Traditional methods are also still popular, with 73% using newspaper/magazine ads, 78% using in-house referrals, 58% using professional associations and 55% using job fairs (Solving the Riddle, 2008). (See Table 5.1, p. 82).

Four factors influence which method(s) of external recruitment an agency will select to recruit candidates for a vacancy. First, how many dollars are available to be spent on recruiting. There are varying costs for print ads, many job board postings, travel to job fairs, and employment agencies.

Second is the time available to fill the position. According to the 2008 EDGE Report, it takes firms on average 4.5 weeks to fill a clerical full-time positions and 9 weeks to hire a manager (Robert Half International, 2008). If a quick turnaround is needed in filling the position, then it would not be wise to choose a venue that takes more time to reach the candidate market than others.

The third factor is the market that the agency needs to reach to fill the position. The target market for recruiting summer-day-camp counselors is high school and college students who can be easily reached with local methods. In contrast, if an agency is hiring a new golf pro, a much wider market needs to be reached. A national job board, specific to golf professionals, would be most appropriate for it would allow a search to be nationally in scope, but limited to those with the required golf credentials.

And lastly, the level of the job will influence which recruitment strategy(ies) would be best. It is common for most non-exempt positions (those eligible for overtime according to the Fair Labor Standards Act) to be recruited at the local level, while salaried professional positions (exempt positions) will be more complex in scope (Arthur, 2001).

Agency Websites

One of the easiest and most economical ways for an agency to recruit externally, as mentioned earlier, is by using the agency website. Many job seekers

Table 5.1
Recruiting Resources and Techniques to Be Used in the 12 Months Ahead (Overall and by Number of Employees)

	Number of Employees					
	1- 199	200 - 599	600 - 1,799	1,800 - 6,999	7,000 or more	Overall
Newspaper/magazine ads	59%	80%	84%	86%	73%	73%
Radio/TV ads	4	10	16	14	36	11
Online recruiting (Internet job sites)	70	88	90	81	91	82
Company Web site	79	88	84	100	100	87
Headhunters	45	51	61	62	45	52
Kiosks	2	2	6	19	9	5
Job fairs	23	61	74	71	91	55
Looking online for résumés/passive candidates	29	34	39	52	64	38
Professional/industry association	48	59	61	71	64	58
Recruit "alumni"	25	24	23	14	64	26
In-house job referrals	75	83	84	67	91	78
Recruit at colleges/high schools	34	61	81	90	73	60
Internships	29	56	71	71	73	52
No recruiting planned	2	-	-	-	-	1
Other	5	7	-	5	-	4

Source: IOMA's 2008 Guide to HR Benchmarks

identify the agency or type of agency they wish to work for and directly investigate possible openings at their site. In the past, telephone calls and walk-ins were most common. But today, applicants expect to be able to find employment information on the Internet and preferably on a potential employer's website. A park district in a community of about 27,000 had over 600 hits in the first month after staff posted openings on their website.

Listing employment opportunities on an agency website also makes it easier for applicants to gain a greater understanding of the agency. Most agency websites contain information about an agency's mission, history, programs, facilities, hours of operation, and staff, all of which can help potential applicants decide to apply. Besides posting the job online and allowing online application, using the agency website expands your ability to recruit candidates. You may present information in a more detailed and appealing manner. For example, Big Brothers, Big Sisters of Eastern Missouri is a non-profit agency that highlights the "benefits section" of their posting in such a way to reach their target market (see Figure 5.2).

In using an agency website as a recruitment tool there are some key principles to remember. The search for job openings on the website must be easy. You do not want to lose potential applicants because they find navigating the system frustrating. If applicants apply online, it is important to respond quickly. Notify them of the receipt of the application and any missing information they still need to submit. Keep the posting of available openings current. If not, job seekers may perceive the agency as unorganized and unprofessional. If dollars exist, utilize an applicant tracking system that lets you eliminate those not qualified and easily organizes the database for staff use. For those disqualified, be sure to notify them promptly (Lawerence, Sauser & Sauser, 2007).

Internet Job Sites

Increasingly popular among both employers and job seekers are Internet job sites. The first of the big three (Monster, CareerBuilder, and HotJobs) was Monster.com, which went online in 1994. These sites attract job seekers by allowing them to search a massive database of jobs and post a standardized

Benefits

Big Brothers Big Sisters of Eastern Missouri not only provides competitive salaries for its employees, the agency also provides a wide assortment of benefits. These benefits help reduce risk for employees should they experience health or long-term medical problems, provide retirement income, help balance work and life, and appreciate and reward great work.

Medical & Dental Insurance
The Agency pays 100% of the health and dental insurance premium for all employees. Additional coverage, paid for by the employee, is available to spouses and dependents.

Life Insurance
A life insurance policy is purchased by the Agency for each employee.

Short Term & Long Term Disability
After three months of employment, each employee is provided with short-term disability insurance. After one year of employment, each employee is provided with long-term disability insurance.

401k
After one year of employment, each employee is eligible for participation in the Agency's 401k plan.

Work/Life Benefits
Big Brothers Big Sisters expects its staff to be committed to the highest standards and be willing to go far beyond what is typically expected to meet the needs of our children, families, and volunteers. In turn, Big Brothers Big Sisters' Board of Directors and Leadership Team believe that the agency must do its very best to take care of its committed and talented staff. The following is a list of some of our Work/Life benefits.

- Time Benefits
- Vacation Days
- Sick Days
- Personal Days
- 10 Calendar Holidays
- Birthday Holiday
- Funeral Leave
- Flexible Schedules, when possible

Peace of Mind Benefits
- Covered and Secure Parking
- Business Casual and Casual Dress Code, including the ability to wear jeans and agency branding t-shirts and sweatshirts!

Sample of "Everchanging" Fun Benefits
- Halloween Party, Potluck Lunches, Sporting Event & Concert Tickets, Movie Matinees, Bowling & Staff Variety Show
Other Benefits
- Mileage Reimbursement

If you are interested in learning more about a future with Big Brothers Big Sisters of Eastern Missouri, click the following links:

| Careers | Culture | Benefits | Current Job Openings | Internships | Administrative Volunteers |

Source: www.bbbsemo.org

Figure 5.2
Big Brothers Big Sisters Website Information

résumé for free. Employers pay a fee to list their job in a standardized listing and search the database of résumés. The fee to post may range from $99 to $500, depending on type of job and length of posting. The entry for lifeguard listed on the next page is a sample of how the position might appear on, say, Monster.com (see Figure 5.3, p. 84).

It is the popularity of these job sites that has led to both their major drawback and their major advantage. The drawback is that due to the vast number of job seekers using the site, employers may receive far too many applications from unqualified applicants.

The advantage, though, is that the increased number of individuals in the database allows the employer to reach a more diverse applicant pool.

In recent years, "niche boards," or more clearly focused Internet job seekers, have evolved to provide a better target market for employers. In recreation, sports, and leisure services, many professional associations facilitate job boards. For some positions, an agency might choose to post on one of the major job sites, as well as on a niche board. The most popular websites are listed in Figure 5.4, p. 84.

Lifeguard

Walt Disney World® Resort Lifeguard

With 5 beaches, 10 marinas, more than 50 resort pools and 2 water parks, the Walt Disney World® Resort has everything, from lazy rivers to wave pools, to make Guests' dreams come true. Lifeguard responsibilities include ensuring the well-being of our Guests, keeping pool areas clean, answering Guest questions, providing information and assisting in boat or towel rentals. Lifeguards may also have the opportunity to work in a variety of locations throughout property and in different positions, including Pool Attendant, Slide Operations, and Marina Operations.

Paid certification training is provided by Ellis and Associates and conducted over three consecutive days weekly.

Lifeguards now receive a starting rate of $8.05/hour for Shallow Water and $9.00/hour for Deep Water.

Full-time Cast Members may also be eligible for medical, dental, and vision coverage; plus paid vacation and sick leave. All Cast Members receive theme park admission and discounts at select dining, merchandise and recreation locations.

For more information and to apply online, visit WaltDisneyWorld.jobs

©Disney is an equal opportunity employer. Drawing Creativity from Diversity.

Figure 5.3
Walt Disney World Lifeguard Ad

Professional Networking Sites

There are two types of applicants in the recruitment process. "Direct applicants" are the individuals who apply for the position without being contacted by anyone at the agency. "Referrals" are the applicants who have been encouraged to apply. It is in hopes of developing this second group, "the referrals," that an agency may choose to use a "professional networking site" in its recruitment. *LinkedIn.com* is presently the most popular professional online network. The purpose of a professional online network is to allow individuals to stay in contact with colleagues, increase the size of their professional network, find and exchange ideas, and explore opportunities (Berkshire, 2005). On *LinkedIn*, individuals create a professional profile page including their résumé. Users are also able to seek "endorsements" or public references from those they network with on the site. Two unique components on the profile page provide more information about the individual's skills and abilities. The first is the "Box" which allows users to post samples of their written work. The second is "SlideShow," where users can post PowerPoint

Young Non-Profit Professionals Network
    www.ynpn.org
Community Career Center
    www.nonprofitjobs.org
Diversity at Work
    www.diversityjobs.com
Human Service Career Network
    www.hscareers.com
USA Jobs
    www.usajobs.gov
Association of Experiential Education
    www.aee.org
Wilderness Education Association
    www.weainfo.org
Association of Outdoor Recreation
    www.aore.org
Backdoor Jobs
    www.backdoorjobs.com
College Grad
    www.collegegrad.com
Recreation Internships
    www.schlags.com/paul/internships
Therapeutic Recreation Directory
    www.recreationtherapy.com/rt.htm
Job Monkey
    www.jobmonkeyjobs.com/GetJobs.rs
Recreation and Park Jobs
    www.recreationandparkjobs.com
N.R.P.A. National Recreation and Parks Association
    www.careercenter.nrpa.org
Coolworks
    www.coolworks.com
Student Conservation Association
    www.thesca.org
College Career Center
    www.collegerecruiter.com
After College
    www.aftercollege.com
The Outdoor Educational Resource
    www.outdoored.com
Indeed.com
    www.indeed.com
National Intramural and Recreation Sports Association
    www.nirsa.org

Figure 5.4
Niche Boards

presentations they have created. Employers and/or their staff who are members of professional networking sites can actively seek qualified candidates and encourage them to apply. Recently, *LinkedIn.com* added a job board, which would also allow agencies to also recruit "direct" applicants through the site.

Public Employment Agencies

Employers now have two avenues available for recruitment through government-supported employment services. State governments, in conjunction with the U.S. Department of Labor's Employment and Training Administration, operate local employment offices, often called "Job Service," to help individuals find work and to help employers find qualified workers. Public employment agencies provide their services for free to both job seekers and to employers. Employers may post their jobs and state employment agencies will match the jobs to qualified job seekers. If necessary, the agency staff can pre-test and/or pre-interview individuals to see if they are acceptable for consideration. The advantage of the state employment service for an employer is that it gives the employer access to a large, usually diverse, labor pool for recruitment at no cost. However, all individuals receiving unemployment compensation are required to register as active job seekers with their state employment agencies. Thus, the major concern with the state employment agency is that in reaching their goal of "putting people to work", they may too often recommend unqualified or poorly qualified individuals to employers (Noe, et al., 2007).

The second public employment agency available to employers is the "One-Stop Career Center." In 1998, the federal government passed the Workforce Investment Act to overhaul the country's job-training system. These centers differ from the traditional state employment services in that greater emphasis is placed on skill assessment and training. All individuals, including youth, who register at a "One-Stop Career Center" are assessed at the "core service" level. If an individual is founding lacking in skill and wants additional training, the case manager can make a decision to approve state-financed training through an approved provider. Employers who post their vacancies with "One-Stop Career Center" may reach a more highly motivated labor pool because no one is required to register with One Stop and there is greater emphasis on individual assessment and training (Llorens & Kellough, 2007).

Private Employment Agencies

Private employment agencies are more commonly used for professional positions. These agencies are for-profit ventures and, as such, charge for their services. Most agencies specialize in particular fields or professions. There are agencies for specific populations such as minorities, women, or older workers.

In recreation, sport and leisure service agencies, private employment agencies are most often used for the recruitment of a Director or CEO. The agencies that specialize in the recruitment of executives are often referred to as "search firms" or "head hunters," as they locate candidates from those already employed in the relevant field. In working with a search firm, it is important to have a "written contract" detailing what services the firm will provide and at what cost. The employer (often the board of the agency for this level of a search) needs to clearly identify the job responsibilities and explain the key requirements for the position to the search firm. A quality search firm is able to tap a large and talented pool of candidates in a timely and effective recruitment process.

Colleges and Universities

Colleges and universities offer excellent opportunities for recruitment. Many recreation and sport agencies actively seek college students for seasonal, part-time, and entry-level positions. Residential camps have long used "Camp Days" on college campuses to meet, recruit, and interview counselors and program staff. Walt Disney World has representatives make presentations across the nation on college campuses to recruit a pool of potential applicants. Large companies such as Marriott and Hilton attend university "Career Fairs" to recruit entry level staff. An agency wishing to expand the diversity of its workforce can actively recruit at a college or university which has a student body of those they wish to reach.

The best way to recruit on college campuses however, is through the appropriate academic department. For summer-day-camp staff, contacts might be made with the Departments of Recreation, Kinesiology, Elementary Education, and/or Social Work. The faculty and staff are more likely to be aware of current and former students who are looking for jobs. Departments and/or student organizations often maintain job boards for their majors.

Developing partnerships with academic departments for internships is yet one more way an agency can expand its recruitment efforts. Internships provide an employer with a unique look at an individual's strengths and abilities. Even if there are no openings at the time the students completes the internship, future contact is easily possible.

Public and nonprofit recreation and sport agencies might find it just a bit easier recruiting on college campuses as a result of the College Cost Reduction and Access Act of 2007. This act discharges any remaining debt after ten years of full-time employment with public service for individuals with direct federal loans or consolidated federal loans. Public service jobs include full-time employment with local state or federal government or with agencies which meet the criteria of Section 501 (c) (3) of the Internal Revenue Code of 1986 ("Public Service," 2010).

Professional Associations

Professional associations play a key role in the recruitment of full-time professional staff. Not only do professional associations maintain job boards, they hold annual conferences at which "job fairs" allow employers the opportunity to meet and recruit qualified candidates. Agencies or individuals who belong to professional associations pay a reduced fee to post an opening or participate in a job fair. The network with an association provides greater opportunity for referrals and references of potential candidates.

Print Ads

While the Internet is now the more common method of recruitment, print ads are still quite common. Seasonal, part-time, and lower-level full-time positions are the most likely to be advertised in the classified section of local newspapers. The advantage of classified ads is that they target specific geographic areas and reach a great many people (Noe, et al., 2007). Due to the nature of classified ads, they are the shortest in length of all job announcements.

Print ads in professional association publications are usually limited to professional positions. Again, cost and space will dictate how much detail is given. However, in professional publications, few abbreviations are used and greater care is given overall layout and design (see Figure 5.5a and Figure 5.5b). The limitation of ads in professional journals and newsletters is the lead time required for publication. Most are monthly publications and some are only quarterly.

Job Announcements

Prior to initiating either the internal or external search for any new employee, the employer must prepare what is known as a "job announcement." It explains the position that the agency wants to fill, identifies those qualifications necessary to meet the job responsibilities, and tells the applicant how and where to apply for the position. It is necessary to prepare the job announcement in order to know what to include in the online posting, print ad, or career fair materials. Similarly, the job announcement is the most critical item in contacting employment agencies and educational and professional institutions.

Job ads and job announcements may include the same basic information, although the cost of advertising may dictate a more condensed text for the ad. The following elements are found in most job announcements.

LIFEGUARD: CITY OF DALLAS

Lifeguard, part time. Minimum age of 15. Serves as a part-time Lifeguard, for the Dallas Aquatic Center. Preference given to those possessing current lifeguard certification, CPR for the Professional Rescuer First Aid or equivalent. Applicant qualification includes successfully passing a verbal, written and water skills test as well as a pre-employment drug test prior to employment.

For an application and more information contact the City Manager's Office, 187 SE Court Street, Dallas, Oregon 97338. Phone 503-831-3598 or visit the City of Dallas Web page (www.ci.dallas.or.us). Faxed applications or e-mail will not be accepted. Position open until all vacancies filled. EOE.

Figure 5.5a
Example of a Classified Ad

---

1. **Job Title.** Every position has a title or classification and applicants often search for positions by the job title.
   Examples:
   Park ranger, fitness director, receptionist, recreation therapist.

2. **Essential duties.** Job titles are often misleading and do not always mean the same thing to every employer or prospective applicant. It is necessary to explain the major duties and responsibilities of the specific job for the applicants.
   Examples:
   Patrols campground and lake area, enforces park regulations, supervises maintenance crew; Recruit, train and supervise officials, schedule leagues and tournaments, evaluate fields and gymnasiums.

3. **Requirements.** This element explains both the minimum and the preferred qualifications the applicants must possess to accomplish the specific job duties or functions. These would include knowledge, skills, experience, and any special certifications or credentials.
   Examples:
   Knowledge of programming, Bachelor's degree in Recreation, two years' experience in athletic programs, computer experience, current CPR certification; preferred: ability to speak Spanish.

4. **Closing date to apply.** Naturally, the applicants need this information to know when to submit their résumés or completed application forms. Some agencies will indicate a time as well as a date.

Position Announcement

The Ohio State University

Title: Fiscal Officer – Recreational Sports

Job Requisition Number: 347529

Function Statement/Summary of Duties:

Manages the Department of Recreational Sports resource management operations; oversees fiscal-related customer service and systems support; collaborates with Recreational Sports and Student Life management to recommend/set financial goals, objectives and strategic plans; identifies and coordinates approved revenue generation and/or expenditure reduction opportunities/initiatives; oversees fiscal status and direction; performs financial analysis for decision making/ pro-forma and capital plans; reviews and approves transactions and provides approved transactions to appropriate Student Life fiscal support staff for entry into the University's accounting system; obtains/maintains recreational sports fiscal and other related benchmark information; recommends and coordinates budgets, fees, rates and contracts; provides payroll services oversight; oversees unit resource management staff to ensure they are trained and work well together as an effective team; ensures compliance with unit, Student Life, University, State and Federal fiscal related laws, guidelines, rules, internal controls, policies, and procedures; assists with overall marketing initiatives; generates financial reports and tracks/communicates fiscal status to unit; ensures fiscal resource management staff maintain appropriate files and documentation retention schedules; assists with and reviews financial reconciliations; oversees/tracks equipment inventory; assists with capital project planning, analysis and financing; participates in professional organizations.

Essential Duties:

50%   Develops, directs, and provides oversight for administrative and operational processes; Develops long- and short-term financial goals, objectives, and strategies; maintains an operation and environment that meet compliance standards; implements and maintains information systems and associated interfaces to support business transactions; evaluates effectiveness of services through ongoing quality-improvement methodologies; manages budgets, negotiates vendor contracts, and maintains inventory control systems; develops and implements capital expenditure plans.

45%   Directly manages fiscal resource support functions, including billing, procurement, payroll services, and finance; establishes fees and projects revenues and expenses; prepares and analyzes budget variance and other financial reports; implements and trains leadership regarding Student Life, University fiscal policies and procedures; develops, implements, and audits accounting, inventory, reconciliation, operations and systems; reviews and approves purchasing, accounts payable, and inventory transactions. Supervises staff, including recruitment, supervision, competency assessment, training, and coordination of staffing assignments; monitors performance and provides feedback on a regular basis.

5%   Serves as member of department and University committees as assigned; participates in orientation and other Student Life activities; collaborates with campus programs and provides practicum experience opportunities for undergraduate and graduate students; performs other miscellaneous duties or projects as assigned by supervisor.

Education/Knowledge/Skills:

Bachelor's Degree in Accounting, Business, or equivalent education and experience required; MBA or equivalent education and experience desired.

Required: 3–5 years business management experience; considerable knowledge of accounting principles and applications; supervisory and administrative experience; capital planning, financial analysis and organizational budgets experience; advanced Microsoft Office application experience.

Desired: Working knowledge of PeopleSoft; knowledge of University policies & procedures; management, motivational, interpersonal, and supervisory skills desired; demonstrated record of consensus building and team problem-solving utilizing the diverse backgrounds and contributions of all staff; demonstrated record of upholding high standards of customer service; demonstrated excellent written and verbal communication skills.

Anticipated Hiring Salary:

$65,000.00–$70,000.00

Benefits:

The university offers a comprehensive benefits package including: medical, dental, vision, and life insurance; tuition authorization, paid vacation and sick leave; 10 paid holidays; and Ohio Public Employees Retirement System (OPERS) or Alternative Retirement Program (ARP).

For More Information Contact:

David Wiseley   wiseley.1@osu.edu   (614) 292-7250

For Consideration:

Visit: www.jobs.osu.edu and follow the instructions to apply, referencing job requisition number 347529. The Ohio State University will **only** accept applications and materials submitted electronically through our human resources link.

Application Deadline: October 18, 2009.

The Ohio State University is an Equal Opportunity, Affirmative Action Employer. Women, minorities, veterans, and individuals with disabilities are encouraged to apply.

Figure 5.5b
Example of a Professional Journal Announcement

Examples:
Closing date: June 30, 2012; Application deadline is 5:00 P.M. Friday, February 24, 2012.

5. Where to apply, how to apply, whom to contact. Employers may allow applicants only one method of application, such as applying online, or they may give the applicants several options. Many organizations use different methods for different positions. If an agency has the material sent to a post office box or e-mail address that does not clearly identify the hiring agency, it is called a *blind ad*.

Examples: Follow the link and complete the online application; Send cover letter, résumé, and copies of applicable certifications to Human Resources, City of Whatnot, 515 S H St. Whatnot, IA 50060. The applications may be obtained by calling (515) 961-1234 or from the city's website at www.Cityofwhatnot.org.

6. Salary information. Applicants may not be interested in applying if the pay scale is too low or below what they are already earning.

Examples:
$32,000 to start; $8.75 per hour; salary range $55,000–$70,000; base salary plus commission on sales; GS-7.

7. Job benefits. Often the employee benefits or job benefits are more attractive than the salary and serve to attract applicants. Key and unusual job benefits should be identified.

Examples:
Full medical benefits including dental and optical, free use of resort golf and tennis facilities, housing provided, excellent opportunity for immediate advancement, on-site daycare available.

8. Equal opportunity statement. This message implies that the employer is aware of EEO requirements and strives for equal treatment.

Example:
Equal opportunity/affirmative action employer; EOE.

9. Background Check Statement. If a background check is required for the position, it is best to inform all potential applicants of this.

Examples:
A criminal background check is required of all NOLS employees; A standard background check is a prerequisite to employment.

Agencies may choose to include additional information in their job announcements, such as characteristics of the agency, or the community in which the agency is located. As mentioned earlier, posting on the agency website allows the agency to share a great deal of information with potential applicants. Many of the Internet job sites allow for additional entries by employers beyond the basic information.

APPLICATION FORMS

Agencies often choose to ask applicants to complete a required application form rather than submit a cover letter and résumé. A standardized application form has several advantages: (1) It enables the organization to standardize its request for factual information so that every applicant has the same opportunity to present the same type of job-related experience. (2) It reduces human errors in subjectively evaluating résumés that are either too cluttered with irrelevant information or present very impressive data in only one area related to the position being sought. (3) It helps ensure that the organization's search for background information is legal under EEO laws.

An application blank is one of the best ways to obtain factual information. A good application blank will include the following sections:

1. *Equal Opportunity Affirmative Action Employer phrase* printed conspicuously somewhere on the form. Recent forms have expanded on this phrase. "Qualified applicants are considered without regard for color, religion, sex, national origin, age, disability, or any other basis protected under federal and state law."

2. *Demographic questions* concerning date of application, position for which applicant is applying, and applicant's name, address, and contact information. This section might also ask a question about whether the applicant can legally work in the United States with respect to American citizenship, permanent resident visa, or other legal category. Also, employers often need to know if the applicant has served in the U.S. military service in order to satisfy veterans' preference laws.

3. *Agency policies and job-related questions* ask the applicants to indicate if they possess the required credentials for the position and understand unique agency policies. For instance, if driving is a required part of the job, the form should ask for information about a current driver's or chauffeur's license. If the agency requires employees to live within a specific geographic area or has a policy addressing nepotism, the form may ask applicants to indicate they are aware of, and understand, the policy. It is illegal to ask any of the following questions on an application form: marital status, maiden name, number of children or plans to have children, type of military discharge, medical issues, arrest record, and convictions (unless nature of the crime is relevant to the position). It is also illegal to ask applicants to attach a photograph to an application (Craig & Vodanich, 2004). Sometimes employers use "disclaimer statements" believing that they can ask sensitive "business-necessity" or job-related questions which are ordinarily considered discriminatory. EEOC officials have cautioned that disclaimers on application forms carries no protection from future charges of discrimination.

4. *Educational questions* that seek information pertaining to job-related duties and responsibilities. The nature of these questions is important. Requesting the type of institution and education attained would be appropriate if the position requires documentation of minimal or a preferred competency in a professional or skilled occupation. It is illegal to ask the dates of attendance at an educational institution, though this still remains on a few forms not recently reviewed.

5. *Employment data* seeking the applicant's employment history, beginning with the present and most recent employer. Some organizations require all job-related experience back to the first job, including part-time, summer, military, and significant volunteer work. Other organizations are interested only in full-time work experience for a designated period of time, such as ten years. The detail requested on every job might be extensive, such as description of duties, responsibilities, accomplishments, salary, number of employees supervised, budgetary responsibilities, and reason for leaving. Other forms simply ask for employer's name, address, dates of employment, and job title.

6. *Skills or abilities inventory* requesting the applicant to check or indicate present skill levels. These may include ability to teach or coach recreational activities, such as scuba diving, sailing, softball, volleyball, orienteering, and so on. Summer playground programs and camps will often ask applicants to respond to such questions. Clerical staff might be asked to indicate their skill level with software programs and maintenance staff their level of experience with different pieces of machinery.

7. *Reference information* is usually requested near the end of the application form, asking for the names and contact information of persons who have knowledge of the applicant's work but are not related to the applicant.

8. *Authorization, certification statement, and signature* from the applicant that all information provided is complete and true to the best of the applicant's knowledge. This section may include statements or insert affidavits, such as the following:

    (a) I understand that as a condition of employment all new hires will be expected to pass a drug test.
    (b) I understand that a condition of employment is residency within the county limits within (time period) of employment.
    (c) I authorize my former employers to give any information regarding my employment.
    (d) I understand that a background check is a prerequisite for employment.
    (e) I understand that, if employed, I will be on probation for a period of (number of months), and during that time, I am subject to being discharged for any reason.

The entire tone of the application blank, should reflect that screening and selection decisions are based on job-related qualifications and conditions and are not, therefore, subject to illegal discrimination. An example of an excellent application form can be found at www.urbanaparks.org/employment.

EEO Compliance Sheets

The collection of certain information (race, gender, national origin, etc.) is sometimes needed to comply with EEO regulations. Agencies need to keep the collection of this data separate from the application materials so those in the hiring process to do not have access to it. Applicants also are to be informed that their cooperation in reporting this data is totally voluntary. If an HR department is initially handling the applications, the request for this information might be requested at the same time as the application is being completed. The HR department would separate this information from the application before the application is forwarded to the hiring supervisor. Agencies who are not large enough to have HR departments can do this by giving or sending applicants a postcard on which to indicate the required data and ask them to mail it back anonymously.

Recruitment Evaluation

If recruitment is to be successful, it is important that an agency periodically review its recruitment program. What is it about recruitment that should be evaluated? It is not simply enough to say that recruitment is successful if a position is filled. There are many components to successful recruitment. Recruitment evaluation should examine the following factors:

1. Quantity of applications. How many properly completed applications were received for the position advertised? And, was that a reasonably good number for that type of position?

2. EEO Goals. How well did this particular recruitment effort do in achieving the goal of equal employment opportunity? If an affirmative action plan is in place, how well did the effort do in following the plan?

3. Quality of the applicants. How well-qualified were the applicants who applied for the particular position? Was the pool exceptional or was the pool so weak, you decided to re-advertise?

4. Cost per applicant. How did the cost of the recruitment effort compare to the number of overall applicants? How did the cost of recruitment compare to the number of *qualified* applicants?

5. Amount of time. How did the amount of staff time spent on recruitment compare to the results?

6. Source of applicants by method. How well did each of the different methods of recruitment do in generating applicants?

Summary

1. Recruitment is attracting qualified applicants for vacant positions and is an ongoing process in most recreation and sport settings.

2. EEO and AA are two different terms. EEO refers to non-discrimination, while affirmative action refers to active steps to maintain diverse workforce.

3. Managers need to be aware and remain current with federal and state legislation impacting personnel decisions.

4. E-recruitment is the fastest growing means of recruitment and often offers agencies the best method to share information about the agency and the position.

5. The method of recruitment selected will depend on dollars, time, applicant market, and level of the position.

6. Job announcements are developed using job specifications and qualifications identified in the planning phase of the staffing process.

7. Application forms are an effective means of gathering information from the applicant and it is important that legal guidelines be followed in designing such forms.

8. EEO compliance sheets allow agencies to track the needed information for reporting equal employment data.

9. The evaluation of recruitment should include several elements to ensure that recruitment is successfully meeting all of its goals.

DISCUSSION TOPICS:

1. What is recruitment and how has it changed in recent years?

2. What should be included in a job announcement?

3. What are some advantages and disadvantages to always hiring from within? Always hiring externally?

4. If you cannot hire full-time employees to meet the workload, what are your alternatives? Discuss the pros and cons of each option.

5. What is e-recruitment and how can it help with recruitment?

6. Design and describe a recruiting process for hiring employees for a summer camp staff.

7. Discuss how college recruiting can be done more effectively.

8. Assume that you are the director of a fitness facility in the geographic area in which you now live. You would like to hire more minority staff at your facility. What specific methods and sources would you use to recruit minorities?

9. A new minor league baseball team is starting up in your community. You have been asked to help design a recruitment process for hiring all hourly support staff (ticket sellers, ticket takers, concession staff, ushers, parking attendants, grounds crew). They expect to hire about 200 part-time individuals. What would you recommend?

10. Identify the legal issues that one needs to consider in recruitment and sate how they can be addressed.

REFERENCES

Aldrich, N. (2008). Job application/applicant tracking software: Saving time, saving trees! *Illinois Park and Recreation Association's Administration and Finance Section Newsletter, 13*(3), 1–2.

Arthur, D. (2001). *The employee recruitment and retention handbook.* USA: American Management Association.

Berkshire, J. (2005). 'Social Network' recruiting. *HR Magazine, 50*(4), 95–98.

Bingham, B., Ilg, S., & Davidson, N. (2002). Great candidates fast: Online job application and electronic processing. *Public Personnel Management, 31*(1), 53.

Bobinski, D. (2006). *Strategic screening and hiring: Six steps to finding the best applicants for your organization.* Boise, ID: Leadership Development Press.

Burns, P. & Schapper, J. (2008). The ethical case for affirmative action. *Journal of Business Ethics, 83,* 369–379.

Craig, W. J., & Vodanovich, S. J. (2004). Personnel application blanks: Persistence and knowledge of legally inadvisable application blank items. *Public Personnel Management, 33*(3), 331–349.

Crompton, C., & Kaczynski, A. (2003). Trends in local park and recreation department finances and staffing from 1964–65 to 1999–2000. *Journal of Park and Recreation Administration, 21*(4), 124–144.

Gutman, A. (2009). Major EEO issues relating to personnel selection decisions. *Human Resource Management Review, 19,* 232–250.

Hirsch, E. (2009). The strength of weak enforcement: The impact of discrimination charges, legal environments, and organizational conditions on workplace segregation. *American Sociological Review, 74,* 245–271.

Kim, S., & O'Connor, J. G. (2009). Assessing electronic recruitment implementation in state governments: Issues and challenges. *Public Personnel Management, 38*(1), 47–66.

Klaff, L. G. (2004) New internal hiring systems can reduce cost and boost morale. *Workforce Management, 83*(3), 76–79.

Kovach, K., Kravitz, D., & Hughes, A. (2004). Affirmative action: How can we be so lost when we don't even know where we are going? *Labor Law Journal, 55*(1), 53–61.

Lawrence, J. D., Sauser, L. D., & Sauser W. I. (2007). Recruiting strong applicants: Process, prospects, challenges. In R. R. Sims (Ed.), *Human resource management: Contemporary issues, challenges and opportunities*. Charlotte, NC: Information Age Publishing.

Llorens, J., & Kellough, E. (2007). A revolution in public personnel administration: The growth of web-based recruitment and selection processes in the federal service. *Public Personnel Management, 36*(3), 207–221.

Noe, R.A., Hollenbeck, J.R., Gerhart, B., & Wright, P. M. (2007*) Fundamentals of human resource management*.(2nd ed.). New York, NY: McGraw-Hill Irwin.

Piotrowski, C., & Armstrong, T. (2006). Current recruitment and selection practices: A national survey of fortune 1000 firms. *North American Journal of Psychology, 8*(3), 489–496.

Public Service Loan Forgiveness. (2010). *FinAid*. Retrieved from http://www.FinAid.org

Pynes, J. (2009). *Human resources management for public and nonprofit organizations*. (3rd ed.). San Francisco, CA: Jossey-Bass.

Riccucci, N. M. (2007). The legal status of affirmative action in employment. In R. R. Sims (Ed.), *Human resource management: Contemporary issues, challenges and opportunities*. Charlotte, NC: Information Age Publishing.

Sandler, S. (2008). Solving the riddle of recruiting and retention. *HR Focus, 85*(4), 12–15.

Solving the riddle of recruitment and retention. (2008). *HRFocus, 85*(4), 1, 13–15.

The edge report 2008. (2008). *Robert Half International & CareerBuilder.com*. Retrieved from http://www.rhi.com/EDGEReport2008

6

EMPLOYEE SELECTION

The recruitment of applicants is only the first step in filling a vacant position. The next step is the *selection* process. The vast number of seasonal, part-time, and entry-level positions in recreation and sport makes personnel selection a major responsibility for supervisors and managers. New managers are often excited to be in the position of deciding whom to hire. The roles have switched, and they are now on "the other side" of the desk, reviewing applications and asking the interview questions. But how do new managers make sure they hire the best person? Is selection as simple as reading applications and asking questions? Is an interview just asking questions? Are reference checks really necessary? Keep in mind, if the wrong person is hired, it costs the agency time and money.

The selection process is complex. It involves screening, interviewing, and evaluating candidates for a position and making the selection based on pre-established qualifications (Pynes, 2009). Any screening techniques a manager uses must comply with the Equal Opportunity Commission's *Uniform Guidelines on Employee Selection Procedures* (Muller, 2009). The individual responsible for filling the position is expected to gather accurate information with which to fairly evaluate the candidates and make the selection decision.

This chapter will assist you in understanding how to design a rating or evaluation system, gather additional information on the candidate, conduct an interview, extend an offer, and orient a new hire.

Hopefully, the recruitment effort from Chapter 5 generated a quality pool of applicants for the vacant position. It is possible, though, that you may encounter a search where none of the original applicants meet the minimum qualifications. In this situation, a decision will need to be made to either, lower the minimum requirements, extend the search process, or search internally for someone to train. However, such situations are not often common in recreation and sport.

JOB ANALYSIS

Job analysis is part of both recruitment and selection. In Chapter 5, we explained how the job analysis was used to write job announcements. In this chapter, we see how the job analysis is used to establish the rating system for evaluation of applicants, the selection of screening techniques, and the questions to be asked in the interview.

The goal of the job analysis is to clearly identify the job tasks and responsibilities of the position (Dixon, Sheng, Calvin, Dineen, & Tomlinson, 2002). This begins with a thorough review of the job description. Ideally, the job description contains a complete list of the job duties for the position. If possible, also speak with individuals who are in, or have held, the position to see if any changes need to be made, as jobs often evolve over time. Conduct a job analysis each time a full-time permanent position becomes available. Job analyses of the many seasonal and part-time positions in leisure services should be done periodically.

Understanding the job enables you to identify the "required" and "preferred" qualifications for the position. These qualifications then become the basis for candidate evaluation and screening. All screening decisions are to be based on job-related criteria, not on a supervisor's personal preferences. Using *job-relatedness* as a guide assists managers in limiting discrimination and finding the best match. The point is to fill the *position*, not replace the *person* who just left.

EVALUATING CANDIDATES

The importance of clearly identifying the criteria to be used in evaluating candidates cannot be underestimated. It is only when you know what you are looking for that you can decide how well an applicant will perform if selected for the job. Let's say you are going to hire a Fitness Assistant Manager. After conducting the job analysis, you select the following qualifications:

- Bachelor's degree
- 1 to 2 years of experience or training
- Knowledge of fitness
- Excellent customer service skills
- Certified or able to be certified in CPR
- Strong writing skills for reports, business correspondence
- Effective presentation skills with clients, customers
- Ability to price, calculate interest, discounts, commissions
- Strong problem-solving skills
- Proficient in Microsoft procedures; preferred experience with Rec-Trac

As a manager reviewing applications, how will you decide who should be the candidates for an interview? The first two qualifications can be screened by a simple yes or no. The remaining eight qualifications, though, will require closer scrutiny and evaluation.

It is not enough to just know *what* you are looking for; you must also decide the *importance* of each qualification (Walker, 1998). The 10 criteria listed above are not equally important. For the position of Fitness Assistant Manager, one would argue that knowledge of fitness is more important than, say, report writing. This is not to say that report writing is not valued, but rather to hire someone with strong writing skills and little or no knowledge of fitness would most likely frustrate the clients.

Once you have identified the criteria and importance of each, an applicant rating form, such as the one in Figure 6.1, can be developed. When there are a number of applicants, which is often the case for positions in leisure services, it is important to be organized and consistent in evaluation. A rating form allows the manager to evaluate applicants fairly and it easily produces a ranking of the applicants. If more than one rater will be using the form, all raters should have a clear understanding of the criteria and rating system. Referring back to the Fitness Assistant Manager, do all raters have the same perception of the criteria, *knowledge of fitness*, and what constitutes *meeting expectations* versus *exceeding expectations*?

Even when a rating form is used, subjective judgment will always remain in the process. There are mistakes raters can make. The common rating errors are (Yusko & Goldstein, 2007):

1. *Contrast Effect* occurs when candidates are compared to each other and not to the rating form. For example, a person of average qualifications is evaluated more highly when preceded by a poor candidate.

2. *Central Tendency* is when the evaluator rates most candidates in the middle of the evaluation form. This is more common if the criteria are poorly defined.

3. *Similar-to-me* bias occurs when the evaluator is inclined to give candidates higher ratings because they have something in common (alumni of same school, gender, etc.).

4. *Leniency/Severity* is when raters are easier or more severe than other raters. Panel interviews have multiple raters. Large agencies may have more than one person conducting interviews for a position with multiple vacancies (counselors, lifeguards).

5. *Halo/Pitchfork* is when the information about one dimension affects the ratings of others. For instance, a candidate may have strong writing skills, so you believe he/she must also be a strong public speaker.

6. *Primacy/Recency* is when comments made by the candidates at the beginning or end of the interview disproportionately sway the rater's scoring.

When hiring staff, managers or supervisors may be asked to give preference to certain applicants. A family member or close friend might ask you to give their daughter or nephew a summer job. The practice of selecting someone solely on familial relationships or friendship is called "nepotism." Or, you might be asked to hire someone whose parents assisted the mayor win the recent election. "Patronage" is showing favoritism as a reward to someone for their support. Both situations ignore the use of job-related criteria and should be avoided if at all possible. Agency personnel policies should address the topics of nepotism and patronage.

Position: Fitness Assistant Manager   Applicant: _____

Evaluator: J. D. Warner   Date: 1/25/12

Core Criteria:
  B.S. Degree   Yes   No
  1 to 2 years experience/training   Yes   No

If applicant fails to possess above criteria, exclude the applicant from the consideration.

Criteria	Weight*	Supporting Evidence	Lacking Evidence	Rating**	Subtotal
Knowledge of fitness	3	• B.S. degree in Kinesiology • 1 year, personal trainer • ACE certified	None		
Customer service skills	2	• 1 year, personal trainer • Campus job @ Bursar's Office • Wait Staff 1 year	Response to interview questions—quick temper		
Communication skills	3	• A's in Comp and Speech courses • Reference praised written work	No experience with large group presentations		
Math skills	1	• B's in Math courses	No pricing experience		
Problem-solving skills	2	• Handled facility scenario well • Provided examples of problem solved in earlier jobs	Only above note on other scenario		
Microsoft/RecTrac	3	• Microsoft used at prior employment uses for personal computer	Knows of RecTrac and has only workshop exposure		

*   Weighting scale for selection criteria: 3 - very important; 2 - important; 1 - marginally important

** Rating scale: 4 - clearly meets selection criterion; 3 - meets selection criterion to a substantial degree but not totally; 2 - partially meets selection criterion; 1 - meets selection criterion only slightly; 0 - does not meet selection criterion

Figure 6.1
Sample Applicant Rating Form

FALSIFICATION OF INFORMATION

A note of caution: do not assume all the information you receive from applicants is true. Believe it or not, major studies have found that from one-third to one-half of all résumés contain overstated, misleading, and/or false information, intentional omissions, and blatant errors (Kerr and Nixon, 2008). The same phenomenon occurs with application blanks where you ask candidates for specific information. Verifying and clarifying the information submitted by the applicants is an important element of the screening process. Sometimes the fabrication is minor, such as slightly overstating job responsibilities in an earlier job. Other times, the dishonesty can be much more damaging for your agency, such as lying about having proper certifications or training. It is the agency's responsibility to properly screen candidates and this includes verifying certifications and other job requirements.

SCREENING TECHNIQUES

Having established the criteria for selection, you can now begin the process of screening applicants. The application form or résumé is the first technique used in the screening process. The initial screen is whether the applicant meets the minimum qualifications. In the case of the Fitness Assistant Manager, applicants who do not possess a Bachelor's degree or the 1 to 2 years experience or training would automatically be deleted. Many employers also eliminate candidates at this initial stage if they leave items blank, have omissions or time gaps between jobs, or submit an application or résumé with poor appearance.

Once the applications have been reviewed, a supervisor may use any number of additional screening techniques. The most common is the personal interview, but there are others, and some are used before deciding whom to interview. These include *reference checks, Internet searches, skill tests, work samples*, and *telephone pre-interviews*. Two legal screening steps, *background checks* and *employment eligibility verification*, usually only occur with the final candidate(s). Which screening techniques will be used, and how involved they will be, depend on the level of the position, the time the technique requires, the number of vacancies, the skill of the hiring supervisor, and any legal requirements for the position or the agency.

References

It is most common for candidates to be asked by the employer as part of the application process to provide references. However, an employer may also ask applicants to sign a release giving permission to contact *all* former employers. If applicants are asked for references, the request is either for reference names and contact information or letters of reference. With the contact information, the manager either personally contacts the reference or a form is sent for the reference to complete and return.

In contacting references, you may find that some references will only verify the job title and dates of employment for the candidate. This is because employers are worried that they will be subject to possible defamation lawsuits if their comments contribute to individuals not being offered a job. In actuality, however, the number of successful defamation lawsuits is quite low. However, some states do have laws limiting what employers can say about an employee (Woska, 2007).

The dilemma for you as a supervisor in hiring staff is that you have a duty to protect your customers and other employees. If you breach this duty, you and your agency might be found guilty of *negligent hiring*. This means employers have a legal duty to use reasonable care in employee selection so that others are not subject to harm. Reference checks, even if limited in the information generated, are an expectation of the court (Woska, 2007). You will find most recreation and sport agencies have operating guidelines for checking references, including who may conduct the reference check and what may be asked. In large agencies, the Human Resource department may handle all reference checking.

Whoever conducts the reference calls may only ask questions about only observable job-related behaviors (Fernando, Groysberg & Nohria, 2009). They may not ask for general comments or broad opinions from the references. Questions need to be confined to specific things the candidate did. Maybe the single best question to ask a former employer is, "Would you hire this person again?" Place all job-related information gathered during a reference check in the applicant's file. A sample reference check guide is provided in Figure 6.2.

Applicant's Name: Position Applying For:

Former Employer Contacted: Name of the Contact Giving Reference:

Telephone: Reference Check Conducted By:

Date:

---

1. When did [Applicant] work for your company?   From   To

2. What was [Applicant]'s position/title?

3. What was your working relationship with [Applicant]?

4. What type of work did [Applicant] do?

5. Did [Applicant] miss a lot of work? Was [Applicant] frequently late? Were there any issues?

6. Did [Applicant] get along well with management and coworkers?

7. Did [Applicant] supervise employees? How effectively? If I spoke to those employees, how would they rate [Applicant]'s management style?

8. How did [Applicant] handle conflict? How about presssure? Stress?

9. Can you describe [Applicant]'s experience working as a member of a team?

10. Would you rehire [Applicant] if the opportunity arose?

11. Why did [Applicant] leave your organization?

12. Is there anything I haven't asked that you would like to share with me?

Figure 6.2
Reference Checking Form

Internet Searches

In Chapter 5, employers were encouraged to use the Internet to recruit applicants. However, in screening applicants, employers need to proceed with caution if they plan to search the Internet to investigate candidates. While there is nothing illegal about using the Internet to screen candidates, you can not "Google" indiscriminately. Employers need to understand that Internet searches, especially ones done on social networking sites, could result in discrimination lawsuits. The reason is that the search could be "perceived" to have influenced the selection decision on a non-job-related factor (race, gender, age, etc.). If you choose to use the Internet, you must do so for all the applicants being considered at that stage of review.

A 2009 survey by CareerBuilder.com found 45% of employers using social networking sites to check on job candidates: a three-fold increase since 2007 when only 12% were using such sites. The three most common sites used by employers were Facebook (29%), LinkedIn (26%), and MySpace (21%). Of the employers who use social networking sites to screen applicants, 35% eliminated candidates as a result of something found. Some of the reasons employers gave for not hiring as a result of the search included provocative or inappropriate photographs or information, lying about qualifications, possessing poor communication skills, having links to criminal behavior, and drugs/alcohol abuse. However, an Internet search can also provide positive information for employers about candidates. In the same CareerBuilder.com study, 39% of the supervisors searching online found support for candidate qualifications, 35% found evidence of good communication skills, and 19% found good professional references. Agencies would be wise to clearly identify their policies for acceptable use of Internet sites to guide staff in screening applicants (CareerBuilder.com, 2009).

Tests

It is legal to ask applicants to take tests as part of the screening process. Any required test must be valid, reliable, and related to required job skills. Tests are given to assess how well an individual will perform on the job. The results allow employers to see who is most qualified for the position. There are any number of tests an employer could select to use as long as they measure a bona fide occupational qualification (BFOQ). Many private companies offer validated tests for measuring personality, integrity, language

arts, aptitude, and more. Skill tests in recreation and sport may include physical ability tests for lifeguards, word processing for secretarial staff, personality in the resort setting, etc.

Large employers often use electronic testing to expedite the screening process. With online testing it is important to include a statement such as "falsifying information or enlisting the assistance of another will disqualify you from consideration." Depending on the content of the test, a second round of testing should be done in a proctored environment to verify the initial score (Mooney, 2000).

A required medical exam may only occur after an offer has been made to a candidate. It can be a condition of employment and as such, failure to pass the medical exam would result in the offer being rescinded.

Telephone Pre-screening Interviews

Employers usually conduct pre-screening telephone interviews when there are too many well-qualified candidates to interview personally. A telephone interview allows an employer to verify the information submitted on the application, confirm the applicant's continued interest in the position, and ask initial job-related questions. Usually telephone interviews are shorter than in-person interviews. However, for higher-level, or extremely competitive, positions, the interview may run longer than an hour and be conducted by a panel of individuals, not just a single individual. Telephone interviews are subject to the same legal guidelines regarding questions and record-keeping as a face-to-face interview, as they are used to screen who will be further considered for a position.

Work Samples

There are a number of types of work samples used most often to assess candidates for full-time permanent positions. Agencies use work samples to get a better perception of the applicants' actual abilities before deciding whom to interview. Agencies may select one or more of the following methods (Pynes, 2009):

1. *In-basket exercises.* This activity requires applicants to respond to a number of items that might be found in the "in-tray" of the vacant position. The exercise measures the skills of task prioritization, written communication, and judgment.

2. *Leaderless group discussions.* A group of candidates for the same position are brought together and asked to solve a problem that requires cooperation. No one is designated as the leader. The purpose of this exercise is to measure oral communication, leadership, persuasiveness, adaptability, and teamwork skills.

3. *Planning exercise.* Applicants are given basic information and asked to plan a program to meet certain goals. This task looks at programming skills, creativity, and attention to detail.

4. *Analysis exercise.* Used most often with upper-level positions. Applicants are given the description of an organization and situation. They are then asked a variety of questions such as how to improve relations, revenue stream, and/or structures.

5. *Task performance.* This is different than the planning exercise in that applicants are given information and asked to develop particular work products (i.e., news release, brochure entry, tournament schedule, pricing guide).

6. *Lecture/presentation.* Applicants are given a set topic and asked to prepare a presentation. Depending on the amount of public speaking required in the new position, applicants may be given the topic before they arrive.

7. *Simulations.* Applicants participate in a role play with individuals duplicating a scenario likely to occur if hired for the position. The simulations need to be standardized and the same script is used for all applicants.

Employment Eligibility Verification

Individuals who are working in the United States must be legally eligible to do so. All employers with four or more full-time employees are required by the Immigration Reform and Control Act to complete Employment Eligibility Verification forms (Form I-9) for all employees, even those who are United States citizens (Muller, 2009). An employee completes Section One of the form within the first three days of reporting to work. The employer is responsible for the rest and for confirming eligibility.

To assist employers, there is an electronic eligibility verification system called E-Verify. The service is provided by the U.S. Citizenship and Immigration Service (USCIS). It provides an automatic link to federal databases and is a free service. In large agencies, HR departments handle the verification paperwork and process. In smaller agencies, the Business Manager or Superintendent may handle it.

Background Checks

Background checks are becoming increasingly common in the field of Recreation and Sport. Many states now *require* employers to conduct background checks on individuals hired to work with children (Background Checks, 2006). In the private sector, about 80% of large companies and 66% of small companies use background checks to screen candidates (Noe, Hollenbeck, Gerhart, & Wright, 2007). A wise move for any agency that does not already have a procedure for background checks is to check with their state's Department of Labor for what should and should not be done. Some states' statutes specifically prohibit asking about arrests, convictions that occurred well in the past, past juvenile records, and sealed records.

Since delving into an individual's background can be a precarious endeavor, most recreation and sport agencies use third parties to conduct the background check. Many agencies utilize the background check service available through state police departments. Others hire independent firms. The Boys and Girls Clubs of America require its affiliates to use Intellicorps Inc.

It is the responsibility of the hiring agency to obtain the permission of the candidate for the background check. This release might be part of a standard application form or a separate release form (see Figure 6.3). Guidelines and further information about background checks may be found at:

- www. privacyrights.org
- www.intelius.com
- www.abika.com
- www.peoplefinders.com
- www.easybackgrounds.com

I hereby authorize [Name of Company] and/or any of its officers, employees, or agents to investigate my background, references, character, education, past employment, and/or criminal records in order to confirm my qualifications for employment as represented on my résumé and/or employment application, and/or in my employment interview.

By signing below, I release [Name of Company] and/or its officers, employees, and/or agents, as well as any person or entity providing information on my background pursuant to this acknowledgment form, from any and all liability in relation to the information obtained from any and all of the above referenced sources used.

Applicant's Signature: _____   Date: _____

Applicant's Full Legal Name: _____

Applicant's Current Address: _____

_____

How long at this address? _____   Driver's License No.: _____   State of Issue: _____

Date of Birth: _____   Social Security No.: _____

Source: www.govdocs.com

Figure 6.3
Background Check Acknowledgment Form

The Interview

The employment interview is perhaps the most widely used selection technique (Judge, Higgins, & Cable, 2000). Interestingly, applicants perceive interviewing as a fair technique and expect interviews to be part of the selection process (Macan, 2009). While employers use the interview to elicit information about the candidate, the applicant uses the interview to gain information about the agency and possibly meet a future supervisor.

The interview differs from the other screening procedures in that it has a social component. It is this social element that sometimes misleads employers to think of interviews in a casual manner. The interview is not just a "conversation" with the applicant, but a screening tool which will strongly influence the selection decision. As such, the EEOC considers employment interviews as equal to pre-employment testing in needing to be objective and fair. It is a mistake to think that no planning is needed prior to interviewing candidates.

Interviews that are well planned and structured have higher validity (Macan, 2009). Structured interviews provide uniformity and consistency across all the candidates and enhance the interviewers' ability to assess with greater accuracy. A structured interview is a more professional and detailed interview, which puts the candidates at ease as they can sense order and direction. The interviewer uses a pre-established

interview guide and if needed, takes notes during the interview. Note-taking is important as it improves your memory, helps you summarize key points, improves the accuracy of your assessment, and meets legal requirements (Yusko & Goldstein, 2007). Finally, structured interviews enable agencies to better comply with legal mandates and record keeping.

Procedural Outline for the Interview

Structured interviews are well planned and follow a consistent format. There are seven basic stages to an employment interview.

1. *Welcome.* At this time of the initial stage the interviewer makes an introduction, giving both their name and job title. The interviewer takes a few minutes with ice breaker questions to help the candidate relax. Common ice-breakers are "Did you have any trouble finding the place?" or "What do you think about our weather?" Much better ones can be developed from the applicant's résumé or current events. "I see you attended Southern Illinois University. I've always wondered, what's a Saluki, your mascot?" "Do you have a favorite Best Picture at the upcoming Oscars?"

2. *Information about the job.* Before asking candidates to respond to questions about

the job, a brief description of the job should be given. This information may include a short description of the agency, the job title of the position, information about basic job duties (including number of staff or participants responsible for), and how the position fits in the overall organization. This transition alerts candidates to the more formal part of the interview and gives all candidates the same basic information to use in responding to questions. For administrative positions, information about the job is usually sent to candidates prior to the interview.

3. *Assess candidate's abilities.* This is the major section of any employment interview and where the candidates are asked a series of pre-determined questions. Prior to starting with questions, mention should be made that the interviewer will be taking some notes during the interview. Interview questions must all be legal and worded in such a way as to encourage candidates to share detailed responses. (See next section, Designing Interview Questions). Questions should be asked in a logical order and provide the interviewers with information about the candidate's ability to do the job, motivation for the job, and their adaptability. During this stage, the interviewer reviews a portfolio if one is brought by the candidate.

4. *Salary/benefit information.* Even though this information may have been listed in the job announcement, it is important to verify with the candidate the particulars for the position. If a range of salary is offered, be sure to clearly state the criteria used to determine where someone would fall in the range. At this time it is also appropriate to share any special training opportunities or professional memberships that would be given to the individual hired.

5. *Solicit candidate's questions.* Ask if the candidate has any questions or concerns that have not been addressed, or if she/he has any additional information to offer.

6. *Selection process.* Share with the candidate the selection process and their status. Be sure to explain how long the process will take, what it entails, and how she/he will be informed of the decision. It may be something like "We are interviewing seven candidates this week for the first round. Telephone calls will be made next Monday to the final three candidates for second round interviews. Those interviews will take place next week and we anticipate making a decision by the following Monday. All candidates not contacted by telephone will receive letters."

7. *Terminate.* Close the interview by thanking the candidate for their interest and by referring once more to the next step to occur in the selection process.

Designing Interview Questions

Selecting and wording the questions to ask during the interview is a critical part of the pre-interview process. An interviewer must decide *what* to ask and *how* best to ask the question. *What* to ask is best ascertained by returning to the job analysis and qualifications. If you are looking for an art instructor for children's programs, then it would be important to inquire about art education and experience with children. In the case of the Fitness Assistant Manager, the questions should cover customer service skills, written and oral communication, and pricing and computer experience, as well as knowledge of fitness. Questions that are asked during an employment interview must relate to the job. Table 6.1 provides a list of topics that may be illegal for interviewers to address unless worded correctly.

Interviewers also need to consider *how* they will ask a question in the interview. Of little value are closed-ended questions. These are questions that can be answered with a simple yes or no. "Do you have experience working with children?" "Are you comfortable working in customer service?" While some candidates may elaborate in their response beyond a simple yes or no, the question itself does not encourage applicants to do so. Much stronger are questions worded with lead-ins such as: "Tell me about ...", "Give an example ...," or "Describe a situation where...". Questions that begin with such phrases will provide the interviewer with much greater information related to the candidate's abilities.

Table 6.1
Interview Questions (Acceptable vs. Unacceptable)

SUBJECT	ACCEPTABLE	UNACCEPTABLE
Name	Can ask if applicant has ever worked for the company under another name.	Have you ever had any other names?
Birthplace	No acceptable questions.	Where were you born? Where were your parents born? Requiring a birth certificate.
Age	Can ask if the applicant meets any age-requirement conditions of the job.	How old are you? Any questions attempting to determine the age of the applicant are unacceptable unless BFOQ relate (e.g., being at least age 21 to serve hard liquor at a golf course).
Religion	No acceptable questions unless it is a bona fide occupational qualification (e.g., counselor at a religious day camp).	Questions about religion generally or about what days the applicant may need off for religious observance.
Work Schedule	Can ask if the applicant meets the attendance requirements of the position.	Any questions about health conditions that would lead to absences from work.
Race	No acceptable questions.	Any question seeking to elicit what race the applicant is or other questions indicating race or color.
Photographs	Unacceptable unless BFOQ (e.g., some sort of acting role).	Please attach a photograph.
Citizenship	The only acceptable question is whether the applicant will be able to prove that he or she is employable in the event he or she is offered the job. Employment authorization and identity must be verified and Form I-9 completed within three days of when the individual begins employment.	Any questions asking or seeking to elicit what nationality the applicant is.
National Origin	Languages that the applicant can read, write, or speak and his or her level of fluency.	Any questions about the applicant's national lineage of his or her date of entry into the United States. Any questions concerning the national origin of the applicant's spouse or mother. Any questions such as, "What is your mother tongue?"
Education	Applicant's educational background.	When did you graduate from high school? When did you receive your college degree?
Experience	Can ask questions like: What is your work experience? Why did you leave your job?	What type of discharge did you receive from the military?
Arrests	In most states, no acceptable questions.	Have you ever been arrested?
Felony Convictions	Can ask about felony convictions in all states, may only disqualify applicant for a job-related reason and not just because of the conviction itself.	Have you ever been indicted for a crime?
Relatives	Names of any relatives employed by the company.	Are you married? What relatives live with you? With whom do you reside?
Physical Conditions	Can you perform the essential functions of the position for which you are interviewing with or without a reasonable accommodation?	Are you disabled? Are you healthy? Any pre-job offer questions concerning workers' compensation?
Memberships	Do you belong to any professional or other organizations that you consider relevant to your ability to do the job?	To what clubs or social organizations do you belong?

In an interview for the art instructor you might say:

"Describe for me your art training or teaching experience."

"Give one example of an obstacle you may encounter when teaching a student."

In an interview for the Fitness Assistant Manager you might say:

"Tell me about any experience you have had in previous jobs where you were responsible for pricing items, collecting money, or making change."

"Describe for me what you think makes for outstanding customer service in a fitness facility."

The interview will consist of a number of questions. In recreation and sport settings it is common to include some scenario questions, especially with young, or less experienced, candidates. These individuals may not be able to give you an example from prior experience of, say, how they handled a rain delay. But, if presented with a situation surrounding a rain delay, they would be able to indicate to you how they would act if such a situation were to occur. In asking scenario questions, it is best to provide key pieces of information so that answers may be compared across candidates. Rather than ask "Tell me how you would settle a fight on a field trip." Consider asking; "Tell me how you would handle a situation on a zoo field trip when two ten-year-old girls in your group of eight start yelling and hitting each other as you wait in a long line at the concession stand."

Also, be careful not to ask leading questions such as: "You intend to get your CTRS certification, don't you?" The applicant clearly knows by the wording the answer you want to this question.

In reviewing each question selected for the interview, consider the following:

1. Is it related to the job or setting?

2. Is it legal?

3. Will it help assess the candidate's ability, motivation or adaptability?

4. Is it likely to be found on the application form or résumé? (If so, no need to ask)

5. Is it something the applicant can answer? (Is it realistic to expect candidates to be able to answer the following question? "Why do you think the board has cut our budget?")

6. Is it repetitious? (Have you in essence asked the same thing in an earlier question?)

7. Is it open–ended? How is it worded?

Although all candidates are to be asked the same interview questions, follow-up probes to their responses may differ (Yusko & Goldstein, 2007). And, while the questions will be listed in a set order in the interview guide, it is OK to change the order depending on the flow of the interview. For example, in response to a question early in the interview, the applicant for Fitness Assistant Manager might mention a public presentation he/she gave on nutrition. So, rather than wait until later in the interview, you move up your questions related to oral communication. Figure 6.4 contains a sample interview guide for the position of dance instructor.

Scheduling the Interview

Prior to conducting the interviews, a decision will need to be made regarding the type of interview, the location, and the amount of time to allocate for an interview. There are three basic *types* of interviews: *one-to-one*, *panel*, and *serial*. A panel interview, sometimes also called a board interview, consists of 2 or more interviewers who get together to interview a candidate and combine their ratings in an overall score. Serial interviews are when multiple interviewers evaluate the same candidate but do so sequentially (Macan, 2009). A candidate may be scheduled for a two-hour block and meet with four different individuals for 30 minutes each.

Where an interview takes place may influence how effective it is. In many recreation and sport settings, office space is shared or the supervisor's desk is located in a high-traffic area. In these situations it would be best to see if an agency conference room or other setting may be reserved. Select a location with privacy, minimal distractions, and comfort for the applicant. Sitting on the bleachers in a deserted gym may provide privacy, but will it be comfortable for the applicant? Wherever an interview takes place, be sure to arrange for no interruptions or calls (Arthur, 1998).

How much time to allocate for an interview is usually a function of the position and the number of vacancies to fill. A state park director will allocate less time per interview to hire eight summer crew

Introduction and Ice Breaker

Job Info

About Park District Dance Program

☐ ☐ ☐ ☐ ☐ ☐

√ 750 students √ 3 dance studios √ 5 & 18 week session √ Recital is the weekend after Mother's Day	√ Classes range in times 45 minutes to 1 1/2 hours depending on the levels. Instructors are paid for the actual class time plus an additional ☐ hour

Tell me about yourself

What made you decide to apply for this position?	
Why do you want to work for the park district?	
Describe for me your formal training/teaching experience in dance (age/levels).	
What range of ages have you taught? What ages/levels do you prefer to teach?	
How much supervision have you typically received in previous jobs?	
Tell me about your experience with children. Why do you want to work with children?	
How is your level of patience (tying shoes/getting them ready for the next phase of class)?	
When would you approach a parent regarding their child who does not seem to be interested in the class?	
How would you go about creating a lesson plan? (Example: BTT I: 3–4 year olds)	
(We normally start out with Tap Ballet Tumbling.)	
Describe for me how you react when you receive constructive criticism.	
The reason I asked is that we have a VERY open policy when it comes to improving our dance program. We feel it is best to address concerns or even shortcomings whether brought up by parents or the instructor themselves.	
Tell me about your experience with recitals (measuring, costumes, costume needs, music, etc.).	
Teaching dance is a long-term commitment. Is there anything you foresee that may prohibit you from meeting your obligations, if hired (other jobs, studios, etc.)?	
What is your availability? AM AFTERNOONS PM WEEKENDS	

What questions do you have for me?

Provide information on selection process.

Thank candidate.

Source: Arlington Heights Park District

Figure 6.4
Dance Instructor Part-time Interview Guide

members than to hire a single year-round naturalist. When scheduling interviews, it is best to allow for a brief break between candidates. This allows interviewers the time to make final notes and to prepare to greet the next candidate. Also, if by chance an interview runs long, it is easier to get back on schedule.

Conducting the Interview

A challenge for interviewers is that initial impressions influence post-interview evaluations. What happens is called *self-fulfilling prophecy*. Managers with positive impressions of a candidate will be tempted to look favorably toward them during the interview and will retain the information from the interview to confirm that initial feeling (Judge, Higgins, & Cable, 2000). The same process occurs if the manager has a negative, or less positive, initial view of the applicant. This is part of human nature and why so many articles are written for applicants about making a good first impression. But, first impressions are not always accurate. A résumé may list impressive work experience but during the interview one might find the candidate responds poorly to questions. On the other hand, a candidate with little experience to date on a résumé may demonstrate a much better understanding of the job, handle the interview well, and possess the necessary skills to be the best match for the job.

Ideally, an employment interview should be a smooth, easy, flowing discussion. For this to occur, interviewers need to be familiar with both the questions they plan to ask, so they do not sound as if they are reading them, and they need to be familiar with the application/résumé of the individual they are to interview. An interview will be less choppy if the interviewer uses transitions. They can be as simple as "Now, I would like to ask you a few scenario questions" or more complex ("You just told me about working at a camp and now I'd like to ask you about your outdoor skills").

Encourage the applicant to talk by head nodding, offering probes, and giving a candidate time to formulate a response. Possible probes to use are "I see," "Really," "I didn't know that," and "Is that right?" It is not necessary to probe or comment on each of the applicant's answers. Sometimes interviewers will respond to an applicant's answers with "Good answer," "Great job," "I like that" or other similar comments. Their intention is to help the candidate relax and feel comfortable, but what happens is the applicant reads too much into the comments and experiences greater disappointment if not offered the job.

An interviewer may become uncomfortable if there is silence and feel the need to jump in and re-ask or re-phrase a question. But, it is important to give applicants time to develop their thoughts. If candidates are unclear about a question, they will speak up. Also, avoid interrupting applicants even if their answers prompt a thought or additional question for you. Make a note to yourself if you are concerned you will forget to ask the question.

Immediately following the interview, the interviewer(s) should review notes of the interview and enter their score on the evaluation form. Panel interview members should discuss briefly their reactions after each interview and individually complete their evaluation sheet (Dixon, Sheng, Calvin, Dineen, & Tomlinson, 2002). Evaluating after each interview minimizes the chances of committing rater errors.

Strong interviewing comes with practice, but new managers can improve their interviewing skills by remembering a few general principles of effective interviewing.

1. Prepare and be organized
2. Ask only relevant questions
3. Keep a friendly but neutral demeanor
4. Let first impressions fade
5. Schedule interviews carefully to avoid fatigue of multiple interviews
6. Allocate the appropriate amount of time for the interview
7. Honestly describe the job and agency policies
8. Take adequate and consistent notes
9. Evaluate candidates against the criteria

The interview is not only a time for a candidate to be evaluated. It is also a time when the candidate develops an impression of the interviewer and the agency.

Extending the Offer

After all candidates have been interviewed and all information gathered, the interviewer should review interview notes and all other data to make a final selection decision. It is important that you first notify the chosen candidate and confirm their acceptance of the job before notifying the other candidates. It is possible that the top candidate may accept another agency's offer or decide the position is not really what he/she was seeking. Once verbal agreement is reached, a written offer needs to follow. The letter of offer should include: job title, salary, probation terms and conditions, department if the agency is large, the date, time, and place to report to work, and anything they may be required to bring the first day. If this letter is sent by someone other than the immediate supervisor, the supervisor should also receive a copy. When the verbal offer is extended, any additional screening still to occur, (drug test, medical exam, background check) needs to be reiterated (Muller, 2009).

Too often individuals who apply or interview for positions never hear from the agency. If possible, alert all applicants of their status. If the agency uses an electronic applicant tracking system, this is an easy thing to do. If not, it is imperative that all individuals who participated in pre-screening work exercises and/or interviews receive notification from the agency. An agency should never fail to follow up with a candidate.

Orientation

A new hire may have some idea what to expect on the first day at a new job, but it will still be stressful. To help a new employee get off to a good start, it is essential that the agency provide a strong orientation. In doing so, the agency demonstrates its commitment to seeing new employees succeed.

Orientation is the process by which a new employee is familiarized with the agency, job duties, coworkers, employment policies, safety procedures, breaks, vacation schedules, and more (Giacalone, 2009). The orientation should be prepared and well-planned before a new employee's arrival. The orientation may be done by one person or by a number of individuals. Allowing a new employee to interact directly with the Business Manager to complete required documents and receive keys and agency ID lets the employee become familiar with staff and understand who is responsible for what. As you can see by the list for the Western Dupage Special Recreation Association, there are many topics to be covered with new employees. WDSRA provides its employees with an extensive and thorough orientation (see Figure 6.5a, p. 106 and Figure 6.5b, p. 107).

The immediate supervisor will want to discuss the job and performance expectations with the new hire during orientation. When orientation is over, the immediate supervisor will want to continue a close relationship with the new employee for the first few months. Some settings will provide additional support

for a new hire by also assigning another staff person to be a mentor for the new hire.

With the high cost of recruitment and selection, an agency wants new employees to succeed. An effective orientation enhances the agency's chances of retaining new hires and increases their acceptance by other staff (Caruth, Caruth, & Haden, 2010).

Summary

1. The selection process involves screening, interviewing and evaluating candidates for a position and making the decision based on pre-established criteria.

2. Job relatedness is important in that selection decisions must be related to bona fide occupational qualifications.

3. An evaluation system should be developed to identify clearly the criteria and importance of each to be used in the selection process before screening begins.

4. Subjective judgment leads to common rater errors in candidate evaluation.

5. One-third to one-half of résumés received by employers misrepresent the candidate.

6. Screening techniques include application forms or résumés, references, Internet searches, tests, work samples, telephone pre-interviews, employment eligibility verification, and background checks.

7. In addition to asking applicants for references, employers should have applicants sign a release allowing them permission to contact all former employers.

8. Using the Internet to investigate applicants is legal if based on job-related criteria and is done equally for all candidates.

9. Tests may be given to applicants to assess how well they will perform on the job if the tests have been established as valid and reliable measures of the criteria.

10. Telephone interviews are subject to the same legal requirements as personal employment interviews.

11. Work samples used as screening techniques include in-basket exercises, leaderless group discussion, planning exercise, analysis exercise, task performance, lecture/presentation and simulations.

Orientation Assignments

Supervisor– INTRODUCTION TO WDSRA

Welcome Packet (obtained from HR)
Tour of WDSRA Office
Introduction of Staff
Mailboxes/Mail System
In/Out Board
Library/Resource File
Lunchroom
Calendar/Datebook
WDSRA Directory
Opening/Closing Office
Agency Regulations Sheet
Recreation Policy and Procedures Manual to include:
  1. Recreational Operations Procedures Manual
  2. Safety Manual
  3. Vehicle Manual
  4. Crisis Manual
  5. Sign off for Manuals

H.R. Manager – PERSONNEL

Physical Results Received
Criminal Background Check
Status Change Form
Pay Periods
Direct Deposit
Name tag/Name plate/Business card
Emergency Contact Information
Personnel Policy/Employee Benefit Handbook
Medical, Dental & Vision Insurance
Life Insurance
Disability Insurance
Pension Plan
FSA Cafeteria Plan
457 Deferred Comp
Vacation Days
Personal Days
Sick Days
Reporting of Vacation, Personal & Sick Days
Administrative Time
Holidays
Professional Development Fund
Resignations, Grievances, Discipline, Terminations
Tuition Reimbursements
Employee Assistance Program
Additional Miscellaneous Benefits

Business Manager – FINANCE

Work Orders for Building Maintenance
Agency Credit Card
Agency Phone
Purchase/Checks
Facility Room Request
Work Order Requests

Safety Coordinator – SAFETY PROCEDURES

Safety Manual
Issued First Aid Kit
Safety Program Elements
Safety Infractions
Fire Drills
Office Safety
Personal Protective Equipment
Accident Investigation & Reporting Procedure
Safety Guidelines
Emergency Procedures
Infectious Disease Guidelines
Safety Goals
PRDMA Introduction

Vehicle Coordinator – VEHICLE PROCEDURES

Vehicle Log
Road Checks
Driver Abstract
Vehicle Orientation to all vehicles
Employee Gas Card-Policies & Procedures
Mileage Reimbursement Procedures

Office Staff – OFFICE PROCEDURES

Copy Machines
Fax Machine
Postage Meter
Phone System
Laminating Machine
Personal Calls
Project Assistance by office staff
Registration Procedure
Requesting Office Supplies
Equipment Check-out
Office Procedures Manual (If Applicable)

Figure 6.5a
Orientation Assignments

Orientation Assignments

Technology Manager – COMPUTER PROCEDURES

Log-in for network/Outlook
Personal File in O and I Drives
Intro to O Drive/ Central Agency File/ Forms File
WDSRA Outlook Address book for all staff
Set Up Voice Mail
Introduction to RecTrac
Introduction/Review of Word and Excel
Intro to budgeting system
Internet access
Review of technology use policies/procedures

Executive Director – SUMMARY

A.D.A.
Budget
Channels of Communication
Service Philosophy
WDSRA History
Park District Overview/Member Districts
Public Image
Professional Organizations
Questions & Answers

Supervisor – JOB DESCRIPTION

Review Duties & Responsibilities
Public Image
Attendance
Punctuality
Goals & Objectives/Work Plans
Performance Evaluations
Filing System
Word Processing Procedures
Written Procedures
Equipment Location
Professional Memberships
Specific Departmental Safety Rules
Program Guidelines
Program Forms
Staff Review
Program Planning Procedures:
  1. Blurbs (Spareware)
  2. Budgets (Excel)

Office Staff – OFFICE PROCEDURES

Copy Machines
Fax Machine
Postage Meter
Phone System
Laminating Machine
Personal Calls
Project Assistance by office staff
Registration Procedure
Requesting Office Supplies
Equipment Check-out
Office Procedures Manual (If Applicable)

Inclusion Manager – INCLUSION

Inclusion Manual
Inclusion Training

Supervisor – FORMS

Accident Report
Blurb Worksheet
Computer/Data Entry Request Form
Long Distance Phone Call Log
Purchase & Payment Request
Scholarship Request Form
Work Order Form

Source: Western DuPage Special Recreation Association's Orientation Checklist

Figure 6.5b
Orientation Assignments (cont'd)

12. Employment Eligibility forms are required of all employers with 4 or more full-time employees.

13. Background checks are required for many positions in leisure services, and agency policies for conducting background checks should be carefully followed.

14. The structured interview enhances the interviewer's ability to assess accurately and is easier for the applicant to follow.

15. Employment interviews should follow a set order, contain only job-related questions, and be consistent across all candidates.

16. Interview questions should be selected before the interviews begin, related to BFOQs, and worded in such a way as to elicit information from the applicants.

17. The location and timing of an interview may influence the interviewer's ratings and candidate's performance.

18. A written offer should follow a verbal acceptance from the individual selected and all other candidates should receive notification of the selection decision.

19. Orientation is the process by which a new employee is familiarized with the agency, job duties, coworkers, employment policies, safety procedures, breaks, vacation schedules, etc.

Discussion Topics

1. When evaluating a candidate, what might you do to avoid committing common rater errors?

2. You are responsible for hiring several seasonal employees and know you will have a large number of applicants; how might you screen the applicants?

3. What are the issues for employers with Internet searches of potential candidates?

4. Why structure an interview?

5. If you are the coordinator for a panel interview, how would you prepare the other panel members?

6. When do you think reference checking should occur?

7. What are the advantages to using an applicant evaluation guide to rank candidates?

8. During an interview, what are the mistakes the interviewer might make?

9. What should be considered when selecting the questions to ask applicants in an interview?

10. If you've had an interview that was poorly conducted, what about the interview made you feel that way?

11. Why should an employer notify candidates not selected for an interview?

12. Once a new employee is hired, how would you orient the new staff member?

References

Background Checks. (2006). Background checks are increasingly required. *HR Focus, 83*(5), 11–15.

CareerBuilder.com. (2009, August 19). *Forty-five percent of employers use social networking sites to research job candidates, CareerBuilder survey finds.* Retrieved from http://www.careerbuilder.com

Caruth, D. L., Caruth, G. D., & Pane Haden, S. S. (2010, March/April). Getting off to a good start. *Industrial Management, 52*(2), 12–15.

Dixon, M., Sheng, W., Calvin, J., Dineen, B., & Tomlinson, E. (2002). The panel interview: A review of empirical research and guidelines for practice. *Public Personnel Management, 31*(3), 397.

Fein, R. (2000). *101 Hiring mistakes employers make and how to avoid them.* Manassas Park, VA: Impact Publications.

Fernando-Araoz, C., Groysberg, B., & Nohria, N. (2009). The definitive guide to recruiting in good times and bad. *Harvard Business Review, 87*(5), 74–84.

Giacalone, K. (2009). Making new employees successful in any economy. *T+ , 63*(6), 37–39.

Judge, T. A., Higgins, C. A., & Cable, D. M. (2000). The employment interview: A review of recent research and recommendations for future research.

Human Resource Management Review, 10(4), 383–406.

Kerr, K. M., & Nixon, W. B. (2008). Background screening myths. *Retail Merchandiser, 48*(4), 23–25.

Macan, T. (2009). The employment interview: A review of current studies and directions for future research. *Human Resource Management Review, 19,* 203–218.

Mooney, J. (2002). Pre-employment testing on the internet: Put candidates a click away and hire at modem speed. *Public Personnel Management, 31*(1), 41–51.

Muller, M. (2009). *The manager's guide to HR: Hiring, firing, performance, evaluations, documentation, benefits and everything else you need to know.* New York, NY: American Management Association.

Noe, R. A., Hollenbeck, J. R., Gerhart, B., & Wright, P. M. (2007*) Fundamentals of human resource management.* (2nd ed.). New York, NY: McGraw-Hill Irwin.

Pynes, J. (2009). *Human resources management for public and nonprofit organizations.* (3rd ed). San Francisco, CA: Jossey-Bass.

Walker, D. (1998). *Selection interviewing: The essential guide to thinking and working smarter.* New York, NY: American Management Association.

Woska, W. J. (2007). Legal issues for HR professionals: Referencing checking/background investigations. *Journal of Public Personnel Management, 36*(1), 1–12.

Yusko, K., & Goldstein, H. (2007). Strategic staffing: Talent acquisition in the 21st century. In R. R. Sims (Ed.), *Human resource management: Contemporary issues, challenges and opportunities.* Charlotte, NC: Information Age Publishing.

MOTIVATION

There is no greater asset for a leisure service agency than a motivated workforce. David Stern, director of Guest Relations for the Seattle Sonics, stresses to his employees that those employees, not the customer, are NUMBER ONE. He realizes that a workforce composed of employees who value themselves, who feel capable and in control, will be "problem solvers," and thus will provide a positive experience for the customer (Fisher, 2004). How often have you encountered a poorly motivated employee at a site and thought to yourself, "I'm not coming back"? Or how often have you worked with someone who is not motivated? You and other employees most likely become frustrated, and maybe angry, as you take up the slack. What is it that makes some employees work and others not?

While much has been written about motivation, what do we really know about motivation in the workplace today? How do managers and supervisors influence employee motivation? What are the key principles for successful employee motivation? What might be the common mistakes for managers to make? These are the questions this chapter will address.

WHAT IS MOTIVATION?

Motivation is an internal state or condition which propels one into action. The term motivation comes from the Latin word 'movere,' which means to move. But just deciding to move or act is not all there is to motivation. There are three elements to motivation: effort, direction, and persistence. "Effort" refers to that which prompts or *initiates* behavior. For example, many individuals make the decision to get in shape, and often do so at the beginning of the year. "Direction" is that which focuses or *guides* the behavior. In the pursuit of getting in shape, there will be those who gather information on proper diet and exercise and plan a program. There will be others who decide to just join a gym, start working out and fail to learn how to work out or lift weights correctly. They are doing something,

but they are not moving in a direction to effectively reach their goal. "Persistence" is the ability to *sustain* or maintain a particular behavior. As we know, New Year's resolutions are often hard to keep. Even those who thoroughly researched proper diet and exercise are challenged with staying on the program.

Extrinsic and Intrinsic Rewards

A manager has two types of rewards in developing employee motivation: extrinsic and intrinsic. In this context, "extrinsic" refers to items external to the individual and in the workplace. These might be a paycheck, time off, or a public word of praise from the director. Not all employees value extrinsic rewards equally. For some, time off is most important and thus would be the prime motivator. For others, maybe young professionals still paying off school loans, a bonus or salary increase would be the greatest motivator.

"Intrinsic" factors are those found within the individual, such as *pride* in being able to mentor others, a feeling of *accomplishment* for completing a difficult assignment or *connectedness* in feeling part of a strong staff team. As is the case with extrinsic rewards, employees vary in terms of which intrinsic rewards serve as motivators. Not only do employees differ on the feelings which serve as intrinsic rewards (e.g., pride vs. accomplishment), they also differ on what gives them that feeling. One employee who values connectedness might get it from serving on work teams while another might get the feeling only from social, non-work related interactions with coworkers.

THEORIES OF MOTIVATION

Unfortunately there is no single perfect theory which explains motivation. Motivation is not easy to see or measure directly. Motivation is common to all humans but uniquely different for each. The challenge for managers is to create an environment which facilitates motivation for all employees. To be able to do this, managers need a broad understanding of motivation. Theories of motivation provide some insight for managers and supervisors to better understand the motivation of their employees.

Nine theories related to motivation are discussed in this chapter. The first two are known as *prescriptive* theories, as they tell the manager how to act. The next four are known as *content* theories because they discuss what is inside an individual that results in motivation. The final three theories are called *process* theories, as they look at how motivation works.

Prescriptive Theories

Scientific Management

There are two early ideas of management that have influenced the thinking of today's supervisors about motivation in the workplace. Fredrick Taylor, father of "scientific management," offered a rather mechanistic view of employee motivation (Sutherland & Canwell, 2004). He argued that if you train your employees to do the task efficiently and offer a wage incentive (more dollars for greater productivity), your employees will be motivated to perform. Of course, we now know that there are several flaws with this line of thinking. First, pay is not a motivator for everyone. As a college student with limited funds, you may question this, but studies consistently show pay is not listed by employees as their primary motivator at work (Society for Human Resources Management, 2009). Second, this theory ignores the impact of working in a group or with others. Employees are often influenced by fellow workers to "try harder" or "lighten up." Third, it is difficult to apply this theory in the service setting where the employee's work is an interaction, not a product. Taylor developed his theory with brick layers and could easily design an incentive program on the number of bricks and quality of installation. But, in leisure services the work of recreation therapists, outdoor leaders, or community directors is not as easily quantified.

And yet, some managers still cling to the belief that all they need to do to encourage productivity from their employees is offer more money.

Theory X and Theory Y

Another major idea of management is Douglas McGregor's Theory X and Theory Y approaches to managing or leading people (Sutherland and Canwell, 2004). McGregor says managers handle people based on their basic assumptions. A Theory X manager believes employees dislike work, must be coerced to work, and in fact, prefer to be treated this way. Theory Y managers, in contrast, believe that people like to work, have creativity and imagination, and they seek independence. McGregor's theory also has weaknesses. Primarily it looks at the manager rather than the employee and is rather a simplistic approach to the complexity of human nature. While Taylor and McGregor's theories are about management and not motivation per se, you will see reflections of these theories in today's workplace.

Content Theories

Hierarchy of Needs

Abraham Maslow's Hierarchy of Needs is the most well-known theory of motivation (Porter, Bigley, G., & Steers, 2003). It simply addresses the question: what is it that arouses an individual? Maslow says there are five basic needs and that they must be satisfied in order. That is, lower-level needs must be met before higher-level needs can be. Also, once a need is met, it no longer motivates us. The five needs, in ascending order of importance, are:

1. *Physiological needs.* These needs include food, water, and shelter. In the workplace these might include clean air, appropriate breaks, or comfortable air temperature.

2. *Safety needs.* These needs include a wanting to feel safe and free from anxiety. These could include freedom from threats from coworkers or clients, safe working conditions, or job security.

3. *Social needs.* These needs reflect our desire to belong to groups and be part of a social network. On the job, these could include getting to know coworkers or feeling part of a team.

4. *Esteem needs.* These needs relate to any feelings about ourselves such as self-confidence and adequacy. On the job these might be met with a promotion or staff award.

5. *Self-actualization needs.* The highest level of need is to strive to one's full potential as a human being. These may be seen in the desire for a challenging work assignment or the creation of a new service/program.

Maslow's theory, while widely known, has limitations. The basic premise of the theory is that all of us would be motivated by the same things and in the same order. Yet, think of the many victims of Hurricane Katrina or other national disasters, who display a greater need for family and friendships than a need for water or shelter. Or think of all your fellow classmates and the many differences in what motivates them. However, Maslow's hierarchy is still useful as a general model, despite the many exceptions to it that can always be identified.

Alderfer's ERG Theory

The ERG Theory, proposed by psychologist C. P. Alderfer, is a popular adaptation for the work setting of Maslow's Hierarchy Theory (Porter, et al., 2003). Rather than five levels, Alderfer collapsed the needs to three:

1. *Existence needs.* These needs are a combination of Maslow's physiological and safety needs.

2. *Relatedness needs.* These needs are the people-oriented or social needs from Maslow's hierarchy.

3. *Growth needs.* These relate to the growth of the human potential including Maslow's esteem and self-actualization needs.

While Maslow's theory sees a progression from "lower" level to "higher" level, Alderfer believes there is also a process called "frustration-regression." That is, if one is frustrated in meeting a higher-level need, a lower level will emerge as the key motivator. In recreation, leisure, and parks, an employee might strive to win the Creative Program Award (*growth need*) and yet realize his/her supervisor's lack of willingness to approve new ideas limits the chance of winning. And so, instead, the employee may find motivation from being part of an outstanding team (*relatedness need*) and seeing the agency receive recognition when it wins an Outstanding Agency Award. The ERG theory also differs from Maslow's theory in that Maslow sees only one need in existence at a time. Alderfer says that it is possible to have more than one need operational at a time.

Two Factor Theory

If someone told you that pay is not a motivator, what would you say? It is not surprising then that Frederick Herzberg's theory of job motivation is a most controversial theory of motivation (Basset-Jones & Lloyd, 2005). The theory came about after Herzberg asked employees two very simple questions: "Can you describe in detail when you felt exceptionally good about your job?" "Can you describe in detail when you felt exceptionally bad about your job?" In the answers, he discovered two sets of factors in the workplace which he called "motivators" and "hygiene factors."

Motivating factors are those elements unique to the job itself. They include opportunities for achievement, personal growth, recognition, the work itself, and advancement. Herzberg argues that it is these factors that motivate employees to *exceptional* performance.

In contrast, hygiene or maintenance factors are elements of the environment or situation. They include such factors as agency policies, salary, working conditions, fringe benefits, job security, and status. These factors are not related to the productivity of the employee, but rather are necessary components to keep employees from being *dissatisfied*. Employees expect the hygiene or maintenance factors to be at a certain level. Even if they are met, however, this only results in employees being satisfied, but not motivated. Herzberg contends only the "motivators" make a difference in employee motivation.

Cirque de Soleil, the highly popular show of circus acts and street entertainment, might be a prime example of this theory (Nohria, Groysberg & Lee, 2008). Its employees are allowed great input into the staging of performances and are allowed to move between shows to learn new skills. Even though the rehearsals and shows are physically grueling, the performers stay motivated and turnover is low. Or consider that a 2002 study of nonprofit organization employees found over 60% were motivated to take their job to "make a difference" and not by salary or benefits (Mann, 2006).

Learned Needs Theory

David McClelland identified three needs present in all individuals: achievement, power, and affiliation (Porter, et al., 2003). He argues that individuals acquire these needs over time and that they are influenced by the culture or society they experience, especially in the early years. A high need for *achievement* would include needs such as finding solutions, completing different tasks, receiving concrete feedback on performance, setting moderately difficult goals, and taking risks. An employee with a high need for achievement would be motivated by a difficult task, but given a mundane or easy task he or she may lose interest and perform below an acceptable level. Such an employee might excel when asked to design a section for the agency website but, when asked to submit just a program description for the brochure, procrastinate due to lack of motivation.

The need for *power* is characterized by a desire to control the environment and/or the behavior of others. Employees with a high need for power are likely to want to give directions to others and to desire supervisory roles. They tend, also, to be eager to share their ideas and to volunteer for projects or chair committees.

The need for *affiliation* reflects the employee's need to establish and maintain a social network. Employees with a high need for affiliation are interested in the feelings of coworkers and want approval and support from fellow employees and supervisors. These employees enjoy working as part of a team and are influenced by friendships. An employee with a high need for affiliation is not likely to be motivated to complete the task of inventory if asked to do so. However, if a fellow employee is also assigned, the task becomes more desirable.

McClelland's theory has no hierarchy. He believes that all three needs are present in employees and may compete with each other. In other words, more than one need may be operational at a time.

Process Theories

Expectancy Theory

Rather than look at what motivates us as the previous theories did, V. H. Vroom examines the process of how an employee is attracted to a task and how much energy the employee will put towards the task (Sutherland & Canwell, 2004). Vroom designed his theory with the idea that employee performance is the result of the employee's personality, knowledge, skills, and experiences. He says that motivation is dependent upon an individual's belief that certain outcomes will occur. But how does an employee come to that belief? There are three factors which interact to form the belief. *Expectancy* is the employee's perception that the effort he or she puts forth will lead to a certain level of performance. *Instrumentality* is the employee's perception that there is a connection between his/her performance and a desired outcome—such as a promotion, a bonus, or a different position. *Valence* is the extent to which the outcome is valued by the employee. Just how much does the employee want the promotion? For motivation to occur, all three factors (Expectancy, Instrumentality, and Valence) must be present and need to be high.

The Expectancy Theory breaks down employee motivation and illustrates the many different ways a manager might influence the motivation level of their employees. With the Expectancy Theory of motivation, a manager might use the following questions as a guide:

Expectancy

1. Did you clearly explain, and does this employee understand, the task they are to do?

2. Does this employee have the skills and confidence to complete the task successfully?

3. Does this employee need additional training?

Instrumentality

1. Is this employee aware that there will be a certain outcome (praise, time off, etc.) if the task is done successfully?

2. How confident are you that the promised outcome will occur?

3. Has this employee seen this outcome occur in similar situations before?

Valence

1. What rewards are important to this employee?

2. Is this employee motivated by public or private recognition?

3. Over time, has the importance of different rewards changed for this employee?

Equity Theory

Equity Theory (Adams's) is attractive to managers and supervisors for its simplicity (Ambrose and Kulick, 1999). Basically the theory states that people react to "fairness," especially in the workplace. Employees compare their level of effort and any outcomes received (bonuses, pat on the back, mention in the agency newsletter) with the work of fellow employees and their outcomes. If an employee perceives an inequity, he/she will act to reduce it. Suppose, for example, that several employees occasionally take long lunches and only one is approached by the manager. He or she might see this as unfair. As a result, the employee might drop their effort at work. On the other hand, if, at the time annual raises are given, an employee learns of someone receiving a large raise who they perceive works harder, they might be motivated to raise their performance level in the coming year if they wish to receive a larger raise.

This is no different than what happens in the classroom. If students feel they've been graded unfairly they might give up, saying "what's the use." However, if they feel the grading is fair, they may see a fellow student do well on a particular test, know they are just as capable as that student, and thus be motivated to study harder for the next test and improve their grade.

Reinforcement Theory

Reinforcement theory, most often associated with the work of B. F. Skinner, assumes that decisions about what to do are based for the most part on the consequences or results of past behavior (Porter, et al., 2003). For example, a pool director is looking for a substitute for an absentee lifeguard. Who he/she will call first is most likely going to be the employee who has said yes before. Reinforcement theory, however, is not based only on the positive experiences in one's past. There are four possible reinforcements to a behavior.

1. *Positive reinforcement.* A positive response is given to a particular behavior. In the case above, the supervisor had heard yes in the past, so the behavior was repeated.

2. *Punishment.* A punishment is given with the expectation that a certain behavior will be stopped. Issuing warnings and docking pay are often used to minimize tardy arrivals at work.

3. *Negative reinforcement.* This reinforcement involves avoiding negative consequences. In other words a behavior will be stopped because a negative stimulus will be removed. A maintenance employee will no longer disregard OSHA guidelines on wearing goggles to avoid being reprimanded by the supervisor.

4. *Extinction.* This reinforcement is when rewards are withheld to influence behavior. Supervisors are not eligible for conference support unless their payroll has been entered on time. It is important to note that while this strategy may result in the extinction of late payroll submissions, it may extinguish other positive behaviors. Will a supervisor just turn something else in late instead?

KEY PRINCIPLES

As managers or supervisors in recreation and sport, you need to remember that you can be either the most motivating or de-motivating factor for your employees. It is true that managers and supervisors greatly influence the actions of their employees. As you supervise staff, remember the following:

1. *Understand motivation.* Motivation comes from within an employee. A manager should not think of motivation as "a problem to be solved," but rather that "an employee needs to be understood." A supervisor's role is to create the environment for employee motivation to occur. As situations arise for you as a manager, think of how they fit into the theories/models presented in this chapter.

2. *Know your employees.* The strongest message in research on employee motivation is the importance of recognizing individual differences within your employees. Managers need to know what employees value in work and the stressors that might limit their performances. Not all employees value all elements of work the same. Look at the 13 items listed in Figure 7.1 on page 116. How would you respond? How do you think your fellow classmates would respond?

   Besides internal motivation, there are factors that limit or inhibit an employee's motivation both on and off the job. At work, an employee might be excited to work on a task until they discover they lack the proper software or that a co-worker is always late in providing needed information. A sport coordinator might want to start all events on time but is limited when an official is late. An employee with a sick child at home or an aging parent might be distracted at work.

3. *Develop a relationship.* It is not enough to just know your employees. As important is the employee's perception of their relationship with you, their supervisor. This is not to say that you must like all employees equally, but you do not want an employee to sense your dislike. Employees attribute 50–70% of the agency's emotional climate to their boss

Think in terms of your first professional job following graduation. Indicate the top 5 job factors for you. (1 = Most important).

It is important to me to have a job that:

____ Provides good career opportunities
____ Allows me to work for a supervisor I respect
____ Is valued by society
____ Allows enough leisure outside the job
____ Consists of interesting tasks
____ Provides high income
____ Allows me to work independently
____ Provides me with a feeling of contributing something useful
____ Allows me to work in a healthy work environment
____ Includes a high sense of responsibility
____ Includes a lot of direct contact with other people
____ Provides high job security
____ Allows me to be of help to others

Adapted from: Quaquebeke, N., Zenker, S., & Tilman, E. (2009).

Figure 7.1
Work Values Inventory

(Kroth, 2007). Employees need to believe that a supervisor is willing to listen and will respond to all fairly. Research has found that employees who feel positive toward their supervisors are more likely to be honest, contribute new ideas, and speak up. As a supervisor or manager, you might ask employees to anonymously complete a questionnaire such as the one in Figure 7.2 to be better understand their perceptions.

4. *Use positive communication.* People enjoy praise. Universal Studios has managers give out "Applause Notes" to staff who perform well. Universal also has a peer-to-peer appreciation program with "SAY-IT cards" (Someone Appreciated You). Some retail businesses have "Working Hard Cards" that are cut and printed to look like currency. When a supervisor sees an employee doing something very well, she/he immediately gives the employee the card which is worth 30 minutes of time off. Employees may collect up to 8 cards and cash them in for time off. There are rules on lead time for schedules to be adjusted and the cards have no monetary value.

As a manager, it is important that you use the right words in giving praise. Explain clearly why the praise is being given. "I think your special event at the high school was a great success because you had students from first-year students to seniors in attendance." "You are an exceptional employee because I saw that you stayed late on Friday to help Sandy with payroll."

5. *Adopt meaningful incentives.* Money is the most often considered incentive. In 2003, 77% of companies used merit pay (Pfeffer and Sutton, 2006). Yet there are many incentives beyond money. Some can be fairly simple. For example, to encourage lifeguards to be on time, use a sign-up sheet upon arrival for assignments. Or at staff meetings periodically, though not too often, share comments from patrons. You may want to consider going beyond the general reading of letters and e-mails. Why not consider a video of patron comments about their use of a facility or participation in a program? Let employees see and hear the benefits of their work.

There are many other low-cost incentives: a flexible schedule, customer choice awards, singing telegrams of praise, a parking space, recognition on the agency website, a tree planted in their honor, movie passes, take-out meal gift cards, ice cream breaks, car washes by supervisors, time off to volunteer, etc.

6. *Accept limitations.* An employee's performance is a function of both motivation and ability. An employee may be motivated, but lack ability. There may be times that tasks need to be assigned to other employees or an employee needs to be transferred to a new position. Factors external to the workplace present the greatest challenge for the manager as there is sometimes nothing you can do. While managers cannot step in and fix family problems or resolve health issues, managers can be creative in allowing time for counseling appointments or accepting conference call attendance at staff meetings.

Directions: Please circle or mark the correct answer for each question. Please respond according to how you normally feel about your manager. Complete anonymously and return to _____ no later than _____.

Awareness – Do you feel your manager notices or is interested in your work?

	Strongly Disagree	Disagree	Undecided	Agree	Strongly Agree
My manager seems to notice what I do.	1	2	3	4	5
My manager probably doesn't know my name.	1	2	3	4	5
I can get my manager's attention when I need to.	1	2	3	4	5
I feel like my manager ignores me.	1	2	3	4	5

Importance – Do you feel your manager seems to care about what you want, think, or do?

	Strongly Disagree	Disagree	Undecided	Agree	Strongly Agree
My manager doesn't care what happens to me.	1	2	3	4	5
My manager is proud when I succeed.	1	2	3	4	5
My manager will go out of his/her way to help me even if it is inconvenient.	1	2	3	4	5
My manager is willing to listen to me and help me when I have a problem.	1	2	3	4	5
My manager cares enough about me to give me helpful feedback if I need it.	1	2	3	4	5
My manager needs me.	1	2	3	4	5
My manager thinks I'm important enough to invest in me.	1	2	3	4	5
My manager listens to me.	1	2	3	4	5

Reliance – Do you feel your manager relies on you?

	Strongly Disagree	Disagree	Undecided	Agree	Strongly Agree
My manager asks my advice on important matters.	1	2	3	4	5
My manager turns to me when he/she needs help.	1	2	3	4	5
My manager trusts me with important information and tasks.	1	2	3	4	5
My manager believes he/she can count on me.	1	2	3	4	5
My manager thinks I make a valuable contribution to our program.	1	2	3	4	5

Source: Kroth, M. (2007). The Manager as Motivator. Westport, CT: Praeger. "Mattering: Empirical Validation of a Social-Psychological Concept." (2004). *Self & Identity, 3*(4): 339.

Figure 7.2
Do Your Employees Matter to You?

Common Mistakes

Just as there are things managers can do well in motivating employees, there are also things they can do poorly (Nicholson, 2003). Listed below are some of the common mistakes to avoid.

1. *Denial.* Too often managers choose to turn their heads when an employee lacks motivation or seems frustrated with their relationship with their boss. Ignoring the problem limits the effectiveness of your agency. If an employee appears to lack motivation, speak with the employee and see if you can facilitate a change in their level of motivation. Don't dismiss or ignore how an employee or your staff perceives you because you believe the perception is wrong. Their perception is what is real to them. You need to understand why that perception exists and act to change it, if possible.

2. *Over-praise.* It is not uncommon for managers to over-praise. In an effort to build "self-esteem" and "self-confidence" of employees, some managers praise lavishly. As a result, some employees are not able to see a distinction when praise is warranted. They expect praise for minimal performance. The phrases "I'm here, aren't I" and "I tried" are common. Some people think just "showing up" for work warrants recognition as well as "trying," regardless of the outcome of their efforts. Some would say an environment of "employee entitlement" exists in such settings. Praise should be given to employees when it is *deserved*, not because it is expected. If praise is given indiscriminately, it quickly loses its effectiveness as a motivator.

3. *Poor communication.* The communication mistakes that managers often make related to motivation are over-talking, repeating the same conversation, and holding back information. In discussions with employees about their motivation, managers need to listen. Employees can, and should, share the most. In other words, the employee should be doing most of the talking. Sometimes managers find themselves repeating the same conversation with an employee. When

this happens, a light should go on for the manager that the employee is not hearing the message. Managers may think they can "sell" or "persuade" an employee to see their side for a solution if they keep repeating it. However, what needs to happen in this situation is a whole new conversation. Finally, managers need to be willing to share information with their staff. This could be as simple as updating all employees on a new hire to giving periodic budget updates. Employees are motivated if they feel they are trusted and working as part of a team.

4. *Over-reliance on incentives.* Not all employee-performance problems can be solved by money. A 2005 study by the Society of Human Resource Managers found "neither money nor non–monetary rewards were effective in improvement of motivation in underperforming workers" (What are the best ways to motivate your top performers?, 2005). With a truly underperforming worker, it is best to see if internal factors can be identified by the employee rather than assuming external incentives always enhance performance. Employees who join an agency for "the money" will leave an agency for "the money" (Pfeffer & Sutton, 2006). Incentives are not a panacea for motivational issues. Interestingly, studies have shown that intrinsic interest in a task often drops when extrinsic rewards are offered (Mann, 2006).

Summary

1. A manager's responsibility is to facilitate a motivating work environment.

2. Motivation is an internal force unique to each employee.

3. Both intrinsic and extrinsic rewards serve as motivators, but primary motivators vary greatly among individuals and thus are hard to predict.

4. Theories related to motivation differ depending on whether they are prescriptive, content, or process theories.

5. Scientific Management encourages managers to motivate employees with pay-incentive plans.

6. McGregor's Theory X and Y holds that managers are influenced in their actions as a result of their basic beliefs about employees.

7. Maslow's Hierarchy of Needs states individuals are motivated in ascending order by physiological, safety, social, self-esteem, and self-actualization needs.

8. The ERG theory collapses Maslow's theory to three needs: existence, relatedness, and growth. The needs exist in no set order and more than one may be operating at a time.

9. The Two Factor Theory distinguishes between hygiene factors and motivators. The theory cautions managers to examine the difference between employee satisfaction and employee motivation.

10. The Learned Needs Theory stresses the importance of society and culture in influencing the development of three basic needs (achievement, power, and affiliation).

11. The Expectancy Theory is based on an individual's perception of outcomes. For example, employees must believe they are capable, see a connection between their actions and a possible reward, and value the reward.

12. Equity Theory argues that individuals are motivated by their perception of fairness.

13. Reinforcement Theory proposes that individual actions are based on reinforcement, both positive and negative.

14. Managers play a key role in employee motivation. There are things they can do to enhance employee motivation, as well things they can do which limit employee motivation.

DISCUSSION TOPICS

1. Define motivation, intrinsic rewards, and extrinsic rewards.

2. What is the difference between prescriptive, content, and process theories of motivation?

3. Why do you think Maslow's theory is so well-known? What do you think of the theory?

4. Which theory of motivation best explains your behavior today in class?

5. Think of people who have motivated you (teachers, coaches, parents, etc.)? What did they do to motivate you?

6. What some things that motivate you? What are some things you have seen motivate others? What do you think are things which motivate everyone?

7. If you think pay is a motivator, why do you think not all professional athletes become free agents?

8. Which theory of motivation seems most valid to you and why?

9. Do you think where you worked in recreation and sports would influence whether one theory of motivation is more applicable?

10. When were you most motivated on a job? When were you least? What role do think your supervisor played in either of those cases?

11. What factors do you think a manager or a supervisor can control that impact employee motivation?

12. Is there a difference in motivation between the "have to do" things versus "excited to do" things at work? Explain.

13. Which of the manager mistakes do you think you might be most likely to make?

REFERENCES

Ambrose, M. & Kulick C. (1999). Old friends, new faces: Motivation research in the 1990s. *Journal of Management, 25*(3), 231–292.

Basset-Jones, N., & Lloyd, G. (2005) Does Herzberg's motivation theory have staying power? *Journal of Management Development, 24*(10), 929–943.

Fisher, A. (2004). A happy staff equals happy customers. *Fortune, 150*(1), 52.

Kroth, M. (2007). *The Manager as Motivator*. Westport, CT: Praeger.

Mann, G. (2006) A motive to serve: Public service motivation in human resource management and the role of PSM in the nonprofit sector. *Public Personnel Management, 35*(1), 33–48.

Motivation Secrets. (2003). Motivation secrets of the 100 best employers. *HR Focus, 80*(10), 1–15.

Nicholson, N. (2003, January). How to motivate your problem people. *Harvard Business Review, 81*(1). 57–65.

Nohira, N., Groysberg, B., & Lee, L. (2008). Employee Motivation. *Harvard Business Review, 86*(7/8), 78–84.

Pfeffer, J., & Sutton, R. I. (2006). *Hard facts, dangerous half-truths, and total nonsense: Profiting from evidence-based management*. Boston, MA. Harvard Business School Press.

Porter, W., Bigley, G., & Steers, R. (2003). *Motivation and work behavior*. (7th ed). New York, NY: McGraw Hill.

Quaquebeke, N., Zenker, S., & Tilman, E. (2009). Find out how much it means to me! The importance of interpersonal respect in work values compared to perceived organizational practices. *Journal of Business Ethics. 89*, 423–431.

Society for Human Resource Management. (2009) *2009 Employee job satisfaction: Understanding the factors that make work gratifying*. Retrieved from http:// www.shrm.org/ research

Sutherland, J. & Caldwell, D. (2004). *Key concepts in human resource management*. New York, NY: Palgrave Macmillan.

What are the best ways to motivate your top performers? (2005). *HR Focus, 82*(1), 9.

Wiley, C. (1997). What motivates employees according to over 40 years of motivation surveys. *International Journal of Manpower, 18*(3), 263–280.

PERFORMANCE APPRAISAL

When asked to identify the highlights of their jobs, most supervisors would not likely list employee evaluations as one of their favorite responsibilities. Similarly, employees typically do not like the experience of having their job performance evaluated by their boss, colleagues, or anyone else. Despite these apprehensions toward evaluations, most organizations require their employees to undergo a performance evaluation at least once a year, and, they task their supervisors with the responsibilities of rating their subordinates' performance and conducting feedback sessions on a regular basis. Regardless of the contention, evaluating job performance is considered by management to be one of the most important aspects of supervising recreation and leisure services employees. Without an effective performance appraisal system, management decisions regarding promotions, pay increases, terminations, and employee motivation and development will most likely be questioned and quite possibly challenged by affected employees.

In this chapter we will present valuable information that recreation, park, and leisure services professionals need to know about understanding performance appraisal systems. We begin by introducing the nature of performance appraisal systems and discussing why it is important for professionals to have a working knowledge of the process of assessing performance. Considerable attention is given to the criteria and methods for measuring performance and the various sources of information that organizations use to collect performance data. To complete the chapter we present guidelines for conducting appraisal interviews and giving appraisal feedback.

NATURE OF PERFORMANCE APPRAISAL SYSTEMS

In an employment context, the *performance appraisal* is an evaluation of an employee's on-the-job behaviors and skills. Management uses a performance appraisal

as a tool to inform an employee of the changes that are needed to lead to his or her higher job performance. Organizations are quite diverse with regard to their approach in planning and conducting employee performance appraisals. Some organizations have an informal, casual approach to performance appraisal, while others have a formal, structured system of appraisal. As an example, many private, not-for-profit organizations that have a small operation and employ only a few employees may conduct performance appraisals infrequently and may not have a formal appraisal system at all. If appraisals are given to employees working for these small companies, they may be handled casually whereby supervisors provide performance feedback as incidents, both good and bad, during the year. Most large organizations—and certainly local, state, and federal governments—take a much more formal approach to appraising employee performance. Typically, these organizations have a structured and systematic appraisal process that is conducted at least once a year, and some require formal evaluation to occur biannually or quarterly.

Regardless of whether organizations are public or private, whether they employ a large number of full-time and seasonal individuals or just a few, they should develop and implement a performance appraisal system. Professionals working in the field of recreation, parks, and leisure services should understand the characteristics and purposes of a performance appraisal system, and appreciate why employees, supervisors, and upper-level administrators benefit from studying the intricate details of an organization's performance appraisal process.

CHARACTERISTICS OF PERFORMANCE APPRAISAL SYSTEMS

There are three characteristics common to effective performance appraisal systems.

1. *Performance appraisal systems are formal and structured.* Having a formal, structured appraisal process means that an organization has a defined way of evaluating performance and providing evaluative feedback to their employees within a predetermined review period. In a formal, structured system, employees know why they are evaluated, what will be evaluated, how they will be evaluated, who will be conducting the evaluation, and how often the evaluation will take place. In essence, assessing performance is serious business, not just a single activity that is done by supervisors on a whim without reason. Organizations, including small and mid-sized operations that have traditionally relied on an informal, unstructured approach to performance appraisal face a challenge in creating a formal framework and training their supervisors to provide performance feedback in such a way that employees can improve their work performance.

2. *Performance appraisal systems focus on job-related performance.* A valid appraisal system evaluates the employee's *performance*, not the employee. As such, the performance appraisal is based on a thorough analysis of a person's job wherein management identifies the job traits, job skills, and job behaviors of each position. Performance appraisals are not biased against personal factors such as an employee's age, sex or sexual preference, attractiveness or personality, race or ethnic background, religion, political orientation, or any other illegal discriminating factor.

3. *Performance appraisals are conducted by supervisors and managers who have requisite knowledge and skills for evaluation practices.* Competent and well-trained supervisors are essential to an effective performance management system. Organizations are responsible for providing ongoing training and support for their managers who have responsibilities for all aspects of performance appraisal, including assessing performance, giving feedback, conducting an appraisal

interview, setting goals, and resolving performance problems. Without credible supervisors, employees lose confidence in a performance appraisal system. Roberts (2003) states that appraising employee performance tests the skills of supervisors, and if this function is handled poorly, the benefits of appraisal can be lost and employee motivation can be reduced.

Purpose of Performance Appraisals

Organizations use performance appraisals as a means to accomplish three important objectives. First, supervisors evaluate an employee's job performance to determine the extent to which he or she is performing the position's assigned duties and responsibilities, and to provide feedback to guide an employee toward improved performance. It is unrealistic to assume that employees will know every aspect of their job duties and responsibilities—and also perform according to management's expectations when they are first hired. Through an effective performance appraisal system, employees gain an appreciation of job-related behaviors and skills that management believes are essential toward achieving organizational success.

A second important objective of evaluating performance is to give management opportunities to get to know their employees in ways that can bring mutually exclusive benefits to both employees and management. Management continually seeks talented and highly motivated individuals who can bring recognition to the organization and have potential for promotion. Similarly, employees are searching for ways to better utilize their talents, improve their chances for promotion, and increase their compensation. Through an ongoing evaluative process which has a constructive feedback technique, supervisors gain an appreciation of the skills, abilities, and ambitions of their employees, and help develop their employees' potential through coaching, identifying training and development needs, and providing rewards and recognition for distinguished performance. Employees can take advantage of the evaluative feedback to further develop their strengths, address and hopefully resolve weak performance areas, and gain higher-level skills that are crucial for a future promotion. When it works well, an employee appraisal system provides a win-win experience for both management and employees.

The third objective for conducting performance appraisal is for management to use the evaluative information generated through the performance appraisal process to document decisions in numerous areas of human resources management. The results of a performance appraisal are customarily used by managers to determine whether a person receives a salary increase and how much, and whether a person has the talent to advance to a higher-level position. Managers may also use appraisal data to make decisions related to discipline, layoffs, terminations, and changing an employee from probationary to regular status. It should be understood clearly that performance appraisal does not exist in isolation from other important management functions.

IMPORTANCE OF STUDYING PERFORMANCE APPRAISALS

It is essential for recreation and leisure services employees to have fundamental knowledge of performance appraisal systems regardless of where their position is located on the organizational hierarchy. Understanding performance appraisals enables individuals to perform at a higher level whether they are employees, supervisors, or upper-level administrators.

Although it is important for employees to know about an organization's performance appraisal system, most new employees are too busy with their job responsibilities to seriously examine the finer details of the performance system until after their first formal appraisal. However, having knowledge about the various aspects of the appraisal, such as the criteria for measuring performance, the methods of evaluation, and the sources for obtaining appraisal information, enables an employee to become an active contributor to the formal review session. Rather than sitting passively and receiving evaluative feedback from an immediate supervisor, informed employees take the opportunity to participate in the appraisal process, ask questions, and seek advice that may be critical to improved performance and advancement.

Recreation and leisure services professionals serving in positions that carry supervisory responsibility and that require them to conduct performance evaluations also benefit from studying the organization's appraisal process. Usually, supervisors are trained informally on how to conduct these evaluations; that is, they may receive brief instructions from their immediate supervisor or from someone from Human Resources, the forms they are to use, and the timetable for conducting the evaluation. Supervisors who take the initiative to learn more about performance appraisals including various methods for assessing performance, providing feedback, and techniques for resolving performance issues of problem employees, are much more likely to acquire skills that enable them to be more effective in coaching and mentoring employees toward a higher level of performance.

Understanding performance evaluation is also important for professionals in upper-management positions who are responsible for developing and designing a performance appraisal system. This is especially true of professionals who own or manage a private organization offering recreation services, or for professionals who direct an independent public agency. Although in some cases these top administrators have the assistance of outside consultants, or can request assistance from representatives in the Human Resources office, they must understand performance appraisal in great depth.

We feel that it is essential for recreation, parks, and leisure services personnel in management to have a basic knowledge of performance appraisal and evaluation. Not only will this enable them to benefit personally as a recipient of an appraisal, but also will allow them to engage as an informed participant in evaluating others, or in designing and implementing an appraisal system.

In developing a solid performance appraisal system, one of the challenges organizations face is determining the criteria for measuring an individual's job success. The next section examines the type of criteria used in performance measures and the numerous problems that exist with each.

CRITERIA FOR MEASURING PERFORMANCE

The criteria used by organizations to appraise employee performance are based on the duties, responsibilities, and tasks that are assigned to an individual. Typically, organizations develop job descriptions that serve as a concise delineation of each position, including the essential job duties and responsibilities, the standards required to perform the job functions, and the performance indicators. Management develops the criteria for performance appraisals based on the job-relevant information contained in the job descriptions. For example, an essential job duty and responsibility of an events manager is to plan, organize, and evaluate special events and festivals, and to oversee the operation and success of all events. The goal of the performance appraisal then is to measure the degree to which an employee is performing effectively the essential job functions for which they are responsible. In other words, the question answered by a performance appraisal for an event manager is: how effective is the individual in planning, organizing, and evaluating events and festivals?

For a performance appraisal system to function effectively, the appraiser and appraisee must mutually review and agree upon the job functions and/or job description assigned to the employee. If appraisal criteria are developed around specific job duties and responsibilities that are not clearly known or understood, employees will more than likely perceive the evaluation criteria as unfair and inaccurate. Quarles (1994) states that inequity or unfairness in the evaluation criteria used in the promotion and reward system leads to dissatisfaction with those criteria and may contribute to such outcomes as reduced commitment, job dissatisfaction, and the desire to resign.

Criteria are the standards on which decisions or judgments about an employee's performance are made. Customarily, three types of criteria are used to measure performance: 1) personality traits, 2) job behaviors and work characteristics, and 3) goals and objectives.

Personality traits

Organizations have used personality traits as criteria for performance appraisals for many years. Traits such as conscientiousness, optimism, enthusiasm, cooperativeness, and getting along with others are popular attributes that organizations adopt as criteria to evaluate recreation, parks, and leisure services employees. Personality traits are important because they influence behavior associated with an employee's performance. Mount, Barrick, Scullen, and Rounds (2005) state that personality traits influence choices that individuals make, such as which job tasks to engage in, how much effort to put forth in those tasks, and how long to remain engaged with those tasks. To evaluate personality traits as they apply to an employee's job performance, a supervisor assesses the employee's efforts and determines the extent to which the employee demonstrates a given trait.

Although personality traits are easily understood by employees and supervisors and can be evaluated with little effort and time, they have several serious weaknesses as they apply to evaluating a person's job performance. First, personality traits are ambiguous and the vague nature of these terms makes the appraisal process highly subjective. For example, several different supervisors might have several different interpretations of the personality trait "getting along well with others." Supervisors who are outgoing and gregarious may like employees who easily initiate conversations with a lot of different people, easily respond when other people initiate conversations, and seek out advice or opinions from others. Extroverts may not appreciate as much, or rate exceptionally high the performance of an employee who is quiet, low-key, and has little to say.

Second, another weakness of using personality traits for an appraisal system is that they may not necessarily be relevant to successful job performance. It is quite possible that two different employees with completely different personalities can perform the same assigned tasks equally well. The introverted employee described above who may lack exuberance may be just as effective, and sometimes more so, than an employee who is described as sociable, active, and energetic.

The third drawback of using personality traits in a performance appraisal system is that supervisors, acting in the capacity of an appraiser, are put in the difficult position of making judgments of an employee's social reputation, and why the employee behaves in a characteristic way. It is important for supervisors to remember that there are many individual differences, and other external conditions that may impact the relationship between a person's personality and his or her job performance.

Although personality traits may have serious weaknesses when used as a basis for performance appraisals, this does not mean that organizations have discontinued their use. Some professionals believe that personality traits are valid criteria for certain positions, such as camp counselors, lifeguards, coaches, concession-stand workers, and wilderness trip leaders. To avoid a legal challenge, however, organizations that use personality traits for evaluative criteria should 1) demonstrate that the traits are clearly job related, 2) define and explain traits related to specific job functions so that vague and subjective interpretation are minimized, and 3) require appraisal training of supervisors on evaluating personality traits as they relate to specific job functions and giving evaluative feedback to employees. These requirements, however, are difficult to accomplish. In our opinion, the problems associated with the use of personality traits far exceed the benefits, and organizations should seek other evaluative criteria for appraising performance.

Job Behaviors and Work Characteristics

For appraisal purposes, many organizations choose job behaviors and work characteristics for evaluative criteria. Job behaviors such as job knowledge, job skills, quality of work, quantity of work, attendance, punctuality, relationship with customers, and written and oral communication are commonly found on performance appraisals. Some organizations cluster the behavior and work characteristics into a small set of key performance dimensions. As shown in Figure 8.1, Camp Ridgecrest for Boys uses several job dimensions (work habits, job performance, relationship to campers) to cluster the job behaviors expected of summer camp counselors.

Similar to the weaknesses of using personality traits to measure a person's performance, job behaviors and work characteristics can also pose a problem because they can be vague and open to several possible meanings or interpretations. Two supervisors, for example, may have totally different perceptions of the meaning of "quality of work" and "quantity of work" when assessing performance. Without clear criteria, supervisors and employees may perceive the appraisal process as arbitrary.

The advantage that job behaviors and work characteristics have over personality traits is that they focus on the essential job functions that employees perform. If organizations choose to use job behaviors, management should write the evaluative criteria in a way that communicates a specific meaning for a specific job function. For example, if the intent is to evaluate employees' interactions with customers, then specific criteria should be written, such as "employee quickly and completely provides customers with assistance and information; answers all customers' questions knowledgeably; and never avoids, ignores,

or fails to respond to customers' requests for assistance." It is much easier to develop specific criteria for lower-level jobs (e.g., camp counselor, lifeguard) than for highly complex jobs (e.g., director of recreation and parks, event supervisor, athletic director). Miller and Thornton (2006) state that lower-level jobs are more accurately assessed than higher-level ones, and Sturman, Cheramie, and Cashen (2005) add that objective measures of performance may not be very useful in highly complex jobs.

Organizations that adopt worker characteristics and job behaviors as criteria for assessing job performance should develop a training program for supervisors serving as appraisers. It is important for individuals involved in the appraisal process to understand the meaning of the criteria, provide accurate ratings, and give helpful appraisal feedback to their employees.

Goals and Objectives

Many organizations seek to appraise performance by examining the extent to which employees accomplish predetermined goals and objectives that are stated specifically for their position. The main purpose of incorporating goals and objectives into an appraisal system is to align employee performance with the overall goals of the organization. *Goals* are broad guidelines that correspond to desired outcomes that benefit the organization and provide overall direction to the employee in his or her job. *Objectives* are specific, measurable, and relate to a single key result to be accomplished.

Typically, supervisors work closely with each of their employees in setting performance goals and objectives at the beginning of the period of review. In developing objectives that add value to the organization, supervisors should help employees understand how their work aligns with the goals of the department, and how the department's goals relate to the overall success of the organization. Supervisors should also work cooperatively with employees in stating objectives that are specific and measurable. For example, measurable objectives for a facility manager may be to:

- Increase the amount of revenue from new sources by not less than 10%

- Return a net profit of not less than 15% of expenses

- Increase visitor satisfaction to 90% in the category of "very satisfied" on the visitor satisfaction comment cards

Work Habits
Attendance
Punctuality
Consistency of work habits
Personal appearance

Job Performance
Has knowledge of responsibilities
Performs assigned duties
Takes initiative in performing tasks
Maintains a clean/safe environment

Relationship to Campers
Works well with campers
Looks for opportunities to help campers
Puts campers' needs above their own

Figure 8.1
Job Dimensions of Camp Counselors

The goals and objectives are monitored by the employee and his or her supervisor throughout the review period, and modifications are ordinarily made if changes occur because of external circumstances that are beyond the employee's control. For example, a golf superintendent may not achieve his or her revenue objectives due to poor weather conditions, or major renovations that were needed for several fairways, the practice facilities, and the club house.

During the formal appraisal interview, supervisors meet with each of their employees to determine the extent to which an individual actually achieved the pre-set objectives. It is also important for appraisers to discuss the means by which employees reached their objectives. For the next assessment period, new goals and objectives are negotiated, along with the means for achieving those objectives.

The primary advantage of establishing goals and stating specific, measurable objectives is to influence job behavior in a way that produces results that benefit the organization. By linking individual performance to departmental operations, employees are inextricably tied to the overall planning and mission of the organization. In this type of appraisal system, if employees fail to perform, the bottom-line results of the organization are impacted.

The weakness of this type of appraisal system is that it provides very little feedback to employees as to the effectiveness of their day-to-day behavior in achieving their goals. Performance objectives may pressure employees to achieve short-term results at any cost, while damaging an organization's long-term viability. For example, a state park manager may pursue corporate sponsorships as a strategy for increasing revenue in the park, but the neon signs and obtrusive sponsorships of cigarette or alcohol companies may compromise the integrity of the park setting and impact the visitors' experience. When using goals and objectives as criteria for measuring a person's job performance, it is essential for supervisors to place a heavy emphasis on the means as well as the ends for a successful performance.

METHODS OF APPRAISING PERFORMANCE

Another component of a performance appraisal system is the method that organizations adopt to evaluate employee performance. There are many different methods for evaluating performance and in this chapter we will review four individual appraisal methods and two multi-person comparative methods. We also provide a discussion of the advantages and disadvantages of using each of the appraisal methods.

Individual Evaluation Methods

There are four methods that recreation, parks, and leisure services organizations commonly use to evaluate the performance of an employee. Organizations rarely use just one of these methods, but rather integrate various elements for the purpose of collecting evaluative information about an employee's performance.

1. *Graphic rating scales.* Graphic ratings scales are one of the most popular methods for evaluating the performance of employees working in the recreation, parks, and leisure services field. A graphic rating scale consists of a list of criteria measures (e.g., personality traits, performance behaviors, and work characteristics) accompanied by a numerical rating scale. Typically, supervisors rate performance on a 1-to-5 or 1-to-7 Likert scale and provide a single score that reflects the direction and intensity of their evaluation. Figure 8.2 is an example of a graphic rating using a 5-point rating scale.

    There are several advantages of adopting graphic rating scales for appraising performance. First, they are not as time-consuming to develop as some of the other methods we describe in this

Rating Scale				
(5) Significantly exceeds expectations				
(4) Exceeds expectations				
(3) Meets expectations				
(2) Approaches expectations				
(1) Fails to meet expectations				

Performance Behavior	Supervisor's Rating				
	1	2	3	4	5
Consistent and dependable in attendance					
Consistent and dependable in punctuality					
Produces high quality work					
Strives to exceed expectations of all customer groups					
Takes initiative in performing tasks					

Figure 8.2
Graphic Rating Scale

section. Second, organizations prefer graphic rating scales over other appraisal methods because they are easily understood and can be easily administered by the supervisors. The major drawback of using graphic rating scales is identifying a wide variety of valid job behaviors, work characteristics, and personality traits that are specific for an employee's position. Also, if job behaviors and personality traits are not job-relevant or are written in vague terms, they may be interpreted differently by different supervisors. To counter this problem, organizations may provide a comment section under each trait or characteristic listed on the appraisal form that allows a supervisor to elaborate on the details of an employee's performance. On some graphic rating scales, supervisors are required to enter comments on low performance ratings. For example, on a 5-point scale (where 5 is the highest rating), a performance rating of 1 or 2 would require the supervisor to enter a comment to explain the reason for the low rating.

2. *Critical incidents.* The critical-incidents method of appraisal involves identifying and describing specific behaviors of the employee, both positive and negative, that are considered critical to the operation of the organization. This method does not require the supervisor to rate an employee's performance, but rather to describe specific job behaviors and work characteristics that occur when the employee does something really well or when an employee performs in a way that does not meet the organization's standards. Critical incidents, both positive and negative, are recorded by a supervisor as they occur throughout each review period.

The advantage of using this method is that employees are given specific evidence of actions and behaviors that are meeting (or not meeting) the organization's performance standards. Having detailed and specific feedback throughout a review period is very useful in helping employees improve their future performance. Some organizations train employees to keep their own record of critical incidents throughout a review period. This is particularly helpful because it is difficult for most employees to recall performance highlights that occurred several weeks or months prior to their formal review. An employee's incident report is also helpful to supervisors who may need additional evidence in making a fair and accurate appraisal.

Critical incidents may appear to be an ideal method for evaluating employees, but they also have drawbacks. To be effective in appraising performance, supervisors must have good writing skills, and they must be diligent in recording critical incidents throughout the year. If they procrastinate and wait until a couple of weeks before the formal appraisal to recall incidents that occurred months prior, the appraisal will lose detail and accuracy. Also, an appraiser with poor writing skills may not accurately depict actions or behavior that occurred. One of the techniques that many organizations use to negate the problems of this appraisal method is to use incident reporting as an element of one of the other appraisal methods. For example, organizations may adopt graphic rating scales and use critical incidents as a way to provide greater detail on the specific job behaviors or personality traits that are rated.

3. *Essay evaluation.* An essay evaluation requires an appraiser to document in writing the strengths, weaknesses, and characteristics of an employee's performance as they relate to the person's job duties and responsibilities. Since the essay evaluation lacks a standardized format, much flexibility is given to supervisors in evaluating an employee's performance. Supervisors have the freedom to focus on issues or attributes that they believe are most appropriate for a particular employee. The primary advantage of using an essay appraisal is that evaluators have an excellent opportunity to provide rich detail about an employee's job performance. Recording the unique characteristics of an employee's performance can be very useful in helping an employee develop his

or her potential in the job. Supervisors may also communicate specific actions that employees can take to remedy any identified problem areas or deficiencies.

Although essay evaluations have a lot of potential, they also have major limitations. The biggest challenge for management in requiring essay evaluations is that supervisors must be competent in their written communication skills and be able to communicate clearly the evaluative feedback. If supervisors have poor writing skills, they may write a narrative about an employee's performance that may be misunderstood by the employee and that subsequently results in the employee's resentment toward the entire appraisal system as well as the supervisor. Organizations that use the essay format also come under fire because of the subjective nature of the process. Since there is no standardized format, supervisors may emphasize the job behaviors, traits, issues, or problems they believe are appropriate, and management may be faced with the challenge of having as many different evaluations as they have supervisors.

To minimize these limitations, essay evaluations are often combined with other appraisal methods. For example, organizations may use a graphic rating scale for evaluating job behaviors and work characteristics, and include an essay section that allows supervisors to write a narrative about an employee's strengths, weaknesses, and training needs. The intent of the essay is to provide specific feedback on worker characteristics or job behaviors so that employees can improve their overall performance for the next review period.

4. *Behaviorally anchored rating scale.* The behaviorally anchored rating scale, commonly referred to as BARS, is an appraisal method that combines the features of traditional rating scales and critical incidents. In essence, a BARS is a rating scale, but the scale points are anchored with critical incidents. Typically, a BARS (see Figure 8.3) consists of five to nine vertical scales, one for each dimension of actual job behaviors that

exemplify various levels of performance. The scale is anchored by the incidents judged by management to be critical to performance. Critical incidents occur when an employee's job performance results in noteworthy success or failure on some part of the job. Management predetermines the values assigned to each of the incidents according to their importance in job performance. In evaluating performance, supervisors are required to check which statements relate to an employee's performance.

To construct a BARS, management must identify examples (critical incidents) of effective and ineffective behavior related to each job dimension. This task is typically accomplished by involving individuals (supervisors, employees, customers) who have the most knowledge about the employee's job. The critical incidents are then rated on a Likert scale (e.g., 1-to-5 points; 1-to-7 points). Another option is to assign a weighted value to each critical incident depending on the importance of the job dimension to the organization.

There are many benefits of using BARS for performance appraisals. First, the specific job behaviors that are most critical to the job are evaluated by an appraiser. The critical incidents describing effective job behaviors enable supervisors to offer specific feedback so that employees can improve future job performance. The critical incidents also offer employees insight into management's expectations of performance. Employees are better able to set performance goals for themselves rather than totally relying on their immediate supervisor to provide guidance.

The major disadvantage of this appraisal system is that professional expertise is required to construct BARS for any given position. Organizations may need to consult with individuals in the professional field for help in identifying examples of effective and ineffective behavior for specific jobs, and converting the behaviors to performance dimensions. Obviously, the process of constructing a BARS appraisal can be

ELEMENTS OF PERFORMANCE	PERFORMANCE BENCHMARKS			SCORE
	(5)	(3)	(1)	
1. Knowledge of Job	Completely familiar with all policies, equipment, and procedures; competently communicates and performs proper actions as required; understands standards and expectations completely; stays abreast of changes and new developments.	Generally knowledgeable of most policies, equipment, and procedures; understands and uses new information as it becomes available; willing to spend time and effort to maintain current and thorough knowledge.	Possesses marginal or inadequate knowledge of policies, equipment, and procedures; unable to communicate and perform actions as required; does not ask questions or seek information to learn about unfamiliar job aspects.	___
2. Customer Service	Consistently demonstrates good judgment and strong rapport in dealing with customers; consistently handles adverse or pressure situations maturely; always follows-up with customer inquiries.	Responds to customers when asked but does not make special effort to help; provides adequate assistance and information or directs customers to a proven source when asked; generally responds to customers in need of assistance.	Deliberately avoids helping customers; unable to communicate adequate responses to customer requests; unfriendly or intolerant of public contacts; tends to behave abrasively toward customers.	___
3. Personal Appearance	Always meticulous in personal appearance; overall appearance reflects a professional image to the public and can be used as an example for others.	Well groomed; maintains proper and acceptable attire and grooming appropriate to job; personal appearance never detracts from the presentation of a professional image to the public.	Frequently presents a casual disregard for personal appearance; exhibits personal manners not conducive to desirable representation of the organization.	___
4. Relations with Coworkers and Supervisors	Works extremely well with coworkers and supervisors; maintains a friendly manner even when under severe pressure; respected by others; resolves conflicts congenially.	Exercises adequate interpersonal skills with most coworkers and supervisors; makes visible effort to get along with all coworkers and supervisors; never initiates conflicts or controversy.	Exhibits an unfriendly or cynical attitude toward coworkers and supervisors; fails to be a team player; makes little effort to get along with others; does not attempt to resolve conflicts.	___
5. Productivity	Significantly exceeds expectations for quality and quantity of work; produces an exceptional level of work output that is consistently well above the average with necessary promptness, accuracy and attention to detail.	Work output is satisfactory; meets standards with only occasional work to be redone; is dependable to fulfill responsibilities and commitments.	Very slow worker; frequently exceeds the expected time frame to complete tasks; only occasionally achieves rate of production which is considered average; work must be checked constantly and often redone.	___
6. Dependability	Tasks are completed in a thorough and conscientious manner; work expectations exceed requirements and accepted standards.	Generally performs assignments in a competent and complete manner adhering to accepted standards; tasks rarely require revision and are usually completed in a timely manner.	Frequently fails to perform assignments in a thorough, timely, and competent manner; work often fails to meet accepted standards and requirements; puts personal interests ahead of job.	___
7. Flexibility/ Adaptability	Effectively juggles numerous priorities and tasks; readily accepts and supports change; consistently adapts well to changing and or difficult situations.	Can adapt to change when reassigned to nonscheduled duty; learns what is necessary to get the job done.	Looks for reasons why assignments cannot be accomplished; refuses to re-prioritize; does not willingly help others when change occurs; as change occurs, asks "what's in it for me?"	___

Summary Score Rating:

___	Outstanding	(4.5 - 5.0)
___	Superior	(4.0 - 4.49)
___	Satisfactory	(3.0 - 3.99)
___	Marginal	(2.0 - 2.99)
___	Unsatisfactory	(1.0 - 1.99)

Total of All Points ___

Divide by 10

Overall Performance Rating ___

Figure 8.3

Example of Behaviorally Anchored Rating Scale for Seasonal or Part-Time Staff Evaluation very time-consuming. Another drawback of this type of appraisal is that some jobs lend themselves well to BARS scaling while others do not. Developing critical incidents for lower-level positions that have narrowly defined job duties and responsibilities (lifeguard, camp counselor, concession worker) may be less complicated than identifying and weighing the value of all of the incidents that are critical to performance in higher-level positions with complex job dimensions (recreation director, event supervisor). Another limitation of BARS is that appraisals are based on observations of conduct, not on the results achieved. Employees may be doing things right according to the BARS rating, but yet not achieving the outcomes (e.g., increase revenue, decrease operational costs) desired by the organization. To counter the limitations of BARS, many organizations add other components to the appraisal system such as developing goals and objectives, and an action plan for each employee.

Multi-Person Comparative Methods

A major shortcoming of most appraisal systems is that supervisors have difficulty in making clear distinctions among high- and low-performing employees. It is customary for supervisors to inflate the ratings of low-performing employees in order to maintain the overall harmony of the employees in the work group and to avoid the conflict that often results when employees do not receive the ratings they expect. In fact research shows that leniency in performance ratings is the norm rather than the exception in most organizations (Longenecker, Jackson-Jaccoud, Sims, & Gioia, 1992). To address these and other shortcomings of an individual appraisal system, many organizations opt to use a multi-person comparative method which forces supervisors to distinguish clearly employees in terms of their performance. The two multi-person comparative methods that will be discussed in this section are ranking and paired comparison.

1. *Ranking.* In using the ranking method of performance appraisal, supervisors evaluate performance by comparing all employees in similar jobs to determine whether their performance is better than, equal to, or worse than their peers.

For example, if an athletic supervisor has six employees under her direction, the supervisor would rank each employee against all others and place them in order with the highest performing individual receiving the #1 ranking, the second best performer receiving #2 ranking, and so on.

2. *Paired comparison.* Paired comparison is another form of ranking employees that involves comparing the performance of every employee in a work group against everyone else, pair by pair. A tally is kept of the number of times an employee is ranked better or worse, respectively, than his or her coworkers. A technique for conducting a paired comparison is to use a round robin tournament bracket (see Figure 8.4). Each employee is assigned a letter (A, B, C and so on) and then placed in the bracket. The supervisor then makes paired comparisons and circles the letter of the highest-performing employee. This process continues until paired comparisons are made in all rounds. Next, the supervisor tallies the number of times an employee has outperformed a coworker. The tally developed is an index of the number of preferences compared to the number being evaluated. The person receiving the highest number of tallies is considered the highest performer, while the individual receiving the least number of tallies is considered the lowest performer.

The advantage of using multi-person comparison methods for appraisal is to determine the relative value that each employee brings to an organization. These techniques may be especially important to organizations that hire employees for jobs in sales and marketing where employees are expected to produce results. For example, a resort hotel in Orlando, Florida, may use ranking as part of its performance appraisal in the sales and marketing department to achieve an organizational goal of expanding its customer base to new markets in Europe and Asia. Multi-person comparison methods are also a good choice for organizations that need their supervisors to make

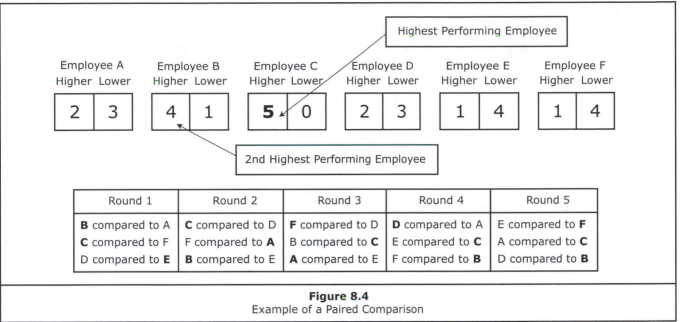

Figure 8.4
Example of a Paired Comparison

clear distinctions among employees by identifying the leaders and the laggards.

Multi-person comparison methods are not without serious limitations. First, if the rank ordering or paired comparisons are made public, supervisors can expect much dissension and angst among employees, especially for those employees performing at an acceptable level. Also, if performance criteria (job behaviors and work characteristics) are not well defined and yet used as the basis for the comparison, employees as well as supervisors may outright reject the appraisal system as neither fair nor valid.

Although ranking and paired comparisons have drawbacks, organizations may consider using them in a restricted (not-for-public scrutiny) fashion to attain certain important organizational objectives. Research informs us that ranking employee performance is more accurate than using rating scales; however, employee rankings should not be used when supervisors provide feedback to their employees (Miller & Thornton, 2006). By ranking employees, supervisors may gain valuable insight into the specific job behaviors and work characteristics that differentiate the top performers from the middle- and low-performers. This finer detail can then be used by supervisors during feedback sessions to help employees gain

an awareness and understanding of specific actions they need to take to improve their overall performance.

THE APPRAISAL FORM

Typically, organizations develop appraisal forms to monitor and evaluate the performance of their employees. As mentioned in the previous section, it is more common for organizations to develop an appraisal system that combines the elements of two or more appraisal methods.

To simplify the performance appraisal process, many organizations have switched from a paper review process to automated and online software programs in order to monitor and evaluate employee performance. The advantages of automated appraisals are that they are easy to access and take much less supervisory time to complete. Employees and supervisors are able to connect to the system year-round and track an employee's progress against his or her goals. Supervisors can add information at any time, including critical incidents. Another benefit of the automated software is that it may improve the quality of appraisals. Many software programs feature a "coaching" advisor that can be used to stimulate thinking and to guide supervisors in writing reviews. Also, many appraisal software programs feature a "legal" advisor that is helpful in flagging illegal or inappropriate words written by supervisors in the comment sections of the appraisal form.

Although employee evaluation software programs can be very helpful, they are not a substitute for the knowledge and experience that supervisors bring to the evaluative process. Supervisors are invaluable in critiquing performance and providing the type of feedback that helps employees improve their overall performance. An entire appraisal system could be doomed if supervisors fall into the trap of "accepting" the default statements without editing the content. Another drawback of an automated system is the training that must take place to teach managers how to use the online system and take full advantage of all the special functions.

Sources of Appraisal Information

Appraisal information for an employee's performance review can come from a variety of sources. In most cases, the employee's immediate supervisor is responsible for coordinating the performance review, but organizations may require their managers to obtain appraisal information from other individuals (peers, subordinates, customers) working closely with the employee. Also, many organizations incorporate self-appraisal as an integral part of their performance review system.

Supervisor's Appraisal

For most recreation, parks, and leisure services organizations, employees are formally evaluated by their immediate supervisor at least once a year, and sometimes more frequently. Immediate supervisors are considered a credible source of appraisal information since they are typically most knowledgeable of the employee's job duties and responsibilities, have the responsibility for assigning work, and most likely know the capabilities of their employees better than anyone else.

There are several good reasons that organizations may seek other sources of appraisal information besides the immediate supervisor's for appraisal purposes. For example, supervisors who are new to an organization or a department, who have not had sufficient time to get to know their employees, may not be comfortable in forming judgments about an employee's performance. In his research, Rothestein (1990) found that upper-level managers are very poor at appraising managers whom they have known and supervised for less than one year.

Another reason for involving appraisal input from appropriate individuals other than the supervisor is if employees do not work in close proximity to their supervisor. As an example, aquatic supervisors employed by municipal parks and recreation departments may have an office and spend a majority of their work day at an aquatic or beach complex, not at the department's main administrative office. Aquatic supervisors may feel uneasy about an appraisal system if 100% of the appraisal information is from their immediate supervisor, there is minimal opportunity for their supervisor to observe their performance, and there is no regular, ongoing feedback. Ilgen and Feldman (1983) found that the probability of appraisal decisions being based on an unrepresentative sample of behavior increases substantially when supervisors lack opportunities to observe their employees. It is extremely important for supervisors to develop an effective system to observe and document employee performance if their appraisal information is the sole basis of the review.

Self-Appraisal

An organization that incorporates self-appraisal as part of its performance appraisal system requires employees to self-evaluate their job performance prior to meeting with their supervisor in an appraisal interview. Supervisors should not assume they know everything there is to know about an employee. As Latham and Wexley (1981) inform us, supervisors rarely have all the relevant appraisal information about an employee. Self-appraisals have the benefit of getting employees to think about all of their work accomplishments, their strengths and weaknesses, the skills they have that might be underutilized, and any additional skills they need to acquire to function more productively. Roberts (2003) states that employees possess valid, unique, and relevant information and insight that is possibly unavailable and unobservable by the supervisor. When they are done well, self-appraisals are a very valuable tool in helping the immediate supervisor to determine the next stage of career growth for an employee.

There are different techniques that organizations use to assimilate self-appraisal into their performance appraisal system. Some organizations require each employee to rate his or her performance against the performance criteria stated on the formal performance appraisal form. A comparison of the employee's ratings vs. the supervisor's ratings for the performance criteria provides supervisors with valuable information that can shape the feedback given to an employee. Another popular technique is to require employees to assess their progress toward predetermined goals and objectives for a given review period. Again, the results are used by supervisors during the appraisal interview to give feedback in order to improve overall performance.

Having employees involved in self-evaluation for performance appraisals has many benefits. First, if employees trust the appraisal process and trust their supervisors, employees are more willing to share candid information about their performance strengths and weaknesses, as well as ways they can improve. Second, employees are more willing to monitor their performance and self-correct throughout a review period, instead of waiting to hear the supervisor's formal assessment. Engaging the employee in meaningful self-appraisal is a win-win for employees and their supervisors.

Peer Appraisal

A peer appraisal involves asking coworkers to provide appraisal information for one of their colleagues under review. To conduct a peer appraisal, organizations distribute an evaluation form that generally contains the same performance criteria found on self-appraisals or on the supervisor's appraisal form. For ease in administration, simple rating scales are commonly used to record the coworker's opinion of an employee's performance. A section for open-ended comments may also be included on the appraisal form to allow coworkers to write more specific detail about their observations. Typically, supervisors collect coworkers' evaluations in advance of the performance appraisal interview with the employee. In most cases the input from peer evaluations is not shared with the employee under review, but rather the supervisor reads through the information on the forms, looks for common threads and other evaluative points that were unknown, and integrates the information into the overall appraisal instrument. Then, at the appraisal meeting, the supervisor discusses the appraisal results and provides feedback to the employee in a confidential, non-threatening manner.

Incorporating peer feedback in an appraisal system has definite benefits. Research tells us that although supervisors have greater experience in appraising performance, the appraisal feedback from peers often has higher validity (Reilly & Chao, 1982). The explanation for this finding is that coworkers often have a greater variety of interactions with the employee which permits finer distinctions among the evaluation criteria. There is also value to peer appraisals when involving individuals in the process who are perceived as credible to the employee. London and Smither (1995) revealed that developmental feedback is not likely to be ignored if the sources of appraisal information includes supervisors and peers because these individuals have more power and status than the employee.

The opponents of this source of appraisal information have definite opinions about why they are reluctant to incorporate peer-appraisal information into formal performance reviews. First, most peers do not want the responsibility of giving appraisal feedback to a coworker. In the field of recreation, parks, and leisure services, it is important for members within a work group to get along well with each other to achieve their goals, and employees may feel uncomfortable in giving negative feedback to a coworker and creating unnecessary tension. Besides the fact that they are busy with their own job responsibilities, some employees may firmly believe that it is management's responsibility to appraise performance, not theirs. Some employees may have little or no interest in helping their peers succeed, especially in highly competitive environments. For example, if the result of an appraisal is used by management to determine the amount of salary increase a person receives, and the funding for salary increases is limited, employees may have little motivation in praising the performance of coworkers or giving feedback to help coworkers improve their performance.

Subordinate Appraisal

Involving employees in the appraisal of their immediate boss provides another source of information for performance appraisal systems. Generally, organizations distribute evaluation forms that contain certain job behaviors and work characteristics of the supervisors that are appropriate for employees to assess. Management may exclude subordinates from the appraisal process if they are in a probationary period and lack sufficient work experience under a particular supervisor. Also, subordinates involved in disciplinary action are excluded from the appraisal process.

Incorporating employee evaluative information in the appraisal of supervisors has several advantages. Evaluative feedback from subordinates offers a unique and relevant perspective of supervisors that may not be available to higher-level managers. The research findings of McEvoy and Beatty (1989) inform us that averaging subordinate ratings of a supervisor's performance is likely to be more reliable than ratings from any one single source. Subordinate appraisal may also be beneficial to higher-level managers in that the appraisal results may give them insight to a supervisor's interpersonal skills. This feedback can be used by management for training programs to improve a supervisor's skills such as listening to employees and responding appropriately, paying attention to the things that are most important to employees, acknowledging and rewarding employees, and developing a culture of friendly collegiality within the organization.

There are many opponents of subordinate appraisals and their concerns are important to know. Typically, subordinates are not in a position to understand the full responsibilities of managers, and are not privy to the important, day-to-day activities that occupy their time. Subordinates' interactions with their bosses may be limited, and when they have opportunities to meet, the discussion is usually focused on the needs of the subordinate. Another drawback of subordinate appraisal is that subordinates may have different motivations in appraising their immediate supervisor. Some subordinates may be truthful in their ratings, but then again, some may fear retaliation if they report negative findings. Some employees may give lenient ratings to gain favor of the supervisor, and yet others may be very strict in their ratings to communicate their resentment of their boss. Bernardine (1986) revealed that subordinate appraisal may not be effective if organizations fail to properly train subordinates in evaluating their managers. His research also tells us that subordinate appraisal often undermines the authority of managers and may hamper efforts in recruiting and retaining managers.

Combination of Appraisal Sources

A widely used method for evaluating the performance of managers and other professional employees involves obtaining feedback from a group of individuals (e.g., coworkers, bosses, and subordinates) who interact regularly with the person being evaluated and have an understanding of that person's job duties and responsibilities. By utilizing a combination of sources for obtaining appraisal feedback, supervisors can gain a more comprehensive understanding of a person's work performance from a variety of perspectives. In fact, Reilly and Chao (1982) found that the validity of peer evaluations is often higher than that obtained from supervisors. Their research attributes the higher validity to the greater variety of interactions with peers which permits finer distinctions to be made among the evaluation criteria. In more recent research, Seifert, Yukl, and McDonald (2003) found that feedback from a variety of sources is useful when it comes from both bosses and subordinates rather than from the subordinates alone.

A popular multi-rater appraisal program is called *360-degree feedback*. As the name implies, a 360-degree assessment examines a person's performance from every perspective. In conducting a 360-degree evaluation, an appraisal form that contains questions covering a specific set of behaviors or skills is distributed by the supervisor to various groups of informed people (coworkers, subordinates, and other managers). Raters are asked to evaluate an individual's performance and to provide written comments. The supervisors responsible for collecting the appraisal data and providing feedback to the employee review the appraisal information and incorporate it into the formal appraisal form. Supervisors must use good judgment when receiving negative feedback about an employee. They may rephrase responses to make them more appropriate, or they may discount disparaging comments from raters who are perceived as biased or uninformed. Confidentiality is an important aspect of 360-degree feedback for both employees and raters. Steps must be taken to ensure that information obtained in the appraisal is considered privileged, and under no circumstances publicly disclosed in a manner that would identify any rater.

As you can see, multiple sources of information are available to supervisors to fully and accurately assess the level of an individual's job performance. The challenge for supervisors is to examine carefully all of the data, decide what information should be communicated, and decide how it should be expressed to the employee on the appraisal form and in the appraisal interview.

THE APPRAISAL INTERVIEW AND GIVING FEEDBACK

A major component of a formal performance appraisal system is the *appraisal interview* in which a supervisor discusses an individual's job performance and provides specific feedback to each employee under his or her direction. As mentioned earlier in this chapter, most organizations require a formal performance appraisal including an appraisal interview at least once a year, but a few require them more frequently, usually on a semi-annually or quarterly basis.

Benefits of Appraisal Interviews

Both supervisors and employees can benefit from an effective appraisal interview. For supervisors, appraisal interviews provide an opportunity to:

1. Get to know the individual performer and learn more about the talent he or she brings to the organization

2. Communicate how well the individual is performing the assigned job duties and responsibilities compared to the performance standards for that position

3. Communicate the individual's performance strengths, any difficulties or weaknesses, and identify ways an individual can correct performance problems

4. Recognize and praise an individual's contributions to the organization

5. Discuss training and development ideas that could address the individual's performance deficiencies and/or help the person improve performance and advance to the next level

6. Negotiate goals and an action plan for the next review period

7. Listen to and exchange views and opinions about the job, the department, and the overall performance of the organization

Effective appraisal interviews also benefit employees in many ways. They provide an opportunity for employees to:

1. Gain their supervisor's perspective on how well they are performing the assigned job duties and responsibilities, and meeting management's expectations

2. Receive feedback regarding their strengths and weaknesses, and learn ways in which they can improve their job performance

3. Exchange opinions and views with their boss about work-related issues and concerns they have with their job, their peers, their subordinates, and other managers

4. Gain a better perspective of their job and how it fits in to the department and the entire organization

5. Get to know their immediate supervisor on a one-to-one basis and learn about his or her perceptions of their job performance, job priorities, and management style

6. Discuss education and training ideas to improve skills and abilities

7. Discuss career growth, direction, and advancement

To achieve all the potential benefits that an appraisal interview can provide, it is essential for supervisors to understand the process of planning and conducting an effective appraisal interview. In this section, we will present guidelines for preparing for the appraisal interview, conducting the appraisal interview, and following up on the results.

Preparing for the Appraisal Interview

Supervisors tend to underestimate the amount of time and effort it takes to prepare adequately for an effective appraisal interview, and this is especially true if they conduct performance reviews only once a year. It is not unusual for supervisors to wait until just days before a scheduled appraisal interview to begin thinking carefully about the work that needs to be completed to conduct an effective review session. When sufficient preparation time is not given prior to an appraisal interview, supervisors often do not invest the time needed to study all the relevant information that is available on an individual's performance to ensure an overall fair assessment. Also, without adequate time to prepare, supervisors may evaluate a person's performance based on incidents that they can remember—usually ones that have occurred most recently—and yet these events may not necessarily provide a comprehensive and fair assessment of the individual over the entire review period.

Preparation for appraisal interviews is essential if supervisors expect to sustain good working relationships with employees and have the outcomes of the appraisal interview shape their employees' future performance. In preparing for the interview, supervisors should consider the following guidelines:

1. *Review data from the previous review period.* In preparing for an appraisal interview, supervisors should review pertinent information from past evaluations to remind them of the employee's career goals, performance strengths, and any weaknesses and deficiencies. If there were any issues from an employee's previous performance appraisal that required follow-up, supervisors should evaluate the progress that has been made on each one.

2. *Review data for the current review period.* A good source of objective data for an appraisal interview is the critical incident notes, both positive and negative, that were kept throughout the review period. Besides the critical incidents, supervisors should also compare an individual's goal accomplishments against the expectations for the current review period. Any extenuating circumstances, such as a major injury or illness that may have impacted an employee's performance should be noted by the supervisor.

3. *Enter tentative comments on the formal performance appraisal form.* In preparing for an appraisal interview, supervisors draft the formal appraisal document, including any written feedback that will be communicated to the employee. Once the draft is complete, the supervisor should give the employee a copy of the document to review before the formal appraisal interview takes place.

4. *Anticipate emotional reactions.* Another critical step in preparing for an appraisal interview is to anticipate the emotional reactions of an individual to the written appraisal document, as well as the verbal feedback that will be communicated during the review session. Employees receiving negative feedback often react with shock and anger, especially if the feedback is unexpected and they feel offended. Employees may react to negative comments by wanting to argue points and defend their performance. In anticipating an employee's emotional reactions, a supervisor's challenge is to remember to stay calm, stay focused on the facts, and guide the employee toward understanding the changes that are needed to improve his or her performance. Supervisors should show empathy toward an individual but resist the temptation of being drawn into an argument.

5. *Schedule the interview.* In scheduling appointments, supervisors should give employees several days of advance notice prior to the appraisal interview. This strategy allows the employee an opportunity to reflect upon the supervisor's tentative appraisal and shape a response. When scheduling the interview, supervisors should be proactive in encouraging employees to participate fully in the appraisal interview by asking them to think about (1) how well they performed during the review period, (2) any issues that may have impacted their performance, (3) ways to improve performance, and (4) goals for the next review period. Frequently employees want to talk informally with their supervisor as soon as they receive the draft document; however, it is best for supervisors not to engage in this type of dialogue until the actual appraisal interview. In scheduling appraisal interviews, supervisors should allow adequate and uninterrupted time for a full discussion of the issues. Also, it is best to conduct performance appraisal reviews in a private office where the employees have the undivided attention of their supervisor.

Investing time in preparing for an appraisal interview sends a clear message to everyone that a supervisor values his or her employees enough to give them the care and attention they deserve. The next phase of the appraisal process is communicating performance feedback to employees through the appraisal interview.

Conducting the Appraisal Interview

Most supervisors and employees are anxious about meeting together for a face-to-face appraisal interview. This is true for inexperienced supervisors conducting their first formal appraisal, as well as for supervisors who have many years of appraisal experience. As for employees, poor performers may have a solid reason for their apprehension about a one-to-one appraisal interview with their boss, but overachievers also are often unsettled and uneasy about the appraisal session until it is finished. It is important for supervisors to understand the anxiety, apprehension, and sometimes fear that employees feel about an appraisal interview, and to find ways to focus on making the actual appraisal interview positive and productive. We suggest the following guidelines for conducting effective appraisal interviews:

1. *Establish ease and set the tone for the meeting.* Throughout an appraisal interview,

supervisors should make a special effort to develop a friendly, constructive, and supportive atmosphere to relieve tension and put the employee at ease. Supervisors typically initiate the discussion by clearly explaining the purpose of the interview and then, rather than rushing into any specifics, drawing the individual into a more general discussion of overall performance. Staying positive and encouraging employees to engage in a meaningful discussion about their work and career goals is an excellent way to set the tone for the meeting.

2. *Give effective appraisal feedback.* Providing effective feedback is vital in helping individuals improve their job performance. In the absence of feedback, poor performance may result because either the employees are not aware that they are failing to meet the organization's performance standards, or they may not possess the skills, abilities, and/or motivation to perform at the expected level. Employees need and want feedback that is timely, specific, and presented by a credible source.

Timely feedback. Supervisors should give ongoing feedback in "real" time as close as possible to when performance incidents occur during the review period. Supervisors who make a habit of providing meaningful feedback on an ongoing basis find that employees learn what is expected of them, and are more inclined to use the appraisal interview to discuss their strengths and successes, as well as their deficiencies and failures. If supervisors expect employees to use the feedback as a basis for making changes to improve their job performance, then supervisors they should not hold back their criticism until an appraisal interview. For example, it is absurd for a supervisor to wait until an appraisal interview to recognize and praise an employee for her superior performance in conducting a major fundraising event. Likewise, a supervisor would be remiss in not sharing constructive criticism with an individual who is talented but lazy and unwilling to carry his fair share of the workload. Successes

and failures need to be highlighted by the supervisor during an appraisal interview, but this occasion should not be first time that an employee receives the feedback. Withholding feedback not only impacts individual performers, but also may have a dramatic effect on the performance and morale of others within the work group. Employees need effective feedback, both positive and negative, on a timely, ongoing basis.

Specific feedback. Employees benefit when their supervisor's feedback is specific and behavioral in nature. Kopelman (1986) states that feedback needs to be specific and tell employees how far they are from a performance criterion. For example, if an organization sets a performance standard that, "employees shall demonstrate organizational citizenship behaviors," and an employee has gone out of his way to show that he is a team player, a supervisor would want to praise his performance by giving him specific feedback. This feedback could be as simple as saying: "Aaron, I appreciate the way you volunteered to help Miley meet a critical deadline when one of her key staff members was in the hospital." This type of feedback that is linked to a positive organizational outcome, and described in terms of the behavior that is desired, is much more effective than saying to Aaron: "you are a helpful person." In giving specific feedback, supervisors should also communicate the impact the employee's behavior has on others. If, for example, attendance has increased at a facility, or revenue has exceeded expectations as a result of an employee's actions, then the employee needs to hear specific feedback about the positive reviews the department has received. Likewise, if parents become irritated because a swim instructor has arrived late on several occasions to a children's swimming lesson class, then the negative publicity and its impact on the organization needs to be communicated to the instructor.

Present feedback from a credible source. Employees are much more likely to make changes to improve their job performance when feedback is presented by a credible source (Ilgen, Fisher, & Taylor, 1979). Most professional employees want to perform well in their jobs and will heed the advice of trusted and respected supervisors when they offer suggestions for improving performance. However, when supervisors lack credibility, employees often complain that feedback is inaccurate and unfair, and may state emphatically that the entire performance appraisal system is meaningless. The challenge for organizations is to educate supervisors about the importance of establishing credibility with their employees, and provide training and support in conducting effective appraisal interviews.

3. *Allow the employee to react to the feedback.* Supervisors should conduct appraisal interviews in ways that encourage employees to participate actively in the discussion, offer their views and opinions, and rebut, if necessary, any information that is perceived as inaccurate or biased. During the dialogue, supervisors must be ready to listen to and react to employee feedback. Supervisors do not necessarily need to agree with an employee's opinion, but at a minimum, they need to acknowledge the message the employee is communicating, as well as the feelings that are associated with it. When employees present information that sheds new light on a performance issue, a supervisor should not hesitate to amend the appraisal document if necessary, and thank the employee for correcting a misperception. It is important for employees to feel that an open and honest line of communication exists with their supervisor during an appraisal interview. When there is mutual respect between supervisors and employees, two-way feedback in an appraisal interview benefits both parties.

4. *Completing the appraisal interview.* Before ending the appraisal discussion, supervisors should make sure that an employee has a clear understanding of his or her overall effectiveness, and negotiate the goals and the action plan for the next review period. After the appraisal

discussion, the supervisor is responsible for updating and finalizing the performance appraisal form. Both the supervisor and the employee should sign the appraisal form. An employee's signature on the form does not mean that he or she agrees with the appraisal, but rather it acknowledges that the supervisor has shared the appraisal results with the employee. In most formal performance appraisal systems, employees are given the opportunity of providing a written response to support or rebut the supervisor's appraisal and attaching it to the final form. It is a standard operating procedure for organizations to provide an employee with a copy of the final appraisal form after each review.

After a performance appraisal interview, supervisors may feel a sense of relief to have that task completed. In reality, conducting the appraisal interview is just one step in the performance management cycle. The next important phase is ensuring accountability by following-up on results.

Following Up on Results

Supervisors are responsible for keeping employees accountable for results throughout a performance review period. On an ongoing basis, the supervisor should meet with each of his or her employees to update the action plan and document the progress on previously agreed upon goals and objectives. At times during the year, action plans and performance goals may be adjusted by the supervisor if extenuating circumstances beyond the control of the employee occur. By following up on results and promoting regular communication and feedback, supervisors have an easier time holding employees accountable for their actions.

The impact that a well-planned and well-executed performance appraisal system can have for both the employee and the company should not be overlooked. Supervisors should be diligent in maintaining accurate records of employee performance during a review period so as to provide employees with clear examples of how to improve their performance. When employees know specifically what actions were beneficial to an organization, and which actions were not desirable, there is a greater chance they will be able to modify their behavior to meet the organization's performance standards. Employees who can meet this standard are an asset for the company, but they can also themselves advance in their organization.

Summary

1. A performance appraisal is an evaluation of an employee's on-the-job behaviors and skills.

2. The purpose of conducting performance appraisals is to determine how well individual employees are performing their assigned duties and responsibilities and to provide specific feedback that guides employees toward improving their overall performance.

3. Performance appraisal systems are formal and structured so that employees know: how often evaluations will be conducted; what behaviors, skills, or traits will be evaluated; who will be involved in the evaluation; and what process will be used to conduct the evaluation.

4. The three criteria that are used to evaluate employee performance are: personality traits, job behaviors and work characteristics, and assigned goals and objectives.

5. Although personality traits are commonly used to evaluate employee performance, they have serious weaknesses and may not necessarily be relevant to assessing job performance.

6. Job behaviors and work characteristics focus on essential job functions that employees perform such as quantity and quality of work. As evaluative criteria, job behaviors and work characteristics work much better for lower-level than for highly complex jobs.

7. Goals and objectives are often used as a dimension of the performance appraisal process and are most effective if written in specific and measurable terms and agreed upon by both the employee and his or her supervisor. A major drawback of holding employees accountable to their goals and objectives is the fact that some employees may behave in ways that focus on short-term results that may damage the long-term viability of the organization.

8. There are several different methods for appraising employee performance and each has its advantages and disadvantages. Rather than relying on just one method in assessing employee performance, organizations are much more likely to integrate various elements from both individual evaluation methods (graphic rating scales, critical incidents, essay evaluation, and behaviorally anchored rating scales) and multi-person comparative methods (ranking and paired comparison).

9. Graphic rating scales are widely accepted as a way of assessing employee performance especially because they are easy to understand and use. The major shortcoming of graphic rating scales is identifying valid job characteristics, job behaviors, and personality traits for each unique job within the organization.

10. Critical incidents and essay evaluations require supervisors to document in writing specific evidence of actions and behaviors of the employee that are meeting the organization's standards. The advantage to both of these methods is that employees receive concrete feedback about their job performance. To achieve success with these methods, supervisors must have good writing skills and be diligent throughout the review period in recording incidents and writing a meaningful narrative.

11. Behaviorally anchored rating scales use critical incidents in describing and rating effective job behaviors. The advantage of using BARS is that critical job behaviors that are most critical to performance are evaluated. The major drawback to BARS is that professional expertise is required to construct a BARS for any given position in the organization.

12. Leniency is the norm rather than the exception when supervisors evaluate their employees using graphic ratings scales, BARS, critical incidents or narrative essays. As a way of addressing the leniency issue and making clear distinctions between high and low performing employees, organizations often require their supervisor to rank employees or conduct paired comparisons.

13. Automated software for conducting performance appraisals has its advantages in making appraisals easy for supervisors to access and complete, but they are no substitute for the knowledge and experience that supervisors bring to the evaluative process in critiquing performance and providing performance feedback.

14. An employee's immediate supervisor is the primary source of information for an employee's performance evaluation, but organizations may also require performance feedback from the employee's peers, subordinates, and/or customers.

15. Seeking sources of appraisal information from someone other than an employee's immediate supervisor is particularly important if a supervisor has been employed less than a year and has not had sufficient time to get to know their employees.

16. Self-appraisals require an employee to self-evaluate their own job performance. Employees have insight into their strengths and weaknesses that is valuable in helping an immediate supervisor to determine ways of helping them improve their job performance.

17. Peer feedback in an appraisal system is most beneficial to employees when individuals involved in the process are perceived as credible.

18. Subordinates bring unique and relevant performance feedback to a supervisor's evaluation even though they may not fully comprehend their boss's job duties and responsibilities. It is the responsibility of higher level managers to filter and then use subordinate feedback in ways that help supervisors improve their overall performance.

19. A 360-degree feedback system uses evaluative feedback from a variety of informed people (coworkers, subordinates, customers, other managers) to assess an employee's performance.

20. Supervisors conduct appraisal interviews to discuss an individual's job performance and provide specific feedback. Most organizations require an appraisal interview at least once a year, but the appraisals can occur more frequently (semi-annually or quarterly).

21. In preparing for an appraisal interview, supervisors are responsible for reviewing pertinent information from past and current review periods, drafting tentative comments on the formal appraisal document, and then scheduling the interview with the employee.

22. A critical step for supervisor in preparing for a one-on-one appraisal interview is anticipating the emotional reactions of each of their employees to the written appraisal document. The supervisor's challenge is to empathize with the employee but at the same time to stay focused on the changes that are needed to improve performance.

23. In conducting performance appraisal reviews, supervisors set the tone for the meeting by providing a supporting environment that motivates the employee to engage in a meaningful discussion about their strengths, weaknesses, and accomplishments.

24. During a performance appraisal review, supervisors are responsible for giving performance feedback to their employees that is factual, timely and specific. Throughout the review session, supervisors listen to the reactions and comments of their employees and should not hesitate in making changes to the appraisal document if new light is shed on a performance issue.

25. After the performance review has taken place, supervisors are responsible for keeping employees accountable to the action plan and documenting progress on previously agreed upon goals and objectives.

Discussion Topics

1. What are the characteristics of an effective performance appraisal system?

2. What are the different criteria used by instructors to evaluate student performance in college courses? What weight (points, percentages) are assigned to the criteria?

Do the criteria provide a fair and accurate assessment of student performance?

3. What type of criteria should be used to measure employee job performance? Should the same criteria be used of all employees? Should the criteria be weighted and if so, how?

4. What are some of the problems that occur when personality traits are used as a criterion for performance appraisals? In what type of jobs, if any, would personality traits be appropriate for evaluating job performance?

5. What are the benefits of using goals and objectives as a major component in evaluating an employee's job performance? What are the drawbacks?

6. Why should employees maintain a record of critical incidents that occur during an appraisal review period?

7. What type of jobs in the field of recreation, parks, and leisure services lend themselves well to BARS scaling? Why?

8. Why should managers use ranking or paired comparisons to evaluate job performance?

9. How important are self-appraisals as part of a performance appraisal system? What are the issues with self-appraisals from an employee's perspective? From the supervisor's perspective?

10. Who should be involved in evaluating the performance of an employee? What are the advantages and disadvantages of having individuals other than the employee's immediate supervisor give appraisal feedback?

11. What are some of the problems that might surface when subordinates are asked to provide appraisal feedback about their immediate boss?

12. Why is it important for supervisors to invest time in preparing for an appraisal interview? How far in advance of the actual date of the appraisal interview should a supervisor begin to prepare?

13. When providing appraisal feedback, why is it important that supervisors refer to specific behavior rather than make vague, general statements?

14. How should supervisors deal with employees during an appraisal interview when they disagree with the performance appraisal ratings and want to argue each point?

15. What options are available to an organization if an employee's annual performance appraisal is due, but his supervisor is new to the organization and has not had sufficient time to observe and evaluate his performance?

16. What options are available in conducting performance appraisals when a person who was just promoted to a supervisory position is responsible for conducting appraisals of employees who are experienced and have been employed for several years?

17. What actions should employees take if their supervisor refuses to meet with them to discuss the results of their performance appraisal?

18. What action should supervisors take to hold employees accountable for the predetermined goals and action plan?

REFERENCES

Ilgen, D., & Feldman, J. (1983). Performance appraisal: A process focus. In L. L. Cummings & B. M. Straw (Eds.), *Research in organizational behavior* (pp. 349–371). Greenwich, CT: JAI Press.

Ilgen, D., Fisher, C. D., & Taylor, S. (1979). Consequences of individual feedback on behavior in organizations. *Journal of Applied Psychology, 64,* 349–371.

Kopelman, R. E. (1986). Objective feedback. In E. A. Locke (Ed.), *Generalizing from laboratory to field settings* (pp. 119–145). Lexington, MA: D. C. Heath.

Latham, G. P., & Wexley, K. N. (1981). *Increasing productivity through performance appraisal.* Reading, MA: Addison-Wesley.

Longenecker, C. O., Jackson-Jaccoud, A., Sims, H. P., & Gioia, D. A. (1992). Quantitative and qualitative investigations of affect in executive judgment. *Applied Psychology: An International Review, 41,* 21–41.

Miller, C. E., & Thornton, C. L. (2006). How accurate are your performance appraisals? *Public Personnel Management, 35*(2), 153.

Mount, M. K., Barrick, M. R., Scullen, S. M., & Rounds, J. (2005). Higher order dimensions of the big five personality traits and big six vocational interest types. *Personnel Psychology, 58*(2), 447.

Quarles, R. (1994). An examination of promotion opportunities and evaluation criteria as mechanisms for affecting internal auditor commitment, job satisfaction, and turnover intentions. *Journal of Managerial Issues, 6*(2), 176.

Reilly, R. R., & Chao, G. R. (1982). Validity and fairness of some alternative employee selection procedures. *Personnel Psychology, 35*(1), 1–62.

Roberts, G. E. (2003). Employee performance appraisal system participation: A technique that works. *Public Personnel Management, 32*(1), 89.

Roberts, G. E. (1992). Linkages between performance appraisal system effectiveness and rater and ratee acceptance: Evidence from a survey of municipal personnel administrators. *Review of Public Personnel Administration, 12*, 19–41.

Rothstein, H. R. (1990). Inter-rater reliability of job performance ratings: Growth to asymptote level with increasing opportunity to observe. *Journal of Applied Psychology, 75*, 322–327.

Seifert, C. F., Yukl, G., & McDonald, R. A. (2003). Effects of multisource feedback and a feedback facilitator on the influence behavior of managers toward subordinates. *Journal of Applied Psychology, 88*(3), 561.

Sturman, M. C., Cheramie, R. A., & Cashen, L. H. (2005). The impact of job complexity and performance measurement on the temporal consistency, stability, and test-retest reliability of employee job performance ratings. *Journal of Applied Psychology, 90*, 269–283.

9

COMPENSATION

'Wages,' 'salaries,' and 'employee benefits' are terms that are used collectively to describe an organization's compensation program. In this text, *'compensation' is defined as all the monetary rewards, both direct and indirect, provided to employees*. Direct monetary rewards include wages and salaries but also other types of cash rewards such as performance-based wage increases (e.g., bonuses, merit pay), overtime pay, paid vacations and holidays, retirement pay, and paid sick leave. Indirect monetary rewards that organizations may make available to employees include health insurance and life insurance as well as other supplemental insurance programs such as dental, vision, and cancer insurance; a company-issued laptop computer, cell phone, and other wireless smart devices; a company vehicle to use during business hours; free or reduced charges for access to recreation areas, facilities and equipment; paid memberships to professional organizations; and paid expenses for conferences, certifications, training, and development.

Offering well-designed and competitive compensation packages have advantages for both organizations and their employees. For organizations, a compensation program is critical to their ability to attract, motivate, and retain quality employees. Without competitive salaries and a solid offering of employee benefits, organizations find it difficult to compete in today's marketplace for highly qualified job candidates. Organizations know that employees who are well-qualified often "shop" until they are offered a compensation package that not only meets their immediate needs but also has built-in incentives for retaining productive employees for many years.

Compensation packages are equally important to employees, regardless of their position or level of responsibility in an organization. Most employees depend on a compensation program to pay living expenses such as rent (or home mortgage), utilities, car loans and insurance, food, clothing, and to pay off student loans or credit card debt. Besides this, most individuals want a salary that gives them sufficient income to enjoy life (dine out, go to the movies or dancing, take a vacation) and contribute toward a savings account for them and their families.

In most cases, recreation, park, and leisure services managers are not responsible for designing compensation programs or determining the policies and practices for their operation. These decisions typically rest with top-level management and compensation specialists either employed or contracted by the organization's human resources office. However, managers are involved in making salary and wage decisions that impact their employees, such as determining starting salary or wage rates of those newly hired. They are also responsible for recommending salary increases for employees based on performance-based criteria established as part of an organization's performance appraisal system. In addition, recreation, park, and leisure service managers play a critical role in communicating compensation matters to potential and current employees. The more that managers understand the features of a compensation program, the better they are able to communicate the value of the package that otherwise may go unnoticed by employees and potential job candidates. For example, a manager may highlight an organization's tuition reimbursement program to a prospective employee who is interested in obtaining a master's degree or a specialized certification but cannot afford to pay the cost. A manager may show a breakdown of out-of-pocket expenses for tuition and books that the employee will save by taking advantage of the tuition reimbursement program.

Oftentimes recreation leisure service managers are not expected to be experts in designing compensation packages and understanding specific details of every employee benefit program. However, they will be most effective to an organization if they have a basic understanding of the primary aspects of compensation and are able to communicate the benefits to current and prospective employees.

In this chapter, the essential information for understanding compensation is presented. In the first section we discuss the major factors that affect a compensation system. In section two, we discuss designing a compensation system. Augmenting salaries and wages is discussed in section three and employee benefits are presented in section four. Major federal legislation impacting wages, salaries, and employee benefits are covered in the last section of this chapter.

Factors Impacting a Compensation System

Organizations often have less control over the wages, salaries, and employee benefits they pay than most people realize. Both labor unions and market forces influence how recreation and leisure service organizations can compensate their employees. A third factor, compensation philosophy, also influences wages and benefits, but it is one that organizations can control.

Labor Unions

Many recreation, parks, and leisure service organizations have all or some of their employees covered in a collective bargaining unit represented by a union or employee association. Employees covered by a labor contract will have the general level of their salaries and benefits negotiated by the union. For example, the base pay of all Recreation Specialists in a municipal parks and recreation department falls within a salary range with minimum annual earnings of $30,098 and maximum pay of $43,451. Although the pay range is established by negotiated contract, recreation and parks managers of the municipal department maintain the authority to hire new employees at a pay rate within the salary range and appraise employee performance on a regular basis, usually once or twice annually.

Union representatives typically push hard for reward systems that emphasize equality wherein all salary and wage increases are distributed equally among all workers. In a union environment, reward systems based on individual work performance are fiercely resisted by labor unions (Calo, 2006). An example of a reward system that is typically supported by union representatives is a step-increase program. Each job is assigned a pay category and each pay category is identified by a grade, say 1 through 15. Within each grade are 10 steps. Based on an individual's time in a particular grade, permanent employees are eligible to go up steps within their pay grade. After one year, an employee can move from Step 1 to Step 2, 3, and then to Step 4. A pay system may require two years of employment to step up from 4 to 5, 6, and 7. Generally, labor unions are not supportive of performance-based (merit) reward systems wherein salary and wage increases are determined on the quality and quantity of work performed by employees covered by the union contract and evaluated by their managers. Labor representatives claim that most performance appraisal systems are inadequate due to judgments made by managers that are subjective. A manager's bias and prejudice against an employee often leads to unfair discrimination in performance-based reward systems.

The general level of compensation that an organization provides its employees in a collective bargaining agreement depends largely on that organization's power relative to the union. For example, if management is not perceived as particularly powerful but the union is, then most likely the union will be successful in negotiating higher salaries and wages and benefits for its covered employees each time the union contract is renewed. At times, management may be forced to adjust salaries of employees not covered by the collective bargaining agreement, especially if the salaries of managers begin to lag behind those of the covered employees whom they supervise.

Market Forces

The economic law of supply and demand has a great deal to do with the compensation levels paid by recreation, park, and leisure service organizations. As it applies to the labor market, the law of supply and demand means that in any free market, the relationship between supply and demand impacts wages and jobs. A change in either the supply or the demand for workers disrupts the equilibrium in the market and usually leads to a change in wage levels and/or jobs. In the labor market of recreation, parks, and leisure services, the law of supply and demand predicts that if the supply of workers increases then wages for similar work can be expected to fall, and vice versa. For example, our field has an unusually large number of job opportunities for part-time, seasonal, and temporary workers, especially in the summer. If the supply of high school and college-aged workers available in a community for camp counselor positions is greater than the number of camp counselor jobs, then wages are kept low. In fact, most summer camps pay minimum wage or in some cases sub-minimum wage to youth workers employed as camp counselors or counselor trainees. On the other hand, if the demand for lifeguards and swimming instructors is high but the supply of certified lifeguards and water safety instructors is low, wages increase. Many local governments' recreation and park departments compete for the short supply of certified aquatic personnel in their communities and pay above minimum wage to attract these workers. In fact, some employers establish incentive programs to retain certified lifeguards and swim instructors, such as paying minimum wage to first-year guards and then increasing the wage rate for each year of experience.

Compared to the number of lower-level part-time and seasonal positions available, the Bureau of Labor Statistics (U. S. Department of Labor, 2008a) reports that administrative and management positions in the field of recreation, parks, and leisure services are in limited supply and wage rates of professional positions are kept low. According to the Bureau of Labor Statistics (BLS), the greatest opportunities for entry-level administrative and management positions such as recreation supervisors and park managers are for workers with a baccalaureate degree and good job experience in part-time and seasonal recreation and park jobs. The BLS Occupational Outlook in 2006 revealed that the greatest supply of recreation positions is within local government, with approximately 32% of Recreation Workers employed by local parks and recreation departments. Another 10% were employed in not-for-profit organizations such as YMCAs, Boys and Girls Clubs, and Boy and Girl Scouts. In 2006, approximately 70% of Recreational Therapists were employed in nursing and residential care facilities and hospitals (U.S. Department of Labor, 2008b).

Although numerous new jobs have opened up in the recreation, parks, and leisure services field over the last several decades, the supply of people wanting administrative and supervisory jobs is high relative to the demand. In other words, even though demand has been good, supply has been even greater. The oversupply of professional workers in recreation, parks, and leisure services positions has contributed to keep salaries relatively low. In 2006 the Bureau of Labor Statistics' Employment Outlook showed that the annual salaries for entry-level recreation positions are lower than those paid to entry-level workers in other fields. For example, in 2006 the median annual earnings of recreational therapists was $34,990. According to the U.S. Department of Labor (2009), this figure is lower than median salaries for social workers employed in local government ($43,500), public school teachers ($43,580 to $48,690), and employment, recruitment and placement specialists in local government ($40,660).

There are several reasons that may explain why the supply of professional workers in the field of recreation, parks, and leisure services is greater than the demand. The leisure services field tends to provide its professionals with numerous non-compensation related rewards, both intrinsic and extrinsic, that are attractive to many people. Intrinsic factors refer to the actual job tasks performed by workers; extrinsic factors refer to the context or conditions where work is performed. Many people want professional responsibilities like those in recreation and leisure services jobs that provide opportunities for obtaining intrinsic rewards, such as making a difference in the lives of others and performing work that is enjoyable, interesting and psychologically rewarding. The extrinsic rewards of leisure services jobs such as working with peers, supervisors, and subordinates who share the same passion for serving others, and working at job sites that are located on, adjacent to, or close by parks, athletic fields, aquatic centers, tennis courts, golf courses, and fitness facilities, are also very appealing to many people. Many administrators and supervisors in this field value their jobs so much that they choose to remain in lower-paying positions even when opportunities for higher-paying professional jobs become available.

Another reason for an oversupply of professional workers in the leisure services field is the lack of a formal control for testing competence and admitting workers to the professional ranks. In many other professional fields, such as those producing teachers, social workers, accountants, and nurses, stringent state and licensing requirements—which include education, examination, and experience—are required to employ and retain professional workers. People who decide to become public school teachers, for example, must meet minimum state requirements such as holding at least a bachelor's degree and demonstrating mastery of professional preparation and education competence by achieving passing scores on statewide professional education tests. The formal controls established by each of these professions reduce the "supply" of workers admitted at the professional ranks.

The field of recreation and leisure services has not yet established stringent requirements to regulate people wanting administrative and supervisory jobs. The National Recreation and Park Association has a national certification program to certify park and recreation professionals (CPRP—Certified Park and Recreation Professional) but most employers advertising jobs do not list CPRP as a job requirement for professional positions. Some employers, particularly those in local government parks and recreation departments, may list CPRP as a "preferred" requirement, but most will employ individuals who are otherwise qualified without certification.

Qualifications to become CPRP-certified are not as rigorous as other comparable professional certification programs. Qualifications for the CPRP certification include those with a bachelor's degree or high-school degree, full-time experience in the field, and a passing score on the national certification examination. Today, it is common to find many CPRP-certified administrators and managers at the professional ranks who have baccalaureate degrees from a variety of majors including physical education, sports management, public administration, business, and human resources management. As stated above, without a formal control for testing competence and admitting workers to our professional field, we are providing open access to people without certification and with various levels of education and experience, which disrupts the equilibrium of the free market and creates an oversupply of workers for a limited number of professional jobs. Thus, supply is not equal to the number of trained recreation, parks, and leisure services workers available for employment; rather, it is equal to the total number of persons having a high school or college degree with job experience in the field.

Finally, some individuals who have hiring authority in our field are not sufficiently aware of the recreation field and may not fully appreciate the value of hiring professionally trained workers. This point is frequently illustrated in the private sector, especially with commercial recreation. Assume that a wealthy entrepreneur who owns a River and Trail Expeditions company enters into a concession agreement with the National Park Service to operate guided rafting and hiking expeditions at several national parks located in Utah, Arizona, Colorado, and Alaska. This entrepreneur might entrust the management of day-to-day operations of this business to a friend or family member, or perhaps hire a person with a business background. If employers are unaware of the benefits of hiring professionally trained personnel, the field will continue to experience an oversupply of workers and lower wages.

Designing a Base-Pay Program

Up to this point, we have examined several factors that affect the level of compensation paid to recreation, parks, and leisure services personnel. In this section, we will focus on the design of a base-pay program. A compensation program consists of a compensation philosophy and the policies and procedures related to the allocation of base pay (salaries and wages) to the people performing the various jobs in an organization.

Compensation Philosophy

One of the major components of a compensation plan is the underlying compensation philosophy and objectives. The responsibility for establishing a compensation philosophy rests primarily with upper management. For recreation and parks organizations, the compensation philosophy should communicate a fundamental belief that qualified employees are essential to the business of providing quality programs, facilities, and services. An organization's philosophy may also address the importance of competitive salaries, wages, and benefits in attracting, hiring, and retaining highly qualified employees.

Compensation objectives should be aligned with the organization's strategic goals and objectives. They are stated in broad terms and serve as a guide for the design and evaluation of a compensation program. One important objective that should be addressed in a compensation plan relates to pay equity. *Pay equity,* also referred to as *comparable worth,* means that individuals performing the same or similar work should receive the same compensation regardless of their age, sex, race, marital status, national origin, and other unfair discriminating factors. From an employee's perspective, being treated fairly is associated not only with how well a position pays relative to other positions within the organization (*internal equity*), but also how competitive the pay is with market rates outside the organization (*external equity*). This particular compensation objective should serve as a guide for organizations in designing a pay system that treats employees fairly and to some degree achieves both internal and external pay equity.

Developing comprehensive compensation philosophy and objectives is difficult and time-consuming for management. However, without a rationale behind a compensation plan, organizations tend to establish wage rates in a haphazard fashion with little consideration given to how one small change in the compensation program can have rippling effects among employees at every level of the organization's hierarchy.

Alternative Base-Pay Arrangements

The recreation, park, and leisure services field is extremely diverse and a wide range of compensation programs exist. As depicted in Figure 9.1, most compensation programs can be placed on a continuum ranging from very informal and arbitrary on one end to very formal systems based on the notion of comparable worth on the other end. In between are those programs that informally attempt to make pay decisions based on comparable worth.

To illustrate the informal, arbitrary system depicted on the left end of the continuum, consider a private, profit-making recreation organization in a small city. In this organization, different employees doing the same or similar work are paid very different wages. Two managers employed in different functional areas of this organization are paid different wages for similar job duties and responsibilities. As the budget is prepared each year for this organization, managers are asked to submit recommendations regarding their employees' salaries. Together with each recommendation is a written justification or performance appraisal which supports the recommendation. For this organization, performance appraisals are informal and not well done, and the written statement is an undocumented, vaguely written opinion. The chief executive for the organization reviews the recommendation and makes the final decisions. The chief executive has had very little training in compensation administration. He bases his decisions on his managers' recommendations but also takes into consideration the labor market and the factors related to supply and demand. Employees occupying hard-to-fill jobs are paid more; those in the easy-to-fill jobs are paid less. The chief executive decides to keep pay raises low this year in order to add on several new programs.

Although flexible, easy to establish, and easy to administer, an informal, arbitrary pay program usually leads to favoritism, discrimination, unfair politicking, and game playing. The only people who seem to like this type of compensation program are the chief executive and the employees who directly benefit from the arbitrary practices.

The middle of the continuum represents compensation programs that are informally administered, and a pay rate is assigned to a position based on its *comparable worth*. A compensation system based on comparable worth means that pay is allocated based on each position's relative worth compared to all other positions. Jobs that are more complex and judged to be more important to an organization are generally assigned a higher pay rate. For example, if the responsibilities, skills, and training required of the aquatic superintendent position are more highly valued than those of a community center director, then the aquatics position would be assigned a higher pay rate. To determine the comparable worth of each position, a careful analysis or *job evaluation* is made of each position. Typically, organizations hire consultants to conduct job evaluations. The process involves rating job dimensions such as (1) job duties and responsibilities and (2) job qualifications (education, certification, training, experience), and then ranking all jobs. Based on this job evaluation, salary ranges are then established. We discuss this process in more depth in the next section.

It is common in the recreation, park, and leisure services field to find compensation programs that are informal and based on job-evaluation features (see middle of the continuum in Figure 9.1). Typically, organizations try to rise above the informal and arbitrary approach to assigning compensation seen on the left of the continuum, but fall short of a formal system based on comparable worth on the right of the continuum. Although the formal system takes more time to design and administer, it eliminates many of the aforementioned problems created by the informal systems.

Formal Base-Pay Systems

The far right of the continuum in Figure 9.1 represents organizations that have a formal pay structure that is based on the concept of comparable worth and developed using a systematic process of evaluating, ranking,

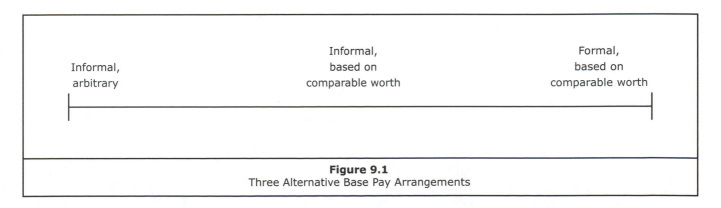

Figure 9.1
Three Alternative Base Pay Arrangements

and classifying jobs and assigning pay levels. Typically, large organizations and especially local and state governments have structured pay systems that would fall at this end of the continuum. To design this type of formal pay system, four basic tools are needed:

1. Job descriptions
2. Job evaluation
3. Job classification
4. Pay structure

Job Descriptions

A *job description* is a statement delineating the duties, responsibilities, and qualifications of a specific position. Job descriptions have two primary components—*job content* and *job specifications*. Job content is information pertaining to a specific job such as a job title, purpose of the job, and the essential job duties and responsibilities. *Job specifications* define characteristics required of the employee to perform the job competently. Specifications that are frequently listed on a job description include the minimum educational and experiential qualifications required by the person in the job; the knowledge, skills, and abilities required for the job; and the salary range. Maintaining updated job descriptions is critical to designing a structured pay system based on comparable worth. More detailed information about job descriptions is provided in Chapter 4.

Job Evaluation

Job evaluation is a systematic way of assessing the relative worth of various jobs within an organization. Determining the "worth" of a job is performed by ranking or rating of what is termed "compensable" factors (Milkovich & Newman, 1987). The relative importance of a job, the skill, responsibility, and effort required of an employee to perform a job, and working conditions are all measures used to measure job worth.

A number of different methods have been developed for performing job evaluations. The two most common methods of job evaluation are job ranking and point evaluations. *Job ranking* is a process where jobs are compared to each other based on the overall worth of the job to the organization. Once the ranking takes place, the jobs are grouped according to their worth to the organization and are then placed in a hierarchy. Another method of job evaluation is *point evaluation*, which involves assessing a set of compensable factors like the skills, responsibilities, effort, education, and experience required of an employee

Pay Band	Working Title	Band Class Title (Job Family)
A	City Manager	City Manager
	City Attorney	City Attorney
B	Assistant City Manager	Assistant City Manager
	Director–Management & Administration	Senior Executive Director
C	Police Chief	Public Safety Chief
	Director–Parks & Recreation	Executive Director
D	Assistant Director-Parks & Recreation	Director
	Manager–Capital Projects	Director
E	Superintendent–Athletics	Senior Manager
	Superintendent–Recreation	Senior Manager
	Superintendent–Parks	Senior Manager
F	Supervisor–Park Operations	Manager
	Supervisor–Parks Construction & Maintenance	Manager
G	Supervisor–Golf Course Maintenance	Assistant Manager
	Supervisor–Aquatics	Assistant Manager
	Supervisor–Recreation	Assistant Attorney
H	Supervisor–Tennis Operations	Team Leader
	Supervisor–Recreation Center	Team Leader
	Supervisor–Athletics	Team Leader
	Supervisor–Swimming Pool Complex	Team Leader
I	Assistant Supervisor–Tennis Operations	Associate
	Assistant Supervisor–Recreation Center	Associate
	Foreman–Golf Course Maintenance	Specialist
	Parks Construction Trades Worker	Senior Technician
J	Pool Maintenance Specialist	Technician
	Athletic Specialist	Technician
	Mechanic I	Mechanic
K	Maintenance Repair Worker	Assistant Technician
	Receptionist	Office Assistant
	Recreation Leader	Group Leader
L	Accounting Clerk	Clerk
	Custodial Worker	Service Worker

Figure 9.2
Pay Bands and Band Class Titles

performing a particular job. Based on the compensable factors, points are assigned to the job. For example, specialized jobs that require certifications (e.g., wilderness first responder, water safety instructor) are awarded higher points than more general recreation positions such as a recreation aide or custodial worker. Based on a point system, the jobs are then placed into a pay grade or pay-band hierarchy.

Job-evaluation methods differ considerably and each has advantages and disadvantages. We will not present a detailed discussion of these methods primarily because human resource specialists or consultants are typically those responsible for performing job evaluations, not recreation professionals. However, it is important that recreation professionals understand that each job evaluation method will ultimately produce an overall ranking of positions as they compare to one another. Once the basic classification is established, it usually needs only minor modifications from time to time. As new jobs are established by an organization they are evaluated and inserted into the existing classification scheme.

Job Classification

After jobs are evaluated and ranked, they are assigned to a job classification. Job classification systems "define the value of jobs, people, or teams with written standards for a hierarchy of classification level" (Heneman, 2003). Jobs that are similar in terms of their relative worth to the organization are grouped into what is called a job grade or band class. For example, in Figure 9.2, the various positions for a municipal parks and recreation department are grouped into 12 pay bands with Band "A" representing jobs with the highest compensation and Band "L" denoting those at the lowest pay level. We can assume from this classification plan that the position of Supervisor of Tennis Operations and the Supervisor of a Swimming Pool Complex were classified in Band "H" because they were similar in the level of difficulty, the qualifications required of the person performing the work, and their importance to the organization.

Pay Structure

The next step in the design of a formal compensation program is to define the level of compensation for each job grade or band class. In some cases, one salary is established for all positions in a pay band but more frequently each band is represented by a salary range, as shown by Figure 9.3. Notice that each of the 12 pay bands (A through L) corresponds to a prescribed range of pay including rates for hourly, monthly, and annual. A pay range is provided so that employees within a band class can improve their salaries as they gain experience and excel in their job performance. *Minimum* is the lowest rate paid to any employee within that pay grade; *maximum* is the highest rate paid to an employee in that pay grade. As shown in Figure 9.3, the next band of similar jobs would include increased duties and responsibilities and thus constitute a higher pay band. It should be noted that job classification plans and pay structures reflect organizational policy and therefore must be officially approved by the appropriate policymaking group or person.

Some organizations have a pay structure that includes a range of steps for each broad category of

Band	Hourly Min ($)	Hourly Max ($)	Monthly Min ($)	Monthly Max ($)	Annual Min ($)	Annual Max ($)
A	41.39	112.38	7,174	19,479	86,091	233,750
B	33.39	76.74	5,788	13,302	69,451	159,619
C	28.78	66.15	4,989	11,466	59,862	137,592
D	24.82	57.06	4,302	9,890	51,626	118,684
E	21.40	49.18	3,709	8,525	44,512	102,294
F	18.46	42.42	3,200	7,353	38,397	88,234
G	15.92	36.56	2,759	6,337	33,114	76,044
H	13.71	31.52	2,376	5,463	28,517	65,561
I	11.82	27.17	2,049	4,709	24,586	56,513
J	10.20	23.44	1,768	4,063	21,216	48,755
K	8.82	20.20	1,529	3,501	18,346	42,016
L	8.15	18.70	1,413	3,241	16,952	38,896

Figure 9.3
Broad Band Pay Plan Band Ranges

Grade	Step 1	Step 2	Step 3	Step 4	Step 5	Step 6	Step 7	Step 8	Step 9	Step 10
1	17,540	18,126	18,709	19,290	19,873	20,216	20,792	21,373	21,396	21,944
2	19,721	20,190	20,842	21,396	21,635	22,271	22,907	23,543	24,179	24,815
3	21,517	22,234	22,951	23,668	24,385	25,102	25,819	26,536	27,253	27,970
4	24,156	24,961	25,766	26,571	27,376	28,181	28,986	29,791	30,596	31,401
5	27,026	27,927	28,828	29,729	30,630	31,531	32,432	33,333	34,234	35,135
6	30,125	31,129	32,133	33,137	34,141	35,145	36,149	37,153	38,157	39,161
7	33,477	34,593	35,709	36,825	37,941	39,057	40,173	41,289	42,405	43,521
8	37,075	38,311	39,547	40,783	42,019	43,255	44,491	45,727	46,963	48,199
9	40,949	42,314	43,679	45,044	46,409	47,774	49,139	50,504	51,869	53,234
10	45,095	46,598	48,101	49,604	51,107	52,610	54,113	55,616	57,119	58,622
11	49,544	51,195	52,846	54,497	56,148	57,799	59,450	61,101	62,752	64,403
12	59,383	61,362	63,341	65,320	67,299	69,278	71,257	73,236	75,215	77,194
13	70,615	72,969	75,323	77,677	80,031	82,385	84,739	87,093	89,447	91,801
14	83,445	86,227	89,009	91,791	94,573	97,355	100,137	102,919	105,701	108,483
15	98,156	101,428	104,700	107,972	111,244	114,516	117,788	121,060	124,332	127,604

Figure 9.4
Annual Rates by Grade and Step

jobs. In Figure 9.4, jobs are classified according to pay grades rather than pay bands. The entry step for a new employee is normally the first step of the range defined for the classification of the position. Step increases provide a way by which employees receive salary or wage increases as they gain experience and reach higher levels of job performance in their job duties. For example, after completing a probationary period, employees can move from Step 1 to Step 2 and earn approximately a 3% pay increase. After a year of satisfactory performance, employees may increase from Step 2 to 3 with another 3% increase. Additional steps may also be included for meritorious performance. People who do not have satisfactory performance usually remain in their step, or may be demoted to the next lower step. The U.S. government has a base general schedule pay scale with which many people are familiar. The General Schedule contains 15 grades, ranging from GS-1 (least difficult position) to GS-15 (most difficult). All of the pay grades have 10 pay steps.

Augmenting Salary and Wages

Increasing salaries and wages is another important component of a comprehensive compensation plan.

Salary and wage-rate increases are not guaranteed by employers but most organizations establish a system for increasing pay rates on a periodic basis to motivate and retain quality employees. The two major classifications of pay increases are performance-based and non-performance based.

Performance-based increases are linked to how well an employee performs the essential duties and responsibilities of his or her job. Most organizations have a system in place for awarding *merit* increases based on the quantity and quality of work performed. For convenience in administering a merit program, many organizations use their existing annual performance-evaluation procedure to obtain individual performance ratings, and then assign an amount or percentage of wage or salary increase based on the rating. For example, an annual increase between 5% and 10% of base salary may be awarded to employees receiving superior performance-evaluation ratings. Besides rewarding individual performance, some organizations use a team-based incentive program to recognize and compensate staff members based on their contribution to a team effort.

Non-performance based salary and wage increases are awarded for reasons that are not based on performance. At periodic times organizations may adjust salaries upward based on increases in the cost-of-living for rent, fuel, clothing, food, and other living expenses. The amount of a *cost-of-living adjustment* (also referred to as COLA) is generally related to the Consumer Price Index. The Consumer Price Index is tracked by the U.S. Department of Labor and represents changes in the prices paid by consumers for a representative sampling of 80,000 different goods and services—from gasoline to milk to doctor bills. The salary increase is usually given to all employees regardless of their position on the hierarchy and is typically a percentage (e.g., 3%, 2.5%) of an employee's base salary.

Another non-performance-based pay increase that is commonly awarded is termed an *across-the-board increase*. An across-the-board pay hike occurs when the same salary increase is given to all employees within a particular job classification. Across-the-board salary increases are awarded based on criteria established by the organization. For example, organizations may grant an across-the-board increase to all employees based on salary ranges. Employees in Pay Band "A" through "D," the positions of highest worth to the organization, may receive a lump sum base pay increase of $250, whereas employees in lower pay bands, Pay Bands "E" through "L" may be awarded a $500 pay increase.

Across-the-board pay increases are commonly awarded based on pay compression. *Pay compression* occurs when there is only a small pay difference among employees regardless of their qualifications and experience. Pay compression can exist in many different forms, but the major one impacting recreation and parks organizations involves paying higher, market-rate salaries for new employees, without adjusting the salaries of long-term employees occupying positions within the same job classification. Employee morale is seriously affected when new employees with limited experience are compensated at a pay rate that is the same or higher than senior professionals who have several years of job experience. To strive toward equity, management uses across-the-board increases to augment salaries of long-term employees who have performed well but whose salaries have not kept pace.

Longevity, or length of service to an organization, is another reason for awarding salary and wage increases. The justification for increasing salaries and wages based on longevity should stem from the fact that an employee's knowledge of an organization increases over the years, and not just from the fact that the individual has spent more time in the organization. A set amount or percentage of salary or wage increase is typically given for longevity, and occurs automatically for employees who have satisfactory performance and have been employed for the required length of time. As shown in Figure 9.4, a step system may be used to award longevity increases.

EMPLOYEE BENEFIT PROGRAMS

Benefits are a form of compensation (in addition to basic wages and salaries) that is given to employees as a reward for their service to an organization. According to the U.S. Bureau of Labor Statistics, employee benefits have accounted for 30.3% of employer costs for employee compensation in 2009. As a portion of total compensation, benefits have been increasing over the past several decades at a much faster rate than wages and salaries. Ironically, many current and prospective employees do not place a high value on their benefits. Most employees, especially young professionals just entering the field, are far more concerned about the level of their base pay.

Employee benefits typically refer to health insurance, life insurance, retirement plans, paid leave, and other such programs that are provided by an employer. Benefit programs are not awarded based on performance (how well employees perform their job), but rather are given to employees based on such factors as their status as either a full-time or part-time employee, their job classification (senior management vs. non-management), and the length of time they have worked for the organization. Employee benefit programs are expensive for employers to offer and represent a sizable portion of an operating budget. Due to the rapid increase of healthcare costs, organizations are constantly changing the benefit program by eliminating some of the options, reducing the range of coverage available to employees, and increasing the employees' share of the cost.

The cost of each of the options in an employee benefit plan may be paid by the employer or employee, or shared between an employer and employee (e.g., 80%/20%, 65%/35%). For example, organizations typically cover 100% of the costs of offering paid leave for vacations and holidays; however, the cost of providing health care and life insurance is typically split between an employer and employee. Employees are usually responsible for paying the full cost of optional insurance plans (vision, dental, cancer) offered through the organization at a low, group rate. Because organizations are buying insurance premiums in bulk, they are much more likely to offer competitive rates to employees for insurance programs compared to an insurance company selling an individual policy to a customer.

Employee benefit plans differ widely and some organizations are more generous than others in covering employees. Eligibility for benefits typically depends on several factors including an employee's work status and his or her tenure with the organization. Permanent, full-time employees are typically entitled to the full-range of benefits offered by an organization. The more generous organizations also extend certain benefits like medical coverage to the employee's family, including a legal spouse and children. Part-time employees who occupy a permanent position and are regularly scheduled for 20 or more hours per week may be entitled to receive partial benefits. Because of the increased costs of providing healthcare coverage, a large percentage of part-time employees are required to pay the full group-rate cost for medical, dental, and vision benefits if they are offered by an organization. Part-time employees who work seasonal positions (camp counselors, lifeguards) rarely receive benefits even if they are regularly scheduled for a 40-hour work week. Organizations may specify the length of time an employee must work before they become eligible for certain benefits. For example, tuition assistance (paid tuition for courses leading to a master's degree) may not be available to permanent, full-time employees until they have worked for the organization for one year.

Most employers are interested in offering not only good salaries to their employees but also a competitive benefits package. In a competitive job market, an attractive benefit package along with a good salary is critical in attracting, motivating, and retaining the most skilled, experienced, and talented employees.

Employer-Sponsored Benefits

Organizations voluntarily offer a wide variety of healthcare plans, pension plans, and other health and employee benefit services. Employees are not required to participate in the benefit programs and services offered by their employer, but most people enthusiastically participate even if it reduces a portion of their income because of the competitive (group) rates that companies are able to obtain on the various benefit options. The employer-sponsored benefit programs that are discussed here include healthcare insurance, life insurance, disability insurance, supplemental insurance, retirement pension, and paid time off. A listing of many other health and employee services that

are commonly offered by organizations is provided at the end of this section.

1. *General healthcare insurance.* Providing access to a quality healthcare insurance plan at an affordable price is one of the most valuable benefits that organizations can offer employees and their families. Most employer-sponsored healthcare insurance plans cover employees for medical services such as doctor's visits, hospital stays, and other medical treatment costs, as well as the cost of prescription drugs.

The cost of general healthcare insurance coverage in America is expensive, and the fees and charges for medical services continue to spiral upward each year. Although most organizations are able to negotiate healthcare insurance premiums at a group rate, they may not have the financial resources available to give healthcare insurance free of charge to their employees. Most organizations share the cost of purchasing healthcare insurance premiums with those employees qualifying for the coverage. For example, organizations may split the cost by paying 80% and employees paying 20%, or 65%/35%, or 50%/50%. Employers use automatic payroll deductions to claim the employee's portion of the cost of the healthcare insurance plan. Not all employees are offered access to company-sponsored health-insurance plans. Most organizations provide coverage only to permanent employees working full-time (40-hour work week). Employees classified as temporary and part-time do not usually qualify for company-sponsored healthcare insurance plans.

There are two types of healthcare insurance plans that most organizations offer—HMO (health maintenance organization) and PPO (preferred provider organization). To participate in an employer–sponsored healthcare insurance plan, eligible employees are required to elect one of the plans that best suits them and their immediate family (if family coverage is offered). While the core benefits between the PPO Plan and the HMO plans are similar, differences do exist. Both plans contract with networks of providers (primary physicians, labs, specialists) to deliver medical services at a pre-negotiated fee. HMO plans require employees to use an exclusive network of providers for services with very few options for using professionals who are not part of the network. With PPO plans, employees typically have the option of using out-of-network providers, but they may incur additional costs for those services. Most PPO plans allow employees to visit specialists without approval from a primary care physician; most HMO plans require employees to first obtain a referral from a primary care physician to have treatment by a specialist covered under the plan.

Under the provisions of a PPO, employees usually pay an *annual deductible* (e.g., $250/individual; $500/family) for medical services before the plan begins paying. Coverage under standard HMOs requires no annual deductible for either individual or family coverage. Most HMO and PPO plans are similar in the *co-payment,* the set dollar amount an individual or employee pays for network doctor's office visits, emergency room services, and prescription drugs. For example, an employee covered by either a PPO or HMO plan may have a co-payment of $15 for each visit to a primary care physician or pay $10/retail for a generic drug prescription.

Healthcare insurance plans may require covered employees to pay a *co-insurance,* which is a percentage of the medical costs, based on the allowed amount, for certain services. For example, under some plans an eligible employee is charged 10%, 20%, or 30% of the cost of the medical service he or she receives. In many healthcare plans, employees must satisfy a *co-insurance maximum* for a calendar year before the insurance plan will pay 100% of the employees' covered medical expenses. For example, let's say a PPO plan sets a maximum of $2,500 for individual co-insurance per year. For comparison, let's say a HMO sets $1,500 maximum for co-insurance. The 10%, 20%, or 30% the employee pays on each claim is the amount that is applied to the co-insurance maximum. Once these dollar amounts total the maximum ($2,500 for PPO or $1,500 for HMO), the plan begins paying 100% of the employee's covered medical expenses during the remainder of that calendar year. The annual dollar limit an individual or family pays in co-insurance or co-payments is also referred to as an *out-of-pocket maximum.* Typically the out-of-pocket maximum is higher with PPO plans compared to HMO plans.

2. *Life insurance.* Life-insurance coverage compensates a surviving spouse or another designated beneficiary in the case of the death of an employee. Cash redeemed from a life insurance policy is usually applied to "final" expenses associated with the employee's funeral, medical bills, student loans, credit card and other debt. A spouse or other beneficiary may also use the life insurance benefit to pay toward the cost of their own living expenses (e.g., mortgage, car loan).

The amount of life insurance paid at death is generally tied to an employee's salary. For example, organizations may have a life-insurance policy that allows an amount equal to one and one-half times the employee's salary to be paid upon death. In this case, if an employee earns $50,000 a year, a beneficiary would receive a $75,000 benefit if she died. In addition, some organizations allow employees to purchase additional life insurance beyond the basic coverage at a discounted group rate.

Organizations typically purchase life-insurance premiums from private insurance providers. While some organizations offer life insurance coverage to eligible employees at no cost, most organizations share the cost with employees. For example, let's say an organization pays an annual premium of $150 for a life insurance policy for a 28-year-old employee and requires the employee to contribute one-third of the cost. If the agency pays two-thirds of the premium (approximately $100), the employee pays the remaining balance of $50 through automatic payroll deductions ($4.17/month).

Each organization establishes employee-eligibility criteria to access life-insurance coverage. Most often, permanent employees working full-time are eligible for life-insurance coverage. The cost of the life-insurance premium is usually based on an employee's age and annual salary.

3. *Disability insurance.* A disability-insurance plan establishes a safety net for eligible employees by replacing a sizeable portion of their income in the event they become disabled and cannot work due to an illness or injury. The amount of coverage and the premium for long-term disability insurance is typically based on an employee's annual salary and age. While some organizations may pay the full cost of long-term disability insurance premium for eligible employees, most make disability insurance available as an optional program, allowing employees to purchase coverage at a group insurance rate.

4. *Supplemental insurance.* Organizations may offer eligible employees the opportunity to participate in a number of other optional insurance plans including dental, vision, cancer, and hospitalization. For most supplemental insurance plans, employees are responsible for the full cost of coverage but can obtain lower premiums through the employer's group rate.

5. *Pension plan.* A *pension* is a sum of money paid regularly by an employer to an employee who has retired and is eligible to receive the retirement benefit. For many retired Americans today, a pension payment is another important source of income in addition to Social Security. Employers are not required to offer a pension plan and roughly half of all privately employed workers in the United States have no employer-provided retirement plan. Employers voluntarily establish and maintain pension plans, and determine the eligibility criteria for employee participation. Most organizations define an eligible employee as a person who is classified as permanent and working full-time (e.g., 40 hours a work week). While most employers allow new employees to immediately participate in the pension plan, other employers require new employees to wait (3 months, 6 months, 1 year). Another important criterion for eligibility is the organization's requirement for vesting. *Vested* is a term that refers to the number of years an employee must work (e.g., 1 year, 5 years, 10 years) before he or she is entitled to receive benefits at the time of retirement. As is typical of most pension plans, employees forfeit the opportunity to receive any type of pension benefit if they leave or lose their job before they become vested. In some plans, the employer makes 100% of the retirement contributions on behalf of the employee. In other plans, both the employer and employee make contributions. A final option is pension plans that are primarily funded by the employee with little or no contribution made by the employer.

Most pensions can be classified as either a defined-benefit plan or a defined-contribution plan. In a *defined-benefit pension plan*, employers make all contributions toward the plan and guarantee a fixed amount of income for eligible employees when they retire. There is no need for the organization to manage separate retirement accounts for each employee because the money to support a defined-benefit pension plan is generally administered through a trust established by the employer. Defined-benefit plans are popular among medium and large companies with 500 or more employees, as well as with large state and local government employers. In defined-benefit pension plans, the amount of fixed income an employee receives at retirement is usually derived from a formula that has three primary factors: the employee's length of service to the employer, the employee's age, and the employee's average earnings for a certain period of time (e.g., last 5 years).

Defined-contribution plans are much different from defined-benefit plans because there is no guarantee of a fixed amount of income for retired employees. Separate retirement accounts are established for each employee and the pension amount an employee receives in retirement is dependent on several factors, including the amount of money that is contributed to the account over time by the employee and/or employer, the type of investments (e.g., money market funds, mutual funds, stocks, and bonds), and the performance of the investments over the years. In many defined contribution plans, employers provide several investment options, and the employee has the responsibility of deciding where to make the contribution. There are many different types of defined-contribution pension plans with a variety of alphabet soup labels: 401(k), TSA, ESOP, SEP, SIMPLE, profit sharing, and money purchase plans.

Employees voluntarily participate in contributing a portion of their earnings toward a pension plan for several different reasons. Besides the interest in old-age security, many employees participate because they can reduce their taxable income by the amount contributed to the retirement plan. Another motivating factor is that many employers match some portion of the employee's contribution with cash or company stock. The amount of money voluntarily contributed each year by an employer to an employee's pension plan is often tied to the company's level of profitability. Generous employers match employee contributions dollar-for-dollar. The national average for employer contributions is 50 cents per dollar, up to 6% of the employee's earnings. If employees terminate employment before becoming vested with the agency, they are given a refund for the money they have personally contributed to the pension plan, but may forfeit all or a major portion of the employer's match.

6. *Paid time off.* Most organizations have several different programs for allowing employees to take paid time off during the year. These benefits are typically awarded to only those positions designated as full-time and permanent. The most common type of paid leave programs are:

Annual leave. Paid leave for vacation (or for other personal matters) is a very popular benefit provided by an employer. The number of paid leave hours for annual leave generally increases with the length of service to the organization. Many organizations require new employees to wait a certain period of time (3 months, 6 months, 1 year) before earning paid leave. For example, new employees may begin earning 10 days (80 hours) of annual paid leave after they have completed their probationary period of 3 months. However, after 5 years of continuous service, employees may earn 12 days of annual leave, and after 10 years they may earn 15 paid days. Many organizations allow an accumulation of a limited number of annual leave hours from year to year. "Use-it-or-lose-it" is a term that is often associated with the use of annual leave and refers to an employer's restriction on the number of paid leave hours that can be accumulated from year to year. For example, some employers require their employees to take a minimum number of paid leave hours, say 40 hours, each calendar year. If an employee chooses to use only 35 hours of annual leave then he will forfeit the other 5 hours. There is no penalty for not forfeiting annual leave hours; the employee will again accumulate hours in the next calendar year.

Holiday leave. Another very popular benefit for staff members is paid leave for holidays. Certain holidays during the year (e.g., New Year's Day, Memorial Day, Independence Day, Labor Day, Thanksgiving, Christmas) are designated by the organization for paid leave. If staff members are required to work on a holiday for a special event, or for whatever reason, another day off with pay is offered.

Sick leave. Most organizations have a paid-leave program to compensate staff members for time missed from work due to personal or family illness. The amount of paid leave a staff member may earn is typically based on the length of service to the organization; the rate is stated in terms of hours per month. For example, a new employee may earn 8 hours a month for sick leave (96 total hours for the year). Also, some organizations have a sick-leave provision that allows staff members to accumulate a limited number of unused sick-leave hours over the years, and use them in situations where extended leave is needed, such as during pregnancy or a serious illness. In addition, organizations may have a policy that allows staff members to be paid for all, or a portion, of the unused sick-leave hours at the time of termination from the organization.

Bereavement leave. Most organizations offer paid leave to staff members to grieve a death in their immediate family. Most policies allow for three days of paid leave for each bereavement occurrence.

7. *Other health and employee services benefits.* Other health and employee services benefits that are commonly offered include:

Mileage reimbursement for use of personal vehicle. Many employees in the recreation, sports, events, and park-services field drive personal vehicles for job-related duties. This is especially true of supervisors or managers who are responsible for a variety of facilities and programs in a particular district or regional service area. Most organizations have a policy for mileage reimbursement (e.g., 50 cents/mile), although not all employees are covered. The amount of mileage reimbursement paid to employees generally lags behind the standard deduction allowed by the Internal Revenue Service, and falls further behind when considering the actual per-mile cost of owning and operating a vehicle.

Vehicle assignment. Many employers assign a company-owned vehicle to their senior-level managers and pay for the fuel. Another alternative is for employers to make available to senior managers a company-owned fleet vehicle for use during the business day.

Memberships to professional associations and societies. Many organizations value the benefits associated with memberships to professional recreation, park, and leisure services associations and societies. These organizations encourage professional participation by becoming an agency member and paying all or a portion of the annual membership dues for designated employees. The types of professional association memberships include but are not limited to the National Recreation and Park Association, state park and recreation associations, the International Special Events Society, the National Intramural-Recreational Sports Association, the Resort and Commercial Recreation Association, and the American Camping Association.

Continuing education, training, and development. Many organizations encourage their employees to pursue academic degrees or certificate programs and to participate in other training and educational programs. This allows employees the opportunity to further their professional development or to maintain their current certification status. Organizations may provide financial support by reimbursing employees for the cost of tuition, educational supplies, and materials. In the event the training program is located out-of-town, organizations may also reimburse designated employees for transportation, lodging, and per diem expenses. The types of organizations that offer continuing education and training programs include professional membership associations, colleges and universities, and nonprofit organizations.

Free or discounted fees for participating in programs and services. Recreation, fitness, resorts, parks, and other leisure service organizations frequently offer the types of programs, services, and rental equipment and facilities that are popular and attractive to employees and their families. As a perquisite of employment, organizations may allow employees and their family members to participate in programs and services or to rent recreation equipment and facilities at no cost or at a rate substantially below the standard charge. To avoid ethical and legal challenges, it is prudent for organizations to develop sound policies and procedures governing the fair and equitable coverage of this benefit.

Uniforms and clothing. Many recreation, sports, fitness, park services, and other leisure service organizations establish a dress code and issue clothing for certain employee classifications where specific identity is desirable.

Employee assistance program. Personal problems come in all sizes, types, and degrees of seriousness, and although most employees can handle their own personal problems, sometimes they want and need professional help. Many organizations offer an Employee Assistance Program (EAP) that provides free and confidential counseling services to employees and their immediate family members as a way of helping them deal with personal difficulties. Typically, EAPs provide problem evaluation, referral, follow-up, and counseling services to help employees dealing with issues such as grief or the loss of a loved one, separation or divorce, alcohol and drug abuse, eating disorders, weight loss, job stress, and other family and marital problems.

Other senior-management perquisites. In an effort to attract and retain talented top-level management officials, organizations often award certain types of perquisites not available to other employees. Executive benefit packages often include, but are not limited to, 100%-paid insurance programs (health care, dental, vision), 100%-paid family healthcare insurance, additional insurance coverage (i.e., life insurance, long-term disability insurance), additional paid leave, and a deferred compensation program. Other attractive benefits include an assigned parking space, GPS navigation system for vehicle, cell phone, purchase card, laptop computer, and other wireless smart devices (e.g., personal digital assistant, smartphone, portable printer) for business related expenses.

Legislation Impacting Compensation

In Chapter 1 we learned that the 1964 Civil Rights Act, the Age Discrimination in Employment Act of 1967, and the Equal Pay Act of 1963 all prohibit organizations from discriminating and paying unfair wages and salaries because of a person's race, color, religion, national origin, age, or sex. In addition there are eleven other major federal and state laws that affect compensation.

1. *Social Security and Medicare.* Both Social Security and Medicare are healthcare insurance programs mandated by the United States government. Social Security is a supplemental retirement system that was established in the United States in 1935. The intent of this program is to provide financial benefits to all workers in the United States. Most workers in the United States receive Social Security benefits once they retire and collect a Social Security check once a month. Workers may also collect Social Security during their working lives if they become disabled and can no longer work. In addition, a spouse or dependent may become eligible for Social Security survivor benefits upon the death of a worker.

    Medicare is a federal health-insurance program that covers most people 65 years of age or older, or those under the age of 65 with certain disabilities. Although Medicare covers most medical expenses such as doctor's visits, hospital stays, and drug and medical treatment costs, it does not cover most medical care given at home, in nursing homes, or in assisted-living facilities.

    Both employers and employees pay taxes required by the Federal Insurance Contributions Act (commonly referred to as FICA) to fund Social Security and Medicare. The Tax Relief, Unemployment Insurance Reauthorization, and Job Creation Act of 2010 reduced 2011 Social Security tax rates for employees and self-employed people by two percentage points, from 6.2% to 4.2% for employees and from 12.4% to 10.4% for self-employed people. This rate applies to the first $106,800 of annual wages. Without further changes in the law, these tax rates will return to 6.2% and 12.4%, respectively, beginning in 2012. Employees pay 7.65% (6.2% Social Security and 1.45% Medicare) of the first $94,200 they earn in annual wages. An employer pays payroll taxes of 7.65%. Employees who earn in excess of $106,800 in 2009 are taxed only for Medicare (1.45%). For these same individuals, employers only contribute 1.45% in payroll taxes toward Medicare. The employee share of Social Security and Medicare taxes is withheld through an employer's payroll deduction plan. Self-employed workers are responsible for paying the federal government the entire FICA tax rate of 15.3%. For example, if an organization contracts with an individual to conduct certain special events during the year then the contracted employee is responsible for paying FICA at the rate of 15.3%.

2. *Unemployment insurance.* Unemployment insurance provides temporary income payments to eligible employees who lose their jobs through no fault of their own, and are able and available to do work. Unemployment checks are typically collected when employees lose their jobs as a result of a company's decision to restructure and downsize, merge with another company, or sell the business. Unemployment payments are intended to serve as temporary income to allow an unemployed worker sufficient time to find a new job without major financial distress

The unemployment insurance program in the United States is based on a program of both federal and state statutes. The program was established by the Social Security Act in 1935 and implemented through the Federal Unemployment Tax Act of 1935 (FUTA). The FUTA imposes a tax on employers who employ at least one person and paid wages of at least $1,500. Each of the 50 states administers a separate unemployment insurance program that must be approved by the Secretary of Labor, based on federal standards.

To support the unemployment-compensation systems, a combination of federal and state taxes are levied upon employers. Employees are not required to pay any part of the unemployment insurance, and employers are prohibited from reducing workers' wages for this purpose. The employer pays for unemployment insurance benefits by making tax payments to a state-administered "Unemployment Compensation Trust Fund," which earns interest on the deposits. Benefits to eligible unemployed workers are then paid from this trust fund. The FUTA tax is imposed at a single flat rate on the first $7,000 of wages paid to each employee. Once an employee's wages for the calendar year exceed $7,000, there is no further FUTA liability for that employee for the rest of the year. The tax rate for unemployment compensation varies depending on the number of unemployment claims filed and the employer's average annual taxable payroll. Employers must pay both State and Federal Unemployment Taxes (SUTA and FUTA).

Laid-off workers do not automatically receive unemployment-insurance benefits. Unemployed workers must apply through their state's Department of Employment Security and qualify for unemployment payments. To be eligible for coverage, unemployed workers must be actively seeking work opportunities. They may not refuse suitable employment, and cannot claim to be unemployed due to participation in a labor strike. Typically applicants are not successful in qualifying for unemployment coverage if they claim that their employer created an intolerable working environment which resulted from a demotion, moderate decrease in wages or benefits, or a reasonable change to the work schedule. In addition, to succeed in obtaining unemployment, employees must not have lost their job because of misconduct at work. Student employees (e.g., graduate assistants, work-study students) hired by a school, college, or university are not eligible for unemployment insurance benefits. Also, students working for credit in a work-experience program such as an internship or field work do not qualify for unemployment insurance benefits.

3. *Workers' compensation.* Workers' compensation provides benefits such as medical treatment, vocational rehabilitation, and income payments to workers who are injured or disabled on the job. More in-depth information is provided about workers' compensation laws in Chapter 2.

4. *Fair Labor and Standards Act (FLSA).* In 1938, Congress passed the FLSA to address low wages and other labor conditions that prevent disadvantaged workers from attaining the minimum standards of living necessary for health and well-being. Today, the FLSA establishes policies and procedures for paying both minimum wage and overtime work while also setting forth child-labor standards that affect full-time and part-time workers. The FLSA covers private employers as well as federal, state, and local governments. By federal law, as of 2009, employers paid a minimum wage of $7.25 per hour. Each state's minimum-wage laws may establish a higher rate of pay, but not a lower one. For example, in 2009 in California, the minimum wage rate was $8.00 per hour.

The FLSA also regulates overtime compensation paid to employees. By federal law, organizations must pay employees not less than one and one-half times the regular rate of pay for all hours worked in excess of 40 hours of work in a work week. For example, Terry is a non-exempt employee working for a private resort and has a regular wage rate of $16 per hour. If she is required to work 50 hours during the week of July 4th to produce a special event, her employer is obligated to pay her for 10 hours at the rate of $24 per hour (1.5 times $16) and 40 hours at the regular rate of $16 per hour. Some employees are excluded from overtime pay provisions under specific exemptions of the FLSA. For example, most executives, administrators, and professionals are designated as "exempt" employees and restricted from earning overtime pay.

Under the provisions of Section VII of the FLSA, state and local government organizations are allowed some flexibility in awarding employees *compensatory time-off* in lieu of overtime pay. Using the above example, if Terry was a non-exempt employee working for a city parks and recreation department, she may be given the option of taking paid time off rather than earning overtime wages. Section VII of FLSA does not provide specific language for governing compensatory time off and overtime pay; therefore, it is the responsibility of government organizations to establish clear policies and procedures for both exempt and non-exempt employee positions.

The Fair Labor Standards Act establishes child-labor standards (including minimum wage and overtime pay) that affect both full-time and part-time youth workers. Under the provisions of the law, employers may pay a *youth minimum wage* above $4.25 per hour to workers under 20 years of age for 90 calendar days—not work days—after they are first employed. After the 90-day period, employers are required to pay minimum wage as specified by the FLSA.

The age of a youth worker determines which child-labor standards apply to the work week. For example, at the age of 18, youth workers may perform any job for unlimited hours. Youth workers who are 16 or 17 years old may also work unlimited hours; however, these jobs must be non-hazardous. At the age of 14 or 15, youth workers are limited during the school year to a total of 18 hours per week (3 hours per day on school days) and must be scheduled for work between the hours of 7 am and 7 pm. During the summer when they are not attending school, 14- and 15-year-olds may work 40 hours per week (8 hours per day) between the hours of 7 am and 9 pm.

5. *Davis-Bacon Act.* The Davis-Bacon Act of 1931 was passed by Congress to address the issue of wage and overtime rates paid by contractors and subcontractors involved in federally funded or assisted contracts in excess of $2,000 for

the construction or repair of buildings owned by the federal government. This legislation requires contractors to pay laborers and mechanics not less than the prevailing wage rates and benefits for corresponding classes of laborers and mechanics employed on similar projects in a community. For example, contractors and subcontractors engaged in maintenance construction projects (restoring historic features, replacing heating and air conditioning units, and resurfacing roads and walkways) at the National Mall and Memorial Parks in Washington, D.C., are required by law to pay laborers and mechanics prevailing wage rates and fringe benefits in the Washington, D.C. area. The Davis-Bacon Act also requires contractors and subcontractors to pay employees overtime wages at the rate of at least one and one-half times their basic rates of pay for all hours over 40 worked on contract-related work in a work week.

6. *Walsh-Healey Public Contract Act (PCA).* The Walsh-Healey PCA establishes minimum wage, maximum hours, and safety and health standards for work on federal contracts in excess of $10,000. The law requires contractors that manufacture or furnish materials, supplies, articles, or equipment to the federal government to pay employees who produce, assemble, handle, or ship goods not less than the prevailing wage rates and fringe benefits in the local community. Covered employees working overtime (in excess of 40 hours per work week) must be paid at the rate of one and one-half times their basic rates of pay. For example, the National Park Service (NPS) established a green cleaning program at Yellowstone National Park and Grand Teton National Park to reduce significantly the toxicity of janitorial products used in park operations. By law, the company that was contracted by NPS to furnish the green cleaning products, as well as companies manufacturing the green supplies used by the contractor, are required to pay their employees prevailing wage rates and fringe benefits.

7. *McNamara-O'Hara Service Contract Act.* The provisions of this legislation target the wages and overtime rates paid to employees of federal contractors providing services to the federal government. By law, contractors doing business with the federal government in excess of $2,500 are required to pay "service employees" in various job classifications the prevailing wage rates and benefits found prevailing in the local community. In addition, service employees working overtime (in excess of 40 hours per work week) must be paid at least one and one-half times their regular rate of pay. Examples of service contracts negotiated by the National Park Service for maintenance of the national parks include garbage collection, janitorial service, and night security and patrol.

8. *Consolidated Omnibus Budget Reconciliation Act (COBRA).* COBRA is a federal law passed by Congress in 1985. It contains a provision allowing employees and their families who had been covered by their employer's healthcare plan to maintain coverage if a "qualifying event" occurs that makes them ineligible for coverage. Divorce, resignation, layoff, discharge, medical leave, death of the covered employee, or a dependent child reaching the age at which he or she is no longer covered are examples of qualifying events. Employers are permitted by law to require qualified employees and their immediate family to pay the full cost of the health plan including the portion previously paid by the employer. When a qualifying event occurs and an employee no longer qualifies for the employer's healthcare plan, the employer is required to give qualified beneficiaries a period of time to decide whether to elect COBRA coverage. COBRA establishes requirements on the length of time that employers must provide coverage to qualified beneficiaries; however, an employer may extend COBRA coverage for a longer period.

COBRA generally applies to group health plans sponsored by private employers with 20 or more employees. The legislation also applies to health plans of state and local governments. The law does not apply to the U.S. government or church organizations.

Recreation, parks, and leisure-service managers can easily feel overwhelmed by the maze of federal and state laws, regulatory agency rules and regulations, and court decisions that govern compensation practices. It is important to realize that few managers are versed in all aspects of compensation and most managers rely on compensation specialists within the human resources office to obtain specific information pertaining to salaries, wages, and individual benefit programs. However, it is of critical importance for recreation, park, and leisure services managers to learn and understand compensation practices so they can use this knowledge as a way to attract and recruit potential employees as well as motivate and retain current employees.

SUMMARY

1. Compensation plans provide information pertaining to employee salaries, wages, and benefits and are designed for the purpose of attracting, motivating, and retaining highly qualified employees.

2. Organizations design compensation plans based on compensation philosophy which emanates from their strategic goals and objectives.

3. Labor unions and the economic law of supply and demand are two factors that impact the level of compensation organizations offer. Labor unions typically push compensation systems that emphasize equality wherein all salary and wage increases are distributed equally among all workers rather than a reward system based on individual work performance.

4. When the supply of workers in the field of recreation, parks, and leisure services increases, then wages for similar work can be expected to fall. Conversely, if the demand for recreation workers such as lifeguards is high but the supply of certified lifeguards is low, wages increase.

5. The supply of professional workers in the field of recreation, parks, and leisure services is greater than the demand due to several reasons including: the intrinsic and extrinsic rewards inherent in recreation jobs; the lack of a formal control for testing competence and admitting workers to the professional ranks that is present in other comparable professional certification programs; and the fact that some individuals who have hiring authority are unaware of the recreation field and may not appreciate the value of hiring professionally trained workers.

6. Designing a formal compensation program involves developing job descriptions, evaluating and ranking the relative worth of various jobs within an organization, assigning jobs to a classification according to written standards, and defining a pay structure for each level of compensation.

7. Performance-based pay increases are based on how well an employee performs the essential duties and responsibilities of his or her job; non-performance pay increases are based on factors other than performance such as cost-of-living adjustments (COLA), across-the board increases, or the length of time an employee has been employed.

8. Eligibility for employee benefits depends on an employee's work status and tenure with the organization. Full-time and permanent employees are typically entitled to the full-range of benefits, whereas part-time and seasonal employees may not qualify for any of the rewards of the benefit programs.

9. The types of employer-sponsored benefit programs that may be offered to employees include healthcare insurance, life insurance, disability insurance, supplemental insurance, pension, and paid leave.

10. Most organizations share the cost of purchasing insurance premiums with their employees who qualify for the coverage. Eligible employees may be charged 10%, 20%, 30% or more of the cost of the medical services. This cost is generally less than the amount employees would pay if they

sought insurance on their own and did not participate in their employer's plan.

11. Pension plans are generally classified as either a defined-benefit or a defined-contribution plan. Most organizations offer a defined-contribution pension plan which requires no guarantee of a fixed income for retired employees. Employees voluntarily participate in contributing a portion of their earnings to the pension plan which may be matched by the employer. The pension amount for retired employees depends on the amount contributed, the type of investment, and the performance of the investments over time.

12. Organizations may offer a wide variety of paid leave programs to their employees such as annual leave, holiday leave, sick leave, and bereavement.

13. Other health and employee benefits that are favored by employees include: a mileage reimbursement program for use of a personal vehicle for business purposes; paid memberships to professional associations; continuing education, training, and development programs; free or discounted fees for employer-sponsored recreation programs and services; company-paid uniforms and other clothing; and an employee assistance program.

14. Employee benefits that are targeted for employees ranked as senior management may include 100% paid insurance programs (health care, dental, vision), electronic equipment (smart phone, computer tablet), purchase cards, and GPS navigation system for vehicles.

15. Social security and Medicare are healthcare insurance programs mandated by the United States government. Both employers and employees pay taxes required by the Federal Insurance Contributions Act to fund these two federal programs.

16. Other federal and state laws that affect compensation include: unemployment insurance, workers' compensation benefits, Fair Labor and Standards Act, Davis-Bacon Act, Walsh-Healey Public Contract Act, McNamara-O'Hara Service Contract Act, and the Consolidated Omnibus Budget Reconciliation Act.

Discussion Topics

1. Why do labor unions favor seniority as the most appropriate basis for salary determination?

2. Do you think the compensation levels paid to recreation, parks, and leisure services professionals would significantly increase if the supply of trained professionals dropped below the level of demand? Explain.

3. If recreation, park, and leisure services employers continue to pay wages that lag behind other human services professions, what might be the long-term effects?

4. Why do you think people choose to spend an entire professional career in the field of recreation, events, and parks, even though their salaries are less than in other professional fields?

5. For a professional career, would you prefer earning less money for a job you enjoy doing every day, or earning more money for a job you don't particularly like? How would your answer be different if you were married or had a partner, and/or had children?

6. If you were a manager of a recreation, parks, or leisure services operation, would you prefer a philosophy of hiring fewer employees but paying them a higher-than-average salary, or would you prefer to have more employees but pay them less than market rate? Why?

7. What are the potential problems associated with an informally organized, arbitrarily administered compensation program? Are there any potential problems with a formal, highly structured pay system? Explain.

8. Should a person's base pay be determined by the notion of comparable worth, or should pay be established based on the market force of supply and demand? Explain.

9. What are the potential problems with a pay system that automatically advances employees who are performing adequately to higher pay levels based on the length of time they have been employed with an organization? What are the arguments for and against this arrangement?

10. What are the arguments for and against a pay program that automatically advances employees to a higher pay level based on the length of time they have worked on the job rather than awarding pay increases based on meritorious performance?

11. What are the potential problems with a job-classification system that designates professional positions in recreation services as exempt and ineligible for overtime compensation? What options are available to employers that have employees classified as exempt and yet work in excess of 40 hours per week on a routine basis?

12. Why do so many people place so much emphasis on the salary of an advertised job rather than considering the importance of a pay package which also includes employee benefits (pension, health insurance, paid leave)?

13. Should public and private employers be responsible for providing health and employee services benefits to their employees? What are the arguments for and against this arrangement? What other options could be explored?

14. What do you think about the future of the federal system of Social Security and Medicare for young professionals today entering in the workforce? What should young professionals do today to ensure adequate retirement income?

15. Pay compression is an issue for long-serving employees whose salaries have not kept pace with that of market-rate salaries paid to new employees. What options are available to long-term employees whose salaries are being surpassed by those of other employees who are newer to the organization?

REFERENCES

Calo, R. J. (2006). The psychological contract and the union contract: A paradigm shift in public sector employee relations. *Public Personnel Management, 35*(4), 331.

Heneman, R. L. (2003). Job and work evaluation: A literature review. *Public Personnel Management, 32*(1), 47.

Milkovich, G. T., & Newman, J. M. (1987). *Compensation*. Plano, TX: Business Publications.

U.S. Department of Labor (2008a), Bureau of Labor Statistics, Occupational Outlook Handbook, 2008–09 Edition, Recreation workers.

U.S. Department of Labor (2008b), Bureau of Labor Statistics, Occupational Outlook Handbook, 2008–09 Edition, Recreational Therapists.

U.S. Department of Labor, Bureau of Labor Statistics, Occupational Outlook Handbook, 2008–09 Edition. Social workers, Teachers, and Human Resources Managers and Specialists.

U.S. Department of Labor, Bureau of Labor Statistics, Economic News Release, 2009, Employer Costs for Employee Compensation Summary.

U.S. Department of Labor, Bureau of Labor Statistics, Consumer Price Index. Retrieved from http://www.bls.gov/cpi/home.htm

U.S. Social Security Administration. Retrieved from http://www.ssa.gov/

U.S. Department of Labor, Employment Standards Administration, Wage and Hour Division, Fair Labor and Standards Act. Retrieved from http://www.dol.gov/esa/whd/Flsa/

U.S. Department of Labor, Employment Standards Administration, Wage and Hour Division, Davis-Bacon and Related Acts. Retrieved from http://www.dol.gov/esa/whd/programs/dbra/index.htm

U.S. Department of Labor, Employment Standards Administration, Wage and Hour Division, Walsh-Healey Public Contracts Act (PCA). Retrieved from http://www.dol.gov/esa/WHD/contracts/pca.htm

U.S. Department of Labor, Employment Standards Administration, Wage and Hour Division, McNamara-O'Hara Service Contract Act. Retrieved from http://www.dol.gov/ESA/WHD/contracts/sca.htm

U.S. Department of Labor, Employee Benefits Security Administration, Consolidated Omnibus Budget Reconciliation Act. Retrieved from http://www.dol.gov/dol/topic/health-plans/cobra.htm

TRAINING AND DEVELOPMENT

10

Today's economic climates, workforce mobility, advances in technology, employee expectations of life/work integration, and pressure from boards of directors to increase productivity have created a culture at work different than any experienced in the past. Gone are the days when an employee was hired, served, and retired from the same organization. Workers' loyalty towards organizations decreased as organizations' loyalty to employees declined through the downsizing, "right-sizing," flattening, and outsourcing tactics that began in the 1980s. Today, employees come into organizations looking for development opportunities so that when they leave, for whatever reason, they leave better prepared to meet their next opportunity. Organizations, on the other hand, need to be agile, adaptable change leaders and position themselves for predictable and unpredictable market conditions. Current financial woes and competitive pressures demand that an organization's employees be knowledgeable, skilled, and

able to deliver results. People drive the systems that make up the organization. As stated by the owner of a company as his employees were leaving at the end of the day, "There goes my business . . . my company's success." Employee skills, knowledge, and motivation determine an organization's future. The success of both the employees and the employer lies in an appreciation for continuous learning and a commitment to development. In this *mutually beneficial relationship*, an organization commits itself to its employees by providing opportunities for growth and development while the employee commits to the organization by learning, improving performance, and adapting to change. See Figure 10.1.

Organizational effectiveness declines if an organization does not invest in developing its workforce. According to PricewaterhouseCoopers, 70% of Fortune 1000 companies cite a lack of trained employees as their number-one barrier to sustaining growth

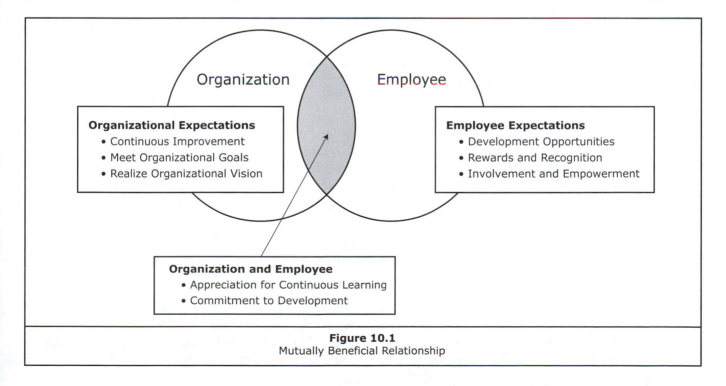

Figure 10.1
Mutually Beneficial Relationship

(Bachman, 2000). Globalization of the recreation and leisure services industry as well as changing service expectations and availability of new equipment put additional pressure on these organizations to prepare employees. Recruiting new employees with needed skills and talent is time-consuming and costly. It would not be cost-effective, motivating for employees, or attractive to potential applicants if an employer fired current employees and hired new workers every time it needed to be responsive to internal and external changes. Businesses that offer ongoing education and training attract new talent and enjoy a higher rate of employee retention along with the benefits of a better-skilled workforce (Prime Learning, Inc., 2001). Employee development is crucial to competitive advantage. This fact not only justifies the need for training and development but demands it. As organizational leaders awaken to this reality, the number of dollars spent on training and development continues to increase. According to the American Society for Training and Development (ASTD), businesses in the United States spent over $134 billion annually on employee learning and development in 2007 (ASTDResearch.org, 2008).

WHAT IS TRAINING AND WHAT IS DEVELOPMENT?

Training and development together comprise the employer's efforts through employee learning to improve present work performance and to ensure future human resource requirements are met. Sometimes a distinction is made between *training* and *development* with *training* more narrowly defined as the acquisition of knowledge and skills to aid in current job performance while *development* is broader, more holistic in scope, and focuses on an individual's life-long learning and deeper growth toward a richer life. Training is often defined as one dimension of development. Yet some experts in the field have said, one trains animals, one develops people. Regardless of what an organization decides to call it—training and development, employee learning, employee development—all training and learning is developmental.

  The above definition serves the needs of both the organization and the employee in their mutually beneficial relationship. The employer prepares for the future by linking training and development needs to organizational goals, while the employee's need for growth is satisfied. People want more from a job than a paycheck. They want greater responsibility, greater opportunity to use personal abilities, and they want

to feel that they are being appreciated and recognized for their efforts by "getting somewhere" (Kent & Otte, 1982). They want to know how they fit into the organization's future. Abraham Maslow might call these employee aspirations "finding self-actualization."

THE BIG PICTURE

To better understand the role of training and development within an organization, it is helpful to have a big-picture view of an organization's structure. An organization is a large system comprised of many smaller systems, each contributing to the organization's mission. Organizational development (OD) is the function focused on improving the performance of these systems and subsystems. Like a physician, the OD specialist is concerned with the general well-being of the organization and leading the necessary change efforts to keep it healthy and strong. The OD specialist diagnoses current conditions and through OD activities, called *interventions*, addresses the gap between desired expectations and the current reality. OD activities include: employee training and development; strategic planning; designing systems, structures and processes (organizational design); leading change; coaching; career development; conflict resolution; team building; leadership development; life/work integration; diversity education; orientation of new employees; and supervisory or management development (see Figure 10.2). Note that *training and development* is one component of OD. Organizational development departments typically report through human resources. Because of the strategic nature of organizational development work, OD departments sometimes report directly to the organization's leaders.

STRATEGIC TRAINING AND DEVELOPMENT

Training and development is both costly and important; therefore, organizations should strive to make every dollar invested produce desired results. Organizations are becoming increasingly more strategic in designing development programs that are in alignment with organizational goals and focused on long-term benefits. Organizations that align their training and development initiatives with their organization's strategy (mission, vision, values, and goals) are referred to as *learning organizations*. With every training and development initiative and dollar spent, the question should be asked, "How does this effort help us attain our goals and advance the mission of

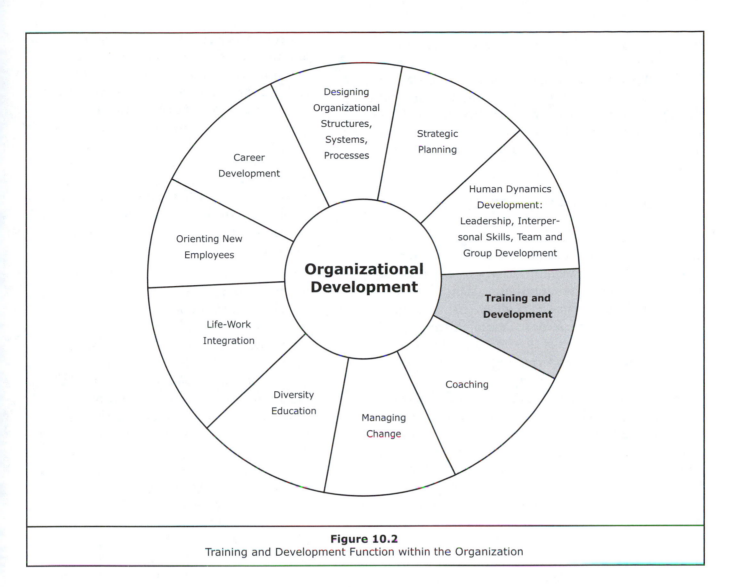

Figure 10.2
Training and Development Function within the Organization

Organizational strategy drives organizational, departmental, and individual goals. Strategic training and development efforts need to align with these goals.

Figure 10.3
Organizational Strategy Drives Training and Development Efforts

our organization?" For example, how might teaching English to housekeepers in an all-inclusive resort in the Mexican Caribbean advance the mission of the organization? Strategically linking training and development activities to organizational goals is critical when identifying and justifying training and development proposals, programs, and activities. See Figure 10.3, p. 167.

LEARNING ORGANIZATIONS

Learning organizations are forward thinking and are not the organizations of the past that eliminated training and development initiatives when times got tough. Learning organizations understand that altering organizational behavior to meet changing needs requires a strong investment in developing employees' knowledge and skills. It is also understood that commitment and support of training and development initiatives are not only the responsibility of the leaders but of the managers, supervisors, and employees as well. Employees are rewarded for learning through recognition, enhancement of job responsibilities, promotional opportunities, or monetary reward. Keeping good employees happy means planning ahead for their future needs and matching their emerging interests and abilities with new job responsibilities. In learning organizations, moving up a hierarchical ladder is not the only path to success.

PURPOSE AND IMPORTANCE OF TRAINING AND DEVELOPMENT

Developing employees carries with it the risk that employees might leave the organization with their new skills to pursue opportunities with other organizations. The following anonymous quote addresses this dilemma in a humorous way. "If you think developing employees and having them leave is expensive, try not developing them and having them stay." The following are sound reasons why human resource development is important.

- *Job performance improves.* Productivity increases when employees receive education in new work methods, new technologies, and interpersonal skills. It has been documented that training reduces accidents, absenteeism, the need for discipline, and grievances.
- *Self-development leads to improved work attitudes.* Self-improvement leads to self-confidence and these two conditions lead to a desire to maintain a high level of performance in order to maintain success and a positive self-image. Employee attitudes are improved if they perceive that the work environment assists and encourages them toward achieving all they are capable of becoming. Today, people join leisure organizations with high expectations of job satisfaction and self-fulfillment. Helping employees expand their abilities increases their motivation and commitment toward the organization.
- *Training and development attract new talent* and develop competent employees to meet future human resource needs. Adaptability not only means training or retraining employees to meet today's expectations, it also means planning ahead to identify future needs. Anticipating organizational expansion, direction, and future staffing needs to support the organization's vision places demands on the employer. Good employee development programs serve as an attraction for prospective employees and an incentive for current employees to stay with organizations. When organizations reimburse employees for tuition and books or provide them with development opportunities such as leadership development programs or coaching, it becomes a more attractive place to work and those organizations tend to attract more and better qualified employees (Mondy, 2008, p. 201).
- *Training reduces turnover and saves money.* Training programs are now credited with strengthening customer satisfaction, contributing to employee engagement, enhancing research and development activities, and reinforcing the bottom line.
- *Training and development contribute to the realization of organizational goals.* Organizational success is directly impacted by an ability to set clear goals and then achieve them. Identifying and building the skills necessary to meet challenging goals are critical. Training and development efforts support the endeavor and are a means for monitoring the progress of goal achievement.

Legal Issues Affecting Training and Development

Employers have a legal obligation to meet certain objectives when designing and delivering training and development programs. Programs must be monitored to ensure against disparate treatment and disparate impact (illegal practices are discussed in Chapter 1). Whether intentional or unintentional, using job-related criteria for entry or completion of training programs that treat members of a protected class differently is illegal. For example, passing an exam written in English would not be fair criterion to determine if a Spanish-speaking groundskeeper knows how to identify the diseases of palm trees. Equal access to training and career development is mandated by Title VII of the Civil Rights Act, the Uniform Guidelines on Employee Selection Procedures, the American with Disabilities Act (ADA), the Age Discrimination in Employment Act (ADEA), and the Uniformed Services Employment and Reemployment Rights Act (USERRA) *as well as other federal and state laws*. Awareness of these laws, along with the required compliance, is expected when preparing and delivering programs. Another example would be accommodating the needs of an employee with a hearing impairment. The decision to adapt a particular training program or tool is one that should be made by the employer after discussing the situation and specific needs with the employee (OSHA.gov, 2005).

Training and Development Process

A strategic training and development process is ongoing, multidimensional, and supports organizational goals. Every work unit should have a well-organized program that includes every employee. Supervisors should discuss development opportunities with each employee on a regular basis. On occasion, management may decide that training is needed for the entire organization or it may focus on targeted groups. Another instance may call for special training of individuals in order to solve problems caused by their performance. For training and development to be most effective throughout the organization, it requires someone or some unit to assume the responsibility of a systematic process that should consist of the following steps: (1) determine the training and development need; (2) establish objectives for the training effort; (3) select the most appropriate type of training program and method of delivery for the situation; (4) implement

the training; and (5) evaluate the effectiveness of the training and development program. See Figure 10.4 , p. 170.

Identifying and Prioritizing Training and Development Needs

Assessing organizational training needs involves examining each situation or the performance issues of employees. In this diagnostic phase, it is critical that the situation be appraised accurately. First, the training specialist must ask the question, "Will training improve or correct this problem?" Only if the answer is yes should the question "What kind of training should be implemented?" be asked. Think of a doctor determining the best course of action for a patient's condition. If the doctor prescribes a decongestant for a broken ankle, the patient's condition won't improve! Initially, a supervisor who conducts a job analysis or performance review may identify specific development needs for a given employee. The training and development specialist serves as an internal consultant in assessing and evaluating the issue and recommending the most appropriate action or intervention. The supervisor may not have the time or expertise to perform those tasks.

Once it is determined that training will help, the following questions should be asked in developing an effective training and development plan:

- What is the training or developmental need?
- How is it linked to organizational goals and organizational strategy?
  - Is it worth pursuing?
  - What is the cost if left alone?
- Who will need to be trained?
- Who will do the training?
- What will be the training format?
- How will the training be evaluated?
- How will we measure the training's effectiveness related to job performance?

Organizational Analysis, Job/Task Analysis, and Individual Analysis are analyses used to determine the training and development needs.

Organizational Analysis

This study typically conducted by an organization's training and development specialist examines

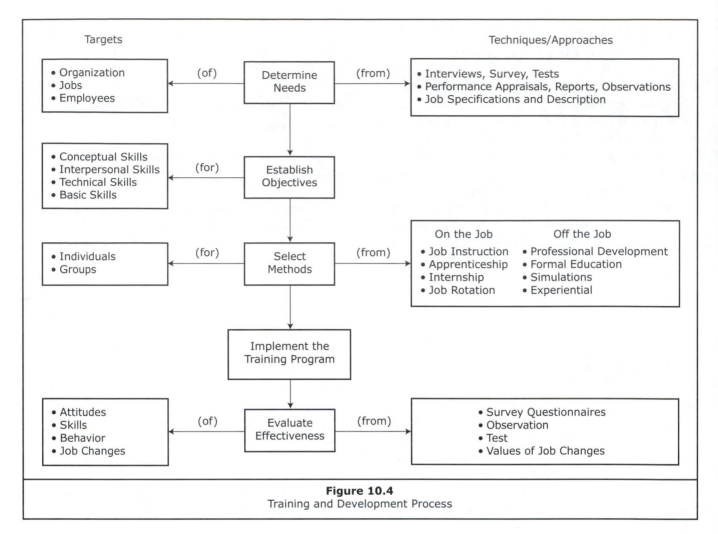

Figure 10.4
Training and Development Process

long-range and short-range objectives for human resource needs; reviews efficiency indexes; and determines the organizational climate by studying patterns of absenteeism, turnover, grievances, accident rates, and general attitudes of employees. These data are indicators of problems, but the problems may not be training related. Although it is not difficult to recognize an increase in on-the-job accidents or a decline in sales volume, it may be difficult to determine the actual cause of these changes and still more difficult to determine whether employee training will solve the problem. A decline in food and beverage sales may be a problem caused by indifferent or unpleasant employees interacting with the public. Customer service training may solve the problem. However, if the decline is due to a deterioration of the food products' quality, then customer service training would not solve the problem of declining food sales.

Job/Task Analysis

Analyzing a job and the tasks performed in those jobs is another way of determining training needs. Job descriptions and specifications are reviewed to gain an understanding of the tasks performed in each job and the skills necessary to perform those tasks. Training and development specialists, in partnership with the supervisor and the employee who actually does the work, are important in this analysis.

Individual Analysis

Individual needs analysis is the third type of review used in determining training and development needs. Relevant questions are, "What kind of knowledge, skills and ability (KSAs) does an employee need in order to perform this task?" and "What needs to be done differently from the way it is being done today?" Individual analyses, sometimes called employee needs analyses, rely heavily on a supervisor's input through performance reviews along with day-to-day observations of the employee. However, assumptions about the employee's performance should not be made without investigating the situation. It is important to involve the supervisor and the employee in the discussion to determine the training need. This interaction builds support for any possible future employee training. Again, before moving forward with a training and development effort, the following questions should be asked: "Is this worth pursuing?" and "What is the cost if left alone?" If the decision is made to implement a training and development activity, then it is critical to consider the following conditions when diagnosing why an employee does not perform as expected:

- Does the individual lack the resources, tools or education necessary to do the job?

- Are there obstacles in the way (e.g., other people; clashing personalities; workload; a clean, safe, supportive environment; personal problems such as family, finances, or health)?

- Does the individual lack the skills or ability (can't do the job)?

- Does the individual lack the knowledge necessary to do the job (doesn't know how to do the job)?

- Does the individual know he or she is expected to do the job?

- Does the individual refuse to do the job? It could be boredom or lack of motivation.

- Is the individual punished when he or she does it correctly?

- Is the individual rewarded or praised even when doing it incorrectly?

- Is the individual ignored whether he or she does it correctly or incorrectly?

- Is the individual getting timely, accurate, specific, relevant feedback when the task is not done as expected?

- Is the individual afraid to do the task or afraid to try something new?

Pooling all of the information obtained from the three needs analyses—organization, job/task, and individual/employee—gives a clearer picture of organizational training and development needs. The training specialist assists the supervisor by conducting interviews, gathering performance data, analyzing job tasks for each position, testing for job task knowledge and skills, and conducting employee surveys. This composite then leads to the recommendations and design of training and development programs or interventions that "close the gap" between the current performance and the desired performance. Through this process known as a *gap analysis*, objectives and priorities for training programs are

established to improve organizational performance by improving employee skill level, reduce deficiencies in performance, and remove obstacles hindering performance. (Figure 10.5)

Prioritizing Training and Development Needs

Cost is often the basis for determining and prioritizing training and development initiatives. Training specialists have methods for calculating the cost of training, the cost of alternatives to training, the cost of substandard performance, and the cost and benefits for individual development. However, not all decisions should be based on their cost-effectiveness alone. The urgency of legal and safety issues, quality of work life, or addressing human interaction situations (such as conflict) take precedence. If one training endeavor must be sacrificed for financial reasons, the impact of its elimination on the organization's performance in achieving its goals must be evaluated. Another consideration in providing and prioritizing training and development opportunities is whether to design and deliver a program using internal resources, to select and hire an external consultant, or to purchase a ready-made program. Cost, quality, and content of such programs must be evaluated before deciding whether to "make" or "buy." Communication with management, supervisors, and employees is important in determining and prioritizing the training needs and should always be based on organizational objectives.

ESTABLISHING OBJECTIVES

Once training and development needs have been identified, concrete, measurable objectives must be established for each training and development program in order to achieve desired outcomes (Mager, 1984). Let us take the example of the previously identified problem, "decline in food and beverage sales." The job/task analysis indicates that one of the most important tasks of snack bar attendants is to serve

| Current Performance | ← GAP → | Desired Performance |

1. Identify the GAP between current performance and desired performance
2. Once the GAP is identified, determine the reason for the GAP by investigating, collecting data, observing, and dialogue
3. Identify possible solutions to close that GAP

Figure 10.5
Gap Performance

customers in a pleasant manner. However, the individual analysis from employee performance reviews reveals poor customer service skills for most snack bar attendants. This suggests the need for customer service training. Or does it? What if 30% of snack bar attendants only speak Spanish? Should their training be oriented toward customer service, conversational English, or a combination? If a snack bar attendant cannot speak English, he can be instructed to smile when approached by customers, but will not be able to respond satisfactorily to customer's questions asked in English. What type of training is appropriate for the snack bar attendant who does speak English?

Training objectives to meet both of these immediate needs might look like this:

1. Develop employee interpersonal skills to demonstrate promptness, enthusiasm, friendliness, and courteousness in responding to customer questions or requests for service.

2. Educate employees on the proper approach and technique to serve customers, handle complaints, and answer questions about other park activities.

3. Teach conversational English to Spanish-speaking employees, focusing on questions asked most frequently by customers.

For the Spanish-speaking employee, development objectives might be stated this way:

1. Learn basic oral communication skills in English sufficient to understand and respond to complex job-related instructions and tasks.

2. Learn basic written communication skills in English sufficient to be able to prepare correspondence and written reports and be able to read employee policy and procedure documents.

In addition to identifying and addressing immediate development needs, each full-time employee should develop an *individual development plan* focusing on his or her long-range development or career aspirations. These plans are created through conversations guided by the supervisor or training specialist where an employee identifies his current skills and abilities, future development or career interests, and written objectives or goals for achieving them.

These long-range plans may take several years to accomplish, but they are aimed at developing present workers into high-performing employees who have a competitive chance for growth, promotion, or movement within the organization. The process involves identifying an employee's current knowledge, skills, and abilities, and identifying practical plans and goals for enhancing preparedness for future opportunities. Objectives should be simple and easily understood, and should specifically identify which new behaviors or skills the employee should demonstrate after completing the training or development program. This planning requires a commitment of time and energy from both the supervisor and the employee. However, as stated earlier with regard to mutually beneficial relationships, both the organization and employee benefit from this formal approach to supporting employee development—the organization ensures people with desired qualifications are available when needed while the employee's need for growth and development is satisfied. This attention to formal career development is important in maintaining a motivated and committed workforce (HR Focus, April 2006).

Major Skills Categories

Skills training refers to the following:

1. *Conceptual skills* such as planning, policy development, and adapting to rapidly changing environments are most needed by middle- or top-level management employees.

2. *Interpersonal skills* such as leadership, communications, and human relations are needed by all employees and especially by supervisors, recreation leaders, volunteer coordinators, and those employees who interact with the public and with other employees on a regular basis.

3. *Technical skills* such as how to organize and schedule events, repair machinery, write bid specifications, propagate plants, and computer skills are needed to perform successfully in specific positions.

4. *Basic skills* such as reading, writing, and listening are necessary to meet at least minimum standards of competency in every job. Good listening skills are essential for all supervisors, and time-management skills are vital to most middle- to top-level managers.

It is the job/task analysis that identifies the skills necessary for every task in the organization. It is the individual analysis that determines which workers need additional training and development to satisfy one or more of the four major skills required for the task. It is the organizational analysis that helps determine the priority of training and development efforts in relationship to their value to the organization.

TYPES OF TRAINING PROGRAMS

After determining what behaviors, attitudes, or knowledge is needed, the next step in the process is selecting the most effective type of program and delivery method for the identified training needs. Budgets and organizational norms may influence the options considered but the fundamental criterion in selecting the training and development method should be its appropriateness to the learning objectives (Laird, Naquin, & Holton, 2003). For example, if getting exercise is the objective, then choosing to ride a power scooter to the store instead of walking or riding a bicycle is not the best choice. Impact on the objective can be enhanced or diminished depending on the method selected. The choices of program types and delivery methods continue to increase and there are advantages and disadvantages to every method. Memberships in professional societies such as the American Society for Training and Development (ASTD) and the Organizational Development (OD) Network help training and development specialists stay up-to-date on their profession and are resources for support, ideas, and networking in considering the options. Some common types of programs and delivery methods follow.

On-the-Job Training

On-the-job training (OTJ) is the most common method of training and developing employees where the person learns a job by doing it. It provides "hands-on" experience that facilitates learning transfer, and employees can be productive while learning the job skills. There are also disadvantages to OTJ training. Although it may appear inexpensive to implement because it does not require off-site facilities like classrooms, OTJ training could result in costly mistakes, damage to equipment, and customer dissatisfaction. Some OTJ methods are expensive in terms of the one-on-one time invested in the process of developing an employee in mastering a new technique or skill.

Supervisory Assistance

The most informal approach to OTJ training is supervisory assistance through day-to-day observation, coaching, and feedback. This technique is effective only if the supervisor provides immediate feedback, takes the time to create feelings of employee self-confidence, and delegates more and more responsibility as the employee is able to handle it. Situational leadership (Blanchard, 1985) is a helpful model for supervisors to use in choosing between a directive, coaching, mentoring or delegating style of leading depending on the employee's motivation and confidence in doing a specific job task.

Informal Training

This type of development occurs when employees share information, tips, and techniques through their own interactions and feedback with each other. Sometimes new employees are assigned to experienced workers for orientation. Demonstrating, asking questions, advising and instruction from coworkers rather than from formal training programs is an inexpensive way to train employees (Mathis & Jackson, 2007). Surveys from the American Society for Training and Development estimate that as much as 80% of what employees learn is through these informal means (Weintraub & Martineau, 2002). Encouraging this type of culture is advantageous for organizations; however, this method of training is difficult to measure, inconsistent, and undependable when specific skills need to be addressed.

Job Rotation or Cross-Training

Another form of OTJ training is job rotation or cross-training in which employees are moved from job to job at planned intervals to broaden their experiences. This helps the employee understand the work of the organization on a larger scale and improves productivity. It is often used to encourage effective teamwork (Vowler, 2005). Organizations also use job rotation and cross-training to prepare employees for future supervisory or management positions.

Several methods combine both on-the-job and off-the-job, or external, training in order to enhance the learning of the participant. Apprenticeships, internships, coaching and mentoring fall into this area of training and development.

Apprenticeships

This training combines OTJ training under the supervision of an experienced master craftsperson or journeyman with related classroom instruction. This learning method is mandatory for more than 1,000 occupations, such as carpentry, plumbing, electrical, culinary arts, electronics, and painting. Apprenticeship programs last from two to five years with four years being the average length. The apprenticeship involves a cooperative relationship between unions, employers, and vocation schools. According to the U.S. Department of Labor's Bureau of Apprenticeship and Training, at least 68% of registered apprenticeship sponsors say these programs help identify needed skills, raise productivity, strengthen worker morale and pride, and improve worker safety (http://www.doleta.gov/OA/, 2009).

Internships

Internship programs (also referred to as fieldwork or practicum) are less formal than apprenticeships, but they do involve an agreement between employers and colleges and universities. This type of OTJ training is frequently found in parks, recreation and leisure settings. Interns receive close supervision from both the employer and the educational institution, and the work schedule is usually varied and carefully planned to provide learning opportunities in all functions within the organization. Interns are usually paid less than full-time employees and/or earn college credits. Many are voluntary.

Coaching

A coach is a person skilled in guiding an individual towards identifying his or her developmental needs or desires and then taking action steps towards achieving these goals. The coach can be the employee's supervisor, a training specialist, an outside consultant, or even a peer (peer coaching). The coaching process is an interactive one where the coach supports, listens, and asks thoughtful questions that evoke responses from the employee intended to illuminate the employee's strengths, hurdles, and ideas. Coaching is effective at all levels and has become an excellent way to develop managers and executives (HR Focus, July 2006). Organizations benefit from supervisors who coach because the process allows for an employee to get individualized attention while the supervisor can learn a great deal about the employee's abilities and motivation. It strengthens the relationship between a supervisor and the employee permitting richer dialogue and feedback to occur. It also helps a supervisor learn more about the processes of motivating, directing, and communicating with employees (Laird et al., 2003). Coaching is time-consuming and requires good coaching skills to be effective. Supervisors may

not have the confidence, experience or knowledge to lead an effective coaching process until they develop their own skills as a coach.

Mentoring

Mentoring is the relationship between two individuals, usually a junior and a senior colleague, or between peers, for the purpose of advising, role modeling, networking, sharing contacts, and supporting. It can occur at all levels of an organization. Mentoring not only benefits the employee but also benefits the mentor and the organization. In helping employees reach their potential, the organization is preparing for future staffing needs and the mentor gets the opportunity to serve as a role model and share his or her knowledge. Some believe that having a mentor is essential to breaking barriers that have challenged under-represented groups in the past. Studies have shown that women who are mentored are more likely to enhance or expand career skills, advance in their careers, receive higher salaries, and enjoy work more (Butler, 2006). As with all methods, mentoring has its disadvantages. It places additional workload and time commitments on mentors who are often strapped for time already, and like coaching, it requires good mentoring skills including strong interpersonal skills.

Supervisory and Management Development Programs

Development programs for supervisors, managers, administrators, and executives are necessary because employees in these positions have tremendous responsibilities leading and in helping employees connect to the organization's vision, mission and goals through the work they do. Oftentimes employees are promoted from within the organization and the skills required for successful supervision may be different than those the employee performed in his or her role prior to the promotion. Preparing and supporting employees who assume these roles is critical. Often, internal training and development specialists plan and deliver customized programs that meet the specific needs of the organization's management.

Leadership Development Programs

As organizations' strategic efforts become more focused, stronger emphasis has been placed on leadership development. Preparing for the future includes encouraging and developing leadership skills of employees who will drive the changes necessary to keep the organization moving forward. Leadership development programs are also part of a talent management strategy called succession planning, designed to enhance the skills of productive, motivated employees to their fullest potential in order to meet future staffing needs. This type of development program satisfies the needs of the employer as well as gives employees greater flexibility and access to more opportunities both laterally and for those interested in upward mobility.

Formal Education Programs

When employees are given leave to return to high school or college to attend classes, it is referred to as *formal education*. Employees may be reimbursed for tuition, materials, and transportation costs. These benefits serve as an inducement to continue formal education. There are distinct disadvantages to all formal education methods of learning. (1) They may require participants to be absent from their jobs, which can be costly to an employer and reduce or delay productivity. (2) The focus of the formal education may not be related to the current job duties of the employee. (3) It is difficult to hold the interest and attention of participants in larger groups for which lecture is a very popular teaching technique. (4) Most of the formal education methods of learning require very good verbal and written skills.

Orientation Programs or Onboarding

Welcoming new employees through *orientation programs* is an important element of recruitment and retention. Orientation programs help employees become productive quicker by offering helpful information, and by engaging them so they feel a sense of belonging and excitement. During orientation programs, employees are welcomed as valued members of the organization. They are provided information about organizational policies, procedures, culture, and goals, giving them an opportunity to ask questions and meet coworkers. This leads to higher job satisfaction and retention. *Onboarding* is the continuation of assimilating the new employee after the initial orientation. It can last up to a year and focuses on further integrating the new employee into the organization. Orientation and onboarding have been shown to reduce employee turnover during the first year of employment (SHRM Learning Systems, 2008, p. 91).

Professional Development Programs

Programs designed to improve organizational performance through improving employee competencies are another important type of training and development program. Examples of professional development programs are skills enhancement workshops, diversity training programs, personal development and team building programs. Also included are conferences, workshops, and forums. NRPA, through its Division of Professional Services, publishes a very detailed calendar each year on scores of state society and regional conferences, workshops, forums, and schools offering development opportunities in recreation, parks, and leisure services. Many of these NRPA educational programs offer continuing education units (CEUs). A CEU represents 10 hours of participation in an organized continuing education program under responsible sponsorship and qualified instruction. The CEU is a nationally recognized criterion of participation in professional development education programs. The NRPA and most state societies also keep record of participation at recognized CEU professional development sessions. Although CEUs cannot be used to obtain degree-granting credit at most universities, they are required by state park and recreation societies that have adopted the NRPA Certification Plan discussed in Appendix F. It is becoming increasingly important for professionals and technicians working in recreation, park or leisure services to participate in those training and development programs that offer CEUs.

Worldwide, Sandos Hotels & Resorts (sandoshotels.com) pride themselves on their attention to employee development. All new employees attend an orientation program called the "Sandos Way" where they are introduced to expected standards of customer service and quality. Depending on the job responsibilities, additional orientation lasting from two to seven days under the guidance of the direct supervisor follows. All Sandos employees are offered opportunities for development enabling them to be considered for promotion within the company. For example, if a Spanish-speaking housekeeper in the Mexican resort of Sandos Playacar learns to speak English or French, he or she has an opportunity to be considered for a host or hostess position in one of the dining rooms. See Figure 10.6 (p. 176) for an example of a Sandos calendar of training and development events.

DELIVERY METHODS

When determining how training will be delivered, the option of using external resources is considered and often used by employers. There are many possibilities for outsourcing training and development

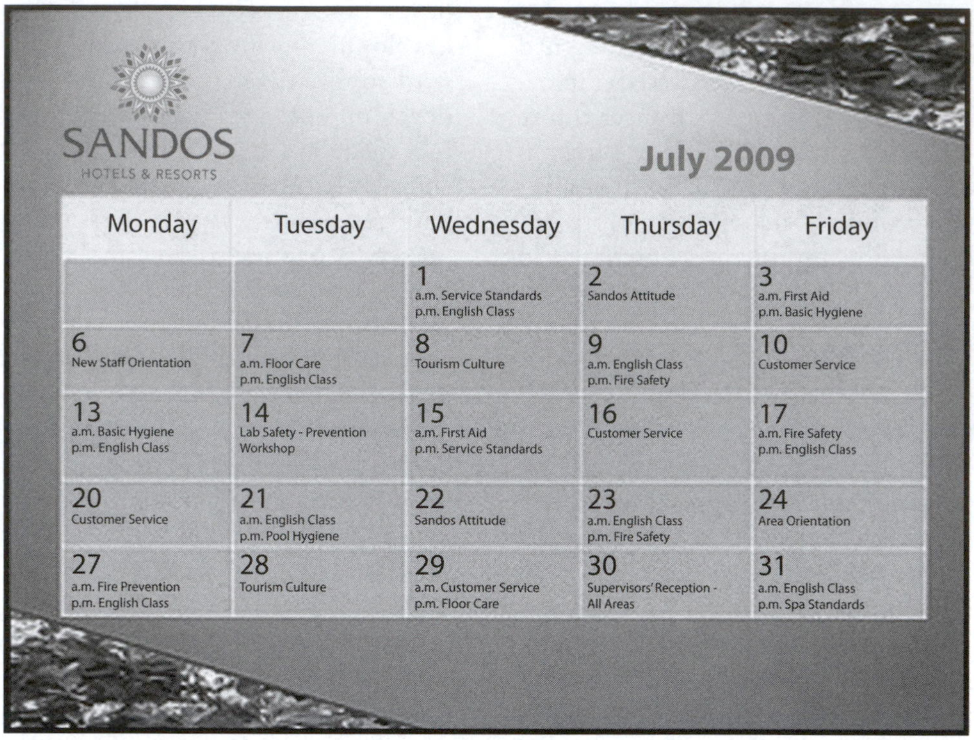

Figure 10.6
Example of a Training and Development Events Calendar

including those offered by colleges and universities, professional associations such as the American Management Association (AMA), the American Society for Training and Development (ASTD), the National Recreation and Park Association (NRPA), and through private independent training organizations and consultants. According to ASTD data, approximately 25% of training expenditures go to outside training resources. However, based on a recent three-year study, there has been a decline in outsourcing of training (ASTD 2008, p. 11). Today's economic environment, in addition to a more strategic focus on expectations of training and development outcomes, may be influencing the decision of whether to use external or internal resources.

Instructor or Facilitator-Led

Instructor-led programs and classes continue to be the most popular method of delivery for training and development needs (Kranz, 2009). A good instructor or facilitator engages participants and creates an environment where participants are excited to learn (Mondy, 2008, p. 206). Face-to-face contact, the opportunity to provide pertinent examples, the occasion for discussing the subject matter, the chance to answer specific questions from the learners, and the

opportunity to provide direct, immediate feedback are the advantages of the instructor-led method. The disadvantages include cost, scheduling conflicts, instructor availability, inconsistent delivery of content from class to class, and the impact on learning related to the personality style of the facilitator.

E-Learning

E-learning refers to the use of electronic technology-based media for the delivery of educational materials for the purpose of learning. Today's rapid growth in technology along with its flexibility has opened the door for this delivery system. One method of e-learning allows for participants to interact together from different locations in a virtual classroom at a specific time led by a facilitator or instructor; another method allows individuals to learn at their own pace. Examples of e-learning include online programs, DVDs, online discussion groups, e-mail communications, CD-ROMs, videos, learning portals, message boards, chat rooms, and podcasts (ASTD Learning System Updates, 2006 & 2009). Some of the disadvantages are that it requires uninterrupted access to computers, a comfort level that all participants may not have with working on computers, and it may not be an effective method when the learning objectives are to change behaviors or to develop interpersonal skills.

Simulated Training

Simulated training is a method in which participants are presented with equipment or situations that are similar to those of real job conditions. Case studies, role playing, behavior modeling, and computer/board games are simulation techniques in which participants solve real-life situations. Simulation is particularly necessary when on-the-job training is too expensive or dangerous. Law enforcement, cardiopulmonary resuscitation, and water safety instruction are examples of situations that require learning through simulation before applying knowledge or skills on the job. Using media such as films or closed-circuit television are excellent tools for simulation training. Employees can observe how a specific operation should be handled as many times as necessary before actually doing it on the job. Audiovisuals are more expensive than case studies but greatly enhance simulation training.

Case Studies

This technique presents specific scenarios in writing to a group of employees. Participants utilize group discussion to analyze and test their ideas. Feedback is immediate. Real-life situations with real-life personalities make the learning more interesting. For example, a supervisor may have to decide on which of several corrective actions are appropriate for a performance issue.

Role Playing

In role playing, employees assume the characteristics of specific persons in a given situation in order to act out a real-life scenario. The purpose is to develop skills such as delegation, dealing with conflict, communication or decision-making. It is also used to increase awareness of other people's feelings during diversity training. Role playing is most beneficial when facilitated by a skilled instructor because many participants are uncomfortable with this technique. Acting in front of others in unpredictable scenarios is nerve-wracking for many and reduces their learning.

Behavior Modeling

Behavior modeling training gives participants the opportunity to copy or replicate observed skills in practice sessions. Behavior modeling has been used to train supervisors in tasks such as conducting performance reviews, correcting unacceptable performance behavior,

delegating work, improving safety habits, overcoming resistance to change, orienting new employees, interviewing applicants, and mediating individuals or groups in conflict (Mondy, 2008). Videotaping participants engaged in role playing is a good way for them to see their strengths and weaknesses and gain helpful insight into different techniques.

Computer and Board Games

These media techniques provide simulated market and environments where employees must compete with each other for limited resources or for a targeted population's leisure dollars. Complex decisions are required in advertising, capital development, pricing, staffing, purchasing, and program offerings. The employee must get actively involved, and active involvement enhances learning. Games are usually interesting because of their realism and competitiveness and are good for developing problem-solving skills and controlling multiple units of data and information overload.

In-Basket Exercises

In contrast, an in-basket exercise is a more solitary activity where an employee is asked to prioritize and then handle a number of items such as e-mail messages, memoranda, reports, telephone messages, and other items of the type that would be found on a manager or director's desk. The trainee must first prioritize the importance of each situation and then recommend solutions and take whatever action is necessary. Management games and in-basket exercises are good training techniques and have proven useful in identifying employees for potential management positions (York, Strubler, & Smith, 2005).

Experiential Learning

Experiential learning is based on the theory that knowledge comes through experience and learning occurs when a person engages in some activity, looks back on how he or she handled the activity, draws some useful insight from this reflection, and then uses this information to change future behavior. Activities are often done in groups with an emphasis on human dynamics and the impact people's actions and behavior have on the group's ability to successfully accomplish a task or assignment. The skill of the facilitator in helping a group process the outcomes is critical and will impact the learning that the participants take away from the activity. Outdoor education programs are founded on experiential learning and use challenge, adventure, and outdoor experiences to help individuals and teams develop (Cornell Outdoor Education, http://www.coe.cornell.edu). *Sensitivity training, psychodrama, transactional analysis, assertiveness training* and *team building* are all experiential learning methods that advocate learning about the self in order to bring about behavioral change.

INCREASING LEARNING POTENTIAL

Selecting the best training method and techniques to meet the stated training objectives does not guarantee the success of the training and development effort. Development and training activities that do not improve job performance are of little value to an organization. The purpose of these programs is for learning to occur. Certain factors must be considered for maximizing learning including the learning environment, approaches to learning by knowledgeable and skilled instructors or facilitators, and the ability, motivation and commitment of the participant to learn.

Learning Environment

Every person who has ever sat for several hours in a hot room on an uncomfortable chair knows that the learning environment can enhance or detract from the learning experience. A room with too many distractions or a seating arrangement that doesn't support the learning techniques used makes it equally difficult for the learner to give full attention to the subject. Any program format that requires intense mental concentration for more than six hours in one day is counterproductive in its design. Similarly, if the employees are isolated for several days and nights in a new environment, special consideration should be given to their "off-duty" needs. If the only recreation option is a bar that serves alcoholic beverages, the facilitator can expect to see a few tired and possibly hungover employees the next morning! Leisure professionals should be able to offer a few recreation and exercise alternatives to television or drinking. Even the food choices offered to participants when planning programs should be considered. Afternoon sessions can drag if participants are served heavy food during lunch breaks. A facilitator was noted for saying, "Hide that cheesecake!"

Approaches to Learning

Maximizing the transfer of learning to participants is the objective of training and development efforts. However, this is not as easy a task as one might hope! Years of study and research have not identified an absolutely foolproof theory about how adults learn (Laird et al., 2003). This never-ending focus on the transfer of learning continues to stimulate the exploration for methods to enhance learning. How learning material is presented impacts the degree to which it is absorbed. For example, if the learning objective is to drive a truck, listening to a classroom instructor talk about how to drive the truck is not going to help the participant become a competent truck driver. Familiarity with a variety of learning principles, theories, and techniques is helpful for designers of instruction when determining the most appropriate method for the situation or learning objective.

Learning Principles, Theories, and Techniques

Learning Styles

Learning styles describe the way individuals learn and their preferred way of taking in information. The three learning styles are visual, auditory, and kinesthetic. Figure 10.7 shows the different characteristics of each style. When working with an individual, it is helpful to know and use their preferred learning style. When working with groups, the training and development delivery for groups should incorporate all three.

Learning Skill

Cognitive, *psychomotor*, or *affective* are the three learning skill domains of human behavior. Identifying the learning skill required for attaining the learning objective is helpful when determining the delivery method or combination of methods to be used in designing the training and development program.

Cognitive Skills: Involve using the mind

- Recite law, policy or safety instructions
- Quote prices to a customer
- Learning another language
- Explain the steps for performing a task
- Calculating employee vacation and sick time
- Trouble-shooting equipment failure

VISUAL	AUDITORY	KINESTHETIC
Learns by seeing	Learns by hearing	Learns by doing
Prefers pictures, diagrams, demonstrations, etc.	Enjoys listening and likes to talk	Prefers hands-on activities, use gestures and is expressive
Likes to see the task being performed before trying	Likes to be given verbal instructions before trying the task, likes to discuss the task before trying	Likes to jump right in and try the task
Distracted by untidiness or movement	Distracted by sounds or noises	Distracted by nearby activity
Difficulty following verbal directions	Difficulty following written directions	Must be actively involved in learning process
Prefers face-to-face meetings	Prefers conversation on the telephone	Prefers walking or participating in activity while talking
Finds something to watch when bored	Hums or talks to themselves when bored	Tinkers or moves when bored
Likes to sit where she can see	Likes to sit where she can hear even if she can't see	Likes to sit where she has freedom to move around or get out of seat

Figure 10.7
Learning Style Characteristics

Psychomotor Skills: Involve using arms, legs, torso, body

- Repairing equipment
- Driving a car
- Cooking a meal
- Using a computer
- Learning yoga or massage

Affective Skills: Involve feelings, emotions, relationship skills

- Increasing self-awareness
- Controlling emotions
- Listening to others with respect
- Practicing empathy
- Learning team building skills
- Understanding impact of personality styles
- Developing ethical practices

Experiential Learning

Today, there is an increased usage of the *experiential learning method*, where the participant is given the opportunity to experience something during the learning in order to maximize the transfer of learning (Laird et al., 2003). This method of learning illuminates the need for expert facilitators rather than presenters who have great platform skills. Facilitation with an emphasis on questioning, listening, feedback, positive reinforcement, and reflection is critical in experiential learning and has the greatest impact on changing behaviors of the learner.

Other learning theories, principles, and techniques for maximizing the transfer of learning suggest:

- Learning objectives should be clearly defined
- Learning materials should be organized
- Exploration and experimentation increase transfer of learning (Allen, 2007)
- Content material should be meaningful and relevant to the learner
- The connection between the training situation and the real-life situation should be clear
- Long stretches of continuous information should be broken up with breaks
- Learners need to know "what's in it for me?"

- Learners already have knowledge and experience—use these to help relate content!
- Learners should be treated with respect, understanding, and genuine concern
- Facilitators be active listeners
- Stimulated and engaged participants learn more
- Using stories for fostering discussion and interaction (Foreman, 2003)
- Playing games involves the senses and fosters high-level thinking (T&D, 2003)
- Learners be given the opportunity to practice skills

Learner Capability and Motivation

Attention to the learning environment, learning principles, theory, and techniques will be useless if the learner does not have the *capability* or the *motivation* to learn the task. Capability refers to an individual's ability—the necessary aptitude, intelligence level, educational level, physical characteristics, manual dexterity, or whatever else is needed to perform the task. If vehicular equipment is designed to be operated by a 5'8" operator, then a 4'11" operator may experience difficulty mastering the clutch while trying to see where to maneuver the vehicle. Equally as important is the individual's motivation and readiness to learn. If an individual does not see the value in learning, does not trust the training, or is unwilling to commit the time or effort, then the transfer of learning is significantly diminished, if not completely absent, and the training and development efforts become a waste of time and money.

Evaluating the Effectiveness of Training and Development

Training and development costs represent major investments for employers. How do organizational leaders know if these investments achieve results? Is it possible to measure the degree to which training and development efforts helped the organization meet business and learning goals? Although these questions are not new, today's economy and competitive pressures require close examination of expenditures. The desire to show a return on investment (ROI) is stronger than ever. Unfortunately, few organizations take the time to effectively measure training and development results. It is not uncommon for organizations to send employees away to expensive, nationally

recognized programs without any attempt at determining how much the employees learned or whether the knowledge gained transferred into better work performance once the employees returned to work. Organizational leaders recognize the value of training and development efforts as reflected by the large sums of money spent on employees each year; however the knowledge of how to effectively evaluate the impact of these efforts is often lacking. According to a study conducted by ASTD (2009) of over 700 organizations, 9 out of 10 respondents reported conducting some form of evaluation following training. Further investigation revealed the evaluation methods used did very little to show the effectiveness of the training and development efforts in terms of impact on organizational goals.

The most widely known model for evaluating training and development efforts is Donald L. Kirkpatrick's Four Levels of Evaluation (Kirkpatrick, 1976). It identifies four levels for evaluating training programs: the participant's reaction to the training (Level 1); the learning achieved from the training (Level 2); the behavioral changes of participants as a result of the program (Level 3); and the results or impact on the attainment of organizational goals (Level 4). See Figure 10.8.

Reaction. Level 1 evaluation is determined by *administering surveys, questionnaires, or by interviewing* participants immediately at the conclusion of the program for their reaction. Typical questions are: 1) What information presented will be helpful to you in performing your job? 2) How effective were the facilitators or presenters? 3) How appropriate were the environment and teaching techniques? Responses to these questions indicate how participants felt about the program and the environment. Ninety-two percent of ASTD's survey respondents reported using Level 1 evaluations in their organizations (ASTD, 2009). Why? Because they are easy to administer! However, research also shows that such evaluations

Level	Evaluates
Level 1: Reaction	How participants feel about the program
Level 2: Learning	How participants increased/changed their knowledge, skills, attitudes
Level 3: Behavior	How participants changed their behaviors on the job
Level 4: Results	How the program impacted the attainment of organizational goals

Figure 10.8
Kirkpatrick's Four Levels of Evaluation

have a low correlation with learning and performance (Laird, et al., 2003). Just because an employee enjoys a particular training effort and finds it fun and exciting is no guarantee that the employee's performance will improve. It is difficult to determine the effectiveness of the training through surveys and opinions. Often referred to as *smile sheets*, these surveys and opinions are not significantly related to an organization's success in meeting objectives and goals.

Learning. Determining how well participants learned information presented during a training and development program is an example of Level 2 evaluation. *Tests* are typically the tool used for this level and are often used for formal education programs, apprenticeships, internships, and simulations. Students are tested to assess if they learned the required principles, facts, concepts, theories, and skills. It is difficult to design a test that measures what it is intended to measure. Assuming that one is developed, it still does not guarantee that the learning will transfer to job application and performance improvement once the employee is back on the job. Learning does not always mean behavioral change. Comparing scores of tests given before and after a workshop would be an indicator of Level 2.

Behavior. Level 3 evaluation examines the change in employee behavior as a result of the training. Behavioral changes are difficult to evaluate because human behavior is often inconsistent. It is also difficult to determine if the training and development effort was the sole reason for an improvement in performance. Factors unrelated to the training program can cause the desired behavioral change resulting in an inaccurate assessment of the training and development effort. Comparing employee performance before and after the training program, interviewing, observing, and follow-up surveys of participants are methods used to identify behavioral change. According to research by ASTD, monitoring performance reviews and linking performance to learning experiences is a useful practice and a good way to support desired behavioral changes and Level 3 evaluation (ASTD, 2009, p. 19).

Results. Assessing training and development efforts in terms of success in meeting organizational goals and business results is Level 4 evaluation. Frequently thought of as the bottom line, this level of evaluation measures training and development efforts in terms of increased productivity, improved quality, decreased costs, reduced frequency of accidents, increased sales, and higher profits or income. One example of a Level 4 results evaluation involves controlled experimentation. This means that the employer would randomly select some employees to receive training, while other employees, representing the control group, would not. Evaluators would establish evaluation criteria to be measured before and after the training to demonstrate changes that occurred as a result of the training and not because of other factors such as changes in routine. Other methods of performing Level 4 evaluation are: measuring customer satisfaction, employee and management perception of the training's impact (anecdotal), actual business outcomes such as sales and revenue, and competency/proficiency levels of employees (ASTD, 2009, p. 21). For example, if the objective was to improve public relations, the evaluation criterion would be a reduction in customer complaints. Strategically, improved business results are the overall reason for training and development efforts, yet Level 4 evaluations are not often conducted. Why not? Linking training efforts to results in terms of impact on organization goals is difficult to do and requires the application of complex models, formulas, and statistical interpretations. Respondents of the ASTD 2008 State of the Industry survey reported that calculating return-on-investment (ROI) of training and development efforts is too complex and time-consuming (ASTD, 2009). The time required to conduct Level 4 evaluations along with their complexity make this level of evaluations costly to implement.

Level 1 evaluations are the most frequently used and there is a significant drop in use of each of the subsequent levels. This is understandable because the difficulty in conducting evaluations increases from Level 1 through Level 4. However, in terms of value to the organization, Levels 3 and 4 are more successful methods of evaluation. Figure 10.9 (see p. 182) shows the four different levels of evaluation with relationship to the difficulty in administering them and their value to the organization. The more accurately an evaluation assesses the effectiveness of training efforts in meeting organizational goals, the greater the value.

It is not fair to say that because training and development efforts are difficult to evaluate they are not valuable experiences. Even though an organization's current evaluation methodology may be flawed or weak, evaluating the effectiveness of training and development is a critical step in the process. Conscientious attention must be given to measuring tangible benefits from training. As organizations continue to pour millions of dollars into training and development efforts, it is important to invest in the evaluation process to demonstrate the positive relationship between

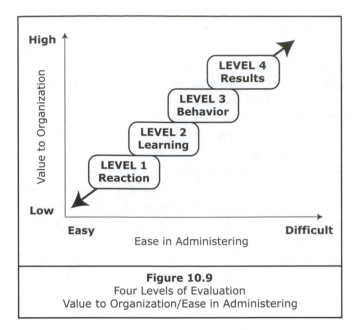

Figure 10.9
Four Levels of Evaluation
Value to Organization/Ease in Administering

training and development programs and improved job and organizational performance. In organizations where training and development specialists perform a solid, accurate analysis of these costs, training budgets seem to remain stable, and even grow when profits sag (Laird et al., 2003). Even more importantly, they consider the money spent on training and development activities as an investment instead of an expense.

Recognizing the importance of investing in the development of people is not new. As stated in an ancient Chinese proverb, "If you want 1 year of prosperity, grow grain. If you want 10 years of prosperity, grow trees. If you want 100 years of prosperity, grow people."

SUMMARY

1. A mutually beneficial relationship exists between an organization and an employee. The organization meets the expectations of an employee by providing opportunities for learning, development, involvement, rewards, and recognition while the employee meets the need of the organization by learning, improving job performance, and adapting to change to help meet the goals and mission.

2. Sometimes the word *training* is used when referring to job-related skills, techniques, or information necessary for employees to perform satisfactorily in their present jobs, while *development* concentrates on preparing the employee to meet the work objective of some future job responsibility. However, all learning is developmental.

3. Organizational development (OD) is the function within an organization focused on the well-being of the whole organization. Training and development is one of many OD activities. Other OD activities include leading change efforts, team building, coaching, life/work integration, organizational design, diversity education, new employee orientation, leadership development, supervisory development, and conflict resolution.

4. T/D improves job performance, work attitude, and self-confidence. These characteristics improve productivity. Training and development efforts attract more and better qualified perspective employees as well as serve as an incentive in retaining current talent.

5. Effective T/D involves a five-step process. First, training and development needs must be determined. Second, objectives must be established that identify which type of skills the employee is to learn. Third, the appropriate program structure and technique must be developed and the right instructor or facilitator identified. Fourth, the training program must be implemented with consideration for increasing the learning potential, and fifth, the T/D program must be evaluated to determine whether the learning objectives established in Step 2 were met.

6. Strategic training and development is linking learning objectives with organizational goals, mission, and vision. Organizations that recognize learning as critical to business success, invest in employee development, and link such efforts to the organization's future are called learning organizations.

7. Job/Task needs analysis identifies which skills at which competency level are necessary to perform each job. Individual needs analysis determines who needs additional training to satisfy those skill requirements. Organizational needs analysis helps determine the priority of training

and development efforts in relationship to their value to the organization.

8. There are many training and development methods and techniques, each with its own advantages and disadvantages. On-the-job training is popular because it facilitates learning transfer by giving the worker hands-on experience.

9. There are several disadvantages of formal group methods of learning, but these can be minimized if the learning technique of simulation training is used rather than the traditional lecture approach. Simulation presents the learners with situations that are similar to their real job conditions and involves them in skill building, knowledge, application, or problem solving.

10. Successful T/D also depends on the selection of a good learning environment free from distractions along with the application of recognized learning principles. Employees will learn best when they are motivated to want to learn, and when they understand why the learning is important.

11. The most common evaluation technique has been to ask the learners if they liked the training and development program and if they can use the material back on the job. This technique does not measure behavioral changes.

12. The best evaluation procedure is one that measures results. Although "results"-oriented procedures are complicated, conscientious attention must be given to measuring tangible benefits from training and development processes.

DISCUSSION TOPICS

1. Why is training and development important to organizations? What are the benefits to the organization?

2. Why is it important to do an analysis of the organization in order to determine training needs? How is this type of analysis related to job analysis and employee analysis?

3. Why is it important to try to increase the learning potential of trainees? How might we accomplish that?

4. Why are the principles of learning important to employee training and development?

5. What role do supervisors play in increasing the learning potential of employees with regard to training and development programs?

6. What are some of the disadvantages of off-the-job training and development?

7. What are CEUs and why have they become important in recent years to the recreation, park resources, and leisure services field?

8. What are the major steps in the training and development process?

9. Why do organizations overlook or lack proper evaluation of employee training and development programs?

REFERENCES

Allen, M. W. (2007). *Do something interesting!* Allen Interactions Inc. Retrieved from http://www.alleninteractions.com, ASTD.

American Society for Training & Development. (2008). *State of the Industry Report.* ASTD Press.

ASTD Learning System Update. (2006). ASTD Press (revised 11-04-2009).

ASTD. (2009, November). *The value of evaluation: Making training evaluations more effective.* Alexandria, VA: ASTD Research.

Bachman, K. (2000). *Corporate e-learning: Exploring a new frontier.* New York, NY: W. R. Hambrecht & Company.

Blanchard, K. (1984). *Leadership and the one minute manager.* New York, NY: William Morrow and Company, Inc.

Butler, K. M. (2006). Today's working women seek mentors, motherhood transition. *Employee Benefit News, 20,* 17–19.

Foreman, D. C. (2003, September). Eleven common-sense learning principles. Training & Development. ASTD Press, pp. 40–46.

HR Focus Human Resource Magazine. (2006, April). Retention and recruitment now top HR professionals' objectives. Vol. 83, Issue 4, p. 8.

HR Focus Human Resource Magazine. (2006, July). For success with corporate coaches, begin with assessment. Vol. 83, Issue 7, p. 8.

Innovative workplace safety accommodations for hearing-impaired workers. (2005). *United States Department of Labor.* Retrieved from http://www.osha.gov/dts/shib/shib072205.html

Kent, W., & Otte, F. L. (1982). Career development: The ultimate incentive. *Advanced Management Journal, 47,* 8–13.

Kirkpatrick, D. L. (1976). Evaluation of training. In R. L. Craig (Ed.), *Training and development handbook: A guide to human resource development.* New York, NY: McGraw Hill.

Kranz, G. (2009, October). Downturn prompts a change in learning initiatives. *Workforce Management Online.* Retrieved from http://www.workforce.com/article/20091027/NEWS02/310279987

Laird, D., Naquin, S., & Holton, E. F. III. (Eds.). (2003). *Approaches to training and development.* New York, NY: Perseus Books Group.

Mager, R. F. (1984). *Preparing instructional objectives.* Belmont, CA: Fearon.

Mathis, R. & Jackson, J. (2007). *Human resource management: Essential perspectives.* Canada: Thomson South-Western.

Mondy, R. W. (2008). *Human resource management.* (10th ed.). Upper Saddle River, NJ: Pearson Prentice Hall.

PrimeLearning, Inc. (2001). *eLearning: A key strategy for maximizing human capital in the knowledge economy.* White paper. PrimeLearningGroup, Ltd.

Society for Human Resource Management (US). (2008). *The SHRM learning system.* Human resource development (Module 3). Alexandria, VA.

Trends. (2003, June). American Society for Training and Development. *T&D Magazine.*

Vowler, J. (2005). Away days promote teamworking. *Computer Weekly.* Retrieved from http://www.computerweekly.com/feature/Away-days-promote-teamworking

Weintraub, R., & Martineau, J. (2002, June). The just in time imperative. *Training and Development,* 52.

York, K. M., Strubler, D. S., & Smith, E. M. (2005). A comparison of two methods for scoring an in-basket exercise. *Public Personnel Management, 34,* 271–280.

DISCIPLINE AND GRIEVANCES

Although organizations expect their employees to abide by established policies and rules, and to carry out their job duties in such a way as to meet acceptable performance standards, the stark reality is that employees sometimes make mistakes and break work rules, and sometimes they are unable or unwilling to meet performance standards. Most employee mistakes are unintentional, minor infractions to the day-to-day operation of the organization, and are relatively easy to resolve. In some instances, employees may not think the performance and conduct standards established by the organization apply to them. At previous jobs they may have committed similar offenses that went undetected or were overlooked by their employer. However, a few employee mistakes represent a major breach of the organization's policies and work rules. These offenses may disrupt the flow of work and endanger the safety and well-being of other employees. Serious misconduct cases which often result in formal grievances are challenging even for the most experienced supervisors to resolve.

No matter what employee mistakes occur—intentional or non-intentional, serious or trivial, they must not be ignored. Supervisors are responsible for acting promptly and resolving discipline problems before they escalate and get out of control. In this chapter we will introduce the nature of discipline in the workplace and discuss guidelines for establishing disciplinary policies, rules, and procedures. We will also present strategies for administering discipline, steps for conducting a disciplinary interview, and principles to adhere to if an accused employee decides to legally challenge an organization's disciplinary policies, work rules, or appeal corrective action taken by a supervisor. Finally, we conclude the chapter by examining employee complaints and grievances and the methods that are commonly used in resolving them.

NATURE OF DISCIPLINE ON THE JOB

One of the important areas of responsibility for supervisors is to motivate and facilitate the productivity of employees assigned to their unit or division. When employees are unable or unwilling to perform the duties of their job and follow the organization's rules and policies, then supervisors must intervene. Not all mistakes require discipline, but all mistakes must be taken seriously. Supervisors are responsible for recognizing employee-discipline issues, investigating the circumstances behind the unwanted behavior, and finding ways to resolve the problem with expediency. In this chapter, we will define *discipline* as formal corrective action taken by a supervisor against an employee who fails to meet the organization's performance standards, policies, and rules. The primary *objective* of administering discipline is to create and maintain a safe and productive working environment for employees.

Historically, discipline has had a punitive connotation for both supervisors and employees. Discipline represented punishment for employees who violated a rule or failed to perform according to the organization's standards. Supervisors often used the threat of punishment to keep employees focused and productive on the job. Supervisors also relied on the fear of punishment to deter employees from misconduct. The form of discipline that focuses primarily on punishment as a way to get employees to do their work and comply with rules and procedures is known as *negative* discipline.

Today, supervisors who depend on negative measures to bring compliance often find that the outcomes of this particular form of discipline have an effect opposite to the one intended. Generally, negative discipline can strain relationships between employees and their supervisors and sometimes, unfortunately, it can create devastating—even irreparable—damage to a trusting relationship. Punished employees often blame a supervisor for not fully understanding an issue and rebuke disciplinary action that is perceived as unfair or too harsh. Disciplined employees frequently respond to their supervisor with anger, resentment, and a desire to retaliate, in either obvious or subtle ways.

Negative discipline may be necessary for serious offenses and mistakes that result from continued carelessness, but a different approach is needed to resolve the majority of run-of-the-mill disciplinary problems that supervisors handle.

Positive approach to discipline. An alternative way to resolve performance and misconduct issues is through a positive approach to discipline. The framework for positive discipline is to create an organizational environment where employees take personal responsibility for their misconduct. Rather than following a traditional approach of resolving behavior problems by applying punitive measures, supervisors seek out alternative corrective solutions, often accepting those proposed by the employee that is being disciplined.

Adopting a positive approach to discipline requires both supervisors and employees to demonstrate self-control and communicate at a mature level. To this end, supervisors take seriously the responsibility of understanding why employees make mistakes and seek out alternative solutions to resolve problems amicably. Moreover, employees accept performance and conduct standards because they want a work environment that is fair, safe, and productive. Here is a case to make the point about a positive approach to discipline.

> An employee (Carol) has received "above average" performance evaluations over the past year. Carol is very bright, performs her job satisfactorily, and is efficient. Over the past couple of weeks the supervisor has observed her playing computer games, sending and receiving personal e-mail and cell phone calls, and spending excessive time during work socializing with others. Rather than treating this as a disciplinary case and applying sanctions, a supervisor using a positive discipline approach may look for an alternative way to resolve the unacceptable behavior. By informally meeting with Carol and discussing the misconduct, a supervisor may learn that Carol is extremely bored with her assigned job duties. Carol shares that she dislikes the lack of variety and the repetitive nature of her work and does not feel like the work is meaningful. With this new insight, a supervisor may suggest ways to expand and enrich Carol's job duties. The supervisor may also invite Carol to propose ways to make the job more challenging and eliminate the inappropriate work behavior.

A positive approach to discipline is an effective way to resolve most, but not all, discipline problems. Supervisors must accept the fact that at times serious discipline issues such as stealing company equipment, coming to work intoxicated, and using a company credit card for personal purchases occur and disciplinary action that is perceived by employees as punitive is necessary and appropriate.

ESTABLISHING DISCIPLINE GUIDELINES

Organizations have the prerogative for deciding what constitutes appropriate conduct for their employees, and generally, top-level management has a responsibility to establish the standards for employee performance and conduct. In many large organizations, representatives of human resource departments often provide invaluable assistance in developing discipline policies, procedures, and rules. They are also available to counsel with management resolving any and all disciplinary issues. In an effort to develop cooperative, win-win relationships, top-level management frequently forms an advisory committee comprised of employees for the purpose of drafting rules that, if broken, will result in corrective action.

Discipline policy and procedures manual. To provide overall guidance and direction to supervisors and employees on disciplinary issues, management is responsible for developing a formal discipline policy and procedures manual. The manual contains pertinent information about the organization's discipline program such as the program's goals and objectives, examples of work-rules violations, an explanation of the corrective action, and procedures for investigating and resolving discipline cases. In a discipline policy and procedures manual, management should include its *philosophy of discipline*; that is, how it intends to deal with performance or work-conduct problems. For example, management may espouse a philosophy that emphasizes a positive approach to discipline in which: 1) employees take personal responsibility for their conduct at work; and 2) supervisors make every effort to understand the reasons why misconduct occurs and pursue corrective actions that are not purely punitive and that resolve disciplinary issues amicably and expediently. Further, management may endorse punishment as an effective disciplinary measure in dealing with only the most serious offenses where an employee's unwillingness to comply with established policies and rules can create an unsafe or unproductive working environment.

It is customary practice for organizations to include discipline policy and procedures as one section of an organization's overall human resources policy and procedure manual.

Elements of disciplinary guidelines. To achieve a healthy, safe, and productive work environment, management must decide what kind of behavior it expects from employees, how to sustain that behavior, and how to maintain consistency in subsequent disciplinary action. A series of questions serve as a guide for establishing disciplinary policies and work rules.

1. Are the policies and rules necessary? To encourage self-discipline and minimize disciplinary action, management should only establish those rules and policies that are necessary to ensure an orderly, efficient, fair, and safe operation.

- For example: Is it necessary, or arbitrary, to have a company rule banning background music from an employee's office due to the noise factor? It may be necessary to have a rule restricting on-duty lifeguards from using earplugs or headphones to listen to music on an iPod or other music device due to safety concerns. However, rather than creating a rule to ban music from an employee's office, management may want to encourage employees to be respectful of others and keep the music volume low.

Rules and policies should be kept to a minimum, and those that are established should be aligned with the organization's goals and objectives. Where behavior is unrelated to the success of the organization, there should be no rules to restrict such behavior.

2. Are the policies and rules reasonable and fair? Organizations aim to establish rules and policies that are fair and can be applied to all employees regardless of their status, job requirements, abilities, race, color, religion, sex, or national origin.

- For example, it might be reasonable for management to establish a rule to ban visible tattoos and piercings for employees who have face-to-face interaction with customers, but management most likely will be challenged if they allow women to sport their piercings and tattoos while precluding men from doing the same.

Employees and management may have wildly different opinions of whether tattoos, piercings, flip flops, muscle shirts, and other clothing options should be allowed, and under what circumstances. Many organizations establish employee advisory committees to help write work rules which will be perceived by employees and management as necessary and reasonable.

3. Are the policies and rules enforceable? In developing discipline policy, managers must be careful to adopt only those work rules and discipline procedures that supervisors can administer fairly among all employees.

- For example, many organizations have a written rule forbidding employees from using company computers, fax, and copy machines for personal business. However, in practice, most supervisors ignore this rule and allow employees to send and receive personal e-mails and, occasionally use the fax and copy machine for personal reasons.

It becomes difficult for an organization to win a case against a particular employee for rule infractions if other employees are violating the same rule and are not disciplined. If this occurs, an organization would most likely be charged with lax enforcement which certainly undermines its reasons for having the rule. There is no reason to adopt rules and policies for employee discipline if they are not routinely and uniformly enforced by management.

4. Are the policies and rules clear? Discipline policy and work rules must be clearly written so employees understand them. Vague language may leave the discipline policies or work rules open to interpretation. It is essential that discipline policy is interpreted the same by employees and supervisors.

5. Are supervisors consistent in their interpretation and application of policies and rules? All supervisors should be consistent in their interpretation and application of disciplinary policies and rules. Inconsistent or arbitrary applications of the policies negatively impacts employees' respect for leadership. Policies quickly lose effectiveness if some rules are enforced while others are ignored, or if harsher penalties are imposed on one employee for a rule infraction, but not for similar misconduct by other employees.

Supervisors should treat employees with the same standards of conduct and judge them by the same rules. Otherwise, employees might find it difficult to distinguish between acceptable and unacceptable conduct in the workplace.

Consistent application does not necessarily mean equal application of corrective action. Equal application implies identical treatment for breaking the same rules. Supervisors must address each rule violation with equal seriousness, and approach employees each time they violate a rule. But, the background and circumstances of each case may require different corrective action.

6. Are supervisors disciplining employees in a timely manner? When supervisors accuse employees of not meeting performance standards or committing a rule infraction, they should take immediate corrective action. *Timely due process* refers to an established course of action that is taken within a reasonable time frame to investigate alleged employee misconduct. Organizations usually stipulate the amount of time (e.g., three to five scheduled workdays) for supervisors to initiate disciplinary action once an accusation has been made against an employee. The legal rights of an employee are violated when a supervisor accuses an employee of wrongdoing and then intentionally waits for a period of time before initiating corrective action.

- For example, if an organization has a policy against installing illegal computer software on company computers and a supervisor accuses an employee of violating that policy, supervisors should not keep the employee under a cloud of suspicion and delay corrective action. Employees are entitled to an impartial hearing or a discipline interview in a timely manner where either guilt or innocence is determined.

Timely due process does not require supervisors to administer discipline on the spot without investigation. However, if supervisors procrastinate for an unreasonable amount of time, others may perceive this lack of action as an indication that the supervisor condones this type of behavior.

It is nearly impossible to write perfect discipline guidelines and cover every possible discipline incident that may occur. For that reason, organizations make it well known that discipline rules and policies serve as a guide, are interpreted broadly, and do not limit management's authority to maintain an orderly, safe, and productive work environment.

Communicating discipline policy. Organizations are responsible for making available discipline policies, procedures, and work rules to all employees and supervisors. Organizations may post disciplinary policies and rules electronically on a web-based site, send electronic memoranda, and make available a hard copy of the discipline policy manual in the administrative office. If changes are made to discipline policies or work rules, organizations are obligated to communicate this information to employees. Organizations may also use other strategies to educate employees and supervisors about discipline policies and rules. Examples of these strategies are listed below.

New-employee orientation programs. Orientation programs for new employees are commonly used as an opportunity to communicate clearly the performance standards and expectations of management, and to acquaint new employees with the organization's rules of conduct. Some organizations require employees at the start of a new job to sign a form acknowledging that they have read and understand the discipline policy and procedures.

Employee-discipline handbook. To protect against legal challenges, many organizations develop an employee-discipline handbook to provide clearly written and specific discipline rules and policies. The employee handbook should be written in a way that presents straightforward, easy-to-understand discipline policies and rules to reach a wide range of employees with different job requirements, abilities, and needs.

Employee training programs. Conducting ongoing training programs and discussing work rules at staff meetings are also techniques used by organizations to reinforce standards of work conduct and performance. Engaging employees in frank discussions about common violations and corrective action, and brainstorming strategies to prevent, reduce, or eliminate misconduct are effective in making known the organization's discipline program. At periodic times management may want to ask employees in different work settings, in different positions, and with different educational backgrounds for an interpretation of the rules and discipline policies. If the answers vary, management may then use the employee feedback to make revisions and provide updates.

Supervisory training. Training supervisors is essential to ensuring the organization's discipline policies and procedures are understood and enforced. It is very helpful for supervisors to meet together and discuss common discipline problems, and learn various techniques to approach and resolve disciplinary cases in a constructive, rather than a punitive way. Effective training builds confidence and enables supervisors to interpret the policies and apply discipline, fairly and consistently, to all employees.

Disciplinary violations. An organization's disciplinary policy usually includes a list of rules that, if broken, result in corrective action. There are differences of opinion about whether or not disciplinary guidelines should include an exhaustive list of rules. Those opposed to a comprehensive list argue that each disciplinary episode is different and must be evaluated according to extenuating circumstances. Further, the absence of a specific violation does not mean an organization condones the behavior, or that employees will avoid disciplinary action if they commit an offense that is not contained in the discipline policy. Those who favor a list of rules argue the case of consistency, that a published list adds credibility to management's efforts to maintain discipline.

Some illegal or immoral acts are considered so obviously wrong that a specific rule may not appear to be necessary. Falsifying official documents (e.g., résumé, employment application, mileage report) and stealing (e.g., office supplies, janitorial supplies, electronic equipment) are decidedly wrong, and it is assumed that most employees should not have to be warned that such behavior is unacceptable. Nevertheless, employees still need to know the corrective action that will be taken if such misconduct occurs.

The need for corrective action is typically the result of employee misconduct in one of four broad areas:

1. Unsatisfactory attendance and punctuality

2. Infractions of organization policies, procedures, rules, or directives governing employee conduct

3. Failure to perform one or more job requirements in a satisfactory manner

4. Offenses or misconduct that violate the general rules of behavior or are specifically prohibited by law

Figure 11.1 provides the reader with an example of employee disciplinary problems.

ADMINISTERING THE DISCIPLINARY PROCESS

When employees are not meeting performance standards or behave in ways that violate policies or work rules, supervisors must follow the organization's established policies and procedures for administering the disciplinary process. One of the first steps in the process is for supervisors to investigate allegations of misconduct to determine an employee's guilt or innocence. If the evidence is convincing that wrongdoing has occurred, the next step is for a supervisor to determine the most appropriate corrective action to take to resolve the problematic behavior. The last step in the

Frequent/habitual lateness to work	Frequent/habitual absence from work
Using company assets for personal benefit	Misusing company time, equipment, vehicles, credit cards
Engaging in unfair and deceptive practices	Illegal use or misuse of technology (cell phones, Internet) at work
Falsifying documents (expense report, résumé)	Accepting "unauthorized" gifts
Releasing "non-public" information	Poor performance of job duties
Sleeping on the job	Possession/use of drugs or alcohol
Insubordination	Damaging or losing company equipment
Abusive behavior toward supervisor/customers	Wasting time (excessive socializing)
Theft	Immoral or obscene conduct
Endangering health and safety of others	Sexual misconduct
Illegal or unethical activities (gambling, pornography)	Possession of firearms on company property without permission
Fighting on company property	Willful destruction of company property

Figure 11.1
Employee Disciplinary Problems

process is for the supervisor to conduct a disciplinary interview with the accused employee to discuss the misconduct and communicate the corrective action.

Investigating Allegations of Misconduct

Management has the responsibility and an obligation to conduct investigations whenever they become aware of alleged employee misconduct. If a charge of unfair discrimination, sexual harassment, or another unlawful act is made against an employee, management is obligated to conduct a thorough investigation until the facts are confirmed and the issues are completely resolved. If complaints are registered against employees for behavior that endangers the safety of others (coming to work under the influence of drugs or alcohol), or if employees are unable or unwilling to be productive and perform their job duties, then it is the responsibility of management to investigate and take corrective action.

The primary purpose of conducting an investigation is to determine the facts surrounding the alleged misconduct so that corrective action can be taken, if necessary. The following points should serve as a guide for the supervisor (or other management representative) responsible for conducting a disciplinary investigation.

1. Determine the nature of a discipline issue. Before accusing an employee of misconduct, and prior to initiating a full investigation, the supervisor must first think carefully about the nature of the incident. Did misconduct actually occur, or could there be some other explanation for the incident? Was the misconduct the fault of only the accused employee, or are others involved? Is the employee taking the blame or being the scapegoat for everyone else? Is the incident critical (e.g., sexual battery/harassment, contraband, theft), or non-critical (misuse of computer/telephones, excessive tardiness, or absences)? When the incident becomes public knowledge, how disruptive will it be to others (coworkers, employees, customers)? Should the supervisor consult with upper-level management to determine who should be involved in the investigation? Who should be privy to the information pertaining to the alleged misconduct or the investigation, if it is

initiated? When investigating a charge of misconduct, supervisors must be very careful not to make snap decisions that they may regret at a later time.

2. Determine if the employee was forewarned about the performance standards or work rules pertaining to the unacceptable behavior. The supervisor must provide evidence that the employee had been forewarned about work rules and performance standards, and that subsequent disciplinary action would follow if unacceptable behavior continued. As mentioned previously, management should keep employees updated of changes to disciplinary standards, policies, and work rules by communicating through official written memoranda, e-mail notices, fliers, and training sessions. If employees are not performing their job duties, then management has the responsibility to provide documented evidence that efforts were made to give feedback to the employee about the changes that were needed to achieve the organization's standards. If employees provide substantial evidence that they were not aware of the performance standards or work rules, or that there were insufficient efforts on the part of management to provide training, then a legal challenge against management could be made.

3. Obtain all relevant documents for the discipline case. The supervisor or person responsible for the investigation should review the organization's policies, procedures, work rules, or practices that pertain to the alleged misconduct. If the discipline incident is related to the employee's poor job performance, the supervisor should examine the employee's past performance appraisals and other evidence (memoranda, e-mail) that documents the history of the problem behavior.

4. Conduct a fair and thorough investigation. If an investigation is warranted, supervisors must be attentive to accuracy and detail, and seek information in a fair, unbiased manner. Employees accused of misconduct are entitled to hear the allegations made against them

and understand the evidence that is collected to substantiate their wrongdoing. Likewise, the supervisor is obligated to listen to an employee's side of the story and understand the evidence that corroborates his or her innocence. If a legal challenge is made after corrective action is taken, management must demonstrate that a fair and objective investigation was conducted.

5. Obtain evidence or proof of misconduct. The best evidence a supervisor can acquire for a disciplinary case is an employee's *confession* of the wrongdoing. A confession is much more legitimate if it is in writing and given voluntarily, without coercion. To protect the accused employee from unfair treatment, a coworker or a neutral third party should be present if the employee wants to confess to the misconduct. The supervisor should make no attempt to threaten an employee or promise leniency to obtain an employee's admission of wrongdoing.

   Without the employee's confession, supervisors may rely on their *personal first-hand knowledge* of the misconduct. If a supervisor has not personally witnessed the misconduct, he or she may question other people (coworkers, volunteers, customers) who were *witnesses* of the employee's misconduct. Without the testimony of witnesses, supervisors may show *other relevant evidence* to prove misconduct, such as e-mail or telephone records, purchasing records, cash-register audit tapes, expense reports, or a doctor's medical report.

   Evidence from any source must be relevant or logically related to the case. Past conduct may be considered in determining appropriate corrective action, but past conduct should not be a deciding factor in whether or not a work rule was actually broken on the date in question. Supervisors must be careful not to lure employees into breaking rules in order to provide evidence of wrongdoing.

6. Document the investigation. The investigating supervisor is responsible for documenting a fair and thorough investigation of the facts and circumstances of the alleged misconduct. The primary reason for documenting the investigation is to avoid problems associated with a legal challenge if one eventually is made. Supervisors should keep all notes and relevant records for each investigation of an alleged misconduct. When interviewing witnesses and the accused employee, supervisors should record objective facts, not feelings or assumptions. Copies of e-mails and other communications exchanged between the investigating supervisor and the accused employee or witnesses should be kept in the file. Copies of all relevant business records are also important for the record. Supervisors may find it very helpful to maintain a daily log pertaining to the case with the date and time that calls are made, meetings are held, or when other investigative action is taken.

7. Maintain confidentiality. The investigating supervisor is responsible for keeping confidential any information gathered during an investigation pertaining to the infraction or disciplinary action. Any papers, notes, tapes, and minutes of disciplinary proceedings should be handled in accordance with federal and state data privacy laws. The supervisor as well as others who are privy to the investigative information should not discuss the case with others within the organization, or with interested parties external to the organization.

   Criminal misconduct. When an employee is accused of committing a criminal act such as a misdemeanor (petty theft, trespassing, vandalism), or a felony (grand theft, illegal drug use, rape), management is legally required to immediately report the allegation to appropriate law enforcement officials. For criminal misconduct, law enforcement officials are responsible for the investigation, and management is then responsible for cooperating with law enforcement by sharing information pertinent to the case. Typically, for criminal misconduct accusations, employees are suspended from work with pay until their innocence or guilt is determined.

Selecting the Appropriate Corrective Action

Although rule infractions and other kinds of discipline problems are disruptive to an organization, some misconduct is more serious and warrants more severe disciplinary measures. It is customary for organizations to provide a broad range of corrective action for a variety of disciplinary problems. Supervisors may choose informal corrective action to address minor infractions, and yet follow formal, progressive steps for dealing with more serious misconduct issues. Supervisors must use good judgment both in making decisions about the approach they will take in dealing with a particular discipline problem, and also in selecting the type of corrective action that is commensurate with the misconduct.

Informal corrective action. On a routine basis, supervisors of recreation, parks, and leisure service organizations face a variety of employee discipline problems that can, and should, be handled without following the formal steps of the organization's disciplinary program. Less serious, first-time offenses such as coming to work late, leaving work early, and sending text messages during staff meetings are prime examples of discipline problems that occur frequently and most likely can be resolved quickly and easily. *Informal corrective action* is a technique used by supervisors to achieve discipline objectives without initiating formal corrective action.

Counseling. One technique that supervisors use to handle minor infractions is employee counseling. *Counseling* is advice that is given to an employee based on the supervisor's judgment of the employee's misconduct. Supervisors typically initiate counseling by having a short and informal counseling session with an employee immediately after the first incident of misconduct. The supervisor may use this session to understand why the inappropriate behavior occurred. Employees may not think what they did is wrong, especially if in previous jobs a supervisor ignored or overlooked minor infractions. Counseling is also a good first step for supervisors to learn about any extenuating circumstances that might explain the misconduct.

- For example, if an aquatics center coordinator is late to work because she depends on the city's bus service to get her to work, and the public transportation system is frequently behind schedule, then the employee has not intentionally broken the rule. This is not to say that the organization will allow the aquatics coordinator to arrive late to work. Rather, the counseling session enables the aquatics coordinator to explain her dilemma and gives the supervisor an opportunity to understand the situation and help work it out if possible. During this counseling session the supervisor may choose to resolve this issue by changing the aquatic coordinator's schedule by 30 minutes so she can arrive to work on time.

Other informal corrective techniques. After counseling sessions, supervisors may also take other informal corrective action without resorting to formal disciplinary action in an effort to keep harmony among employees. Shifting an employee's work schedule or changing the employee's job duties are examples of two techniques that supervisors find successful in achieving discipline objectives. In dealing with less serious discipline problems of part-time employees, supervisors may choose to reduce the number of scheduled work hours per week, or change the person's job duties as ways of communicating dissatisfaction with his or her performance.

Informal corrective action should not be mistaken as a way for supervisors to be "soft" on discipline. To the contrary, it is a positive disciplinary approach that allows supervisors to engage employees in discussion for the purpose of establishing an understanding of the issues, exchanging relevant information, and communicating job expectations.

Informal corrective action taken by supervisors to deal with minor infractions is not documented in writing or recorded on an employee's official personnel record. In those instances where informal corrective action fails to yield the needed improvement in an employee's job performance or behavior, the supervisor then initiates formal, corrective action following the organization's progressive disciplinary process.

Stages of formal corrective action. The goal of a formal discipline program is to help employees understand that a performance problem exists while at the same time documenting the supervisor's effort. Documenting disciplinary problems becomes critically important in the event that more severe corrective action is warranted. The stages of formal corrective action generally involve a sequence of four steps: 1) oral reprimand, 2) written reprimand, 3) suspension, and 4) dismissal.

1. *Oral reprimand.* An oral reprimand from a supervisor is a verbal admonishment about a specific disciplinary problem. An oral reprimand is the least offensive

corrective action and is typically given for minor rule infractions. Playing computer games on an office computer and shopping online for personal merchandise during business hours are examples of employee misconduct that typically result in an oral reprimand for the first incident. Oral reprimands are given for the purpose of sending a clear message to an employee that his or her behavior is not meeting performance standards and/or the conduct is in violation of the organization's discipline policy.

- In using a *positive* discipline approach to an oral reprimand, supervisors should be friendly, ask for and listen to an employee's concerns, and encourage the employee to take responsibility for his or her conduct. Once an oral warning is issued, supervisors should follow up with the employee with some type of friendly contact without mentioning the oral reprimand.

Oral reprimands are documented in writing. A formal disciplinary document signed by both the employee and the supervisor becomes a part of an employee's official personnel record.

2. *Written reprimand.* A written reprimand from a supervisor is an admonishment about a specific disciplinary problem that is put in writing and given to an employee. Generally, it is issued following an oral reprimand when no, or too little, corrective action has been taken by the employee to resolve a discipline issue, or as a first step in disciplinary action for a more serious violation. Unexcused absences from work and failing to call in within the first 15 minutes of the start of an assigned shift are examples of rule infractions that may result in a written reprimand. In a written reprimand, a supervisor is responsible for communicating the facts about an employee's misconduct and calling for the employee to take responsibility for immediate corrective action.

- In adopting a positive approach to dispensing written reprimands,

supervisors may choose to schedule a disciplinary meeting with the employee to further explore the underlying reasons for continued behavior problems, especially if the individual has already been counseled and has received an oral warning. An employee may be experiencing personal problems (e.g., divorce, financial hardship, family illness) and/or may not have the needed skills or experience to perform at a level expected by management. By having a mature conversation about the nature of the disciplinary problem, the supervisor and employee may gain a deeper understanding of the issues and together reach a solution to the problem.

Written reprimands are formally documented, signed by both the supervisor and employee, and placed in the employee's official permanent record. Copies of the written reprimand and any other disciplinary action information are given to the employee and kept by the supervisor.

3. *Suspension.* A suspension is disciplinary action taken by a supervisor to temporarily remove an employee from his or her job for a specific period of time. An employee can be suspended from a job with or without pay. Suspensions typically are administered after employees have received prior oral and written reprimands that have resulted in no (or insufficient) corrective action to resolve the problem behavior.

Organizations may also administer a suspension as a first step in disciplinary action for major offenses such as reporting to work under the influence of alcohol, or for felony violations such as an arrest for possession or sale of illegal drugs. A *suspension with pay* is given if time is needed for a thorough investigation to prove an accused employee's innocence or guilt. A *suspension without pay* is usually administered if an employee knew or reasonably should have known about standards of work conduct and commits a serious offense (fighting on the job, making a verbal threat at work that could potentially result in endangering others). Like all formal disciplinary action, suspensions must be documented and copied for the employee's official personnel record.

A decision-making leave is a type of suspension that can be utilized by supervisors to achieve the organization's discipline objectives. *Decision-making leave* is paid leave for a specific period of time, usually one day, and its purpose is to give employees "one last chance" to make a final decision to either 1) correct behavior and commit to the organization's performance or conduct standards, or 2) resign from the job. Generally, supervisors send employees home for a "decision" day after reprimands have failed to bring about the desired behavior change.

In following formal disciplinary procedures, organizations typically require supervisors to consult with higher-level management, and possibly meet with a representative from Human Resources before administering a suspension. A suspension without pay can create a financial hardship for suspended employees and their families and lengthy suspensions can burden coworkers who frequently perform the work of suspended employees until they return. Management must consider the full ramifications of a suspension before choosing it for corrective action.

At times suspending an employee for disciplinary action may be necessary and an appropriate choice to make; however, supervisors must realize that it is disruptive before, during, and after corrective action is taken. Once a suspended employee returns to work, supervisors must expect to deal with the challenge of making the team work productively together again.

4. *Dismissal.* A dismissal is a formal act of removing an employee from his or her job due to misconduct. Dismissing an employee is the most extreme form of disciplinary action taken by management for the most serious misconduct, such as repeated rule violations, incompetent job performance, committing a major offense (e.g., sexual misconduct, drinking while driving a company vehicle), or a

first-time felony violation (assault that causes serious bodily injury). Usually, dismissals are handled by a higher level of management rather than by the affected employee's immediate supervisor. Representatives from Human Resources are usually involved in meetings leading up to the dismissal of an employee.

Dismissing an employee is one of the most difficult and dreaded responsibilities of a supervisor's job, and yet it serves a very important function for management. A supervisor's primary job responsibility is to achieve results for the organization through the employees in his or her unit. If an employee has a history of poor performance, or has chronic disciplinary issues, the morale of coworkers, subordinates, and customers are impacted. Similarly, if a mismatch occurs and an employee's skill set does not match the level of expertise required for a position, an employee's morale and feelings of self-worth may be low. Dismissal may be exactly the right decision to put the rest of the team back on track and allow the employee to move on.

Frequently employees prefer to resign from a job rather than receive a dismissal notice. Once termination takes place, the disciplinary action becomes a permanent part of the official record which may become a disadvantage to an employee in a future job hunt. If an employee offers to resign before final action is taken on a dismissal, an employer may still document the fact that the dismissal was pending.

Other penalties. Some corrective action taken by supervisors for disciplinary cases are so punitive or negative that we do not recommend their use unless something positive can come from it. Two penalty options that are typically found in a formal discipline program, but which are not often used, are demotions and transfers.

Demotion. A demotion is disciplinary action taken against an employee that results in a reduction in pay, benefits, status, and privileges. Some demotions are not considered punitive or negative. If, for example, an employee does not have the skill set to perform the duties of a job, and has a record of poor performance, he or she may request a demotion to a lower level, or a more manageable position. If the position is available and the receiving supervisor agrees to this corrective action, a demotion in this instance would not be considered negative or punitive.

However, supervisors embracing a positive approach to discipline would find it nearly impossible to use a demotion as a disciplinary penalty to rehabilitate an employee's unacceptable behavior. Most employees perceive a demotion as a stigma that dogs them throughout the remainder of their career. Not only does the demotion impact an employee's current salary, it also affects that person's retirement earnings if the organization makes retirement contributions on behalf of its employees. A demotion often forces the person to be subordinate in rank to former subordinates. This humiliation creates ill-will and a loss of motivation. It stands to reason that most supervisors using a positive approach to discipline would not choose a demotion as an option in their discipline program.

Transfer. A transfer is disciplinary action taken against an employee that results in moving the employee to another unit or division within the organization. Not all transfers are considered punitive or negative. Individuals may request transfers because they believe they would be happier in a different job and under a different supervisor. However, transferring an employee with disciplinary problems to another unit accomplishes nothing more than shifting responsibility for problems from one supervisor to another. A marginal employee that a supervisor does not want should be counseled, disciplined, and even dismissed. A transfer should not be an option unless it is voluntary for the employee, and agreed to by the supervisor of the receiving unit.

Progressive discipline. In selecting the appropriate corrective action to address discipline issues, supervisors should use the least severe disciplinary action they judge is necessary to bring about a change in undesirable behavior. If employees choose not to take personal responsibility for their misconduct, then supervisors should increasingly take more formal disciplinary measures until the employee demonstrates desired behavior or is dismissed. The process of taking increasingly formal action to correct behavior is called progressive discipline. Two key features of progressive discipline are: 1) a progressive series of warning steps, and 2) a gradual increase in the severity of corrective action.

• Let's say, for example, an employee named Tony makes a habit of coming to work late and fails to follow the call-in procedure of letting someone know in advance that he will arrive late. A supervisor may be very annoyed and want to terminate Tony for his blatant misconduct, but progressive disciplinary action would not allow dismissal for the first time the supervisor chooses to discipline Tony for this misconduct. A supervisor would most likely have a counseling session with Tony to discuss the reasons for his tardiness. If there were no extenuating circumstances and the same problem occurs again, a supervisor would issue Tony an oral warning for the rule infraction and remind him of the organization's attendance policy. If a couple of weeks go by and Tony once again starts a routine of coming to work late, the supervisor then progresses to the next step of issuing a written warning. If Tony persists in arriving late to work, the next step his supervisor might take is to put him on a one-day suspension. This gradual and progressive discipline sequence continues until either Tony takes responsibility for his work conduct, or he is terminated.

Although progressive discipline sounds good in theory, supervisors do not frequently deal with disciplinary cases where employees commit the same offense multiple times. Typically, once an employee, like Tony, receives formal disciplinary action for misconduct, he does not repeat that same offense again and if he does, there is usually a long time lapse between violations. Supervisors are much more likely to face the kind of disciplinary cases where employees have a variety of behavior issues which occur at various times. What is important about the concept of progressive discipline is that employees should be given more than one chance to modify their behavior, and supervisors should use progressive corrective action with more formal action at each step if employees choose not to take responsibility for their misconduct.

Extenuating circumstances impacting corrective action. Resolving discipline problems is never quite as simple as it seems due to a number of factors that may mitigate or aggravate a discipline case. A *mitigating circumstance* is a situation or condition that weighs in favor of an employee, and may influence a supervisor to reduce or eliminate corrective action due to compassion or fairness. An *aggravating circumstance* is a chronic situation or condition that weighs against an employee and may influence a supervisor to increase the severity of corrective action. Here is a case in point.

- Suppose an employee, Kiera, has three years of excellent performance evaluations and she is considered by all to be a model employee. However, most recently Kiera is not responding to customer telephone calls or e-mail communications; rather, customers are calling Kiera's coworkers to obtain the information they need. In staff meetings, Kiera is argumentative and does not treat others with the level of respect they deserve. In talking privately with Kiera, her supervisor learns that Kiera's mother was diagnosed with an aggressive cancer and has less than six months to live. Kiera also shares with her supervisor that she is taking antidepressant medication to cope and is having difficulty sleeping at night. Kiera has not shared the news about her mother with any of her coworkers due to the fact that she is not emotionally prepared to become the center of attention and respond to constant questioning.

Even the most experienced supervisors would find Kiera's discipline problem challenging and might be unsure as to how the situation should be handled. Should a supervisor expect Kiera's behavior to change after a counseling session? Should a supervisor consider Kiera's sterling reputation as a mitigating circumstance and refrain from any and all formal discipline? If no action is taken and Kiera's behavior continues to disrupt coworkers and customers, how long should the supervisor wait to approach her again?

As supervisors face difficult employee problems, they have a responsibility to weigh the circumstances of each disciplinary situation to determine the appropriate action to take. Supervisors often seek assistance from upper-level managers or Human Resource specialists to discuss the extenuating circumstances and to brainstorm different strategies to deal with these employees as well as with others who are being impacted (employee's coworkers, customers, and other supervisors). Figure 11.2 provides a listing of common mitigating and aggravating factors that influence a supervisor's selection of disciplinary action.

Off-duty behavior. Supervisors are often tempted to discipline employees for off-duty behaviors that negatively impact the organization and its employees. Questionable behaviors that occur during an employee's non-duty time can tarnish an organization's image, increase an organization's healthcare costs, create discord among employees, and have a negative impact on an employee's job performance (Pearce & Kuhn, 2003). Management often discovers that the task of listing off-duty behaviors deserving disciplinary attention is daunting. Here are four examples of questionable off-duty behavior:

- Should employers have the right to monitor or regulate employees who drink or smoke excessively off-the-job? In the long term, this off-duty behavior will most likely increase healthcare insurance costs for the company.

Nature and seriousness of the offense
Notoriety of the offense and its impact on the organization
Time lapse between disciplinary occurrences
Employee's job level and type of appointment
Employee's past work record (length of service, job performance)
Employee's previous disciplinary record
Employee's attitude (positive or negative) toward improvement
Willingness (refusal) to show remorse for behavior
Effect of the offense on employee's ability to perform at a satisfactory level in the future
Effect of the rule violation on coworkers or customers
Consistency of the penalty with those imposed or other employees in similar situations
Other mitigating circumstances offered by the employee, such as a medical condition, unusual job tensions, personal difficulties (divorce, loss of loved one)

Figure 11.2
Mitigating and Aggravating Discipline Factors

- Should an employer intervene when a high-profile manager is having an extra-marital affair with one of his employees?

- Does an employer have the right to discipline an employee who accesses social networking sites after work hours and posts derogatory remarks about the organization?

- Should employers restrict political activities of employees who are labeled as right-wing or left-wing extremists?

The challenge for supervisors is to determine what they can legally do to monitor and regulate the behavior of their employees during their off-duty time. Some states restrict an employer's right to terminate or discipline employees based on behaviors or incidents that occur off the job. Once the legal context is understood, the organization should have clear policies that address off-duty conduct, and disciplinary procedures that are followed to investigate and document violations. Supervisors should investigate each off-duty incident with the consultation of someone in higher-level management, with a representative from Human Resources, or with the organization's attorney.

The Disciplinary Interview

When employees make mistakes or serious misconduct occurs, supervisors have a responsibility to conduct a face-to-face meeting and a disciplinary interview. A *disciplinary interview* is a meeting between at least one supervisor and an employee for the purpose of investigating and dealing with the employee's misconduct. Depending on the seriousness of the misconduct, management may require a higher-level manager (other than the accused employee's immediate supervisor) to conduct the meeting, and they may request an official from the Human Resources office to attend. The employee may also have representatives present at the disciplinary interview such as an attorney, union steward, or a good friend. When preparing for and conducting a disciplinary interview, there are two important points to consider.

1. *Discipline employees in private.* The disciplinary interview should take place in a private setting (office or conference room) that is located away from coworkers and customers. Disciplining employees in front of coworkers or customers for poor performance or for

work-rule violations is not appropriate, and can be humiliating for an employee. Almost always, employees perceive disciplinary action that is "dished out" by a supervisor in a "public" setting as punishment. Disciplined employees often feel embarrassed, resentful, and may respond with severe negative behavior. A public display of angry feelings and an exchange of emotionally charged words between supervisors and employees serve no purpose in a positive discipline program. An exception is made to this principle when immediate action must be taken by a supervisor to handle misconduct that endangers the safety and welfare of coworkers or customers. In these situations, the purpose of reprimanding an employee in public is to immediately stop the dangerous behavior.

2. *Treat accused employees with respect.* What a supervisor says and how he says it during a disciplinary interview will have a significant impact on an employee. If an employee perceives that the supervisor shows respect and that his motivations in dealing with the situation are genuine, the employee may be more willing to take responsibility for the unacceptable behavior and to work cooperatively with the supervisor to seek a solution that is agreeable to both parties. On the other hand, if an employee perceives the supervisor's behavior as insincere and retaliatory, the employee may resort to arguing with the supervisor and may possibly become belligerent. If the disciplinary interview is not handled properly, the trust and respect between a supervisor and employee can erode and irreparable damage may be done to the relationship.

Preparing for a disciplinary interview. Prior to conducting a disciplinary interview, supervisors need to allow sufficient time to adequately prepare. There is too much at stake not to organize the documents needed for the meeting, and seriously consider the explanations that will be communicated to an accused employee. The following recommendations are offered to supervisors as they prepare for a disciplinary interview.

1. Gather all documents, business records, and written testimony and review them prior to the meeting.

2. Review the accused employee's employment record to determine if other informal or formal corrective action has been taken in the past.

3. Consider the employee's personality and anticipate his or her response to the disciplinary feedback and the possible alternatives for corrective action. Think about ways to respond if the employee cries, argues, or completely withdraws from the discussion.

4. Become aware and self-manage emotions. It is important for supervisors to understand the emotions they are feeling toward the accused employee, and how those emotions may impact the disciplinary interview. If the supervisor is annoyed or angry with the employee, the supervisor needs to self-manage to keep disruptive emotions and impulses under control during the disciplinary interview.

5. Review the organization's formal disciplinary policy and contemplate options for corrective action that fit the misconduct. Consider alternative corrective action that may be more appropriate for the employee and commensurate with the seriousness of the misconduct.

6. Confer with more experienced managers or a specialist in Human Resources to learn creative ways of handling difficult people during disciplinary interviews and dispensing corrective action.

7. Draft an introductory statement. The supervisor's introductory statement sets the tone for an effective disciplinary interview. The supervisor should communicate to the employee the nature of the misconduct and explain that management has the responsibility to investigate such incidents to maintain a safe and productive working environment. The supervisor should tell employees that accurate and truthful responses are expected and assure them that no conclusion will be made until the facts are gathered and analyzed. It is important

for employees to hear during this meeting that the supervisor will conduct a fair and thorough investigation and that all conversations and communications will be kept confidential.

8. Draft a closing statement. In developing a closing statement, the supervisor should make certain that both parties understand explicitly the terms of the corrective action and the next steps that will be taken. The supervisor should also include a point that assures the employee that information about the disciplinary case will remain confidential, and that the employee will be protected against retaliation.

9. Inform the employee of the disciplinary interview. Supervisors should prepare a written memorandum to inform an employee of a disciplinary interview. In the memorandum, the employee should be told explicitly the nature of the misconduct, and the change in behavior that is needed to correct the performance deficiencies. Other points made in the memorandum include the date, time, and location of the meeting, and a list of people attending. The supervisor is obligated to tell the employee that he or she may have representatives present during the meeting. Sufficient lead time should be given to the employee to allow him or her to gather documents, obtain evidence to support his side of the case, and to meet with personal representatives, if necessary.

Supervisors must understand that receiving a disciplinary notice can be distressing for an employee, and handling the notification with the utmost care is expected. Sending a dismissal letter attached to an e-mail message, calling an employee on the telephone, or telling the news to an employee while at lunch, are cold and callous ways for supervisors to communicate.

Conducting a disciplinary interview. The supervisor's goal of conducting a disciplinary interview is to facilitate a change in the employee's behavior in order to maintain a safe and productive working environment. Typically, disciplinary interviews are stressful for both the supervisor and the employee accused of misconduct. Supervisors are anxious about what they say and how it is delivered, how their words and behavior are interpreted, what kind of response they receive from the employee, and what effect the incident has on the morale of others.

Employees are also uneasy about the disciplinary interview, especially if they honestly believe that what they did was not a work-rule infraction or that their level of performance is acceptable. Employees may also have other concerns such as the impact this incident will have on their job security and the effect it has on relationships with their immediate supervisor, coworkers, subordinates, customers, and higher-level managers. In the back of their mind, some employees may be concerned about what to say about their dilemma to family members and their friends.

Several recommendations are offered to supervisors who are responsible for conducting disciplinary interviews.

1. *Make an introductory statement.* At the beginning of the meeting, the supervisor makes an introductory statement by communicating the nature of the misconduct, the responsibility of management for investigating such incidents, and the format of the disciplinary interview. The supervisor should make proper introductions of representatives attending the meeting for both sides. As mentioned before, supervisors should also make a convincing statement that the investigation will be fair and thorough and that the employee is considered innocent until evidence proves otherwise. Employees should be assured confidentiality in the case and must be reminded that retaliation is not tolerated from anyone in the organization.

2. *Present the case.* The supervisor should present documents, business records, and written statements of witnesses that demonstrate that the employee breached work rules or performed unsatisfactory work.

3. *Allow the employee to reply and present his case.* Employees should be given an opportunity to respond to the charges and to provide evidence to support their side. Even if supervisors have personal, first-hand knowledge of the misconduct or have other conclusive evidence, they have an obligation to allow the employee to tell his or her version of the story.

4. *Discuss the case.* In disciplinary cases, it is common for employees to have a different perspective than management on performance standards and work rules. During a disciplinary interview it is important for both sides to have an opportunity to ask questions to clarify the circumstances surrounding the misconduct. Supervisors should ascertain from the discussion whether extenuating circumstances exist and if so, to what extent they explain the misconduct. During the discussion, the supervisor may involve the employee in brainstorming alternative corrective action to resolve the disciplinary problem.

5. *Summarize the findings.* Once the discussion draws to a close, the supervisor summarizes the findings by stating the points that both parties agree to be correct. If new information is brought to the discussion that was not previously known by the supervisor, then the supervisor may need additional time to rethink the options before reaching a decision about the appropriate corrective action.

6. *Inform the employee of the corrective action.* Before the employee leaves the disciplinary interview, he or she must clearly understand the corrective action that will be taken. Any corrective action, such as a written reprimand or other alternative corrective action, should be documented in writing and signed by both the employee and the supervisor. For example, if the supervisor and employee have agreed upon an action plan to resolve unsatisfactory performance, the actions for improvement should be in writing and signed by both parties. For work-rule violations, the supervisor should record the corrective action that will be taken, sign it, and obtain the signature of the employee. Another important point to make is that supervisors and employees need to set future goals so that the same or similar incidents do not happen again.

Dealing with problem employees in a disciplinary interview. Supervisors will face challenges with accused employees who are belligerent, defensive, argumentative, and just plain dishonest. Employees may react to a supervisor by name calling ("the supervisor is so stupid"), making statements of revenge ("I'm ready to wring my supervisor's neck"), making statements about the sense of injustice ("It's not fair and my supervisor is always picking on me"), and dramatizing the importance of small incidents ("my supervisor is making a mountain out of a mole hill"). Supervisors can also expect negative reactions and comments from coworkers ("I'm not being paid enough to do a loser's work") who are asked to carry additional responsibilities of an underperforming coworker. The best approach to take during a disciplinary interview with a difficult employee is not to overreact and become drawn into an emotional battle. Unless supervisors are unusually gifted, they cannot make a defensive employee own up to his or her mistakes, nor can they make a belligerent employee cooperative. If an employee comes to a disciplinary interview and acts rude and obnoxious, the disciplinary interview should be terminated, and the case referred to a higher level of management.

For a discipline program to be effective, policies and procedures must be administered in a way to sustain a legal challenge. It is very frustrating for supervisors to build cases against employees with chronic disciplinary problems only to lose a case as a result of a misstep in administering corrective action. To properly administer disciplinary cases, management must take responsibility for using "just cause" principles to establish disciplinary policy, procedures, and training.

"Just Cause" and its Impact on Discipline

In today's legal climate, employees accused of misconduct have the right to challenge an organization's discipline policy, rules, and procedures if they perceive the supervisor was unfair and did not have a good reason or "cause" for imposing disciplinary action. Typically an organization must prove "just cause" to justify an employee's dismissal, suspension, or any other disciplinary action. The following seven principles are commonly applied to determine "just cause" when deciding discipline cases. If a "no" answer is given to any one question it could mean that a supervisor's reason for disciplining the employee is weak or not warranted.

1. Did the organization forewarn the employee of the possible or probable consequences of his or her actions?

2. Are the employer's policies reasonably related to the orderly, efficient, and safe operation of the business?

3. Prior to administering discipline, did the employer conduct an investigation to determine whether the employee violated or disobeyed a rule or policy? Organizations must demonstrate that a thorough investigation was conducted to determine the guilt or innocence of an accused employee. An exception to this requirement is if an employee is immediately suspended due to a serious violation.

4. Was the investigation conducted fairly and objectively?

5. Did the employer obtain substantial evidence or proof that the employee was guilty of violating or disobeying a rule or policy? The use of rumors, circumstantial or hearsay (secondhand information) evidence is not a good practice and typically does not provide the evidence needed to satisfy the requirement of a fair and objective investigation.

6. Did the employer apply all rules, orders, and corrective action fairly and without discrimination to all employees? In administering discipline, management must demonstrate that performance standards and rules are known to all employees and when standards are not upheld, affected employees are held accountable. Lax enforcement (enforcing some of the rules some of the time) and inconsistency (disciplining some employees for rule infractions but not all) will not satisfy the requirements of this principle.

7. Was the degree of discipline reasonably related to the seriousness of the employee's misconduct or to the record of past service? The key to this principle is whether the corrective action taken by a supervisor is commensurate with the severity of the misconduct. It is important for supervisors to apply the least offensive disciplinary action necessary to gain compliance.

If, for any reason, employees do not agree with the findings of a disciplinary interview or the way it was conducted, they may try to appeal the decision. If an organization provides the employees the option of appealing discipline decisions, the supervisor has a responsibility to make sure the employee understands the appeals procedure and the next step to take in that process.

Appealing Disciplinary Action

Some organizations allow employees to appeal disciplinary action when they believe that a policy or rule is unfair, the investigative procedure was unjust, or they feel the corrective action taken by a supervisor is too severe. The term *right of appeal* means that an organization gives accused employees the prerogative to have a higher authority review a case if they believe they have been disciplined unfairly. Typically, public jurisdictions and organizations with collective bargaining agreements offer right-of-appeal procedures to employees. Non-public and non-union organizations may not offer such an option. There are several mechanisms for allowing employees to appeal disciplinary action (mediation, ombudsperson, hearing officer, peer-decision committees, and arbitration) that are discussed in the next section.

Resolving disciplinary issues is one of the most difficult responsibilities that supervisors face and that is why it is so important for supervisors to have positive relationships with their employees when implementing a positive discipline plan. Promoting a positive approach to discipline and giving employees a voice in resolving disputes helps to dramatically decrease the frequency and seriousness of discipline problems. In this next section we will discuss strategies for managing employee complaints and grievances and for resolving disputes.

Managing Complaints, Grievances, and Dispute Resolution

Most supervisors would prefer to work in an environment where employees are satisfied with their jobs and have nothing but good things to say about each other and their supervisors. However, realistically, a work environment is not perfect and employees often *complain,* that is, they gripe out loud, grumble and express their feelings of dissatisfaction or discontentment about some aspect of work. Supervisors often see a lot of employee complaints as frivolous and are tempted to deliberately disregard them. However,

good managers realize that employee complaints must be taken seriously, and strategies and formal procedures are needed to resolve problems when they first occur. When employee complaints are not resolved satisfactorily, or when an employee believes that an actual or supposed circumstance is serious and cause for a formal protest, then employees may initiate a formal grievance against the organization. A *grievance* is a complaint by an employee concerning the interpretation or application of rules and regulations governing personnel practices, working conditions, workplace rules, or alleged improper treatment.

Resolving employee complaints and grievances is a critical function of management at every level, from entry-level supervisors to upper-level managers. Without an effective system for receiving employee feedback and resolving complaints and grievances, organizations often become a breeding ground for employee unrest and discontentment.

Dispute-resolution program. Many organizations establish a formal dispute-resolution system in the workplace as a way to resolve employee complaints and grievances. A *dispute-resolution program* is a comprehensive conflict-resolution system that typically includes informal and formal methods of addressing and finding solutions to work-related issues. A dispute-resolution program is a valuable management tool and serves three primary purposes. First, a dispute-resolution program provides management the opportunity to learn about problems from an employee's perspective and resolve them before they become too serious. Second, it gives employees an emotional outlet for expressing their dissatisfaction or discontentment with management. Sometimes, employees need the opportunity to release pent-up emotions, and openly gripe and complain to someone in management who will listen to them. A dispute-resolution program can serve this purpose and allows management to make adjustments (e.g., reduce the severity of a penalty, dismiss a misconduct case) if needed. Third, it protects employees from impulsive and unpredictable management actions. Unfortunately, there are occasions when management makes decisions that are not in the best interest of employees, or are designed to intentionally disadvantage one or more persons. Having an effective conflict-resolution system is one way of revealing poor management practices and making adjustments.

Three methods that are commonly used in an organization's dispute-resolution program include the open door procedure, mediation, and grievance procedure.

1. *Open door procedure.* One technique that is commonly adopted by management to focus attention on employee complaints is through the use of an *open door policy*. When organizations have an open door policy, it means that supervisors are accessible and prepared to meet with employees to informally discuss their complaints and receive feedback—whether positive or negative. Organizations choosing to implement an open door policy typically require all of their top-level managers and supervisors to attend training to gain an appreciation of the importance of the open door procedure as an integral component of its dispute-resolution program. The training typically focuses on effectively dealing with employees using the open door procedure to discuss and hopefully resolve their issues. The overall goal of the open door policy is to find solutions to problems early before they become increasing sources of irritation.

   Most successful open door policies have three basic characteristics. First, top-level management must commit to an open door policy and develop sound policies and procedures, provide management training, and then hold their supervisors accountable for its success. Second, supervisors and managers at all levels must embrace the open door policy. They must demonstrate to employees that they are serious about hearing and resolving complaints, and willing to meet and discuss whatever issues employees may have on their minds. Third, employees must trust their supervisor and believe the open door policy is fair and an effective method of resolving their issues.

   Virtually all top-level managers claim to have an open door policy, and yet the effectiveness of open door policies as a formal method of listening to the voice of employees is difficult to evaluate. Organizations cannot assume that because employees use this procedure to express their frustrations to management that the policy is effective. The truth is that a majority of employees would never choose to use an open door procedure to voice complaints or provide feedback.

   After all, they know their supervisors wield a lot of power and have the potential to make their work lives difficult so they may not be willing to become vulnerable by airing their differences to a higher-level manager. There also may be many individuals who believe the open door policy may be good in theory but does not function effectively. The success of the open door policy depends heavily on the attitude and ability of individual supervisors to deal with employees and their complaints. Some, but certainly not all, supervisors have the right attitude and skills to resolve employee complaints effectively. Too many times, supervisors are not tuned-in to their employees and disregard or ignore complaints that are expressed during open door meetings.

   To address the limitations of an open door, more organizations are incorporating an *internal complaint procedure* along with an open door policy (Hendriks, 2000). This business practice requires organizations to develop a formal system for handling employee complaints, including creating a standardized form for registering complaints, establishing procedures for processing complaints, and continually communicating with employees until the complaint is resolved. By having an internal complaint procedure, organizations are assured of having hard evidence when an employee expresses dissatisfaction rather than possibly overlooking comments that were intended to be a complaint in an informal meeting.

2. *Mediation.* Appreciating the importance of having a more formal mechanism for receiving employee feedback, many organizations establish mediation as an option in their dispute-resolution program. *Mediation* is defined as a voluntary process in which two or more parties involved in a dispute work with a neutral third party (*mediator*) in order to help them generate their own solutions in settling their conflict. A mediated agreement usually comes in the form of a consensus of the parties on a proposal that has been developed with the help of a mediator. Mediation is not binding, and either

party has the right to refuse consent on any aspect of the mediated agreement or completely withdraw from the process.

As a method of resolving disputes, mediation has its benefits and limitations. One of the major advantages of using mediation is the non-adversarial approach. The mediator is not expected to make decisions, but rather to work with the two parties to find a solution that is acceptable to both. Since both parties enter mediation expecting the possibility of a compromise, conflict is reduced and the two parties have a much better chance of reconciling the employee-supervisor relationship. Another benefit of mediation is the wide range of solutions that an experienced mediator can bring to the table. Since mediators are impartial and have no reason to endorse one particular result over another, they often bring an array of creative solutions that resolve not only the dispute at hand, but also other problems that may be annoying, but have not yet been formally voiced by the employee. Management also prefers mediation because cases are typically resolved quickly and employees are not left in limbo for several months while a complaint is being investigated.

The major drawback of using mediation to resolve disputes is the possibility of working with an unqualified mediator. If mediators are not competent in mediation, they may create more problems than they resolve. There is a national certification for mediators and it is recommended that professional mediators be used. Another problem is that employers may reject mediation because they do not believe the charge brought against the organization by the employee has merit. Since they do not believe the charge, there is no reason to mediate it. However, whether the manager believes the charge or not, mediation may help to clear up misperceptions and misunderstandings the employee has that is creating the discontent.

3. *Grievance procedure.* A *grievance procedure* is a standardized set of actions or instructions established by the organization that is followed when an employee files a formal grievance. A grievance procedure involves a systematic review and deliberation of an employee's grievance at successively higher levels of management within an organization until the grievance is either denied at the last level, or resolved to the employee's satisfaction.

Typically, grievances result after an employee's complaint has not been resolved either through the open door procedure or mediation. There are many reasons for bringing a grievance against an organization and the most common include:

- Dismissal, demotion, or suspension without pay without just cause

- Discrimination in denial of promotion, transfer, or training; or retaliation in selection for demotion or termination

- Denial of promotion due to failure to post the job announcement

- Violation of the Fair Labor Standards Act, Age Discrimination Act, Family and Medical Leave Act, or Americans with Disabilities Act

- Failure to give promotional priority over outside applicants

- Failure to follow systematic procedures in reducing the workforce during an economic cutback or downsizing

- Denial of a request to remove inaccurate or misleading information from personnel file

- Denial of employment on the basis of illegal discrimination

Formalized grievance systems are adopted by both non-union and unionized organizations. In non-union organizations, the grievance procedure may involve various individuals or groups in resolving disputes. Some organizations use an *ombudsperson,* an official of the organization responsible for investigating complaints and mediating a fair settlement between an employee and management. This official is outside the chain-of-command and knows the organization's policies and procedures as well as the supervisors and managers of the organization. An ombudsperson is given the authority to investigate complaints and grievances, review official records, and make decisions.

Non-union organizations may also use a hearing officer or peer-decision committee to manage problems as they develop. A *hearing officer* is another term for an impartial official of the organization that is assigned the responsibility of hearing complaints and grievances and rendering a decision. A *peer-decision committee* is composed of various combinations of both management and non-management employees. Typically peer committees are advisory in nature and any recommendations they may make are not binding. Final decisions are usually made by upper-level management.

In unionized organizations, the grievance process typically begins when an employee presents a formal complaint in writing to the Step-1 supervisor, normally the employee's immediate supervisor. The formal complaint identifies the employee, also known as the *grievant*, the employee's statement of the grievance (who, what, when, where, how, why), and the employee's explanation for a just and fair solution to the grievance. The grievance form is signed by the grievant and copies are given to the union's representative and the immediate supervisor. At Step 1 the supervisor is given a specific time limit (e.g., 5 days) to make a decision and conduct a conference with the grievant and the union representative. If the employee is not satisfied with the Step 1 answer, then the grievance is forwarded to the designated Step-2 employer representative and the union representative. Unresolved grievances continue through the management hierarchy and ultimately culminate in voluntary, binding arbitration. *Binding arbitration* is the final stage of the grievance process and involves a negotiation in which both the employee and management agree to accept an arbitrator's (impartial observer) resolution of the dispute.

To implement an effective grievance program, unionized organizations must follow the formal grievance procedures established by the collective bargaining agreement. They must have clear, concise, and written grievance forms and procedures that are made available to all employees. The procedures should identify matters that can be grieved by an employee, the time limitations for filing a grievance, and the time limitations at each step of the grievance process. The procedures should also include criteria for employee representation during a grievance discussion.

The desired outcome of a dispute-resolution program is to resolve issues before they become serious, and to avoid situations where an employee is so upset that he or she believes filing a formal grievance is the only option. However, to achieve this goal, organizations must work very hard to provide an optimum working climate where most problems are discussed and resolved when they first surface.

There are several ways to encourage ideas, opinions, and honest feedback from employees. For example, regularly scheduled staff meetings of smaller work units may open the door for employee suggestions concerning work situations. The organization's performance appraisal system provides a good mechanism for valuable feedback. In addition, many organizations implement a "suggestion box" to solicit good ideas or have a "1-800" hotline to accept anonymous complaints. This allows employees to share concerns in a non-intrusive manner. Supervisory and management personnel should also solicit opinions and concerns expressed by employees when they voluntarily terminate or resign.

Finally, in dealing with employee complaints, disputes, and grievances, it is important for supervisory personnel to listen with understanding and empathy, and investigate issues or charges when they occur. Organizations should have procedures to document and maintain written records of complaints or disputes that are processed.

Summary

1. Discipline is considered formal action taken by a supervisor against an employee who fails to meet the organization's performance standards, policies, and/or rules. The objective is disciplining employees is to create and maintain a safe and productive working environment.

2. Negative discipline focuses primarily on punishment as a way of getting employees to comply with rules and procedures however employees typically respond to a supervisor's negative discipline with anger, resentment and a desire to retaliate.

3. Positive discipline aims to create an environment whereby employees take personal responsibility for their misdeeds and supervisors make an effort to understand why employees misbehave and seek alternative solutions to resolve problems amicably.

4. Not all discipline problems are resolved by taking a positive approach. Serious employee discipline issues such as stealing, coming to work intoxicated, and falsifying

official records may be best resolved with disciplinary action that is perceived by employees as negative and punitive.

5. Discipline policy and procedure manuals are developed to communicate an organization's philosophy, goals and objectives of discipline, provide examples of work rules violations and explanations of the corrective action, and make known the procedures for investigating and resolving discipline cases.

6. A series of five questions serve as a guide for establishing disciplinary policies and work rules: Are the policies and rules necessary? Are the policies and rules reasonable and fair? Are the policies and rules enforceable? Are the policies and rules clear? Are supervisors consistent in their interpretation and application of policies and rules? Are supervisors taking disciplinary action in a timely manner?

7. Organizations use various strategies to educate employees about disciplinary policy and procedures including: conducting employee orientation and training programs; developing employee discipline handbooks; and providing disciplinary training to their supervisors.

8. Employee misconduct is often classified into four broad areas: unsatisfactory attendance and punctuality; infractions of organizational policies, procedures, or rules; failure to perform job requirements; and offenses or misconduct that violate the general rules of behavior or are specifically prohibited by law.

9. Management has the responsibility of investigating allegations of misconduct to determine: the nature of a discipline issue; determine if the employee was forewarned about work rules and performance standards; obtain all relevant documents for the discipline case; conduct a fair and thorough investigation; obtain evidence or proof of misconduct; document the investigation; and maintain confidentiality.

10. The best evidence a supervisor can acquire for a disciplinary case is an employee's written confession of the wrongdoing.

11. Management is legally required to report employee criminal acts such as a misdemeanor or a felony to appropriate law enforcement officials.

12. Supervisors often use informal corrective action such as one-on-one counseling to handle less serious, first-time offenses.

13. The four stages of formal corrective action taken against an employee are: oral reprimand, written reprimand, suspension, and dismissal. Each of these stages requires supervisors to document the action in writing and obtain the signatures of both the employee and supervisor on the formal disciplinary document.

14. A decision-making leave is a type of suspension that gives employees "one last chance" to make a final decision to correct behavior and comply with the organization's standards, or resign from the job.

15. In selecting appropriate corrective action, supervisors should use the least severe disciplinary action to bring about a change in undesirable behavior.

16. The key features of progressive discipline is that employees should be given more than one chance to modify their behavior and supervisors should use "progressive" corrective action with more formal action at each step if employees do not take responsibility for their misconduct.

17. A mitigating circumstance is a situation or condition that weighs in favor of an employee and may influence a supervisor to reduce or eliminate corrective action; an aggravating circumstance is a chronic situation that weighs against an employee and influences a supervisor to increase the severity of disciplinary action.

18. Disciplining an employee for off-duty behavior is tricky. Supervisors must understand the legal context and follow the organization's policies for investigating and documenting violations.

19. A disciplinary interview is a meeting between at least one supervisor and an employee for the purpose of investigating and dealing with the employee's misconduct. Supervisors should conduct

disciplinary interviews in a private setting and treat accused employees with respect.

20. In preparing for a disciplinary interview, supervisors need to consider the accused employee's personality and anticipate his or her emotional responses. Supervisors need to understand the emotions they are feeling toward the accused employee and keep their disruptive emotions and impulses under control.

21. Conducting disciplinary interviews is stressful for both the accused employee and the supervisor. Supervisors should assure accused employees of a fair, thorough, and confidential investigation.

22. In dealing with difficult employees during a disciplinary interview, supervisors must not overreact and become drawn into an emotional battle with the accused.

23. Employees accused of misconduct have the right to challenge an organization's discipline policy, rules, and procedures.

24. "Right of appeal" means that an organization gives accused employees the prerogative to have a higher authority review a case if they believe they have been disciplined unfairly.

25. An organization's dispute resolution program is a conflict resolution system that typically includes both formal and informal methods of addressing and finding solutions to work-related issues.

26. An open door procedure is a dispute resolution technique that supervisors use to meet with employees informally to discuss their complaints and receive feedback.

27. Mediation is a voluntary dispute resolution process in which two or more parties involved in a dispute work with a neutral third party (mediator) in order to help the parties generate their won solutions in settling their conflict.

28. A grievance procedure is a dispute resolution technique that involves a systematic review of an accused employee's grievance at successively higher levels of management within an organization until the grievance is either denied at the last level, or resolved to the employee's satisfaction.

DISCUSSION TOPICS

1. What is the difference between a positive approach to discipline and punitive discipline? Which one is the most effective in the workplace and why?

2. What are the common discipline problems of part-time, seasonal employees working at summer camps, youth sports camps, swimming pools and aquatic parks, or amusement parks? What informal or formal corrective action should be taken for these types of discipline problems?

3. What is the responsibility of a supervisor in investigating an employee who has committed a felony or misdemeanor at the workplace?

4. Discuss the steps in a progressive disciplinary procedure for the following employee misconduct: a) using abusive language toward a customer; b) abusing prescription drugs while at work; c) using petty cash for personal reasons; and d) loading illegal computer games and software on a company-owned computer.

5. What mitigating factors would influence a supervisor to reduce or eliminate disciplinary action for an employee who: a) comes to work late at least twice a week; b) sleeps on the job; c) socializes too much during work time; and d) drives a company vehicle with an unauthorized passenger?

6. When might an employer have the right to discipline, including dismissing employees for off-duty misconduct?

7. How much proof should be gathered by a supervisor to satisfy the "just cause" criteria for disciplining employees?

8. Explain the steps followed in a progressive discipline procedure by contrasting one example of serious misconduct, and one less offensive, first-time disciplinary violation.

9. Explain the steps of preparing and conducting a disciplinary meeting with an employee who is not meeting performance standards of her job and has already had several informal counseling sessions about her performance with her supervisor.

10. What negative behavior can supervisors expect from employees being disciplined and how should they be handled? What reactions can be expected of employees who work with the person being fired and how should they be handled?

11. What is the difference between a complaint, gripe, and a grievance?

12. What are the drawbacks of having an open door policy as a means of listening to employee gripes and complaints?

13. What methods can be used by non-unionized organizations to hear appeals from employees who allege their supervisor was unfair in the way the disciplinary incident was investigated?

14. The statement, "grievance procedures are for troublemakers" has been expressed by some supervisors? Do you agree? Why or why not?

REFERENCES

Hendriks, E. S. (2000). Do more than open doors. *HR Magazine, 45*(6), 171–177.

Pearce, J. A., & Kuhn, D. R. (2003). The legal limits of employees' off-duty privacy rights. *Organizational Dynamics, 32*(4), 372–383.

12

EMPLOYEE WELL-BEING

The global financial crisis that began in 2007, the emergence of the H1N1 influenza virus in 2009, and the ever-increasing rate of identity theft are just a few important issues that have affected employee well-being in the workplace. The financial crisis that swept through our country caused many organizations to downsize, eliminate programs and services, and in some cases lay off employees. Regardless of how the economic turmoil has specifically impacted organizations, one thing is indisputable: there is an increase in stresses and burdens in the workplace environment. For example, many who are still employed have faced pay freezes or cuts, the elimination of bonuses and merit opportunities, reevaluation of employee benefits, and/or the reduction of professional-development opportunities (i.e., training and development). Despite these hardships, employees are under pressure to continue being efficient and productive. This pressure can take a toll on the employees' focus on health care. Therefore, it is paramount that recreation and sport managers pay particularly close attention to their employees' well-being.

So what is employee well-being? Gebauer and Lowman (2008) define it as encompassing three interconnected aspects of an individual's work life:

1. Physical health
2. Psychological health
3. Social health

Physical health refers to your employee's overall health, energy, and stamina. Are your employees taking good care of themselves? A 2009 survey by the American Academy of Family Physicians found that doctors were seeing fewer patients during the economic crisis. In addition, more health problems were reported to the astronomical rate of cancellations or postponed preventative care checkups and tests. *Psychological health* refers to your employee's stress, anxiety, intrinsic satisfaction, sense of accomplishment, optimism, confidence, control, and safety issues. Recreation and sport organizations are continually under pressure to "do more with less" as budgets continue to shrink. As a result, employees often stay late, work additional hours on the weekends, skip meals, and give up their exercise regimes, which can compromise their psychological health. Finally, *social health* refers to work relationships, the balance in work and personal life, equity, fairness, respect, and social connectedness. All three of these aspects help us to define and understand employee well-being.

In this chapter, we discuss the importance of employee well-being as it relates to job safety and health, burnout and stress, and wellness and employee assistance programs. We conclude the chapter with a discussion on planning for unplanned circumstances in the workplace.

JOB-RELATED SAFETY AND HEALTH

The terms 'safety' and 'health' are not synonymous. 'Safety' refers to the potential of accidents and injuries that occur within the workplace. 'Health' is related to illness. An accident results in physical injury that is often immediate and noticeable. Illness may be neither immediate nor noticeable and can include both physical and/or emotional illness. Problems in either of these areas may seriously affect the employee's quality of work life.

Although substantial progress has been made in the past to reduce occupational safety-and-health hazards and their effects, the costs are still high. Recently, employers spent approximately $50 billion on workers who were hurt on the job; however, more than 60% of employers found that for every $1 spent on preventative measures against injuries, returns were $2 or more (www.ishn.com, 2005). According to the Bureau of Labor Statistics, nearly 940,000 injury and illness cases were reported in 2008 among state and local government workers. In the same year, approximately 3.7 million injury and illness cases were reported from the private industry. In terms of fatalities, a total of 5,071 work-related deaths were recorded in the United States in 2008, down from a total of 5,657 fatal work injuries reported for 2007. Let us examine more closely the causes of workplace accidents.

Causes of Workplace Accidents

The causes of accidents fall into three categories: (1) unsafe employee behavior, (2) unsafe work environment, and (3) acts of nature. Certain places and certain physical conditions are more likely to produce injuries. In order of decreasing frequency, these include:

1. About 25% of all accidents are caused by improperly moving heavy, awkward material. These sprains and strains are the most common injury in the workplace. In addition, musculoskeletal disorders (MSD) account for 30% of the injuries and illnesses requiring days out of work. According to the U.S. Department of Labor, an MSD is an injury or disorder of the muscles, nerves, tendons, joints, cartilage, or spinal disks.

2. The most dangerous machines are metal- and wood-working machines, power saws, and machinery with exposed gears, belts, and chains.

3. Falls are a major source of accidents anytime that workers climb, descend, or walk on narrow and high walkways. Floors, walkways, and ground surfaces account for approximately 19% of all sources of injury or illnesses (www.injuryboard.com, 2010).

4. Car and truck accidents are the leading cause of work-related deaths. With the increasing usage of cell phones and text messaging while driving, multitasking is causing this rate to continually increase.

There is much evidence to show that young workers, untrained workers, and newly hired workers experience a substantially higher number of injuries than older workers, trained workers, and more experienced workers. Age often has a much greater influence on accident rates than time on the job. Thus, an organization that maintains a well-trained, seasoned workforce is much less likely to have a high rate of accidents.

Occupational Health Hazards

Occupational health hazards falls into four general categories: (1) *physical conditions*, such as noise, heat, vibration, and radiation; (2) *chemicals,* such as dusts, poisonous fumes, gases, toxic metals, and carcinogens; (3) *biological organisms*, such as bacteria, fungi, and insects; and (4) *physical or psychological stress.*

It is more difficult to protect employees from occupational health hazards than it is to safeguard them from injuries. This is because health hazards are frequently hidden and unknown. For example, American industry has produced hundreds of new toxic substances each year. As a result, the Occupational Safety and Health Act (OSHA) requires manufacturers and users to evaluate, label, and classify such substances. Employers must make available the information about hazardous substances to their employees. Park employees who are involved in maintenance will quite frequently use cleaning solvents, gasoline, paint removers, insecticides, herbicides, fungicides and the like. The possibility of hidden dangers with the use of these chemicals is very real.

LEGAL RESPONSIBILITY FOR HEALTH AND SAFETY

The most ambitious governmental attempt to improve health and safety in the workplace was the passage of the Occupational Safety and Health Act (OSHA) in 1970. This act, discussed in Chapter 2, was passed to provide workers a safe and healthful work environment. The act consists of three main stipulations that employers must address:

1. Establish a safe work environment that is free from known hazards and harms to employees.

2. Obey all OSHA standards and regulations.

3. Maintain safety records of injuries and illnesses on the job.

The mission of OSHA is to promote and ensure workplace safety and health, and reduce workplace fatalities, injuries, and illnesses (www.osha.gov). Since the passage of OSHA, workplace fatalities have been reduced by 60% and injuries and illnesses by 40%.

OSHA has prepared regulations and standards which are collected in several volumes that provide guidance for employers. Appropriate regulations and standards for equipment maintenance, work methods, and protective clothing should be written down and communicated to respective supervisors and employees. For example, park construction workers should be told to wear hard hats, machinists should know to wear goggles, and welders should always wear face shields and gloves. It is the responsibility of the recreation and sport supervisor to understand and convey OSHA regulations to all employees in order to provide a safe and healthful working environment.

HEALTH AND SAFETY PROGRAMS

Recreation and sport organizations have a legal obligation to establish an employee's safety and health program. Faulty management policies in the area of safety and health are the basic cause of accidents in the workplace. The plans can be relatively simple for small organizations, or extremely complex at larger organizations. At a minimum, all health and safety programs should comply with governmental standards. We recommend that the principal components of a safety and health program include those identified in Figure 12.1.

Organizational Commitment and Management Support

There has been a great deal of research conducted on the issue of safety management. As illustrated in Figure 12.1, the core of safety management begins with a sincere commitment by the organization and supported by middle management. The organization must decide how comprehensive a program it wants and adopt safety policies to suit its size, circumstance, and financial resources. Recreation and sport organizations with a low accident rate usually have greater management commitment and involvement in the implementation of the program. This involvement and sincere concern about safety serves as a motivational force for all employees. They perceive that management is interested in their well-being as individuals, and those feelings heighten their morale. Employees with higher morale tend to have fewer accidents.

Policies, discipline, and recordkeeping are paramount to the success of safety programs. Employees should be well versed with safety policies and know

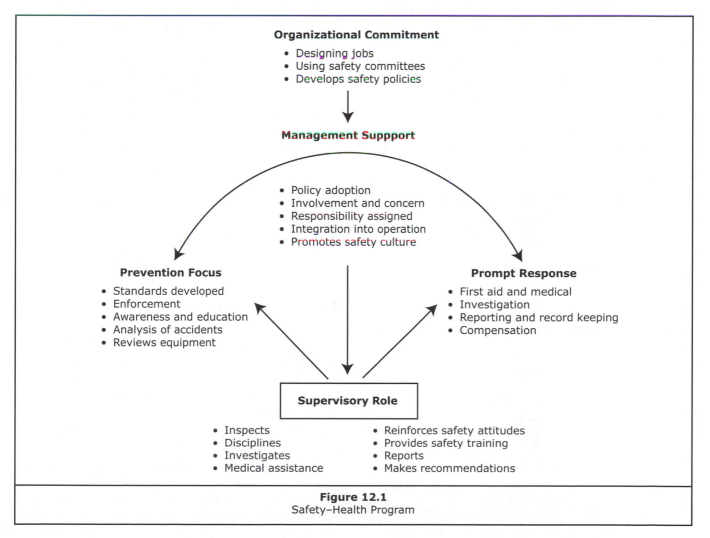

Figure 12.1
Safety–Health Program

what to do when the situation arises. Good record-keeping allows the organization to keep track of data, safety performance, and trends that will be beneficial when evaluating safety programs. Safety training is essential and will reduce accidents. Usually organizations will develop committees to thoroughly investigate safety plans, policies, and procedures. And when accidents do occur, they should be investigated by the safety committee. Typical phases of an accident investigation are identified in Figure 12.2.

Prevention Focus

The key to any safety program is prevention, and well-designed safety plans can reduce not only accidents but the associated costs. Statistics show that accidents tend to decline when supervisors and managers are keenly aware of the importance of safety in the workplace. The approaches to such preventative safety measures may vary from organization to organization. Referring back to Figure 12.1, an organizational and management-driven approach is necessary to convey the importance of safety in the workplace. In addition, a supervisory approach is also needed to reinforce the safety culture within the organization. Reinforcement can be demonstrated by providing employee-safety training programs and rewarding safety through workplace incentives.

Preventing accidents means continually focusing on safety. Awareness can be accomplished on the first day of the job by including safety in orientation and on-the-job training. Ongoing training and education are equally important. Additionally, recreation and sport managers should include accident and safety-related incidents in employee-performance appraisals. As data are collected on accidents and injuries, the supervisor will need to analyze the descriptive reports and statistics to determine where additional recommendations and preventative measures are needed.

Prompt Response

There is no doubt that every organization should have well-known and understood procedures for handling injuries. These procedures can reduce the element of surprise and prevent confusion. Employees injured on the job must receive first aid or medical treatment immediately. If the supervisor is present following minor injuries, he or she should know these procedures, provide first aid, or make sure that the worker receives medical care. Many recreation and sport organizations provide a first-aid area with adequate supplies for treatment of injuries.

Because the supervisor may not be present all the time, every employee should know the procedures and how to get help for an injured coworker. For emergency medical treatment, the numbers (in addition to 911) should be made readily available. A strong case has been made that key employees in every department should receive first aid, cardiopulmonary resuscitation (CPR), and automated external defibrillators (AEDs) training so they may be able to render help to injured coworkers. All injuries, no matter how minor, should be reported. Documentation is essential in establishing workers' compensation claims (see chapter two) especially if medical complications develop later. Almost every organization has its own employee accident/injury report form.

The Supervisory Role

The recreation and sport supervisor often has daily contact with the employees, knows the working environment, and knows each worker's behavior. This makes the supervisor the key person in a health and safety program. The supervisor may not develop the standards, but it is the supervisor who makes sure that they are followed. It is the recreation and sport supervisor who most influences the employee's attitude toward safety and the overall safety program within the organization. The following summarizes the responsibilities of the supervisor:

Accident Occurs in Organization

↓

Investigate the Scene

↓

Interview Line and Staff Employees and Others

↓

Prepare Written Reports

↓

Evaluate and Make Recommendations

Figure 12.2
Investigating an Accident in the Workplace

1. *Sets a good example* by following all safety policies and procedures.

2. *Develops safety inspection schedules* and follows them.

3. *Takes corrective action* when areas or equipment become unsafe or when employees fail to follow safe procedures.

4. *Trains and develops each employee* to be safety conscious by using proper work methods, safety devices, and protective equipment and clothing.

5. *Investigates accidents,* even if they do not result in injuries, so one can determine how they might have been prevented. Evaluate and re-evaluate.

6. *Completes and submits all safety-related reports* and records on time.

7. *Seeks* outside help and advice when necessary.

8. *Understands what to do in case of injuries;* preferably knows first aid and CPR, and how to use a defibrillator.

In addition to understanding the importance of health and safety programs in the workplace, recreation and sport supervisors should be aware of other types of safety concerns such as violence in the workplace, and burnout and stress among employees.

Workplace Violence

Defining workplace violence has generated considerable discussion in the popular press. The media have even coined the term "going postal" to describe violence that occurs in the workplace. Much of the reason for this attention is the reporting of data by the National Institute for Occupational Safety and Health (NIOSH) and others regarding the magnitude of this problem in U.S. workplaces. So what exactly is workplace violence? Some scholars in this area might include in the definition any language or actions that make an employee uncomfortable in the workplace; others might include threats and harassment; and all would agree upon any bodily injury inflicted by one person on another. Although there is a wide spectrum of workplace violence, the NIOSH defines workplace violence as *violent acts, including physical assaults and threats of assault, directed toward persons at work or on duty* (http://www.cdc.gov/niosh).

According to the NIOSH, an average of 1.7 million people are victims of violent crime while working or on duty. An estimated 75% of these incidents were simple assaults while an additional 19% were aggravated assaults. The Bureau of Labor Statistics' Census of Fatal Occupational Injuries (CFOI) reported 11,613 workplace homicide victims between 1992 and 2006. Averaging just under 800 homicides per year, the largest number of homicides in one year (n=1080) occurred in 1994, while the lowest number (n=540) occurred in 2006. So what can recreation and sport supervisors do to protect their employees from workplace violence?

It is important for recreation and sport supervisors to recognize the contributing factors that often lead to workplace violence. In no particular ranking of importance, the following factors are often identified: office politics, monotonous work with little challenge, unpredictable change, long hours, high stress levels, hazardous work conditions, poor management or supervisory styles, and cultures that tolerate violence.

Monitoring Employee Behavior

Supervisors must be in tune with the behaviors of their employees. Most workplace violence can be traced back to preceding signs that were left unattended or simply not dealt with by a supervisor. The 2007 tragedy that occurred at Virginia Tech University clearly illustrates this point. Some behavioral warning signs for recreation and sport supervisors to be aware of include an employee's yelling or screaming, sudden or explosive outbursts, inappropriate comments, crying, depression or withdrawal, regular disregard and violation of policies and practices, and deteriorating work performance and personal appearance. It is especially crucial to observe an employee's behavior if he or she has experienced job layoff, termination, end of a relationship, loss of a lawsuit, or any other traumatic event or humiliation.

Preventative Actions

An employer can take several steps to help reduce the risk of workplace violence but nothing is foolproof. In order to create a safe and healthy environment, organizations should consider developing policies and practices that will help to reduce violence in the workplace. Consider the following statements found in a manual from a local sport complex:

- No guns or other weapons are allowed in or around the sport complex property.

- With sufficient evidence of suspicion, employees must comply with a search for weapons.

- A zero-tolerance policy is in effect for incidents or threats of workplace violence.

- Troubled employees shall be referred to the employee assistance program.

- All supervisors must successfully complete the workplace-violence training program.

A sample workplace-violence policy, provided by the United States Department of Justice (Federal Bureau of Investigation, 2010), is shown in Figure 12.3.

This organization does not tolerate workplace violence. We define workplace violence as actions or words that endanger or harm another employee or result in other employees having a reasonable belief that they are in danger. Such actions include:

- Verbal or physical harassment

- Verbal or physical threats

- Assaults or other violence

- Any other behavior that causes others to feel unsafe (e.g., bullying, sexual harassment)

Post-violence response is just as important as establishing preventative actions. Many organizations have established crisis or violence-response teams. This team can function much like a safety committee, however, the response team requires a specific focus and should have specific training. In this instance, the crisis or violence-response team will investigate threats and incidences that fall within the jurisdiction of workplace violence. In addition, this team may be charged with developing policies and practices, conducting analyses, providing awareness and educational training to staff, and being on-call to diffuse emergency situations.

This organization does not tolerate workplace violence. We define workplace violence as actions or words that endanger or harm another employee or result in other employees having a reasonable belief that they are in danger. Such actions include:

- Verbal or physical harassment
- Verbal or physical threats
- Assaults or other violence
- Any other behavior that causes others to feel unsafe (e.g., bullying, sexual harassment)

Figure 12.3
Sample Workplace Violence Policy Statement

Stress and Burnout

Pressure in the recreation and sport field is inevitable. Employees in our field tend to work during others' leisure time which often includes weekends and holidays. We deal with demanding customers, we have an endless battle with public abuse of parks and facilities, we fight for financial resources like everyone else, and too frequently, we have lower salaries than comparably trained and educated workers. Furthermore, professionals in our field often suffer from "career identity," as they continuously explain to the public, season after season, what we do for a living. All these conditions produce continuous stress that may lead to burnout.

In 2007, the American Psychological Association's (APA) "Stress in America" poll found that one-third of people in the U.S. report experiencing extreme levels of stress. In addition, nearly one in five people report they are experiencing high levels of stress at least 15 or more days per month. As a result, stress in the workplace is costing American businesses $300 billion a year. This is the figure that APA puts on the loss of employee absenteeism, productivity, turnover and the ever-increasing medical costs that are associated by stress in the workplace.

Understanding Stress

According to the American Institute of Stress (2010), stress is difficult to define because it is a subjective sensation associated with varied symptoms. These symptoms often differ from one person to another. For example, situations like shooting a free throw with no time left on the game clock may cause tremendous anxiety for one player yet prove highly pleasurable for another player. The term 'stress' was coined by Hans Selye (1974) and he states that stress is *a response to any demand made on the body which requires readjustment.*

The American Psychological Association claims that stress can be a reaction to a short-lived situation, such as losing a set of keys only to find them later on your kitchen counter, or stress can last a long time if you are dealing with relationship problems, a partner's death, or serious health issue. Chronic or not, stress can play an instrumental role in damaging one's physical health. Miller and Smith (2007) identify different kinds of stress in Figure 12.4, and Figure 12.5 (see p. 216) identifies the physical, psychological, and behavioral symptoms often associated with prolonged stress.

According to the American Psychological Association (2010), there are several ways to help better understand one's stress. By understanding stress in

Acute Stress: Acute stress is the most common form of stress. It comes from demands and pressures of the recent past and anticipated demands and pressures of the near future. Acute stress is thrilling and exciting in small doses, but too much is exhausting. A fast run down a challenging ski slope, for example, is exhilarating early in the day. That same ski run late in the day is taxing and wearing. Because it is short-term, acute stress doesn't have enough time to do the extensive damage associated with long-term stress. The most common symptoms are:

- emotional distress—some combination of anger or irritability, anxiety, and depression, the three stress emotions;
- muscular problems including tension headache, back pain, jaw pain, and the muscular tensions that lead to pulled muscles and tendon and ligament problems;
- stomach, gut, and bowel problems such as heartburn, acid stomach, flatulence, diarrhea, constipation, and irritable bowel syndrome;
- transient overarousal leads to elevation in blood pressure, rapid heartbeat, sweaty palms, heart palpitations, dizziness, migraine headaches, cold hands or feet, shortness of breath, and chest pain.

Acute stress can crop up in anyone's life, and it is highly treatable and manageable.

Episodic Acute Stress: There are those, however, who suffer acute stress frequently, whose lives are so disordered that they are studies in chaos and crisis. They're always in a rush, but always late. If something can go wrong, it does. They take on too much, have too many irons in the fire, and can't organize the slew of self-inflicted demands and pressures clamoring for their attention. They seem perpetually in the clutches of acute stress.

Chronic Stress: While acute stress can be thrilling and exciting, chronic stress is not. This is the grinding stress that wears people away day after day, year after year. Chronic stress destroys bodies, minds, and lives. It wreaks havoc through long-term attrition. It's the stress of poverty, of dysfunctional families, of being trapped in an unhappy partnership or in a despised job or career.

Chronic stress comes when a person never sees a way out of a miserable situation. It's the stress of unrelenting demands and pressures for seemingly interminable periods of time. With no hope, the individual gives up searching for solutions.

Chronic stress kills through suicide, violence, heart attack, stroke, and, perhaps, even cancer. People wear down to a final, fatal breakdown. Because physical and mental resources are depleted through long-term attrition, the symptoms of chronic stress are difficult to treat and may require extended medical as well as behavioral treatment and stress management.

Adapted from: *The Stress Solution*, by Lyle H. Miller, Ph.D., and Alma Dell Smith, Ph.D.

Figure 12.4
Different Kinds of Stress

our own lives, we may become a more effective supervisor to our employees.

Understand how you stress. Everyone experiences stress differently. How do you know when you are stressed? How are your thoughts or behaviors different from times when you do not feel stressed?

Identify your sources of stress. What events or situations trigger stressful feelings? Are they related to your children, partner, family, health, financial decisions, work, relationships or something else?

Learn your own stress signals. People experience stress in different ways. You may have a hard time concentrating or making decisions, feel angry, irritable or out of control, or experience headaches, muscle tension, or a lack of energy.

Recognize how you deal with stress. Determine if you are using unhealthy behaviors (such as smoking, drinking alcohol, and over/undereating) to cope. Is this a routine behavior, or is it specific to certain events or situations? Do you make unhealthy choices as a result of feeling rushed and overwhelmed?

Find healthy ways to manage stress. Consider healthy, stress-reducing activities such as meditation,

exercising, or talking things out with friends or family. Keep in mind that unhealthy behaviors develop over time and can be difficult to change.

Take care of yourself. Eat right, get enough sleep, drink plenty of water, and engage in regular physical activity. Ensure you have a healthy mind and body through activities like yoga, taking a short walk, going to the gym or playing sports that will enhance your physical, psychological, and social health.

Reach out for support. Accepting help from supportive friends and family can improve your ability to manage stress. If you continue to feel overwhelmed by stress, you may want to talk to a professional, who can help you better manage stress and change unhealthy behaviors.

By understanding these seven ways to help manage your own stress, we are more aware of the stress in the lives of others—particularly the employees whom we supervise.

Managing Stress: Awareness and Action

Awareness of stress is the first step in getting control of one's personal life, in recognizing another's distress,

Physical Symptoms Of Stress
- Muscle tension in the jaw and forehead
- Digestive changes, such as constipation or diarrhea
- Dry throat
- Fatigue
- High blood pressure
- Grinding of the teeth
- Headaches
- Indigestion
- Muscle aches
- Pounding of the heart
- Shortness of breath
- Upset stomach

Psychological Symptoms Of Stress
- Anger
- Anxiety
- Apathy
- Cynicism
- Defensiveness
- Depression
- Difficulty concentrating
- Feelings of helplessness, hopelessness, or worthlessness
- Feelings of being misunderstood or unappreciated
- Hypersensitivity
- Insecurity
- Irritability
- Lack of direction
- Pessimism
- Resentment
- Sadness
- Insomnia
- Isolation or withdrawal from others
- Lessened enjoyment of activities that were once pleasurable
- Loss of appetite or, in contrast, overeating
- Loss of sexual desire
- Procrastination
- Readiness to argue

Behavioral Symptoms of Stress
- Increased smoking
- Increased use of alcohol or drugs
- Nail biting
- Neglect of responsibility
- Poor job performance
- Unusually poor hygiene

Figure 12.5
Prolonged Stress Leads to Physical, Psychological, and Behavioral Symptoms

or anticipating the possible distress of employees. The second step is to initiate action to reduce the factors that produce distress. The awareness of personal factors, awareness of organizational factors, and awareness of social factors as they relate to stressors will be discussed next. We conclude this section with actions to reduce stress, such as the act to change attitude, the act to change work habits, and the act to maintain a healthy lifestyle.

Awareness of personal factors. A number of studies have documented that certain events in our lives will lead to stress. In one of the earlier but very influential research studies on stress, Holms and Rake developed the Social Readjustment Rating Scale shown in Figure 12.6. The adapted self-assessment questionnaire gives weights to each of 43 life events. The weights were assigned according to the stressful impact these events have on a person's life. People who score high on this rating scale are more susceptible to illness because they have experienced the most recent change. The more change, the more stress, and the more adaptive the body must become to regain equilibrium. Adaptation consumes energy and when energy becomes depleted, susceptibility to illness increases. Subsequent and more recent validation to the Holms and Rake study have supported the links between stress and illness.

A sensitive supervisor should know if a significant number of these events have occurred to any one employee within a 12-month period. An employee may not be exhibiting symptoms of distress on the job but the supervisor should be aware that the stress exists for the employee. The presence of enough events to attain a score of 150 points indicates that the employee is having to consume much energy in order to adapt to all life changes and faces exhaustion.

Organizational factors. In addition to life-event changes, the working environment also contributes to distress. A job that presents conflicting demands on an employee, offers little variety and autonomy, or produces poor supervision may generate much job stress. The following eight factors have been found to cause distress specifically as it relates to the workplace:

1. Heavy workloads with unrealistic deadlines.

2. Employer's inability to respond quickly because of poor internal communications.

3. Poor feedback on performance.

4. Lack of control over one's work environment and job.

5. Assigned responsibility without authority.

6. Ambiguity in job assignment or role definition.

7. Work location far from central decision making.

8. High competition for fewer available positions.

Awareness of social factors. People are social beings and need interpersonal relationships. These social-support systems are necessary in order to receive love, esteem, and value, and they tend to protect us in times

Listed below are events that may occur over the course of your life. Place a check in the left-hand column for each of those events that have happened to you during the last twelve months.

	Life Event	Point Value		Life Event	Point Value
____	Death of spouse/partner	100	____	Son or daughter leaving home	29
____	Divorce	73	____	Trouble with in-laws	29
____	Marital separation	65	____	Outstanding personal achievement	28
____	Jail term	63	____	Spouse/partner begins or stops work	26
____	Death of close family member	63	____	Starting or finishing school	26
____	Personal injury or illness	53	____	Change in living conditions	25
____	Marriage	50	____	Revision of personal habits	24
____	Fired from work	47	____	Trouble with boss	23
____	Marital reconciliation	45	____	Change in work hours, conditions	20
____	Retirement	45	____	Change in residence	20
____	Change in family member's health	44	____	Change in schools	20
____	Pregnancy	40	____	Change in recreational habits	19
____	Sex difficulties	39	____	Change in church activities	19
____	Addition to family	39	____	Change in social activities	18
____	Business readjustment	39	____	Mortgage or loan under $10,000	17
____	Change in financial status	38	____	Change in sleeping habits	16
____	Death of close friend	37	____	Change in number of family gatherings	15
____	Change to different line of work	36	____	Change in eating habits	15
____	Change in number of marital arguments	36	____	Vacation	13
____	Mortgage or loan over $10,000	31	____	Holiday season	12
____	Foreclosure of mortgage or loan	30	____	Minor violations of the law	11
____	Change in work responsibilities	29			

Score _____

After checking the items above, add up the point values for all the items checked. A high rating would be 300 or more points and a low rating would be 150 or fewer. The authors of this rating scale found that people with a high rating are more susceptible to illness than are those with a low rating.

Figure 12.6
Self-Assessment Exercise on Adaption

of life crises. Ideally, we should strive to belong to a variety of social-support systems at work and during our leisure. All our support systems together should collectively provide *listening* persons, *technical support* persons, *emotional support* persons, and *social reality* persons. When all personal-support functions are not in place, the risk of burnout is greater during distressful situations. The lesson here for the supervisor is to recognize that workers who have lost a loved one or newly hired employees who have moved a great distance to take the new job may be experiencing a loss of support systems. We live in a transient society and being aware of these situations will make a difference in the lives of your employees.

Act to change attitudes. It is also helpful to examine our attitudes about life, our work, and ourselves in order to alleviate prolonged stress. We need to:

1. *Live in the present* and not worry about things in the past. We can no longer change the things in the future we cannot control. Even in the present we must learn not to worry about things beyond our control.

2. *Learn to relax* and do nothing at times—and not feel guilty. This applies to on-the-job moments. As Carl Honore (2004) paraphrases a play on words, instead of saying "Don't just sit there, do something!" say to yourself "Don't do something, just sit there!" Taking five to ten minutes each day to breathe deeply in a relaxed state has a positive effect on reducing stress.

3. *Learn to laugh.* If negative feelings produce bad chemical changes in our bodies, good feelings produce positive changes. We should seek out those who make us laugh, and laugh every day.

4. *Be a positive person* who sees the best in situations and people.

Act to change work habits. Volumes have been written about time management and how to reduce on-the-job stress. We could write a chapter about changing work habits, but here we offer the reader three important suggestions:

1. *Reduce information overload.* The Internet, podcasts, fax machines, cell phones, iPods, text messages, mobile alert notices, etc. all offer a tremendous amount of information overload including a lot of unnecessary noise. Eliminate this environmental noise, which competes for your attention. Noise can include visual distractions such as people walking by, as well as audio distractions such as ringing cell phones or fax machines. Visual distractions also include a cluttered desk and other symptoms of poor organizational skills. Having fewer items on a desk enables the worker to concentrate better on one item at a time.

2. *Use memory aids.* Things-to-do lists, web calendars, and journals are not only helpful but are essential to a busy manager. Schedule similar functions together each day during the same time period.

3. *Concentrate on one thing at a time.* When a person tries to multitask, he or she cannot process any one item effectively. If an overload condition persists over a long period of time, the person will start to make errors, become forgetful, have less tolerance for frustration, and will build resentment toward coworkers. Eventually, tedium or burnout will result.

Act to maintain a healthy lifestyle. You would not be reading this text if you did not already know that everyone needs to recreate and exercise regularly. Recreation and fitness are vital to the well-being of the employee. Walking or climbing a flight of steps several times a day offers a healthy outlet for all the hormones and chemicals the body produces under stress. Physical exercise can help to reduce the symptoms of prolonged stress.

Recreation is also a stress reducer if it is a regular part of one's life. The annual vacation or the occasional weekend trip to the beach or state park is not adequate to reduce stress. A balanced healthy lifestyle should offer social interaction, physical exercise, variety, creative expression, intellectual expression and stimulation, solitary relaxation, and following good diet habits. Too many people under stress watch television as their only recreational activity. The employer and the supervisor may not have much control over an employee's leisure time away from work, but they can counsel workers on the importance and value of maintaining a healthy way of living.

Burnout

Burnout is a state of physical, mental, and emotional exhaustion caused by excessive and prolonged stress (Smith, Jaffe-Gill, & Segal, 2008). When an employee experiences burnout, he or she may feel unfulfilled and that their work has no basic purpose anymore. As a supervisor, it is important to be aware of the employee who appears to lose interest and motivation at work. Moreover, it is important to be aware of feelings of helplessness, fatigue, procrastination, emptiness, and resentfulness. Many of the same strategies to help employees cope with stress may also help the employee who is experiencing burnout.

In an effort to avoid employee burnout, supervisors should create a work atmosphere that promotes a healthy balance between work and family, and between fun and seriousness. Supervisors can create job diversity for employees who suffer from performing repetitive tasks. Cross-training employees within different units or departments may be a possible strategy. Allowing employees to feel as though they have a choice in what they are doing may be helpful. Career counseling and professional development opportunities might prove fruitful, and always remember to recognize and reward employees for their accomplishments and contributions.

The Difference between Burnout and Stress

Although burnout may be the result of unrelenting stress, it is not the same as too much stress. Stress can make an employee feel overwhelmed by too many demands or pressures, but employees who suffer from burnout often do not see hope in their situation and they feel constant emptiness and lethargy. Often employees are not aware that they are experiencing burnout, whereas employees usually know when they are under a lot of stress. Figure 12.7 illustrates some key differences between stress and burnout.

EMPLOYEE WELLNESS PROGRAMS

According to the Society for Human Resource Management, two thirds of U.S. companies offer programs to keep employees healthy, and 66% of those offering programs use incentives to encourage employee participation. Organizations are realizing that focusing on employees' health is less costly than focusing on healthcare costs (www.shrm.org, 2010). Employee wellness programs are designed to maintain or improve employee health before problems arise.

Stress	Burnout
• Feeling overly engaged or involved	• Feeling disengaged
• Over reactive	• Sharp and blunt responses
• Exudes urgency and hyperactivity	• Exudes helplessness and hopelessness
• Loss of energy	• Loss of motivation, ideals, and hope
• Primary damage is physical	• Primary damage is emotional
• May kill you prematurely	• May make life seem not worth living

Figure 12.7
The Differences Between Stress and Burnout

Organizations offer many types of wellness programs including:

- physical fitness
- counseling
- newsletters
- disease prevention
- back care
- stress management
- nutrition education
- weight control
- mental health programs
- medical self-care
- recreation
- alcohol and substance abuse

Healthy employees are more productive and have less absenteeism and turnover. Employee wellness programs often reduce the healthcare cost for the organization; so as healthcare costs continue to climb, more employers are turning to wellness programs as a way to potentially save money. Less healthcare cost could mean higher earnings for the employee.

The National Center for Health Statistics reports that more than 34% of the U.S. population is obese compared to 33% who are overweight. The Center for Disease Control (CDC) reports that 32% of U.S. children fit the definition of being overweight, 16% are obese, and 11% considered extremely obese. Interestingly, the price of obesity in a company with 1,000 employees is about $285,000 per year in increased medical costs and absenteeism. Overall, an estimated $18 billion in productivity is lost due to

health-related issues each year. Armed with statistics like these, there is little reason to dispute why organizations are establishing employee wellness programs (www.cdc.gov/obesity, 2010).

Designing an Employee Wellness Program

Every organization designs their wellness programs differently. However, there are best practices used by companies when designing such programs. These commonly used practices include the following:

1. It is critical to gain the support of executive leaders (and board members) in your organization. Senior leaders must understand the importance and benefits of establishing employee wellness programs.

2. Develop a team of experts to help manage the wellness programs. Oftentimes the teams will include a nutritionist, personal trainer, recreation and sport manager, and other individuals who have special training in the area of wellness and physical fitness. This team of experts should also include employees who have a vested interest in establishing the program.

3. Collect data to evaluate employee health and physical-fitness interests, and the potential health risks. Surveys can be used to gather such data, and health risk assessments can be used to determine what types of programs are needed.

4. Create a strategic plan by starting with a mission statement followed by goals and objectives. What are the program's short-term and long-term goals? Are the goals measurable?

5. Create an organizational culture that appreciates wellness. Develop awards programs, highlight individual and team accomplishments, program special events, and be sure to include employees when developing, implementing, and evaluating wellness programs. The best marketing tool is word of mouth.

6. Constantly review and evaluate the program's goals and objectives. Data that prove results can sway future management decisions.

Several companies are recognized for their commitment to health care and work-life balance.

For example, SAS leads the "Top 100 Best Companies to Work For in 2010" because it offers quality childcare, 90% coverage of the health-insurance premium, unlimited sick days, a fitness center and pool, a lending library, and a summer camp for children. Other notable employee-friendly companies that boast wellness programs include Google, Zappos, and Patagonia.

Substance Abuse in the Workplace

Employee wellness programs are different than employee assistance programs (EAPs). Before we introduce EAPs, it is helpful to understand why employees may need assistance programs. We begin by gaining an understanding of the severity of substance abuse in the workplace.

Everyone experiences personal problems from time to time, and occasionally during a person's life a personal problem becomes so great that it may temporarily interfere with job performance. Divorce, death, or illness of a loved one can affect people this way. Some individuals deal with distressful situations by receiving help while others resort to unhealthy choices such as alcohol or drug abuse. Organizations are morally required to help their employees who are in need of assistance. It is good business practice and it is the humanitarian thing to do. Furthermore, helping employees in need has proven to reduce tardiness, absenteeism, on-the-job accidents, and turnover (Cadrain, 2005). The U.S. Bureau of Labor reports that alcohol and drug abuse in the workplace costs American businesses approximately $81 billion a year in lost productivity.

Substance abuse is the use of illicit substances or misuse of controlled substances, alcohol, or other drugs (Mondy, 2008). The U.S. Department of Health and Human Services says that alcoholism and drug dependence and addiction, known as *substance-use disorders*, are complex problems and people with these disorders once were thought to have a character defect or moral weakness. Unfortunately, some people mistakenly still believe this but most realize this simply is not true. Scientists and medical researchers now consider dependence on alcohol or drugs to be a long-term illness, like asthma, high blood pressure, or diabetes. Most people who drink alcohol drink in moderation, and many people can stop taking drugs without a struggle. However, some people develop a *substance-use disorder*—use of

alcohol or drugs that is compulsive, or dangerous, or both (http://kap.samhsa.gov).

Alcohol Abuse

According to the National Institute on Alcohol Abuse and Alcoholism, alcoholism is a disease that includes one's strong need or urge to drink and not being able to stop drinking once the drinking has begun. Since alcoholism is a chronic disease, it will follow an employee the rest of his or her life.

Research shows that alcoholism is hereditary but just because alcoholism tends to run in families does not mean that a child of an alcoholic parent will automatically become an alcoholic. It is not uncommon for people to develop alcoholism even though no one in their family has a drinking problem. On the other hand, one study found that biological sons of alcoholics are four times more likely to become alcoholics themselves, even if they are raised by non-alcoholic parents (Newhouse, 2003). Interesting findings related to alcohol abuse in the workplace include:

- 40% of workplace fatalities and 47% of workplace injuries are related to alcohol consumption.
- Employees who abuse alcohol are far less productive than those who do not.
- Employees who abuse alcohol use three times as many sick days.
- Employees who abuse alcohol are five times more likely to file workers' compensation claims.
- Stress plays an important role in the employee becoming an alcoholic and the drinking itself produces greater stress.
- Alcoholism is a treatable disease.
- It is estimated that more than 10% of adults who are employed full-time have a substance-use disorder.

(Source: http://pubs.niaaa.nih.gov)

In the early stages of alcoholism, the work pattern varies and may be excellent, poor, or anything in between. Sometimes nervous and irritable, the worker may try to avoid the supervisor. He or she may sometimes come in late, leave early, and take long lunch hours.

During the middle stage of alcoholism the worker may be untalkative but appears all right in the morning, and then will not return from lunch, phoning in sick. The eyes will appear bloodshot or bleary, the hands will shake, and the employee may act depressed. Speech may be slurred or sloppy. Moods will fluctuate, judgment is impaired, and personality changes are noted.

In the last stage, long-term regular drinking increases physiological tolerance so that the employee must drink more to achieve the same effects. The worker may be arrested for driving while intoxicated or is caught drinking on the job. Eventually, the employee is terminated. It is critical that recreation and sport managers understand the legal ramifications of terminating an employee as a result of substance abuse in the workplace. The handling of such cases as they relate to the Americans with Disabilities Act (ADA) will be addressed later in this chapter.

Drug Abuse

From NASA finding a bag of cocaine in a secured area of the Kennedy Space Center to the eight-year-old who brings marijuana to school, drugs can be found just about anywhere. There is no surprise that drugs have found their way into the workplace and this continues to be a serious and growing problem that reflects a national trend. The U.S. Department of Health and Human Service's Substance Abuse and Mental Health Services Administration reports an estimated 14.8 million Americans are current illicit drug users and 77% of these users are employed. Further, the National Council on Alcoholism and Drug Dependence reports that 50% of employees who test positive for drugs in the workplace report using drugs on a daily basis.

A survey by the federal government showed full-time employees who admitted to being current illicit drug users tend to be:

- between the ages of 18 and 25
- less educated
- male
- divorced or never married
- white

Like alcoholics, drug abusers bring their problems with them to work. According to the U.S. Department of Health and Human Services, drug abuse in the workplace lowers work productivity, causes accidents and injuries, increases the absenteeism and turnover, and increases an employer's medical costs. In an effort to have substance-abuse-free workplaces, the *Drug-Free Workplace Act of 1988* was passed, requiring all federal grantees and some recipients of federal contracts to agree to provide a drug-free workplace as a condition of receiving federal money. In a drug-free workplace, there is an established awareness program to inform employees about the danger of drug abuse in the workplace, policies for maintaining a drug-free workplace, counseling, rehabilitation, employee assistance programs, and the penalties that may be imposed upon employees who violate such policies. Figure 12.8 identifies the positive impact of a drug-free workplace.

Employee Assistance Programs

The Drug-Free Workplace Act requires federal employees to have access to Employee Assistance Programs (EAPs), which must be provided by their employers. In addition to federal agencies, the business community has also recognized that many everyday-life stresses can negatively affect employee work performance and the general workplace morale. Thus, many companies—private and public—provide EAP services for their employees. Unfortunately, less than 10% of employees use EAPs, indicating that too many workers do not take advantage of these health benefits. There continues to be a stigma associated with "needing help" and therefore many employees choose not to use these services.

So what are employee assistance programs? Whether managed in-house or outsourced, EAPs furnish professional counselors who provide confidential

---

Drug-free workplace programs include:

- A written policy
- Employee education
- Supervisor training
- Access to assistance
- Drug testing

A successful drug-free workplace program can lead to:

Decreases in:	Increases in:
• Absenteeism	• Productivity
• Accidents	• Profits
• Downtime	• Customer satisfaction
• Turnover	• Health status
• Workers' compensation costs	• Employee morale
• Employee discipline problems	

Source: http://workplace.samhsa.gov/

Figure 12.8
The Positive Impact of a Drug-Free Workplace

assessment and short-term counseling to employees and their families in order to assist in dealing with the following:

- balancing work/life issues
- quality of life problems
- stress and burnout
- work performance difficulties
- family problems
- drug and alcohol abuse
- relationship issues
- elder care, parenting, and childcare
- harassment
- separation and loss
- financial and legal issues
- work violence
- career planning and advice

Employee Assistance Programs (EAPs) are important because they can improve the productivity of workers, increase employee well-being and morale, reduce healthcare costs, absenteeism, and accidents, and empower employees both personally and professionally.

EAPs may be implemented in several ways. For example, some organizations may provide *referral-only programs* whereby the recreation and sport manager may refer employees to community resources, self-help programs, and substance-abuse-treatment providers. *Outside programs* provide crisis intervention, short-term counseling, assessment, and referral to specialized sources of assistance with the use of a consultant or firm providing these services. For example, an employee would access services by calling a toll-free number (made public by the employer) which is in operation 7 days a week, 24 hours per day. Confidential triage ensues and a referral to an affiliated provider will be given to the employee. The professional staff addresses the immediate problem and a referral is made if necessary. If special assistance is required, such as further counseling, the employee is usually granted a maximum number of sessions at no cost. There is usually no paperwork or provider bills involved at this stage and confidentiality is maintained by all parties. Finally, *consortium programs* combine employers, unions, and work-sites, usually within a defined geographical area or a specific industry, to offer assistance services often on a more comprehensive and less costly basis.

In recent years, EAPs have become increasingly vital in helping organizations prevent and cope with workplace violence, trauma, and other emergency response situations. The intent of EAPs is to ensure that employees and family members have access to confidential assistance when they need it and, hopefully, before problems appear on the job. When problems become apparent on the job, assistance programs help to support employees as they address their problems, seek and receive counseling or treatment, and return to work. Offering EAPs sends a strong message that the employers care about their employees, and in return, it can help reduce healthcare and other costs for the organization.

Role of the Supervisor

There are several ways a supervisor may help an employee who has, for example, a substance-abuse problem. However, before the supervisor encourages an employee to seek assistance, we must first understand the legal parameters associated with substance abuse in the workplace. The Americans with Disabilities Act (ADA) directly impacts how a supervisor may handle substance abuse cases. Employees who use *illegal* drugs are excluded from the definition of *disabled* under the act. However, employees who are addicted to *legal* substances (such as alcohol) and prescription drugs (such as pain medication) are considered disabled under the ADA. Furthermore, employees who are recovering from substance abuse are also considered disabled under the act.

So what is the supervisor to do? Most organizations use the *firm-choice option*. This legal option allows the recreation and sport supervisor to confront the employee privately about unsatisfactory work-related behaviors. The supervisor should have concrete data (such as unacceptable number of tardiness, absences) and keep the conversation to unsatisfactory work-related behaviors. Once the employee is confronted, he or she is offered a choice between receiving treatment for the problem or receiving standard disciplinary action. It is important that the recreation and sport supervisor clearly outline the treatment options and discuss the consequences of future unsatisfactory work performance. The supervisor must maintain confidentiality and a follow-up plan of action when using the firm-choice option.

In essence, the supervisor is usually the person who identifies, confronts, and refers the employee for assistance, but also the supervisor must follow up to ensure that the employee is striving to become rehabilitated. The objective of follow-up is to determine whether job performance improves satisfactorily. It is the goal of the supervisor to help the employee return to work and reach his or her potential.

Now that we have a clearer understanding of the impact of the Americans with Disabilities Act (ADA) as it specifically relates to substance-abuse cases, let us move toward the general steps that a supervisor should take when dealing with a problem employee. These steps include detection and confrontation, referral, discussion and consequences, and the follow-up.

Detection and Confrontation

Detecting and confronting an employee who has unsatisfactory work performance are not easy tasks. For example, supervisors may have mixed feelings about confronting the employee who has a drinking problem. They view the alcoholic as a difficult problem, but too often, supervisors tend to look the other way or try to cover up for the employee. Supervisors rationalize that the problem will get better. To make matters more difficult, often times the supervisor may know all about the employee's tragic personal problems. They may know the family and even have spent time drinking with the employee. But sympathy for the problem drinkers is not a good reaction to the problem. It only delays corrective action.

Regardless of the issue that is causing a problem, the supervisor needs to confront the employee with specific examples and recordings of their deterioration of work performance. The supervisor should review all previously documented incidents prior to this confrontation. Reviewing this documentation again during the disciplinary interview may help the employee to understand the problem. Comments should remain job-related. The supervisor is not a professional counselor and moralizing, diagnosing the cause of the problem, or offering specific medical advices should not be attempted. Again, keep the conversation job-related and maintain confidentiality where appropriate.

Referral

Once the supervisor confronts the problem employee, counseling or assistance should be recommended if necessary and appropriate. The supervisor should be familiar with the protocol for initiating the use of employee assistance programs offered by the organization. If the organization does not have access to an EAP, the supervisor should provide the problem employee with the names and telephone numbers of local agencies offering assistance. Most employers offer the employees insurance coverage for counseling by offering EAPs. The supervisor should be aware of all

the alternatives and make these options known to the affected employee.

This step is also difficult for the supervisor because employees often will not admit that they have a serious problem. They may become defensive, hostile, or blame their problems on the supervisor or on situations beyond anyone's control. These are common reactions and should not be taken personally, nor should they elicit supervisor sympathy. During this entire interview the supervisor should remain calm and very supportive.

Discussion of Consequences

Most important, the employee must understand that there is need for job improvement. Continuation of poor performance will most likely lead to termination. The statement to this effect should not be made threateningly, but it must be made firmly. Knowing that job loss is possible frequently helps the employee face the problem and want to seek help.

Follow-up

Once an employee accepts outside help the supervisor can strengthen the rehabilitation process by taking certain actions:

1. Continue to monitor and document job performance. Look for improvement and encourage the worker through positive reinforcement and praise. Corrective discipline should be applied when performance fails to meet expectations or if the employee does not take the EAP seriously. Both continued problems as well as improvements should be documented.

2. Know the EAP guidelines for rehabilitation of problem employees. Be patient and do not expect immediate improvement.

3. Preserve the confidentiality of the employee's personal problem(s) and any specific details that may surface.

Disaster Preparation and Recovery Planning

It may seem rather odd to include a section about disaster planning in this chapter on employee well-being. However, health and safety issues in the workplace must be discussed beyond the planned circumstances. During the past decade, we have witnessed a number of significant natural disasters such as the earthquake of Haiti, hurricane Katrina, major tsunamis, snow storms, and forest fires. Furthermore, there is more concern than ever before about violence in the workplace after the horrific events of Columbine and Virginia Tech University. Concern about terrorism has escalated to an all-time high since 9/11, especially as it relates to threats to air travel. So what does disaster preparation and recovery planning have to do with employee well-being?

Crisis management has become an important issue to many organizations during the past decade. In order for a disaster plan to be used effectively, supervisors must understand the plan and know how to execute it under dire circumstances. Imagine that an employee takes your manager hostage or that a hurricane destroys your fitness center. Are you prepared to respond? Expecting the unexpected and having a well-thought-out plan simply makes good business practice.

There are numerous templates and checklists available that offer assistance in disaster preparedness and recovery planning. Most of the templates have three sections: preparedness, response, and recovery. Preparedness may include protocol and address procedures to getting organized, identifying supplies and equipment, establishing emergency communication systems, assigning response teams, and planning ahead for evacuations. The response section may include a flow chart depicting the emergency response actions, how to implement an evacuation, and reporting procedures. The recovery section includes support services and assistance for employees, and documenting emergency outcomes. Checklists that are applied here typically include categories such as employees, customers, supplies, equipment, property, records, insurance, and supply kit inventory. Since no plan is foolproof, the recreation and sport supervisors should begin by researching available resources to assist in developing a disaster and recovery plan. We recommend the following resources:

The U.S. Small Business Administration (SBA)(www.sba.gov/services/disasterassistance) provides information on how to prepare for disasters and the SBA's disaster loan program, which helps homeowners, renters, and businesses of all size recover from disasters.

The American Red Cross (www.redcross.org) offers free materials regarding disaster planning and recovery.

The Federal Emergency Management Agency (www.fema.gov/business/guide/index.shtm) offers free, step-by-step advice on how to create and maintain a comprehensive emergency-management program.

The Department of Homeland Security (www.ready.gov/business/index.html) shows how to be ready for emergencies. The website includes a sample emergency plan you can use for your organization.

The Institute for Business and Home Safety (www.ibhs.org) and The National Federation of Independent Business (www.nfib.com) offer a variety of tools designed for small business owners to both reduce their potential for loss, should disaster strike, and to reopen quickly, should they be forced to close.

You should also check with your state government home page to see what resources are available. The state website usually consists of your state's name followed by ".gov" (e.g., www.ny.gov or www.az.gov). Look for links to emergency management agencies, public safety departments, and small business offices.

One final note about disaster preparedness and recovery planning concerns the importance of training managers, supervisors, and employees. All of the planning efforts may be wasted if people do not understand what to do should a disaster occur. Training should be ongoing and include topics such as:

- first aid, cardiopulmonary resuscitation (CPR), and automated external defibrillators (AEDs)
- hazardous materials containment
- disaster escape routes
- employer contact communication flow
- recovery and restoration efforts
- re-evaluation and recommendations

Organizations should conduct routine exercises and drills for training purposes. The mock drills may or may not be announced in advanced much like the fire drills used in public schools. Regular tests to ensure proper use of technology (such as text messages, alarm systems) should occur. It is essential to be prepared for the unexpected. Intentional and purposeful training and updating of planning efforts is smart business practice, especially when it comes to the well-being of our employees.

Summary

1. Employee well-being encompasses three interconnected aspects of an individual's work life. These aspects include the physical health, psychological health, and social health.

2. In addition to moral and legal reasons, it is economically advantageous for employers to provide a work environment that supports good health, safety, and employee well-being. To do otherwise costs the employer billions of dollars in insurance premiums, medical claims, and lost productivity.

3. There are three basic causes of accidents: unsafe conditions in the work environment, unsafe employee acts, and acts of nature. By far the major cause of occupational injuries is unsafe human actions.

4. The Occupational Safety and Health Act attempts to prevent work-related accidents by establishing very detailed standards, which are enforced by inspectors who can issue citations and recommend penalties.

5. To reduce job accidents, employers need to be committed to and involved in a comprehensive safety-health program. This program requires an organizational commitment, management support, prevention focus, prompt response, and supervisors who can cultivate a safety-conscious work environment.

6. Workplace violence is defined as violent acts, including physical assaults and threats of assault, directed toward persons at work or on duty. Organizations should have a policy on workplace violence.

7. Stress is any response to a demand made on the body which requires adapting to the demand. Different types of stress include acute stress, episodic acute stress, and chronic stress.

8. Prolonged stress leads to physical, psychological, and behavioral symptoms. In addition, prolonged stress is common in our profession. Management, supervisors, and workers need to understand the nature and symptoms of distress in order to eliminate or reduce job-related stressors. Stressors that cannot be eliminated can be managed through awareness and productive action.

9. Balanced recreational activities, regular exercise, positive attitudes, and efficient work habits can help alleviate prolonged stress.

10. Burnout is a state of physical, mental, and emotional exhaustion caused by excessive and prolonged stress. Stress and burnout are not synonymous.

11. Employee wellness programs are designed to maintain or improve employee health before problems arise.

12. Problem employees do not work up to their potential capacity and experience increased absences and greater incidents of insubordination. Employee programs to help problem employees are called employee assistance programs (EAPs). Whether managed in-house or outsourced, EAPs furnish professionals who can help employees and their families in a variety of areas such as balancing work/life issues, relationship issues, financial and legal issues, career planning, and substance-abuse problems.

13. Drug and alcohol abuse in the workplace costs American businesses approximately $81 billion a year in lost productivity. The Drug-Free Workplace Act of 1988 promotes a substance-abuse-free work environment by providing programs and services for employees.

14. Supervisors need to detect, confront, refer, and follow-up with employees who are not performing satisfactorily at work.

15. The alcoholic is perhaps the most protected problem employee, as many of his or her coworkers and the supervisor tend to ignore or hide the drinking problem. But when drinking prevents the employee from doing the job properly, it is the supervisor's responsibility to take corrective action.

16. Disaster and recovery planning prepares organizations for the unexpected and unplanned circumstances. Most plans

include preparedness, response, and recovery. All of the planning efforts may be wasted if people do not understand their role should a disaster occur. Organizations should conduct routine exercises and drills for continual training purposes.

DISCUSSION TOPICS

1. Why is employee well-being so important to the employer?

2. What is an accident? What is an occupational injury, and what are occupational health hazards?

3. What causes most job-related injuries? What are some examples of poor housekeeping?

4. Give the components of a good safety-health program and discuss the role of immediate supervisor plays in achieving good safety performance.

5. What role does OSHA play in employee well-being?

6. What are the phases of an accident investigation?

7. Why has substance abuse become a major problem? As a supervisor, would you be equally willing to help an alcoholic, a drug addict, and one who is considering suicide?

8. If you were a supervisor and someone came to you needing emotional assistance, how would you respond? Would you feel compelled to give advice or just listen? Do you think people should express their feelings or try to keep them under control?

9. What types of workplace violence are most prevalent in today's society? What can you do as a supervisor to help prevent acts of violence in your workplace?

10. Could you recognize someone who is experiencing stress or burnout? Someone with a drinking problem? Someone who uses illegal drugs or abuses the use of legal drugs? Explain why or why not for each of these questions.

11. If stress is productive and desirable, how can prolonged stress be considered destructive?

12. Is it better to fire problem employees than to rehabilitate them?

13. Can supervisors rehabilitate problem employees? What can a supervisor do when he or she detects a problem employee?

14. Why are employee wellness programs advantageous to organizations? To employees? Why are EAPs advantageous to organizations and employees?

15. Discuss how you might develop a disaster and recovery plan for a recreation and sport organization. What steps would you take to develop this comprehensive plan?

REFERENCES

Accidents in the workplace. (n.d.). *InjuryBoard*. Retrieved from http://www.injuryboard.com/help-center/articles/accidents-in-the-workplace.aspx

Cadrain, D. (2005, August). Helping workers fool drug tests is a big business. *HR Magazine, 50*, 29–32.

FAQs for the general public. (2007). *National Institute on Alcohol Abuse and Alcoholism of the National Institute of Health*. Retrieved from http://www.niaaa.nih.gov/FAQs/General-English/default.htm#whatis

Gebauer, J. & Lowman, D. (2008). *Closing the engagement gap: How great companies unlock employee potential for superior results*. Retrieved from http://www.towerswatson.com/assets/pdf/1550/Viewpoints_1550.pdf

Honore, C. (2004). *In praise of slowness: How a worldwide movement is challenging the cult of speed*. New York, NY: HarperCollins.

Miller, L. & Smith, A. (2007). The different kinds of stress. *Health Place: America's Mental Health Channel*. Retrieved from http://www.healthyplace.com/anxiety-panic/main/different-kinds-of-stress/menu-id-69

Miller, S. (2009). Practices Shared for Lowering Costs, Improving Health. *Society for Human Resource Management*. Retrieved from http://www.shrm.org/hrdisciplines/benefits/Articles/Pages/BestPracticesShared.aspx

Mondy, R. W. (2008). *Human Resource Management* (10th ed.), p. 372. Upper Saddle River, NJ: Pearson Prentice Hall.

Newhouse, E. (2003, Spring). Alcoholism: Its origins, consequences and costs. *Nieman Reports, 57*, 28.

News Release: Workplace injuries and illnesses--2009. (2010). *U.S. Bureau of Labor Statistics*. Retrieved from http://www.bls.gov/news.release/archives/osh_10212010.htm

OSHA 2003–2008 Strategic Management Plan. (n.d.). *U.S. Department of Labor*. Retrieved from http://www.osha.gov/StratPlanPublic/strategicmanagementplan-final.html

Selye, H. (1974). *Stress Without Distress* (p. 17). Philadelphia, PA: J. B. Lippincott.

Serious workplace injuries decrease, but financial impact remains high. (2005). *Industrial Safety and Hygiene News*. Retrieved from http://www.ishn.com/articles/serious-workplace-injuries-decrease-but-financial-impact-remains-high

Smith, M., Jaffe-Gill, E., Segal, J., & Segal, R. (2008). Preventing burnout: Signs, symptoms, causes, and coping strategies. *Helpguide*. Retrieved from http://www.helpguide.org/mental/burnout_signs_symptoms.htm

Stress Tip Sheet. *American Psychological Association*. Retrieved from http://www.apa.org/news/press/releases/2007/10/stress-tips.aspx

Violence in the workplace. (1996). *The National Institute for Occupational Safety and Health*. Retrieved from http://www.cdc.gov/niosh/violintr.html

Workplace Violence: Issues in Response. *U.S. Department of Justice, Federal Bureau of Investigation*. Retrieved from http://www.fbi.gov/stats-services/publications/workplace-violence

13

COMMUNICATION

Communication skills are consistently ranked by employers as the number-one quality they seek in new employees. A Department of Labor study reports that strong communication skills are correlated with career success (Stevens, 2005). Regardless of one's interest area in recreation and sport, communication skills are critically important. Recreation and sport professional are expected to effectively communicate with coworkers, participants, administrators, outside vendors, volunteers, and others. Former Supreme Court Justice John Powell said, "Communication works for those who work at it." But how can one work at communication?

The purpose of this chapter is to help students better develop their communication skills for the workplace. Specifically, the chapter will discuss elements of communication, review basic principles for written business communication, present the "language" of running meetings, offer suggestions for effective presentations, and discuss the importance of behavioral communication related to sound ethical practices for managers.

ELEMENTS OF COMMUNICATION

Very simply, communication is the process of sending and receiving messages. The key elements in the process are a *sender* who encodes a message and a *receiver* who decodes the message. For "effective communication" to occur, both the sender and the receiver need to interpret the message the same (Schermeron, Hunt, & Osborn, 2005).

If we look at communication closely, we find there are many factors which contribute to the likelihood of effective communication. "Congruent communication" is when all the communication sent refers to the same message. A manager may say to an employee, "Come on in, I have a few minutes. What did you want to see me about?" while pointing to a chair for the employee to use and smiling in greeting.

Both the words and the behavior of the manager are saying the same thing: "I want to take time to listen to you." "Incongruent communication" is when the message is mixed. Rather than point to the chair, the manager glances at his/her watch and gives a slight frown but says the same words. The employee will be unsure whether the manager really means what was said. Or, incongruent communication is when the website lists one date for the Easter Egg Hunt and the flyer distributed to schools lists another. As we'll see, the more a manager can send congruent communication, the greater the chance employees will hear the intended message.

"Positional communication" is the concept that receivers react or respond to the sender based on the position or *hierarchical relationship* between the two. For example, if your instructor tells you the test date has been moved you are likely to accept it as true. However, if a fellow classmate tells you the test date has been moved, you will probably double check with either the instructor or another classmate you perceive as conscientious before accepting the date change. Another element of positional communication is that a receiver is more likely to give greater priority in responding to a message from someone in higher position than to a message from a subordinate or coworker.

"Parallel communication" is the use of *more than one method* of communication to send the same message. Let's say you announce at the end of a staff meeting that budget worksheets are due on the 15th. With parallel communication, you also send an e-mail reminding staff of the due date following the meeting. Another example would be when handouts are given to coaches during orientation reiterating the policies for emergency situations in addition to the material being covered in the oral presentation.

Communication Barriers

"Noise" is any disturbance which disrupts the communication process. Noise can be created by the sender, the receiver, or the environment (Schermerhorn et al., 2005). If the sender communicates without thinking, noise could be created by the following:

1. *Timing. When* a message is sent, is under the sender or manager's control. Select a time that is appropriate for the message. If you have an important message, should you catch employees in the hall or as they arrive to or leave work? What's the difference between scheduling staff meetings for Friday afternoons versus Monday mornings?

2. *Audience. Who* is to receive the message is the decision of the sender. It may sound simple, but be sure you are sending the message to the correct audience. Is it appropriate to ask children to check their health insurance before signing up for a sport or should the reminder go to the parents? Should you talk with everyone at a staff meeting about coming in late or do you meet one-on-one with the employee who has been tardy?

3. *Delivery.* If not careful, the sender could encounter several problems in *how* a message is sent. The wording of the message needs to be clear and unambiguous. Suppose a manager asks a staff member to design a new program related to health. The employee produces an excellent program on cardio fitness but the manager is disappointed as he/she really wanted a program on nutrition. Another problem in the "delivery" of a message is to sound condescending. Since managers are in a supervisory role, they also need to be cautious that they do not sound condescending. ("Do you think you can do that?")

Besides poor wording, poor body language inhibits effective delivery. Telling a staff member you are behind them 100%, but failing to establish eye contact as you say it, raises doubt. Smiling and cracking a joke just after talking to seasonal staff about the importance of being on time, may send the message you won't discipline too harshly if they are tardy.

The final part of delivery is the method of communication. The sender should consider both the message and the receiver(s) in choosing which method to use. An e-mail to Program Staff informing them of the new agency contact at the local television station is much more appropriate than an announcement at an all-staff meeting where they might be distracted by others or may fail to spell the name correctly.

Noise may also occur in the communication process as a result of factors related to the receiver. These are:

1. *Selective Perception.* Individuals tend to hear what they want to hear. Lazy listeners tune in for key words. Students, for the most part, stop daydreaming when they hear the instructor say, "Now, this will be on the test." Other receivers have a mindset as to what is important in the message. A fiscally conservative member of an agency board might read the Superintendent of Recreation's report and only look for revenue generated, not attendance numbers or satisfaction ratings.

2. *Emotions.* What receivers are feeling and thinking at the time a message is sent impacts their ability to process a message. An employee, whose child is beginning school, might be distracted the first morning or two as he/she worries about the child adjusting to a new routine. Or, the day after the 4th of July celebration, the Special Events Coordinator, might just be too exhausted to really process much.

3. *Frame of Reference.* A receiver decodes a message by comparing it to past experiences. So if a message is about something the receiver has experienced before, the message will be received. But, if the employee has no frame of reference or a different experience, miscommunication may occur. A new employee who has not yet had the responsibility to "close" a facility for the night may not fully understand what the manager really expects be done. Or, a new employee with experience in "closing" a facility but from a prior job may not complete the tasks in the manner the manager expects.

4. *Overload.* A receiver can only process so much information at one time. If there are too many messages or an overload, some messages will be altered or lost. In the workplace, managers may be able to minimize overload for employees. If not, managers should consider using parallel forms of communication. For example, interns during their first week of internship are presented with all sorts of information. In addition to telling them what programs they will be responsible for, provide them a list with key information highlighted.

WRITTEN COMMUNICATION

Memos, e-mails, and letters are the three most common forms of written communication used by managers. For each there are set formats and guidelines that need to be followed. At home, or with friends, one might communicate in a very casual style and/or abbreviated format. However, on the job one's written communication is part of one's professional image. It is important on the job to follow the common standards for workplace communication. Whether it be a memo, e-mail, or letter, all written communication in the workplace should contain proper spelling, punctuation, and grammar. It is important to proof one's work and if need be, ask for assistance from others (Agnew & Hill, 2009). Remember with written communication the receiver sees only the printed word. There are no facial expressions or body language to accompany the message. Think of the *tone* of the message in selecting the wording.

Memos

Memos (short for memorandums) are short written forms of communication used *internally* in agency (Munter, 2000). That is, they are used to communicate with fellow staff. Memos are used to make announcements, request information, seek input, or summarize data. Memos are written in a clear and concise manner. There are no salutations or greetings and they are often written in a bullet or list style. Agency letterhead or standardized memo stationery is used. The agency word processing program may contain a memo template; such as in Word, the "Professional" memo format. The proper format for a memo is:

AGENCY LETTERHEAD

To:
From:
Date:
Subj:

Text or main message written in paragraph format. Single space with double space between paragraphs.

cc:
Attachment:

The *date* is the date the memo will be distributed. *To* lists the memo recipient(s). If several employees are to receive the memo, list them in order according to their title. If the memo is going to everyone then you can just write "All Staff." *From* includes the full sender's name and the title or position if the recipient may not recognize the sender's name. Once a memo has been written and proofed, the sender initials next to his/her name before the memo is distributed. The *subject* line, sometimes listed as *re:*, contains a brief indication of what the memo is about. It should be descriptive rather than general. Avoid wording like "A quick question." A better subject line entry is "What time is Coaching Clinic?" The *text* is the main body of the memo and follows the four part header in paragraph style. There is no need in a memo to insert a greeting or closing. Following the text the *cc* identifies anyone who receives a copy of the memo who is not part of the "to" line above. *Attachments* indicate any additional material that will follow the memo. For example, the memo may have been about a change in section of the agency's paid holiday policy. To avoid confusion, the sender attaches the complete policy with the change highlighted. See Figure 13.1 on p. 232. If the memo is to be *confidential*, the word 'confidential,' in all capitals, is centered just below the last line of the header (Sabin, 2005).

Business Letters

Business letters are the written form of communication used to communicate with those *outside* of the agency (Munter, 2000). In rare instances, the letter format may be used to communicate with an employee such as with a "letter of reprimand." Business letters are prepared on agency letterhead. The basic components for letter format are *date, inside address, salutation, body, closing, signature, cc* and *enc.* At least two lines beneath the letterhead is the full *date* indicating when the letter

Everlasting Recreation Agency
136 Heaven Rd.
Beautiful, CO 96378

MEMO

To: All Full-Time Staff
From: Shaela Francis, Director
Date: October 1, 2012
RE: Change in Paid Holidays

At Monday's meeting, the Everlasting Recreation Agency Board approved additional paid holidays for all full-time permanent staff. The new policy recognizes Martin Luther King, Jr. Day, the Friday after Thanksgiving, and Christmas Eve. The new policy takes effect November 1, 2012. The revised policy governing paid holidays is attached.

Attachment: Holiday Policy

Figure 13.1
Example of a Memo

is written should be at the top. This is followed at least two lines below with the *name*, *title*, and *address* of the individual receiving the letter. The salutation is "Dear _____:". If you know the person well, it is permissible to use their first name. Otherwise, use the formal prefix Mr., Mrs., Ms., or Miss. In a business letter, the *salutation* is followed by a colon—not a comma, as is the case in personal letters. Skip one line before and after the salutation.

The *body* of the letter contains the main message. Maybe you are writing a letter of reference for an employee or confirming a partnership with another agency. Whatever the letter is about, be sure to include the necessary facts for the reader. "Erin Williams worked for our agency during the summers of 2010–2012." If the purpose of the letter is to result in some action by the reader, clearly identify that action before ending. "Please return the enclosed contract by July 1, 2012." Single space within a paragraph and double space between paragraphs.

The most common *closing* in a professional business letter is "Sincerely." Be careful about using cute or creative phrases such as "Leisurely yours." Four lines below the closing, the name of the sender is typed. The

signature is entered above the printed name. The title of the person may follow on the same line as the typed name or directly beneath. As with the memo, the *cc* is used to identify who else will receive a copy of this letter. If any additional material is included in a business letter, it is identified by *enclosure*. See Figure 13.2.

The preferred style for formatting a business letter is *block style*. This is when all the writing is aligned with the left margin and paragraphs are separated by double spacing. Block is perhaps the easiest style. Modified block style is when the date, the closing, the signature, and printed name are indented to the right half of the page. Semi-blocked or indented style is similar to modified block with one addition: the paragraphs within the letter are also indented.

Business letters should be folded in thirds and placed in a number 10 envelope. The *inside address* (who is to receive the letter) is always single spaced and blocked to the left. Use capitals and smaller letters plus punctuation as appropriate. If the word processing program does not have a template for envelopes, the *inside address* goes four inches in from the left and two inches from the top. The sender's address appears in the upper-left corner (Sabin, 2005).

E-mails

E-mails are electronic written communication used with people both *inside* and *outside* your agency. E-mails are best used for routine updating, scheduling, quick inquiries, and similar items. For other situations you should interact face to face or use the telephone. It is not appropriate to use e-mail to delegate work to an employee, discipline an employee, deliver bad news, or share sensitive information (Lloyd, 2009).

The format for an e-mail is somewhat similar to the memo. The e-mail system provider inserts the date and time an e-mail is sent. The *to* line of the e-mail lists only the individuals you are addressing with the message. Any others who receive the e-mail are entered following the cc, and the receiver will see the names. To send a *blind copy*, meaning the main recipient is not aware a copy is being sent, use *bcc*. It is not recommended that blind copies be sent, but if there is a situation where it is warranted, the mechanism exists. The *from* line includes the sender's name and e-mail address. In an e-mail the *attachments* may be identified before the main text of the message. This depends on the format of the e-mail system provider. The final entry in the header of an e-mail is the *subject line*. Just as with a memo, the entry for this line should be descriptive of the main message.

CUNNINGHAM CHILDREN'S HOME
787 S. RACE ST.
KNOXVILLE, OH 04781

November 2, 2012

Brittany Roberts
715 S. Oakland
Knoxville, OH 04782

Dear Brittany,

On behalf of all the staff at Cunningham Children's Home, please let me say thank you for coordinating this year's Halloween Party. It exceeded all our expectations. The children loved the event and are still talking about the "Sticky Eyeball" contest. There is no doubt that it will become part of all future Halloween events.

Brittany, your work in recruiting and coordinating volunteers was amazing. They all played their parts beautifully and interacted so well with the children. As I mentioned to you at the event, I am happy to send a thank-you to any of the volunteers. Please just let me know their contact information and the notes will go out promptly.

We really are lucky to have individuals such as you who are willing to volunteer so much of your time to create a special event for our children. Thank you, Brittany, for making us all enjoy the world of ghosts and goblins.

Sincerely,

Sean Mercurio, Director

Figure 13.2
Example of a Business Letter

The format for the body of an e-mail differs from a memo. There are a few dissenters, but the vast majority of the experts on e-mail and workplace etiquette recommend including in the body of the message a *greeting* and a *closing*. They can be simple: "Hello Jan," and "Thank you, Bruce," (Lloyd, 2009).

Business e-mails usually have set signature lines pre-set. The signature line follows the main message and should contain the sender's name, title, address, telephone and fax information in block format. The final entry on many business e-mails will be a pre-set disclaimer adopted by the agency for all e-mails sent through the agency's e-mail system (Muller, 2009). See Figure 13.3.

The rules for writing business e-mails are the same as for memos and letters. The writer should always use appropriate language and write in a professional tone. It is not appropriate to use linguistic shortcuts such as "2" for "to," "u" for "you," or "IIRC" for "If I recall correctly." Use standardized capitalization as the use of all capitals in electronic communication comes across as shouting.

Unique to e-mail is the automatic "out of office" reply. A manager or employee who will be away from their desk for the day or longer, should use the "out of office" reply to inform others that they will not be checking e-mail on a regular basis (Lloyd, 2009).

For the most part, e-mail is seen as a positive force in office communication. But, the ease of e-mail may invite quick and heated messages. E-mails that contain sarcasm, insults, or an offensive tone are called *flames*. An exchange of heated e-mails is *flaming*. The most important thing to remember is that if you receive a flame, cool down before responding. Many suggest you follow the 24-hour rule: wait 24 hours before responding to annoying e-mail. It may be best to talk with the person directly rather than send a reply electronically. If you cannot, then use caution in responding. The tone of your voice and inflection are missing so use friendly or neutral language. Avoid creating a volley of heated e-mails. A good reminder is to be more polite than when you speak (Lloyd, 2009).

Misuse of business e-mail commonly occurs; though this does not make it acceptable. A 2010 workplace study by the Ponemon Institute found 42% of employees "frequently" use business e-mail for personal use and another 29% "sometimes" do. A 2009 study by the American Management Association found 89% of employees said they had sent an e-mail outside the agency containing either jokes, gossip, rumors, or disparaging remarks (Mantell, 2010). Employees should understand they are not entitled to privacy or freedom of speech regarding business e-mails. According to the Electronic Communication Privacy Act (ECPA), managers have the legal right to monitor employee e-mail since the employer provides the system. The best solution is for an agency to have a written policy for employees detailing appropriate use of e-mail and the Internet and to be sure they clearly explain the policy to all employees (Desai, Hart, & Richards, 2009).

ORAL COMMUNICATION

Talking is easy, right? Everyone does it. For those who work in recreation and sport, oral communication comprises a major portion of their work day whether it be talking with people face to face or talking on the telephone. But what about the oral communication that is not part of the "typical day"? Facilitating formal meetings or making presentations are not daily occurrences. But, they are two skill areas of oral communication that managers need to master.

Robert's Rules of Order

Meetings are inevitable. There are staff meetings (see Chapter 3), board meetings, task-force meetings, etc. There are one-to-one meetings such as employment interviews or performance appraisals. And, there are single or short-term meetings to solve a problem (Andelman, 2006).

Meetings run the gamut from informal, chatty get-togethers to formal, structured business meetings. How structured and formal a meeting will be depends on the purpose, who will attend, and the agency setting. A small outfitting business may take a much more relaxed approach to staff meetings than a large metropolitan recreation agency. It is the more formal or structured meetings that present a challenge for new managers as they are not quite sure what to do.

This e-mail is intended for the addressee shown. It contains information that is confidential and protected from disclosure. Any review, dissemination, or use of this transmission or its contents by persons or unauthorized employees of the intended organization is strictly prohibited.

The contents of this e-mail do not necessarily represent the views or policies of [insert agency name], or its employees.

Figure 13.3
Example of an E-mail Disclaimer

The classic guide for meeting structure is *Robert's Rules of Order*. Henry M. Robert was an engineering officer in the Army when he was asked to step in and conduct a meeting. Unsure of how to do it; he failed in having a very productive meeting. After that he decided to find out how to do better and investigated parliamentary law. The result was his book, first written in 1876, and now in its tenth edition. The manual offers a basic *order* for business to be handled and explains *language* for the attendees to use to move through the items (http://www.robertsrules.com). While the complete manual is seldom used in recreational and sport settings, there are some basic elements that recreation and sport professionals should understand.

An *agenda* is an outline of the topics to be discussed at a meeting. The general order of meetings according to Robert's Rules of Order should be:

1. Call to Order
2. Approval of Minutes
3. Officer(s) Reports
4. Committee Reports
5. Unfinished (Old) Business
6. New Business
7. Announcements
8. Adjournment

Agendas should be sent prior to the meeting to those who will be attending. In the case of board meetings, the agenda goes to the members of the board ahead of the meeting and is made available to others at the meeting. Many boards have policies that require they receive the agenda one week prior to the meeting so they are prepared and ready to discuss the topics when they meet.

Besides designing a guide for the order of the meeting, Robert's Rules of Order offers a language to use at meetings. Most familiar to many is the phrase "making a motion." To make a motion means someone is asking the group to consider a decision or action. "I move the 2012 budget be adopted." "I move we approve 4% raises for all full-time employees." "I move we table the discussion on fee increases." But, what does the term "table" mean? What happens after a motion is made? What is a "second"? What happens if someone "calls the question"?

This may seem confusing at first but it does not take long to pick up the language of parliamentary procedure (See Figure 13.4, p. 236). At first, Robert's Rules may seem quite stringent and unnecessary. The purpose is not to restrict individuals from participating but rather to establish a mechanism for "constructive and democratic" meetings. The first time you attend a meeting with no order or direction, or a meeting on a controversial issue, you will see the value of Robert's Rules of Order. It becomes easier to keep meetings on track and move toward decisions when some of the elements of Robert's Rules of Order are in place.

Simply, to "table" a discussion means to set aside or postpone further discussion. All motions, including a motion to table a discussion, require a "second." That is, one additional person must support the motion. In a meeting this usually happens immediately when someone other than the person with the original motion, follows the initial motion with the simple word, "second." If there is no second, the motion dies and the topic is no longer discussed by the group. When someone "calls the question" they are attempting to stop the discussion. This move also requires a second. If there is a second, a vote is taken to determine whether discussion should continue. This step is a useful technique if the discussion seems to be going in circles or is limited to 1 or 2 members continually repeating their views.

Presentations

Recreation and sport professionals often find themselves in the situation of preparing presentations. It is not unusual for local service organizations, such as Rotary or Kiwanis, to invite professionals in leisure services to make presentations to their members. When an agency decides to undergo a capital campaign or bond issue referendum, managers make presentations to provide information and gain support. There are all kinds of situations in which recreation and sport professionals make presentations. So, how does a manager best prepare an effective presentation?

First, when asked to speak, it is important to confirm the topic to be addressed, who the audience will be, the amount of time allocated for the presentations, and the location. In asking about the audience, clarify how many there will be, their age, their gender, possibly their educational level, if they know you will be coming, and if they are aware of your agency.

Once a manager knows the "specifics," work on the presentation itself can begin. The overall structure of a presentation consists of three parts: introduction, body, and conclusion. There is no reason to be at a loss for how to begin or introduce a presentation as there are a number of ways to start a presentation (Griffin, 2009).

1. **Motion:** To introduce a new piece of business or propose a decision or action, a motion must be made by a group member ("I move that . . ."). A second motion must then also be made (raise your hand and say, "I second it"). After limited discussion, the group then votes on the motion. A majority vote is required for the motion to pass (or quorum, as specified in your bylaws).

2. **Postpone Indefinitely:** This tactic is used to kill a motion. When passed, the motion cannot be reintroduced at that meeting. It may be brought up again at a later date. This is made as a motion ("I move to postpone indefinitely . . ."). A second motion is required. A majority vote is required to postpone the motion under consideration.

3. **Amend:** This is the process used to change a motion under consideration. Perhaps you like the idea proposed but not exactly as offered. Raise your hand and make the following motion: "I move to amend the motion on the floor." This also requires a second motion. After the motion to amend is seconded, a majority vote is needed to decide whether the amendment is accepted. Then a vote is taken on the amended motion. In some organizations, a "friendly amendment" is made. If the person who made the original motion agrees with the suggested changes, the amended motion may be voted on without a separate vote to approve the amendment.

4. **Commit:** This is used to place a motion in committee. It requires a second motion. A majority vote must rule to carry it. At the next meeting, the committee is required to prepare a report on the motion committed. If an appropriate committee exists, the motion goes to that committee. If not, a new committee is established.

5. **Question:** To end a debate immediately, the question is called (say "I call the question") and needs a second motion. A vote is held immediately (no further discussion is allowed). A two-thirds vote is required for passage. If it is passed, the motion on the floor is voted on immediately.

6. **Table:** To table a discussion is to lay aside the business at hand in such a manner that it will be considered later in the meeting or at another time ("I make a motion to table this discussion until the next meeting. In the meantime, we will get more information so we can better discuss the issue."). A second motion is needed and a majority vote required to table the item being discussed.

7. **Adjourn:** A motion is made to end the meeting. A second motion is required. A majority vote is then required for the meeting to be adjourned (ended).

Note: If more than one motion is proposed, the most recent takes precedence over the ones preceding it. For example, if #6, a motion to table the discussion, is proposed, it must be voted on before #3, a motion to amend, can be decided.

In a smaller meeting, like a committee or board meeting, often only four motions are used:
- To introduce (motion).
- To change a motion (amend).
- To adopt (accept a report without discussion).
- To adjourn (end the meeting).

Source: http://www.portlandonline.com

Figure 13.4
Examples of Key Language in Parliamentary Procedure

1. *Personal reference.* "I'm Erin Williams, owner of Elite Gym here in Dongola."

2. *Reference the occasion.* "I remember my first Earth Day."

3. *Starting statement.* "Leisure is not a right."

4. *Illustration or story (brief but fitting).* "Jamie McDowell is a 47-year-old woman recovering from breast cancer. This past month, for the first time she kayaked a river, completed a teams course and finished an 8,000-foot climb. She loved it all. But, what she told me she loved the most was getting to do all those things with other breast cancer survivors."

5. *Quotation.* "You can discover more about a person in an hour of play than a year of conversation." —Plato

6. *Rhetorical question.* "How many of you as children spent a week away at camp?"

7. *State the main idea.* "Today I'm here to talk with you about the bond referendum to build a recreation community center."

8. *Humor.* Only individuals who tell jokes well should use humor. The humor should fit the occasion and the audience.

9. *A visual aid.* The presentation begins with a short video, PowerPoint, or the speaker holding a prop (kayak paddle, trophy, etc).

The actual text or body of the speech is the longest of the three sections in length and requires the greatest organization of material. The information may lend itself to one of the organizational structures discussed below or the manager may just select one of several possible structures (Griffin, 2009)

1. *Chronological.* With this pattern, the information is organized in the order in which it happened. The historical approach is common if asked to speak generally about an agency or program.

2. *List.* The material in the body of the speech is broken into segments and addressed separately. A presentation encouraging the audience to send a child to camp might discuss who the campers are, staff credentials, the camp facilities, programs offered, and cost.

3. *Acronym.* An acronym is a word formed by the initial letters of several words. In a presentation to summer day-camp staff, the director might use CARE (Children, Attitude, Respect, and Equality) to discuss expectations of the counselors.

4. *Analogy.* An analogy is when a comparison is based on similarity. "The elements of an effective fitness regime may be compared to an automobile tune-up."

5. *Comparison/Contrast.* A very simple technique where the body of the speech consists of information about similarities and differences between two items or situations. In an effort to get an increase in student fees for campus recreation, the director may organize the talk around present offerings and possible offerings with additional money.

6. *Problem/Cause/Solution.* In this pattern the speaker identifies the problem (childhood obesity), discusses the causes (lack of physical activity, poor nutrition, etc.), and offers a solution (Summer Park Incentive Program).

Just as important as the opening of a presentation is the *closing*. The audience should sense a logical flow to the ending and feel the overall message is complete when the speaker concludes the presentation. If one just ends abruptly, the listeners are startled. Always bring a presentation to closure before asking the audience if they have any questions. A presentation may be closed with any of the following:

1. *Summary.* The speaker provides an overall summary of the key elements in the talk.

2. *Question.* The use of a rhetorical question can again be an effective technique. "When will you be bringing your children to Splashin' Safari for a day of family fun?"

3. *Quotation.* Select a quote relevant to the main idea and credit the source. "So as First Lady Michelle Obama recently said, 'This [childhood obesity] isn't the kind of problem that can be solved overnight, but with everyone working together, it can be solved.'"

4. *Statistics.* An impressive number or piece of data may leave a strong image. "Over 14,400 runners participated in last weekend's Illinois Marathon and we aim to see 17,000 on our streets next year."

5. *Refer back to the introduction.* "Jamie McDowell is not alone in the battle against breast cancer. Our outdoor adventure therapy program is here to help the many who battle this frightening disease."

6. *Prophecy.* The speaker makes a prediction. "By this time next year, we will be breaking ground on our new facility."

7. *Pose a challenge.* "Special Olympics cannot exist without the support of organizations. I challenge you Rotarians to match or beat the donation given by Kiwanis."

8. *Make a pledge.* "As the new director of Everglades National Park, I promise to work with all outfitters to meet your needs and protect the ecological balance of the park."

9. *Appeal to their emotions.* This technique can be effective if indeed there is a strong connection between the topic of the speech and the audience's emotions. "If you've enjoyed the laughter you've experienced today, then by all means come to the Comedy Improv Night next Saturday."

Following the conclusion of certain presentations, it is customary to ask the audience if they have any questions. Listen to the question and ask for a clarification if the question is unclear. Repeat the question before responding if you think some in the audience were not able to hear it. If possible include the audience in your answer by use of the collective "you" or an example. When you receive a question you cannot answer, just say so. Indicate you will be happy to follow up if it is a question for which you can get the answer. Speak later with the individual who asked the question and obtain contact information and be sure to send the answer.

Even the greatest presentation will fall short if the delivery is lacking. Public speaking is not a comfortable role for many. In fact, it is often said that public speaking is the number-one fear of most Americans. To combat the nervousness that might surface during a presentation, concentrate on a few principles to avoid a few of the typical pitfalls.

- Speak in an even tone and steady pace
- Enunciate clearly
- Minimize the use of fillers such as "you know", "ok?" and "uh, uh, uh."
- Maintain a relaxed but confident posture with hands out of pockets
- Develop eye contact and use appropriate facial expressions and gestures
- Dress for the setting of the presentation
- Use notes or prepared remarks, if necessary

Very few individuals can speak "off the cuff" and do it well. It is entirely appropriate to use some sort of notes in making a presentation. The key is not to read to the audience, but rather to use the notes as a guide to keep the remarks in order and help you relax. Notes may be made either on cards or 8 ½" x 11" paper. If one will be speaking at a podium it is quite easy to just move one sheet of paper to the side. Or, if there is no podium and you are often nervous when presenting, stiff note cards would be better to use. With both methods, remember to number the pages and use a font size easy to read.

Visual or presentation aids may be used to enhance a presentation. However, it is important that presentation aids be relevant to the topic and not just a gimmick or crutch for the speaker (PowerPoint). When using a visual aid, ensure that all in the audience can see it. Be careful not to stand between the aid and your audience. Always rehearse with a visual aid before the actual presentation. It is best to be familiar with any required technology and always have a backup plan. There inevitably is that one time someone promises to have the equipment there and forgets.

Public speaking is a great way for managers in recreation and sport to promote their agencies and educate others on the values of leisure and sport. While it might be a difficult experience at first, it is one that gets easier with time; especially if you believe in what you are doing.

BEHAVIORAL COMMUNICATION

A manager's behavior is closely observed by employees. The saying, "Actions speaks louder than words," is an apt description of how employees read their supervisors. The situations when behavior becomes the most critical messenger are ethical ones. How a manager acts when there is a right and wrong way to do so sends a powerful message.

Our ethics or moral values are shaped by family, friends, religion, education, social movements, work, and by the actions of celebrities or influentials (Callahan, 2004). Individuals learn from their experiences and develop a moral code or road map which is then reflected in a personal morality, professional morality, religious morality, and legal morality (Kihl, 2007). Professional morality or business ethics "refers to clear standards and norms that help employers to distinguish right from wrong behavior at work" (Sauser & Sims, 2007).

Today headlines are full of scandals in American corporations and government. Sandra Baldwin, head of the U.S. Olympic Committee, was fired for lying about her academic degrees and she is only one of many prominent individuals to do so. Colleges and universities are cited for NCAA violations. 51% of America's high school students believe cheating is not wrong and 85% of college students say one needs to cheat to get ahead. Maybe Robert Merton was correct when he said "A cardinal American virtue, 'ambition,' promotes a cardinal American vice, 'deviant behavior'" (Callahan, 2004).

In the workplace there are five reasons why employers violate ethical standards. The first is poor role models. When employees see top-level managers, and/or immediate supervisors, behave unethically, it becomes much easier for them to act incorrectly.

Second is rationalization. This is when employees justify their actions by comments like: "I'm overworked and underpaid," "No one else will notice or care," or "I deserve this because I'm an excellent employee."

Third is impatient ambition. Some employees are so eager to climb the professional ladder or increase their personal wealth that they are willing to act in an unethical manner. Exaggerating qualifications on a résumé or accepting kickbacks may seem to be acceptable behavior to reach their goal.

Fourth is temptation. If employees work in an environment where unethical behavior could easily go unnoticed, it is much easier to take that first step. Individuals who work away from the main office or are "in the field" are out of sight of their supervisors and maybe even coworkers.

Fifth is unguarded trust. An employee knows he has the supervisor's complete trust and the supervisor would never suspect the employee of such an action. Without the fear of getting caught, it is easier to slip into doing the wrong thing.

Managers and supervisors are often confronted with ethical decisions and are expected to use their moral compass. Carl Skoogland, Ethics Director for Texas Instruments, says, "Ethical managers must know what is right, value what is right, and do what is right." Some of the ethical situations which arise in recreation and sport are listed in Figure 13.5 (see p. 240). Which would you rate as ethical? Unethical? Questionable? Why? Would the setting (resort, public agency, nonprofit club, etc.) make a difference?

Managers must recognize when an ethical issue exists and choose the morally right option. To decide what is the morally right thing to do, ask the following questions:

- Is it legal?
- What is the agency's policy?
- What does my professional association's code of ethics say?
- How will it make me feel about myself?
- What would others, especially my Mother, think?

The last question may seem a bit elementary but the idea is important. Think of someone whose respect you value. How would they react to your decision?

It is possible for managers and supervisors to create "a culture of character" (Sauser & Sims, 2007). To do so, however, takes considerable time and effort. But when morality is embedded in an organization, it influences the thoughts and actions of employees. Employees are much more likely to weigh values of the organization in making a decision about behavior at work (Kihl, 2007). An action plan for improving the ethical environment at work should include:

1. Top-down commitment to ethical behavior with moral leadership.
2. A written code or set of policies.
3. Proper training of employees regarding ethical issues and appropriate actions.
4. Confidentiality and a mechanism for employees to report ethical violations.
5. Policies and procedures to investigate ethical complaints.
6. Consistent enforcement of policies.

In taking the time to develop a culture of character, an agency helps its employees become better people. It is important to help employees understand

Examples of Possible Ethical Issues

- Conducting online personal shopping during work hours
- Having alcohol on company premises, even if one does not drink excessively
- Punching someone else's timecard to cover for them
- Making reasonable excuses to cover for a coworker who is late to work
- Sending out jokes and/or chain letters to coworkers via e-mail
- Passively condoning activities which are contrary to public safety and welfare
- Occasionally taking an extended lunch break to compensate for unpaid overtime
- Listing membership in a professional organization on your résumé even though you no longer belong
- Pretending to be a coworker's supervisor so that you can give him/her a reference
- Failing to inform your employer of paycheck errors or vacation time accrual when they are in your favor
- Using your friendship with a boss or coworker to get special privileges at work
- Accepting compensation from outside sources when it poses a conflict of interest to your employment
- Going to potential job interviews during working hours
- Using one's personal cell phone during working hours
- Telling your boss you're coming back from maternity leave when you know you're not
- Accepting Christmas gifts or other gifts from clients or vendors, even when agency policy prohibits it
- Using a company vehicle for personal business
- Taking home company property (pencils, paper, tape, etc.) for personal use
- Gossiping in the office, even if it tends to impinge on someone else's reputation
- Hiring a family member to work in your department
- Taking periodic breaks by playing games on the computer at work
- Exaggerating or misleading one's skill on a résumé
- Taking a sick day, even when one is not sick
- Accepting outside employment that might impair your efficiency and effectiveness
- Occasionally using use of the agency's copier for personal or community use
- Using funds from "petty cash" for personal or non-professional use
- Borrowing and returning recreation and sporting goods equipment
- Personally participating in programs without paying
- Allowing family or friends to participate in a program or use facilities without charging
- Plagiarizing and violating copyright laws
- In a therapeutic recreation agency, discussing the progress of a client in a social setting outside of work
- Misleading the public or a customer in making false claims about a program, service, or facility
- Falsifying attendance reports for programs or facilities
- Hiring employees in wrong job classifications to pay them a higher wage rate
- Collecting cash from one program and using it for another purpose
- Budgeting money for a popular program and using the money for another purpose

Figure 13.5
Possible Ethical Issues in Recreation and Sport

the difference between what they have a right to do and what is right to do.

Written, oral, and behavioral communication all contribute to one's professional image. There are differences between how one communicates with family and friends and how one should communicate in the workplace. If one fails to recognize the importance of such differences, success in the workplace will be limited. But remember, it is possible to "work at communication."

Summary

1. For effective communication to occur, both the sender and the receiver need to interpret the message the same.

2. Managers should use *congruent* and *parallel* communication and understand the power of *positional* communication.

3. Senders need to consider the timing, audience, and delivery to avoid creating *noise* in the communication process.

4. Four factors which limit a receiver's ability to effectively process a message are selective perception, emotional state, frame of reference, and information overload.

5. Oral, written, and behavioral communication all contribute to the professional image of the manager.

6. All written communication in the workplace should include proper spelling, punctuation, and grammar.

7. Memos, e-mails, and letters have standardized formats and guidelines.

8. Employees are not entitled to privacy when using business e-mail.

9. *Robert's Rules of Order* provides a basic order for meetings and procedures for handling business. There is unique language or terminology to use.

10. It is inappropriate to use personal electronic devices during meetings in the workplace.

11. In making presentations there are several options to use for opening, closing, and organizing material.

12. Public speaking is a great way for recreation and sport managers to promote their agencies and educate others about leisure and sport.

13. How a manager acts when there is a right and wrong way to do so, sends a powerful message.

14. Agencies can create "a culture of character."

Discussion Topics

1. Explain the following terms: congruent communication, incongruent communication, positional communication, and parallel communication.

2. What are the differences between sender and receiver noise in communication?

3. What are your thoughts as a manager about your employees texting during work? During staff meetings?

4. Your new employee has experience in "closing a facility." How might you communicate your agency's expectations in contrast to an employee with no such experience?

5. What are the proper formats for a memo and a business letter?

6. When is e-mail the appropriate technique for communication?

7. Robert's Rules of Order provides a basic format for agendas. What is the format? When might you choose to use a prepared agenda for a meeting?

8. Recreation managers often find themselves giving presentations to groups both large and small. What are possible presentation openings? How might the material or content be organized? How might a manager close a presentation?

9. Why might managers act unethically?

10. Do you agree or disagree with Merton's statement, "A cardinal American virtue, 'ambition,' promotes a cardinal American vice, 'deviant behavior.'?

11. Select 4 situations from the final Table in the chapter and discuss how you would handle?

REFERENCES

Andelman, B. (2006). Meeting effectiveness 101. *Corporate Meetings & Incentives, 25*(12), 20–25.

Callahan, D. (2004). *The cheating culture: Why more Americans are doing wrong to get ahead.* Orlando, FL: Harcourt.

Desai, M., Hart, J., & Richards, T. (2009). An IT manager's view on e-mail and internet policies and procedures. *Journal of Institutional Psychology, 36*(4), 317–322.

Griffin, M. (2009). *Public speaking basics.* Lanham, MD: University Press of America.

Kihl, L. (2007). Moral codes, moral tensions and hiding behind the rules: A snapshot of athletic administrators' practical morality. *Sport Management Review, 10,* 279–305.

Lloyd, J. (2010). Do's and don'ts for using e-mail at work. Retrieved from http://www.hodu.com/email-do.shtml

Mantell, R. (2010, May 2). Watch your e-mails. Your boss is. *The Wall Street Journal.* Retrieved from http://www.online.wsj.com

Muller, M. (2009). *The manager's guide to HR: Hiring, firing, performance, evaluations, documentation, benefits and everything else you need to know.* New York, NY: American Management Association.

Munter, M. (2000). *Guide to managerial communication: Effective business writing and speaking.* (5th Ed.). Upper Saddle River, NJ: Prentice Hall.

Sabin, W.A. (2005). *The Gregg Reference Manual.* New York, NY: Glencoe McGraw Hill.

Sauser Jr., W. & Sims, R. (2007). Fostering an ethical culture for business: The role of HR managers. In R.R. Sims (Ed.), *Human resource management: Contemporary issues, challenges, and opportunities* (pp. 253–285). Charlotte, NC: Information Age Publishing.

Schermerhorn, J., Hunt, J., & Osborn, R. (2005). *Organizational behavior* (9th Ed.). Hoboken, NJ: John Wiley & Sons, Inc.

Stevens, B. (2005). What communication skills do employers really want? Silicon valley responds. *Journal of Employment Counseling, 42*(1), 2–9.

The Official Robert's Rule of Order Web Site. (2010) Retrieved from http://www.robertsrules.com

INDEX

OTHER BOOKS FROM VENTURE PUBLISHING, INC.

21st Century Leisure: Current Issues, Second Edition
by Valeria J. Freysinger and John R. Kelly

Active Living in Older Adulthood: Principles and Practices of Activity Programs
by Barbara A. Hawkins

Activity Experiences and Programming within Long-Term Care
by Ted Tedrick and Elaine R. Green

Adventure Programming
edited by John C. Miles and Simon Priest

Assessment: The Cornerstone of Activity Programs
by Ruth Perschbacher

Beyond Baskets and Beads: Activities for Older Adults with Functional Impairments
by Mary Hart, Karen Primm, and Kathy Cranisky

Boredom Busters: Themed Special Events to Dazzle and Delight Your Group
by Annette C. Moore

Brain Fitness
by Suzanne Fitzsimmons

Client Assessment in Therapeutic Recreation Services
by Norma J. Stumbo

Client Outcomes in Therapeutic Recreation Services
by Norma J. Stumbo

Conceptual Foundations for Therapeutic Recreation
edited by David R. Austin, John Dattilo, and Bryan P. McCormick

Constraints to Leisure
edited by Edgar L. Jackson

Dementia Care Programming: An Identity-Focused Approach
by Rosemary Dunne

Dimensions of Choice: Qualitative Approaches to Parks, Recreation, Tourism, Sport, and Leisure Research, Second Edition
by Karla A. Henderson

Diversity and the Recreation Profession: Organizational Perspectives, Revised Edition
edited by Maria T. Allison and Ingrid E. Schneider

Effective Management in Therapeutic Recreation Service, Second Edition
by Marcia Jean Carter and Gerald S. O'Morrow

Evaluating Leisure Services: Making Enlightened Decisions, Third Edition
by Karla A. Henderson and M. Deborah Bialeschki

Everything from A to Y: The Zest Is up to You! Older Adult Activities for Every Day of the Year
by Nancy R. Cheshire and Martha L. Kenney

Experience Marketing: Strategies for the New Millennium
by Ellen L. O'Sullivan and Kathy J. Spangler

Facilitation of Therapeutic Recreation Services: An Evidence-Based and Best Practice Approach to Techniques and Processes
edited by Norma J. Stumbo and Brad Wardlaw

Facilitation Techniques in Therapeutic Recreation, Second Edition
by John Dattilo and Alexis McKenney

File o' Fun: A Recreation Planner for Games & Activities, Third Edition
by Jane Harris Ericson and Diane Ruth Albright

Getting People Involved in Life and Activities: Effective Motivating Techniques
by Jeanne Adams

Health Promotion for Mind, Body, and Spirit
by Suzanne Fitzsimmons and Linda L. Buettner

Inclusion: Including People With Disabilities in Parks and Recreation Opportunities
by Lynn Anderson and Carla Brown Kress

The Multiple Values of Wilderness
by H. Ken Cordell, John C. Bergstrom, and J. M. Bowker

N.E.S.T. Approach: Dementia Practice Guidelines for Disturbing Behaviors
by Linda L. Buettner and Suzanne Fitzsimmons

The Organizational Basis of Leisure Participation: A Motivational Exploration
by Robert A. Stebbins

Outdoor Recreation for 21st Century America
by H. Ken Cordell

Parks for Life: Moving the Goal Posts, Changing the Rules, and Expanding the Field
by Will LaPage

The Pivotal Role of Leisure Education: Finding Personal Fulfillment in This Century
edited by Elie Cohen-Gewerc and Robert A. Stebbins

Planning and Organizing Group Activities in Social Recreation
by John V. Valentine

Planning Areas and Facilities for Sport and Recreation: Predesign Process, Principles, and Strategies
by Jack A. Harper

Planning Parks for People, Second Edition
by John Hultsman, Richard L. Cottrell, and Wendy Z. Hultsman

Programming for Parks, Recreation, and Leisure Services: A Servant Leadership Approach, Third Edition
by Donald G. DeGraaf, Debra J. Jordan, and Kathy H. DeGraaf

Puttin' on the Skits: Plays for Adults in Managed Care
by Jean Vetter

Recreation and Leisure: Issues in an Era of Change, Third Edition
edited by Thomas Goodale and Peter A. Witt

Recreation and Youth Development
by Peter A. Witt and Linda L. Caldwell

Recreation for Older Adults: Individual and Group Activities
by Judith A. Elliott and Jerold E. Elliott

Recreation Program Planning Manual for Older Adults
by Karen Kindrachuk

Recreation Programming and Activities for Older Adults
by Jerold E. Elliott and Judith A. Sorg-Elliott

Reference Manual for Writing Rehabilitation Therapy Treatment Plans
by Penny Hogberg and Mary Johnson

Service Living: Building Community through Public Parks and Recreation
by Doug Wellman, Dan Dustin, Karla Henderson, and Roger Moore

Simple Expressions: Creative and Therapeutic Arts for the Elderly in Long-Term Care Facilities
by Vicki Parsons

A Social Psychology of Leisure, Second Edition
by Douglas A. Kleiber, Gordon J. Walker, and Roger C. Mannell

Special Events and Festivals: How to Organize, Plan, and Implement
by Angie Prosser and Ashli Rutledge

The Sportsman's Voice: Hunting and Fishing in America
by Mark Damian Duda, Martin F. Jones, and Andrea Criscione

Survey Research and Analysis: Applications in Parks, Recreation, and Human Dimensions
by Jerry Vaske

Taking the Initiative: Activities to Enhance Effectiveness and Promote Fun
by J. P. Witman

Therapeutic Recreation and the Nature of Disabilities
by Kenneth E. Mobily and Richard D. MacNeil

Therapeutic Recreation: Cases and Exercises, Second Edition
by Barbara C. Wilhite and M. Jean Keller

Therapeutic Recreation in Health Promotion and Rehabilitation
by John Shank and Catherine Coyle

Therapeutic Recreation in the Nursing Home
by Linda Buettner and Shelley L. Martin

Therapeutic Recreation Practice: A Strengths Approach
by Lynn Anderson and Linda Heyne

Therapeutic Recreation Programming: Theory and Practice
by Charles Sylvester, Judith E. Voelkl, and Gary D. Ellis

Therapeutic Recreation Protocol for Treatment of Substance Addictions
by Rozanne W. Faulkner

The Therapeutic Recreation Stress Management Primer
by Cynthia Mascott

Traditions: Improving Quality of Life in Caregiving
by Janelle Sellick

Trivia by the Dozen: Encouraging Interaction and Reminiscence in Managed Care
by Jean Vetter